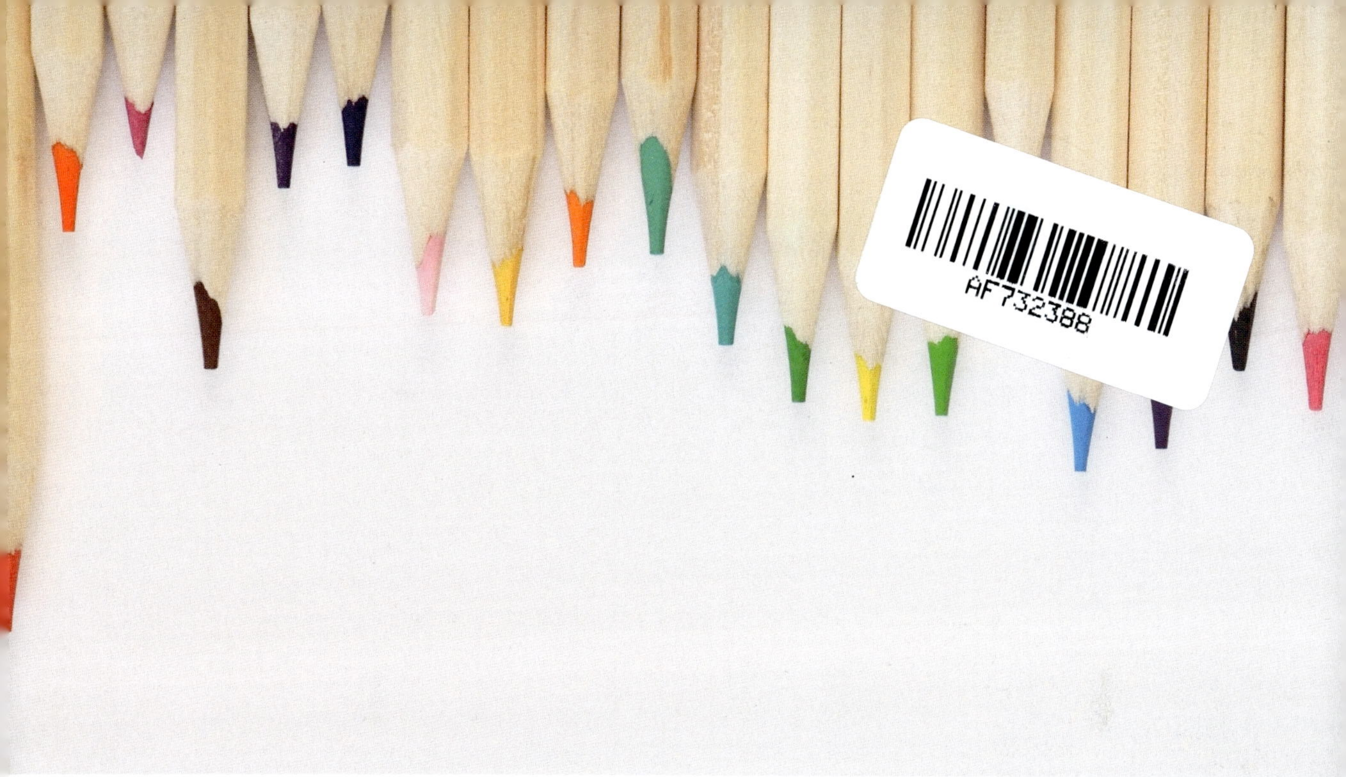

TEACHING CREATIVE WORKSHOPS

IN PERSON AND ONLINE

Patricia van den Akker

HERBERT PRESS
LONDON • OXFORD • NEW YORK • NEW DELHI • SYDNEY

Dedication

To Isobel & Emily.

You are my teachers.

‘Patricia has been at the forefront of advising small businesses on best practice for many years, and this handbook is full of her wisdom for both new and much experienced creative teachers.’

Sarah James MBE, Director of Craft Festival and Find a Maker

‘If there's anyone who knows how to make a living out of your creativity, it is Patricia! As more people opt to turn creative passion into commercial profit, this book can be your guide. It's written by a professional who's been there and done it, and offers top tips plus the all-important inspiring case studies. In short, it's essential reading!’

Emma Jones, Founder of Enterprise Nation

‘This is the definitive guide to how creative practitioners can package their knowledge and experience to create memorable, valuable and enriching courses that people will want to pay a premium for.’

Jo Sealy, Director of To Market, Founder of The Black Artisans, Trustee of Heritage Crafts

‘This book showcases Patricia's drive and energy, in a really practical and inspirational way to help you unleash your teaching potential, identify what you can teach, reach your market, and run creative and powerful workshops. If you've been thinking for a while “I should teach this”, then this book is the answer.’

Tony Quinn, Reader & Course Leader, BA Ceramic Design, Central Saint Martins

‘Having worked with Patricia for several years I am delighted that she is sharing her experience and knowledge to empower others. I am a huge believer in “it is not always what we know but how we deliver it” is what impacts our learners, and this book is a fantastic tool to add to anyone's kit.’

Chris Oliver, Head of Professional Training, The Goldsmiths' Centre

‘In this book Patricia has crafted practical exercises and pragmatic top tips, alongside insights from brilliant professionals and, importantly, guidance on reflection to ensure that you develop skills and put them into practice in a way that is right for you and your business.’

Nicky Dewar, Director of Programmes, Crafts Council

Contents

Foreword

Throughout my life I have had the privilege of not only learning a craft, but also of teaching one, either directly or indirectly, encouraging and influencing people to work with clay as a natural material, and showing what it can truly offer us.

In my capacity as a judge on *The Great Pottery Throw Down* television show, I am in a unique position to observe human behaviour through the lens of the creative process. As the potters enter the television studio and start working with clay, we and the audience witness over the weeks how their relationship with clay develops and how their skills and confidence grow as makers. Of course, due to the nature of circumstance their development is more intense, but regardless all creatives need to overcome challenges and boundaries within ourselves as makers and ultimately humans.

Integral to the creative process is failing, rediscovering, and learning through problem-solving, then hopefully achieving the desired goal. So often in modern life we are told that failure is negative, something to be frowned upon. This, in my view, is nonsense because being creative gives you the opportunity to be completely responsible for your own endeavours, and to learn from your own unique mistakes. This then gives the maker the very thing that takes away the fear of failure, and to see it as a process to achieve higher personal conscientiousness.

Taking part or learning creative skills has many positives that give us the opportunity to expand our imagination, articulate our thoughts and communicate in ways that otherwise may not be available to us.

I often describe my own dyslexia as a superpower, turning what could generally be perceived in society as a hindrance into a real positive. It is through creative endeavours that we can learn many important lessons about ourselves, but also change the narrative to work for us. This, I firmly believe comes from the ability to work and think creatively – in an art studio, and taken beyond.

I discovered my calling that fortunate day I walked into the art room at school, aged 11. Learning a creative subject led me to have more confidence in myself and gave me the ability to push forward in life that I didn't think was possible at the time. It opened up a world of possibilities the very second I touched clay. Clay has been a companion throughout my life, and to this day I am still learning.

In this book Patricia will inspire you to continue to learn to become an even more unique and creative teacher. She will help you offer focus and diversity in your teaching to create a welcoming learning environment for your students, at whatever level they want to explore and expand their own creativity, stories and humanity.

I often think of my art teacher who introduced me to clay, and thank my lucky stars that he had the insight to communicate his teaching and to bolster my learning in this way. I hope you will become somebody's favourite creative teacher too.

Keith Brymer Jones

Master potter, design expert and TV judge for *The Great Pottery Throw Down* since 2015.

Preface

Why I wrote this book

I am a fire starter – that's according to one of my 'teachers', Danielle LaPorte.

She isn't really my teacher in the formal sense as I have never met her, and she doesn't know me. But I have read her books and taken one of her courses, and she has had a huge impact on me in my 25 years as a creative business adviser, trainer and coach. Yes, books can change lives!

I am the director of The Design Trust – one of the UK's leading online business schools for professional creatives. Every year, I work with hundreds of artists, designers and makers, helping them to improve their business skills, knowledge and confidence.

For me, teaching isn't just about building knowledge, skills and confidence: it's about **kindling sparks that light the fire of inspiration** in my clients and students. In turn, they kindle sparks of their own, especially if they teach.

In this book **I want to share with you how creative teaching can be**, from the skills you teach, to why and how you teach – the content, purpose and format you select – and the way you price and promote your teaching. Teaching should be an extension of your artistic practice, as original as your products and art.

While researching and writing this book, I had the immense privilege of interviewing creative professionals about why, what and how they teach. They have all developed truly unique training and made teaching a successful part of their practice. You will find these in-depth case studies and their quotes and tips throughout this book. Talking to them about their teaching has made me even more passionate about sharing inspiring, imaginative training; I hope they will inspire you too.

Teaching creative skills has become very popular in the last few years. Interest in starting hobbies increased during the COVID-19 pandemic, and many creatives launched online courses and workshops to meet the needs of an audience eager for new creative experiences.

But with that increase in popularity comes a downside. Few artists have teaching qualifications or the time to improve their teaching skills and, although learning is popular, without targeted, timely marketing it can be difficult to get 'bums on seats'. Teaching can also be exhausting, especially alongside the demands of a busy creative practice.

I wrote this book for ambitious professional creatives who want to develop their skills and confidence as teachers of adults. Maybe you are thinking about offering training, or perhaps you have started already; you may even have many years of experience.
If you want to deliver workshops and courses (online or in person) based on your unique talents, and you are motivated to become the best teacher you can be, this book is for you.

I will help you to dig deeper into why and what you want to teach to adults, and how to do it well while combining it with your creative practice. I will show you how to price and promote your training appropriately so that you can make a good living from sharing your skills.

I have written the practical handbook that I wish had been around when I started teaching more than 20 years ago. I hope that it will help you learn from both the mistakes and successes I experienced along the way.

Right now, the world needs more creativity, joy and meaning – indeed, it needs more fire starters. Are you with me?

How this book is organised

This book is divided into **three parts** – teaching, money and marketing, and growing your teaching business – each one containing thought-provoking questions, practical creative and planning exercises, common challenges or mistakes, and useful checklists and resources.

Reading is a great first step, but it's only by doing and practising that you will truly improve your own creative teaching practice, whatever level you are at right now.

Throughout this book you will find a variety of exercises that encourage you to reflect and take practical steps forward:

- **Creative Exercises:** core practical exercises to advance you on your teaching journey. These are big, juicy and often challenging creative and planning exercises that will really help you to move forward.
- **Time to Pause:** reflective and stimulating questions to help you dig deeper into your personal teaching journey.
- **Creative Case Studies:** real-life stories from a wide range of creative professionals that will inspire you to find your own purpose and distinctive way of teaching.
- **FAQs:** I answer those questions that people ask me regularly.
- **Top Tips:** helpful hints on avoiding common mistakes and becoming more efficient and professional.

Part 1: Why, what, who, how and where to teach?

In this section, we will look at the foundations of your teaching, and answer some of the big questions:

- **Why do you teach?** What motivates you, and how can this insight help you to create original formats and content?
- **What topics, projects or skills** do you want to teach, and to whom?
- **What are the best formats** or methods for you and your ideal students?
- **Who are your ideal students,** and what do they really want to learn?
- **How will you plan,** organise and pace your training?
- **How will you manage yourself** and your students?

We will also take a practical approach to some of these areas:

- **Preparing for your first workshop,** or revitalising your existing training.
- **Teaching in person or online,** and the pros and cons of each, or combining both.
- **Online teaching methods:** presenting live, creating pre-recorded content, and how to blend both.
- **What equipment you will need** for online training.
- **Understanding some of the fundamental pedagogic frameworks,** and becoming a better, more confident teacher.
- **Managing challenging situations** and accommodating students at different levels.
- **Protecting yourself** and your intellectual property.

Part 2: Money and marketing

In this section, we will ask questions about finances and promotion, including:

- **What costs and income** should you include in your financial forecasts?
- **How can you price your training** to keep it affordable and make it profitable and sustainable?
- **How can you increase your prices,** and gain the confidence to charge what you are worth?
- **How will you position and promote yourself** to attract and retain your ideal students?
- **What are the best ways to market** your training to get 'bums on seats' or fill last-minute places?
- **How will your website attract** your ideal students and make sales?
- **What should you include** on your sales pages to get more bookings?
- **How will you launch** and onboard your students successfully?

Part 3: Taking your teaching to the next level

In this final section, we will look at next steps and investigate opportunities for taking your creative and teaching skills to the next level, to help you grow your business.

How to get the most from this book

I teach by asking questions, sharing different opinions or approaches, and most of all, **spurring my students into action**; I wrote this book with the same intention.

Although it is packed with expert advice, questions large and small, practical activities and strategic exercises, and useful checklists and resources, it's not meant to be prescriptive – there are many ways to teach creative skills, just as there are many ways to use this book.

You can read it from cover-to-cover for an overview, and then return to do the questions and exercises, or you can just dip in and out as you like – for many years to come.

I recommend that you get a gorgeous new notebook or use an online document to make notes on actions and insights, and to keep track of your own progress. Use the 'pauses to reflect' and question, and read the case studies for inspiration.

I especially recommend that you look out for the key **creative exercises**: creating your training plan, lesson plan and filming and content plan (if you decide to teach pre-recorded online training), your annual training plan and annual training budget, your website and future growth plan. These are big, juicy exercises that will really help you to move things forward and put what you are reading into practice.

Please note that some examples and exercises will be given in pound sterling (GBP) later in the book. Simply substitute for your own currency.

Please also note that this book reproduces some online screenshots. By their nature it is not possible to make them 100% crisp for print but they hopefully illustrate the points I am making.

To help you launch your own training sooner I have an extra gift for you: the Teach Your Creative Workshop Toolkit, exclusive to readers of this book. As you work through this book, you can use the Toolkit to access additional downloadable resources, including the templates for the various key creative exercises, checklists, forecasts and more, which I will keep up to date.

You can find the Teach Your Creative Workshop Toolkit on www.thedesigntrust.co.uk/toolkit-for-book-teach-your-creative-workshops (use password: READYFORACTION).

It's free and you can download and print off templates and checklists.

My mission for this book has been to create a truly useful companion for artist teachers to guide and inspire you for many years. I want it to be used, with scribbled notes in the margins and dog-eared corners. I hope that you will share what you learn from it with fellow creative teachers and **join me as part of the global community of fire starters!**

1

Part One: Why, what, who, how and where to teach?

CHAPTER 1

Why teach?

> *'There's something timeless about people sitting in a circle together, making and talking. It's essentially human.'*
> **Ruby Taylor,** artist/maker

'Why teach?' is a very big question with which to kickstart our journey. In this chapter we will focus on what motivates you to teach, placing your unique purpose at the heart of your teaching.

Creative professionals teach for a variety of reasons:

- **To share the skills and passion for their craft** with people who are genuinely interested, and to help or inspire others to become more creative. Teaching is a very meaningful way to use creative skills while making money within the boundaries of existing creative practice.
- **To become a better artist.** As the Roman philosopher Seneca the Younger said, 'While we teach, we learn.' Your students' questions, mistakes and results will inspire you to become a better teacher, and often impact on your own creative work.
- **To make money.** Teaching has become a very popular and reliable income stream for many creative business owners. For seasonal businesses, it can provide an income in quieter selling periods.
- **Creative workshops are social and fun.** Connecting with other makers, regardless of previous experience, is good for everybody's well-being – being a sole trader can be lonely.
- **To improve visibility and credibility.** Creatives who teach have another way to tell their story; students often become customers, and will share their positive experience with others.
- **To showcase skills and expertise, and educate their audience.** Many people want to know more about the creative process. This works well if your work is considered high-end – educating potential clients about what goes into it is often the best marketing tool.
- **To sell related products** such as books, patterns, equipment or craft kits. Adding free online training videos can really increase the value of these products.

- **To build a local or online community.** Teaching is a very sociable activity and nurturing connections can stimulate repeat business or create mission-driven networks that learn and grow together.
- **To leave a legacy or change a life.** Some craft skills are on the verge of extinction and, without training for the next generation, may disappear forever. And we all have that one teacher who made a difference – that could be you!

‘I generally work on my own, which really suits me, but it’s not particularly healthy. Teaching a couple of hours each month is just so satisfying and I get so much enjoyment from it. People who tend to sign up for my one-day cushion-weaving workshops are so lovely. The conversations that happen during the workshops are always uplifting.

From a financial point of view, it’s a really efficient and secure way for me to control my income, but it’s a balance of those two things. I wouldn’t want to be a full-time teacher. That would change everything, as I’d have to wave goodbye to the making. It all works together. I wouldn’t like not to teach, but I don’t want to teach more than I do.’

Angie Parker, textile artist

Below Angie Parker at the loom in her studio.

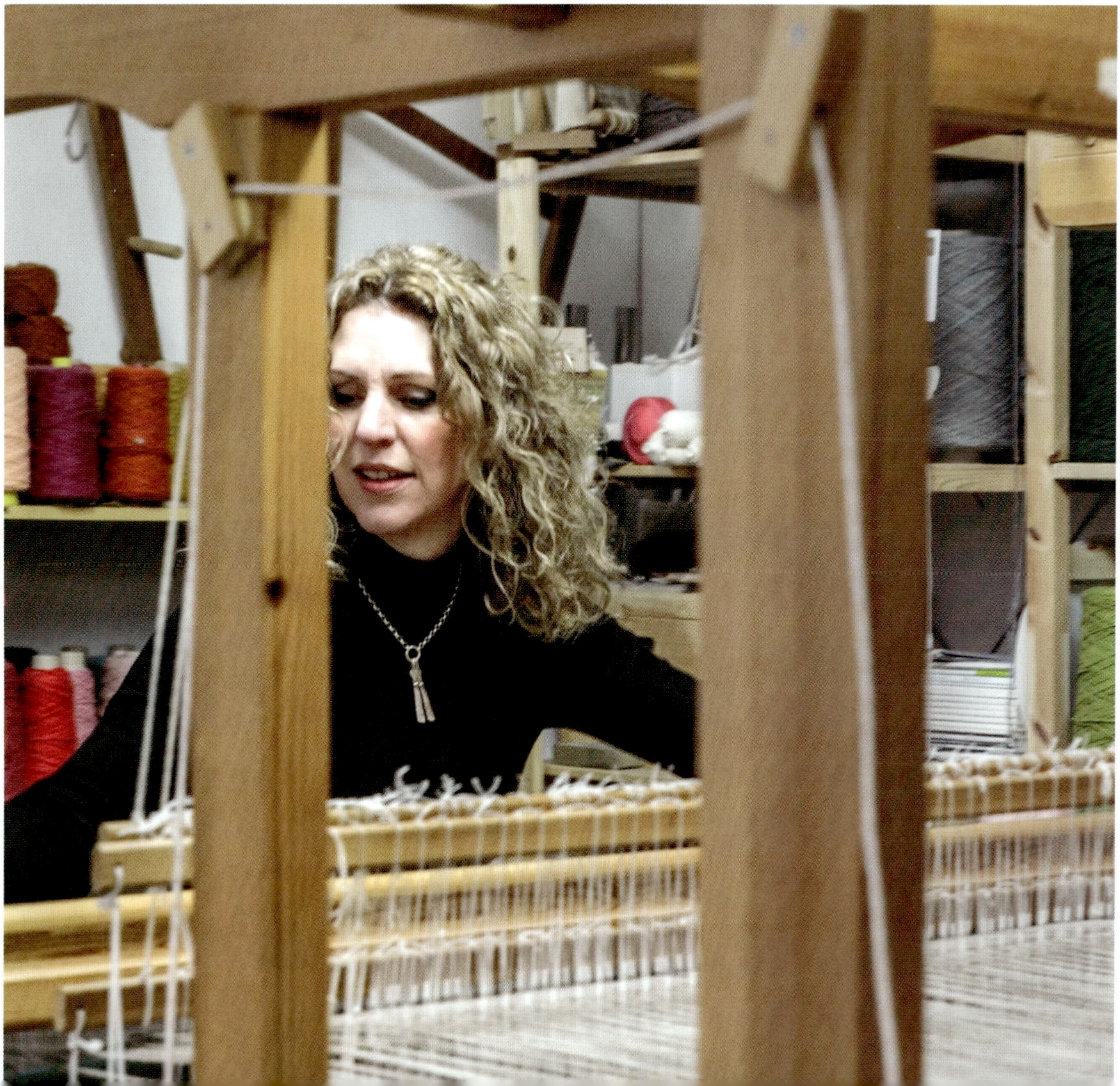

What's your definition of 'teaching'?

Before we dive deeper into your motivations, what do we actually mean by 'teaching'?

It's important to pause for a moment and reflect on this, as teaching is a very broad concept. Of course, it includes in-person workshops and online courses, which will be the main focus of this book, but **there are many other forms of teaching available to you**.

Teaching can include free learning opportunities, such as publishing useful blog posts or e-books; short demos on social media, or hosting virtual live Q&A sessions; demonstrations at craft fairs or in a gallery that shows and sells your work; talks at exhibitions, or taking part in a discussion panel at a tradeshow or conference. Many of the creative teachers featured throughout this book also include writing in their teaching practice.

Time to pause

Get your notebook and identify at least five alternative ways you can share your expertise, skills and knowledge with your existing or potential audience and students.

Include a variety of ideas that you could implement in a few hours, as well as more in-depth approaches.

Why is it important to understand your motivation?

One of the most inspiring aspects of researching and writing this book was interviewing professional creatives and asking this very simple but powerful question: 'Why do you teach?' Their answers were often very personal and revealing.

Your motivation, or your 'why', is your foundation and your purpose. It will give you focus and clarity, connect you with your values and deeper motivations, and inform how your teaching fits into your creative practice. Your 'why' relates to what, who and how you want to teach.

For example, is it your mission to keep traditional skills alive by providing highly specialist expertise to other professionals? Or do you love the idea of reaching out to beginners online and helping their creativity bloom?

Simon Sinek, in his book *Start with Why*, says, 'Very few people or companies can clearly articulate WHY they do WHAT they do. By WHY I mean your purpose, cause or belief – WHY does your company exist? WHY do you get out of bed every morning?'[1]

Simon's Golden Circle concept explains how to **create a stronger, more value-based and purposeful business**. Rather than starting with what you want to teach or create (as many creative businesses do), he suggests that starting with your 'why' will give you a stronger and longer-lasting foundation.

Your motivations will rarely change, while what or how you teach can be flexible. It's easy to change your topics or adapt your format, and there will always be new technical tools or trends to follow (especially online), but **your 'why' will be the anchor that stabilises you**, keeps your approach consistent, and connects you to your core values.

Time to pause

Get your notebook and make time to reflect on your 'why'.

- **Quickly, write down your gut feelings about your own motivations for teaching.** Try to come up with at least three different 'why's. Create a mind map with your three key motivations, then add another level to each of these, noting why each one is important to you. What's underneath? What really drives you? Take the time to uncover some deeply personal insights.
- **If needs be, return to the list of reasons why creatives teach** (on p.14). Use it to help you identify more or deeper motivations.
- **How will knowing your 'why' affect what and how you will teach?** Make that connection and write down your thoughts.

Understanding your "why" will help you to create training that's more unique and in line with your personal values and purpose. It will make you stand out more in a crowded teaching marketplace, and make you personally more fulfilled. And it will help you attract the right students too.

Understanding your 'why' is a fundamental first step that will help you to **identify what, who, how and where to teach your skills**. Are you ready to get there?

First, let me introduce you to silversmith Rauni Higson, who has a very powerful and inspiring 'why' that informs what and how she teaches.

It's an experiment, everyone working, living and eating together, connected through our love of silversmithing. We're learning from each other and, as teachers, get the broadest, most in-depth learning experience. We create a safe space, and people bond and are more open to being vulnerable. We talk about the technical training, but we also discuss difficult client situations or how to cost and price work. It becomes a powerful cauldron of problem solving in a safe environment.

What about your online teaching?

The online teaching started during COVID-19 when I tried to keep the CBS Skills Training Programme running. It was a big learning experience.

I now offer one-to-one bespoke troubleshooting sessions to professional silversmiths on Zoom. I've got some pretty unique, highly developed ways of transmitting technical knowledge and skills to people who are not in the room with me. I live draw diagrams, and use close-up videos and models with cross-sections. We talk through videos together, with loads of reflection and feedback. We even send pieces back and forth in the post, so that I can have a look.

I am using some of the videos I make in these sessions to build a library that I can share with other students. They might become a short course – I have started to work out some ideas around that.

I have found some unexpected benefits of teaching online. For example, when a group of people are working together in a room, there's always a slight competitive undercurrent – to be the first, the best, the most accurate. Some people are overwhelmed by that and find focusing difficult. When I teach one-to-one there is none of that.

When people learn online, they become more self-reliant. They work on their own project with instruction and encouragement from me, but they've had to do so much more independent problem solving. They've probably listened more to their own thoughts. That kind of learning is deep and powerful. It's more self-directed, and that can be a game changer, particularly for introverts.

How do you plan?

I lean really heavily on experience, because I have learnt that we never get as far as we think we will. I try to identify the milestones, and the most important steps that they all need to learn. You can't plan how quickly people will work because some people will pick things up and go with it, and others take much longer.

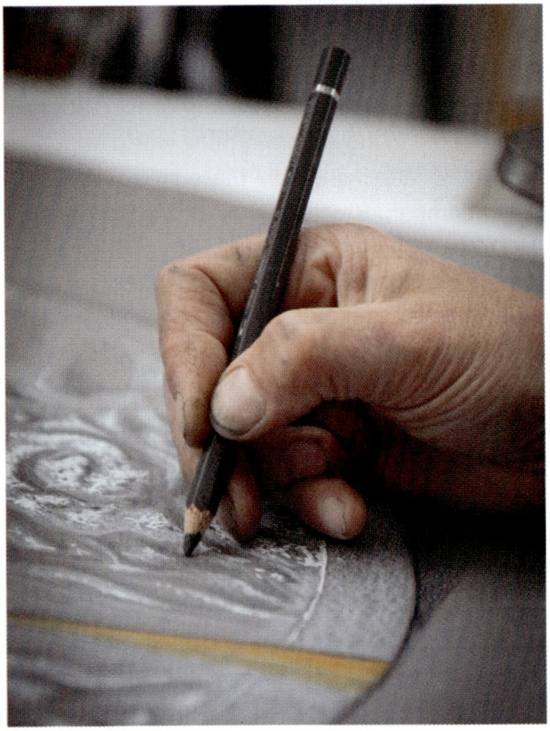

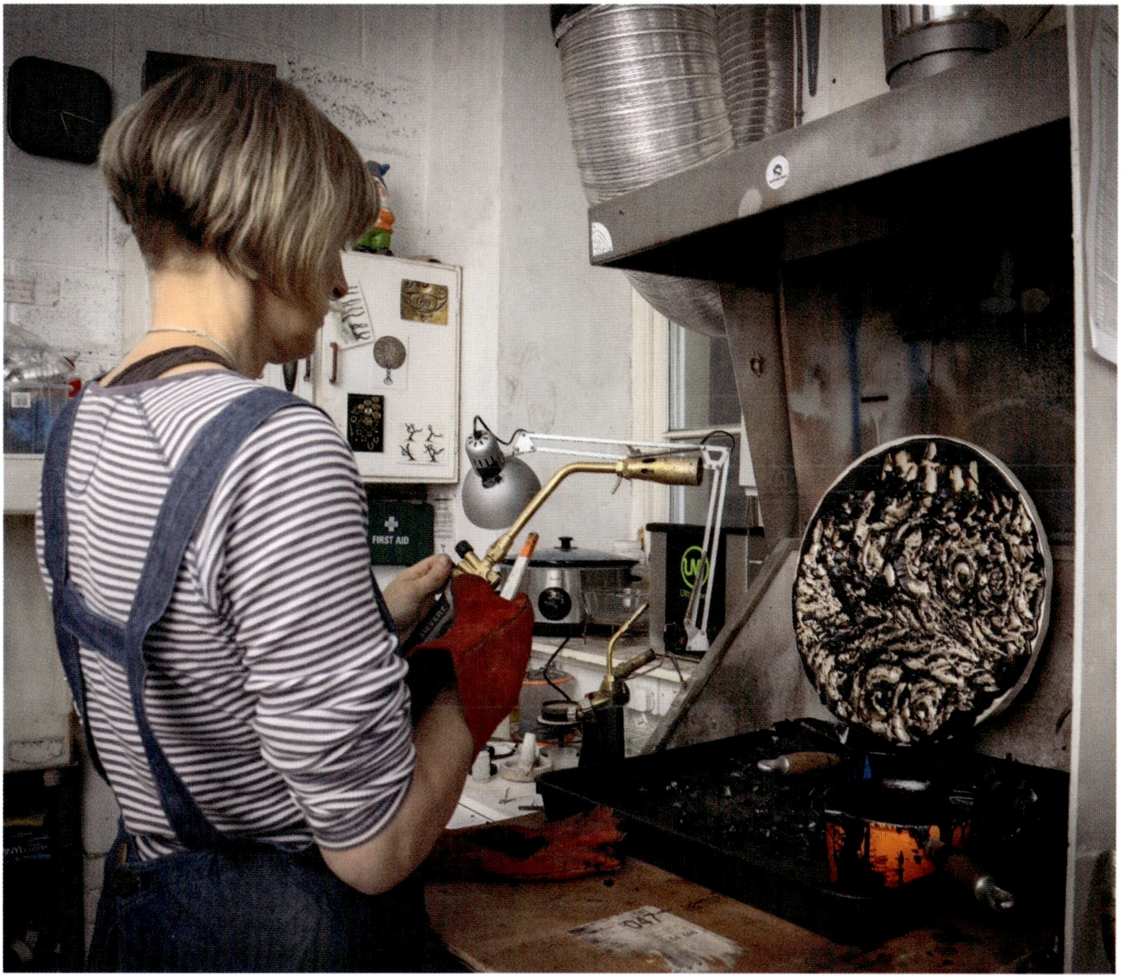

What are your long-term plans?

I want to help people break through both technical and emotional barriers. To achieve mastery, you need to deal with failure. If you work on large-scale silver commissions, you might hold yourself back from trying because the stakes are so high, and things take so long.

I am currently testing an offer of one-to-one problem solving, where silversmiths can come to me with projects they are stuck with. I help them to think ahead, heading off any potential problems before they happen, and I share practical and technical solutions.

Ultimately, I want to build a school here in my valley in Snowdonia (Eryri) in North Wales, to bring people to this amazing, remote place. They can leave their everyday world behind and immerse themselves in the life of a Bronze Age metalsmith in this landscape. The school will also be online so we can reach a global audience. On a practical level, as I get older it makes sense to do more teaching and a bit less making. It's a physical job, and relentlessly making massive pieces to deadlines is intense.

Above Rauni working at the hearth in her workshop.

CHAPTER 2

What to teach

After looking at your 'why', we are going to look at your 'what': **the topics, skills or techniques you want to teach**.

I will encourage you to start looking at similar teaching that's out there already, and there is a great creative exercise coming up that will help you think about what students really want from creative skills training.

What skills do you want to teach?

This might seem like an obvious question, and you might already have some very clear ideas about your themes; however, I want to expand your ideas – creative training can include sharing very different skill types:

- **Technical skills:** mixing colours for acrylic painting; advanced hand-lettering in Procreate.
- **Design skills:** composition for landscape photography; combining visuals and fonts for powerful poster design.
- **Digital skills:** advanced Photoshop tricks and hacks for illustrators; stop-motion films to promote your art.
- **Creativity skills:** exercises for unlocking creativity; creating a true self-portrait.
- **Art/craft/design or cultural history:** remarkable female graphic designers of the twentieth century; an introduction to contemporary Japanese textiles.
- **Professional development skills:** business, marketing or financial planning, or social media skills.
- **Transformative teaching:** students connect with themselves, their identity or background: a mentoring programme for silversmiths; a weekend grief retreat with clay.

I encourage you to think beyond the topics that are most obvious to you.

Start to consider at what level you want to teach – amateur or professional? Have you thought about teaching the history or cultural context within your field of expertise?

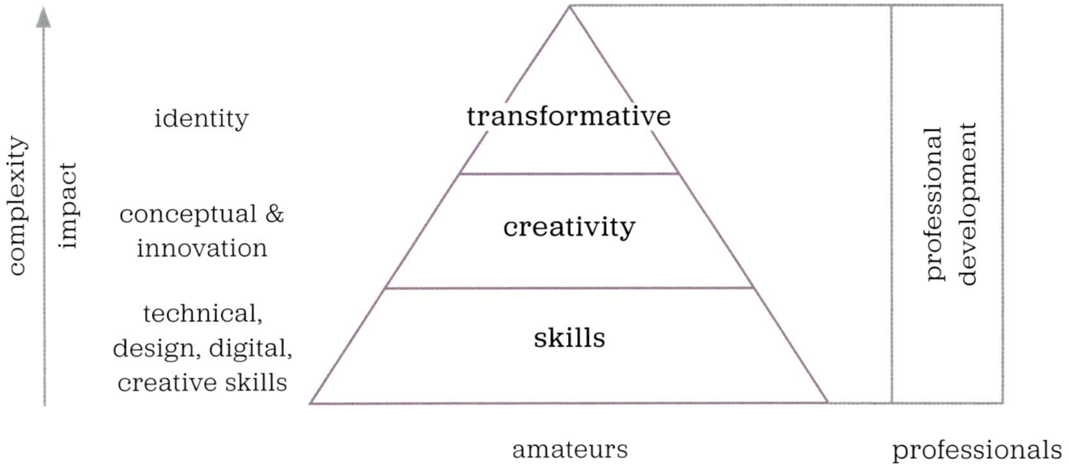

Above What type of skills will you teach to whom?

Choosing your creative topic

Do you find it difficult to decide what you want to teach? It's important at this early stage to explore different topic ideas. Use these questions to dig a little deeper, and generate some ideas that are individual to you:

- **What are you good at?** What do you love to do? Look back at the list of different skills opposite and consider how your skills could apply to them. Don't limit yourself to the obvious.
- **What do you wish somebody had taught you when you were starting out?** Do you remember what you found really challenging? Teach that!
- **Do you have existing clients or students?** Have they asked to learn a specific skill?
- **Do you want to teach what you create as an artist?** Be a little careful about that! I am playing devil's advocate here ... first, you are a lot more accomplished and what's easy for you might be rather difficult for beginners. Second, by teaching your specific skills and approach you might devalue your own work and open the gates to get copied by others. It's important to protect your intellectual property. We will look into this in more detail in Chapter 6.

Top Tip

Even at this early stage, dig deeper and avoid very generic skills, such as 'photography' or 'embroidery'. These subjects are simply too broad and can't be taught in a short workshop. It's time to get more focused.

When thinking about what to teach, take into account how you can personalise your teaching, or make it an extension of your creative practice. Remember your 'why' from Chapter 1 – how can you include your values and motivations more in your teaching? How can you make your training more about sustainability, focus on your eye for detail or encourage individual creative expression?

FAQ: Should I focus on a creative project rather than a skill?

Rather than teaching a skill, focus on a project, especially for workshops (this works particularly well for online teaching), e.g., 'Crochet a Plant Hanger', 'Weave a Cushion in a Day', 'Launch your Etsy site in 30 days'.

Why? Because teaching a project offers clear results, which motivates students as they create a physical piece that they can take home and show off. Incorporating specific techniques within a project will make it more achievable, especially for beginners. And very attractive if they want a fun day out.

Time to pause

Get your notebook and make a note of some initial ideas:

- **What skills, topics or projects are you thinking about teaching?** Will you teach creative or digital skills, or move to a higher level around concepts, or even create life-changing or transformative experiences?
- **Do you know broadly who you want to teach, e.g., beginners or professionals?** We will look at this in much more detail in the next chapter.

Write down between three and five different topic ideas and identify broadly who your ideal students would be for those.

Common mistake: Trying to fit too much in

One of the biggest mistakes many creative teachers make is to try to teach too much in one course. I speak from experience!

In 2012 (yes, I was an early adopter) I was planning my first online course for The Design Trust, about starting a craft business. The first draft lesson plan I created came to over 40 hours of teaching, with 25 video lessons and loads of downloads. I was super enthusiastic and wanted to include everything I knew. I spent many weeks creating this fabulous, all-singing, all-dancing course. But I never launched it. It just became too overwhelming, even for me. And, of course, it would have been far too much for my students too!

If you offer a very broad creative technique as a course, it can take a while before students will see results. **If it looks too complicated or too long, your potential students won't even buy your training.** Offering a specific project or creative technique makes things much more achievable, especially for beginners. Even at this stage, set yourself some boundaries around what you can teach in a limited period.

> *'Over time I've become more relaxed, partly from being more confident with the content. I've distilled more and more of what matters to me in what I offer. My teaching is simplified, but richer. It's easy to try to offer too many things and end up scattered (and shattered).'*
> **Ruby Taylor,** artist/maker

Practical market research

Practical market research can help you to generate ideas for topics, or become more focused. It is a great way to expand your thinking about what and who to teach, to be inspired by what is out there already and to make your training ideas more uniquely yours.

Time to pause

Get your notebook and spend a bit of time researching who is already teaching what and whom in the area that you are considering. Look at the different topics or projects you are currently thinking about.

Use Google, Eventbrite or popular online course marketplaces such Skillshare or Domestika to identify similar training. Try to identify between three and five similar offerings, but look at where your idea can be different, for example:

- **What's the topic or title?**
- **What level is it aimed at?**
- **How long is the training?**
- **Where does it take place?**
- **What's the price?**

Top Tip

Check out Amazon for books with similar content. I regularly look at books for teaching inspiration, to identify the steps involved in getting students from A to B, or to identify what's missing in my own training. Also check the questions or comments that people leave on Amazon or other online forums.

Use the market research to inspire you to become more specific about what, who and how you want to teach – you don't need to spend longer than one hour.

It's not to compare yourself negatively but to show you the variety of what, who and how you can teach on a similar topic.

The reality is that there will be people already out there teaching what you want to teach, so don't let that stop you. In fact, it's a good sign if others are teaching a similar topic as that means that there is more likely to be a market for it!

But the point of this reflection is to **make your training ideas more specific and different** from what's out there already – to make your training more individual to you! We will return to deeper market research in Chapter 8.

Top Tip

Could you try one of your competitors' training or free sessions? Not to copy or negatively compare but to experience different teaching styles and approaches.

You can really learn a lot from being a student. Many of the creatives in the case studies told me how important learning is when you are a teacher. Regularly experiencing first-hand not only how other creative professionals teach, but also promote or manage their training, can really help all aspects of your own teaching practice.

What do your potential students want?

So far, we have looked at why and what *you* want to teach, and at what your competitors are teaching. Now it's time to start thinking about your potential students. How can you be sure that students want to learn what you want to teach?

As teachers, we often make assumptions about what our students know already or what they can do. We have forgotten what we had to learn to get where we are today.

Many of your students will have doubts about their creativity or may lack confidence.

It's often about much more than just learning skills – they want to have an experience! Their 'why' is important too.

> '*My weaving workshops have become more about the atmosphere, to introduce people to the therapeutic side of weaving. To make their life better for those three hours. No one's got time to look at their phone or check the news.*
>
> *It's a proper break from their life. And I have seen friendships start to form in those three hours, which is just nuts.*'
>
> **Angie Parker,** textile artist

Let's get curious about different students' needs and motivation, and the significant impact that has on almost every element of your training.

Read the following four scenarios; observe who the students are and what they really want from the learning experience. Think about how these impact what you offer, where and when, and how it might affect your pricing and marketing.

SCENARIO 1: Creative students who want a fun, half-day creative workshop with friends.

In this case, you need to create a fun, easy training experience that everybody will enjoy, regardless of their expertise. The venue will be lovely, refreshments provided will be delicious, and they will create a product or project to take home at the end.

The ideal group size for this scenario is around six to eight participants so that everybody gets personal attention and feedback when needed. People are more likely to come with a friend or family member, which might change the group dynamics.

These fun beginners' workshops often take place in evenings or weekends. It works very well to offer these as gift experiences, or to offer the opportunity to book as a group.

SCENARIO 2: Students who are looking for a new hobby.

In this case, you can appeal to them by offering a taster workshop, but they will soon want to go deeper into specific creative techniques. These students are highly committed and motivated, and they could learn more through a series of connected workshops or longer courses.

These students will need to be local, although offering courses that run over two days or more will make it easier for people further away to attend. You can sell relevant materials, patterns, books and equipment, and create a series of related online or in-person workshops or courses to keep them coming back.

SCENARIO 3: Students are creative professionals who want to improve their creative, technical, conceptual or professional development skills.
In this case, it's more likely that participants want specialist and personalised training over an intensive day or weekend, or regularly over a longer period, from someone with an expert reputation.

As your training and support will directly benefit your students and improve their own businesses, and as it is more specialist and possibly on a one-to-one basis, you can charge a higher fee. These fees are tax-deductible for them too.

SCENARIO 4: Your clients are organisations or corporate businesses who want to offer creative workshops or activities.
Which galleries or event organisers would be interested in a demonstration or talk given by you? Which businesses are keen to offer creative workshops for their staff to improve well-being, creativity or to have a fun day out? In groups like this the motivation will be very different and often more varied than with people who paid for their own ticket. You will need to create a fun environment where everybody will feel welcome.

Now that you have read these scenarios, start to think about your ideal students.

Get your notebook and write down your own observations, thinking about the following questions:

- **What do they really want from your training, and why?**
- **What impact will this have on what, how or where you teach?**
- **What experience do you want to create for them?**
- **How will this affect the length or timing of your training?**
- **What might this mean for your marketing and pricing?**

We will return to this in more detail in Chapter 3, when we look at customer surveys.

As we have seen in this chapter, **what you teach and who you teach are closely intertwined**. You have already started to explore a bit more about who your ideal students are, and we will get to know them much more in the next chapter.

In the next Creative Case Study, you can read about what and how ceramicist Linda Bloomfield teaches.

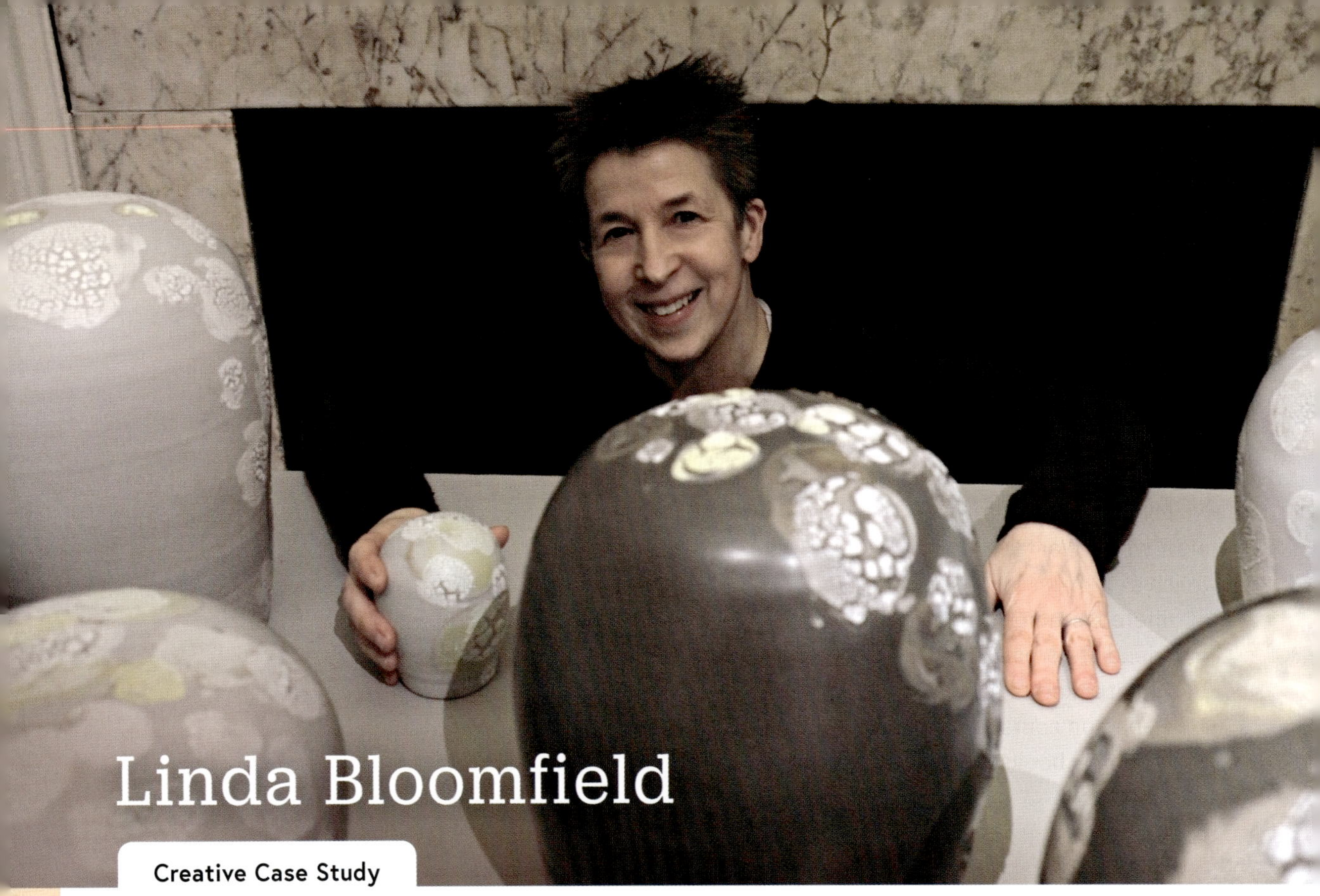

Linda Bloomfield

Creative Case Study

After training as a scientist and starting a family, Linda began making porcelain tableware. She is a ceramic glaze expert who has written various books on the topic. For the last 10 years she has taught at West Dean College, Forest Row School of Ceramics and at pottery studios around the UK and Europe.

Her books include: *Colour in Glazes* (2012), *Science for Potters* (2017), *Special Effect Glazes* (2020) and *Design and Create Contemporary Tableware* (2023), which was co-authored with Sue Pryke.

She sells her porcelain tableware online and through shops, galleries and exhibitions.

You can find more about Linda at lindabloomfield.co.uk

Above Linda Bloomfield showing at COLLECT craft fair.

What and who do you teach?

I am really good at teaching the chemistry of glazes. A lot of people come to ceramics from the art side, so they don't really understand chemistry – I specialise in teaching that. People have told me that when they hear me teach or watch the free YouTube videos, it's not so intimidating.

I don't teach people how to make a beautiful object. It's a chemistry lesson, and students end up with a set of glazes that they can use. It's always an experiment. Sometimes when it fails, you learn more, because you learn what not to do.

My ideal students are quite serious ceramicists. They are usually thinking about having their own studio or getting a kiln, and want to make their own glazes.

Why did you choose ceramic glazes as your topic?

Ever since I was at school, I've been fascinated by both art and science. The career advice I got was to be a colour technologist, and that's kind of what I am. I mix my own glaze colours using raw materials, and I'm still completely fascinated by that. I won't buy a ready-made ceramic pigment.

My first book was on colour in glazes, after which West Dean College asked me to teach a course. Then I started teaching courses at different studios around the UK, and with my friend at Forest Row School of Ceramics. I now get asked to teach internationally too. My in-person courses and online talks are all based on my books.

Below Linda Bloomfield's lava glaze tests at London Potters' glaze workshop.

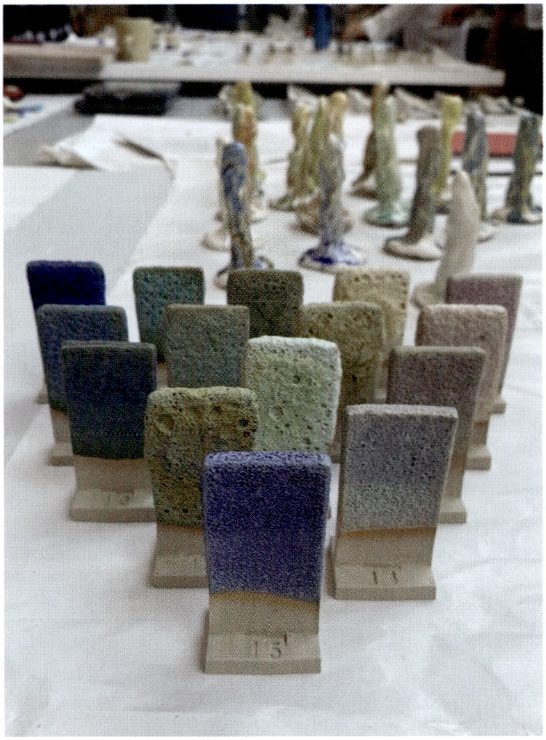

How do you teach?

My workshops are often over two days. On the first day we do loads of testing. It's a bit like cooking – following a recipe, mixing powders and water together – and that gets put onto test pieces. That's one whole day. Then we fire overnight.

On the morning of the second day, we discuss the results and what went wrong, asking questions like, 'How could you make it better?', 'What's your next step?', 'What do you want to develop?' It's all about understanding the chemistry and analysing the results. That's when we delve into the theory.

If the kiln is still too hot, I can do a talk. If the venue doesn't have an electric kiln, then we need to go elsewhere and add a third day for the firing. We use that day in the middle to have a break; sometimes we go to a museum.

How has your teaching evolved?

The first time I did a workshop, I did the theory first, but people did not know what I was talking about. Some people hadn't handled the materials. So, I decided it was much better if I did the practical first, then they can see what these materials are, and touch them. They're all just powdered rocks, but if you've handled them, it's easier to remember their names!

Usually, I have about 12 students per workshop. Each makes five colours and combines them to make another 10 colour combinations. They apply them to tiny little rectangular ceramic test pieces, so it's a full kiln!

I used to do a three- or four-day workshop, but people would run out of steam, so I now run this as a two-day course. It all came about from trial and error, seeing what worked best.

How did you start teaching online?

At the beginning of the pandemic I did The Design Trust's *Teach Your Creative Skills Online* course, and my husband Henry filmed and edited a practical session of me making a glaze, called *How Glazes Work*.

It's a simple, short presentation, crammed with information. I based it on my books and a talk I gave with PowerPoint slides. My online course is four lectures of about eight minutes each. Although it's only 30 minutes long, it took a lot of editing with the slides and the voice-over that we added later.

> *'This short online demonstration works so well because it's so short. And the content doesn't really get out of date so I can sell it for longer.'*

How did you price your training?

I priced the online session based on the price of my books and workshops, the length of the session, one year's access, my experience and the fact that I'm sharing specialist knowledge. With the in-person workshops the students have access to me for two whole days, but for the online session it's just the demonstration part.

As a potter and a writer, I don't have time for much interaction, but students can always email me if they have questions. It's very useful to have it on my website and to direct people to it on social media, and it has paid for itself many times.

For my in-person courses the studios and venues often decide the ticket price. One of them charges nearly double, because they are in central London, but they bring in two technicians and have purchased a lot of new equipment, especially for my courses.

I charge the venues a set daily rate for my in-person workshops. There is often room for negotiation. One venue offered me their space for a free book launch, so I charged less. It also depends on whether they pay travel and accommodation, especially if the venue is abroad.

How do you promote your courses?

My in-person courses are always full. I announce my courses for the next year every September, and I share that via Instagram and on my Facebook Business account.

My venues promote the courses and sometimes their members fill all the spaces up immediately. I sometimes need to do a last-minute call if somebody has dropped out, but that rarely happens.

What do you wish somebody had told you at the start?

You can't please everyone all the time. I've tried. I once had lots of students who were at different levels. I tried to go around them one by one and give them what they needed. That's really hard. Do try and tailor your training to a certain kind of person, and do not have too many people at different levels.

I used to really struggle to not be stressed, especially the night before I had to teach. It's the anticipation of it. It's easier now because I've done it so many times. You can't just say, 'Don't be stressed', because you can't help it.

Opposite Linda Bloomfield at work.

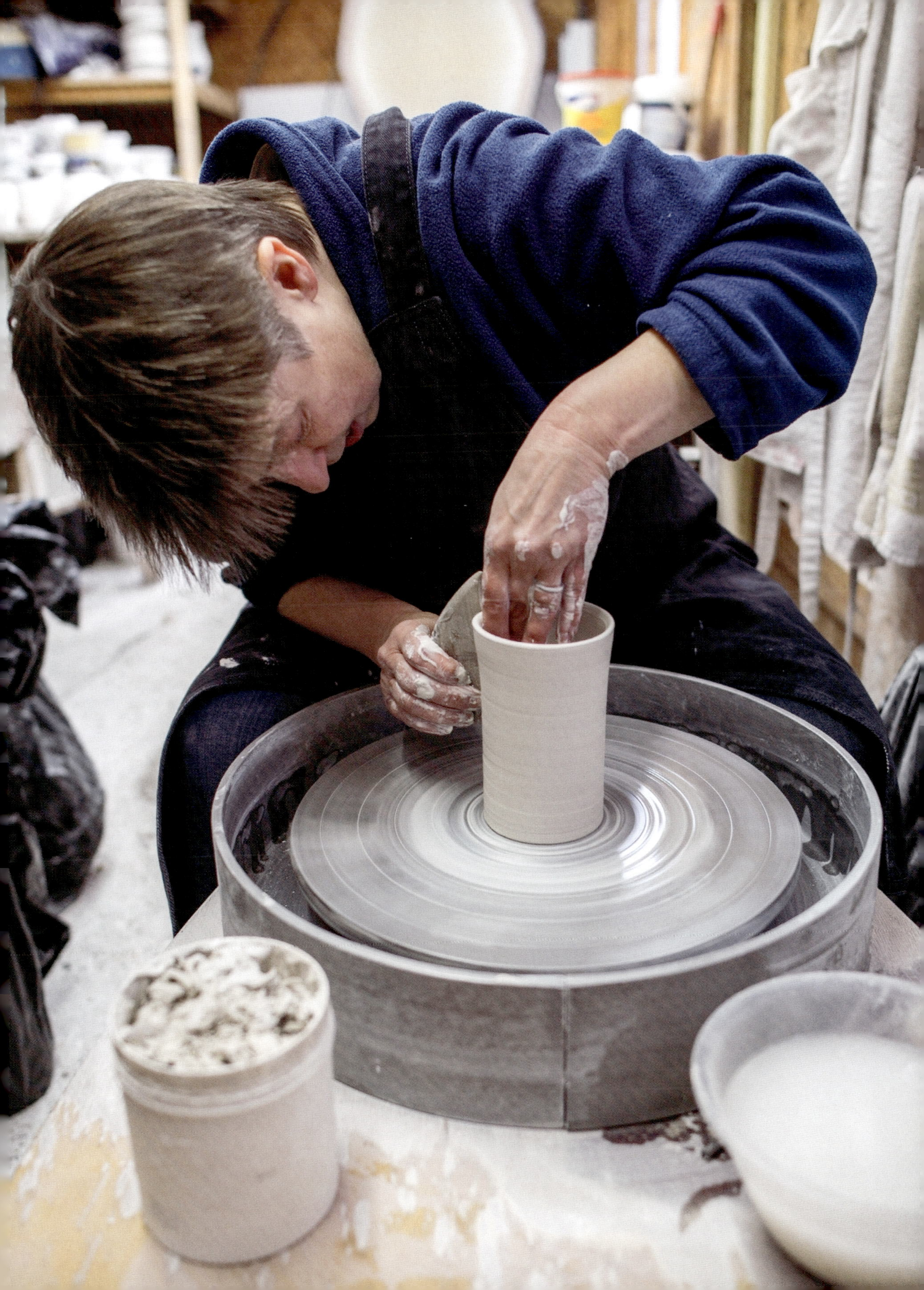

CHAPTER 3

Who do you want to teach?

Are you getting a sense yet for who your ideal students are? Are they hobbyists who want to spend a mindful weekend in the woods creating sculptural forms collaboratively? Or a group of friends who want to push their creativity and express their true selves on a self-portrait weekend?

As we saw in Chapter 2, what you teach and who you want to teach are closely related. In this chapter we will focus much more on who your ideal students are. By the end of this chapter, you will have more clarity on your niche and will start to create your own teaching plan.

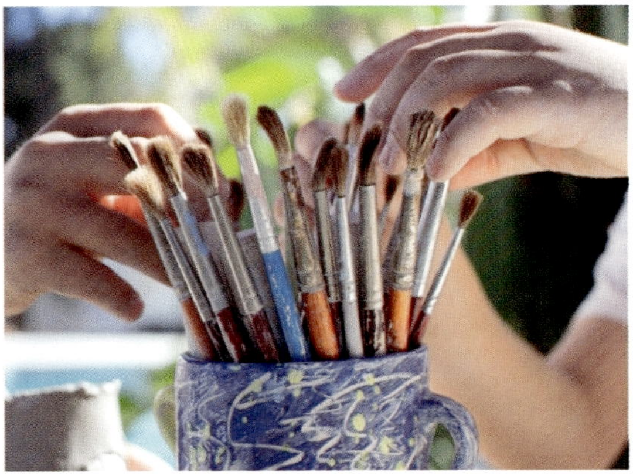

Why is it important to know who your ideal students are?

As you discovered in the scenario exercise in Chapter 2, knowing who your ideal clients are is not only directly connected with all aspects of creating a successful training offer, but also how you will promote and price it. This knowledge determines:

- **Skill level:** are your students beginners, advanced, or fellow artists?
- **Purpose and learning goals:** what do your students know already and what do they need to learn? What do they really want to get from your training? It's often more than just skills!
- **Group size:** How many people can you teach comfortably? This often depends on their skill level, the type of training and your venue.
- **Format and length of course or workshop:** Do they want a one-day workshop with a

friend for their 40th birthday? Or a local six-week course to improve their pattern-cutting skills?
- **Location of training:** Do you have enough local students for longer in-person courses or is the venue and location attractive enough to get students coming to visit especially for that experience?
- **Where and how to promote your training:** Where will your ideal student look for information about training? How can you make your website especially attractive to your ideal students?
- **Price point:** What you can charge very much depends on who the student is, and what and why they want to learn.

How to identify your ideal students

Many creatives find it difficult to identify who they want to teach. It helps if you have some previous teaching experience, or if people have expressed interest in your training ideas. Have clients asked you to teach? Have galleries or event organisers asked you for a talk or a demonstration?

Identifying your ideal students takes a mix of common sense, curiosity and research.

- Based on your current teaching ideas, **what kind of person** do you think would be interested in your teaching?
- **Have you had interest from potential students?** Who are they? What do they want to learn, and why?
- **Do you already have students?** Spend some time finding out about them: their gender, age, personality, values, location. Pay particular attention to students who have come to more than one workshop or course.
- **Who do you like to teach?** Do you have a favourite student? What is it about them that you like and what might they have in common with other ideal students?
- **Do you want to work with galleries, events or studio providers?** Working with trade clients requires a different marketing approach to working with individual students.

Use a combination of facts and assumptions, and start to build up a picture of who your ideal students are.

Use the exercise on p.34 and start to dig deeper into who you want to teach.

Top Tip

Do you find it difficult to identify your ideal students? Your training idea may still be too broad. Revisit your notes on what you want to teach, the purpose and level, and who would be especially interested in this. It's likely that you have a lot in common with some of your ideal students!

Time to pause

Get your notebook and continue to think about your ideal students, answering the questions below.

Try to identify around five specific student groups for the topics you listed earlier (the exercise on p.24). Group similar kinds of students together into specific groups.

- **Get curious about who they are** and add more detail about why they want to learn and what they want to get from your training.
- **Go beyond their gender and age** and think about the problem or challenge they want your training to help them resolve, e.g., organising a fun, creative 30th birthday party.
- **What's important to them?** What do they want from your training? Think more about the scenarios we looked at in Chapter 2, on pp.26–27.
- **Where do they live?** Are they local or further afield but really committed to do a course?

Start to work towards a niche description for each of your ideal student groups, e.g., 'retired female who loves outdoor crafts'; 'somebody who is stuck with a knitting pattern'; 'adults near Manchester who want a creative event to celebrate a family occasion'; 'accomplished embroiderers who want a challenging project'. We will come back to this at the end of this chapter.

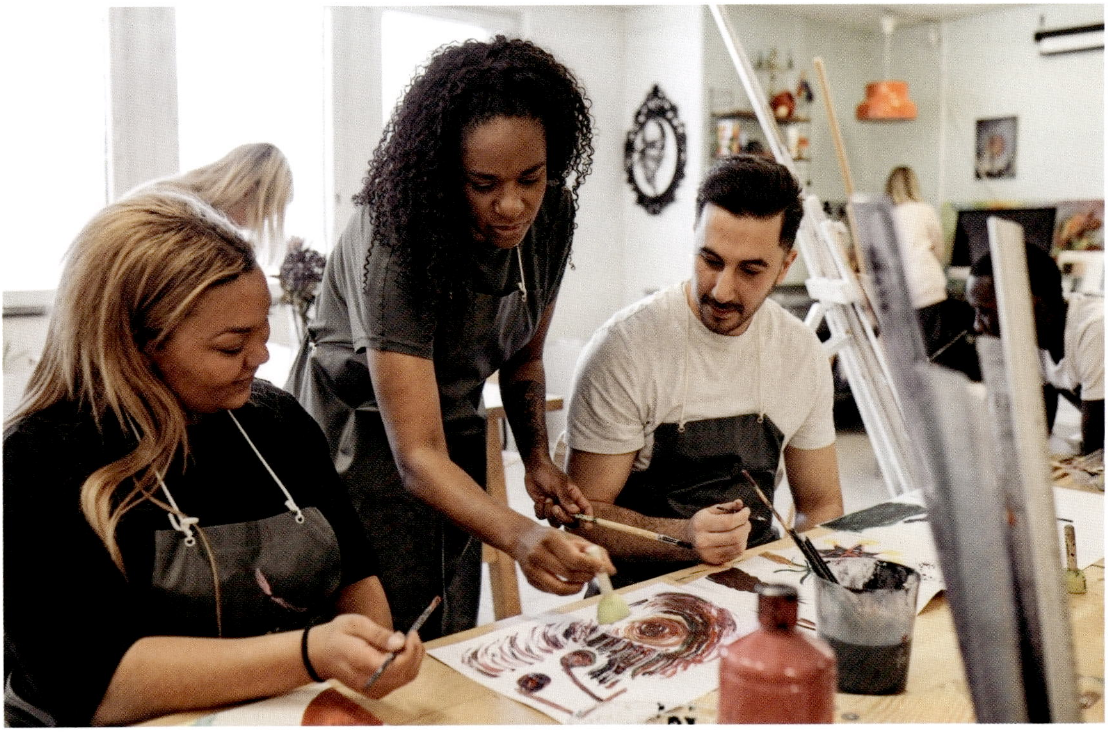

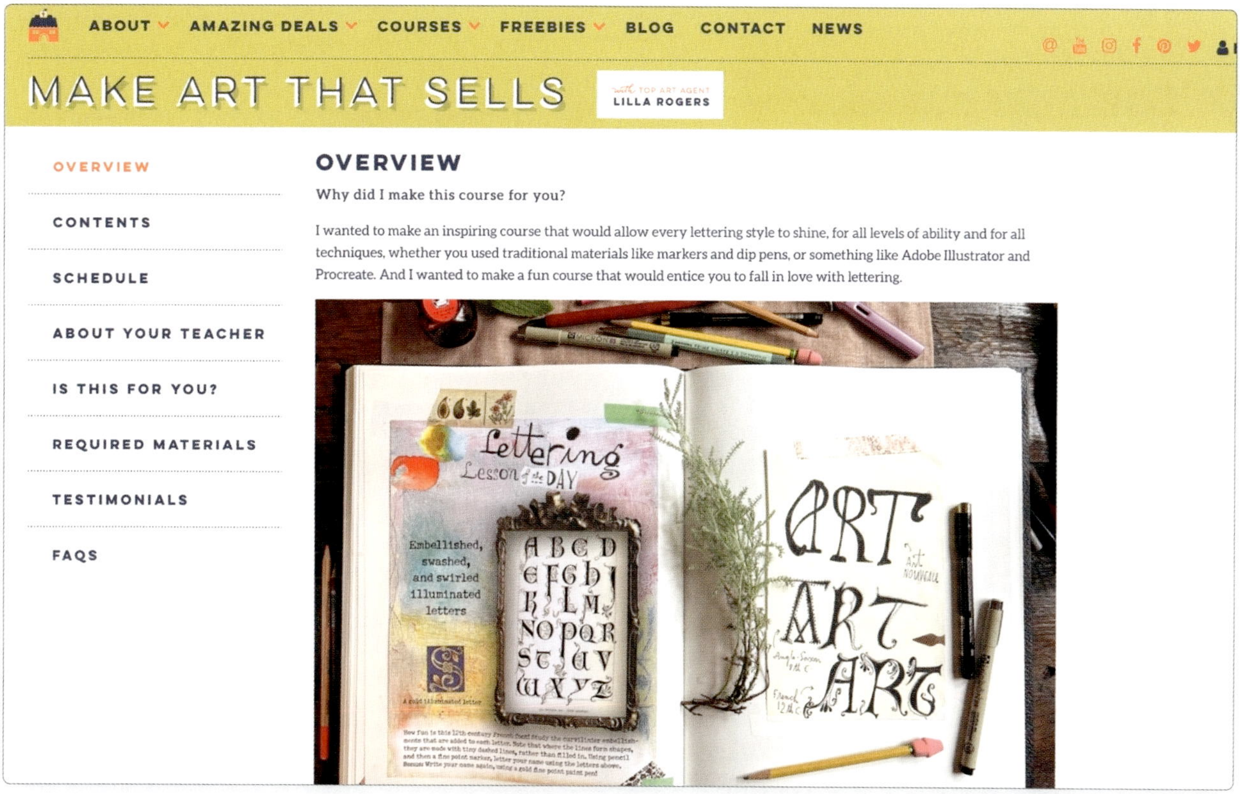

ABOUT AMAZING DEALS COURSES FREEBIES BLOG CONTACT NEWS

MAKE ART THAT SELLS with TOP ART AGENT LILLA ROGERS

OVERVIEW
CONTENTS
SCHEDULE
ABOUT YOUR TEACHER
IS THIS FOR YOU?
REQUIRED MATERIALS
TESTIMONIALS
FAQS

OVERVIEW

Why did I make this course for you?

I wanted to make an inspiring course that would allow every lettering style to shine, for all levels of ability and for all techniques, whether you used traditional materials like markers and dip pens, or something like Adobe Illustrator and Procreate. And I wanted to make a fun course that would entice you to fall in love with lettering.

Above and below Two great examples of ideal client personas for this hand-lettering course on the Make Art That Sells (MATS) website.

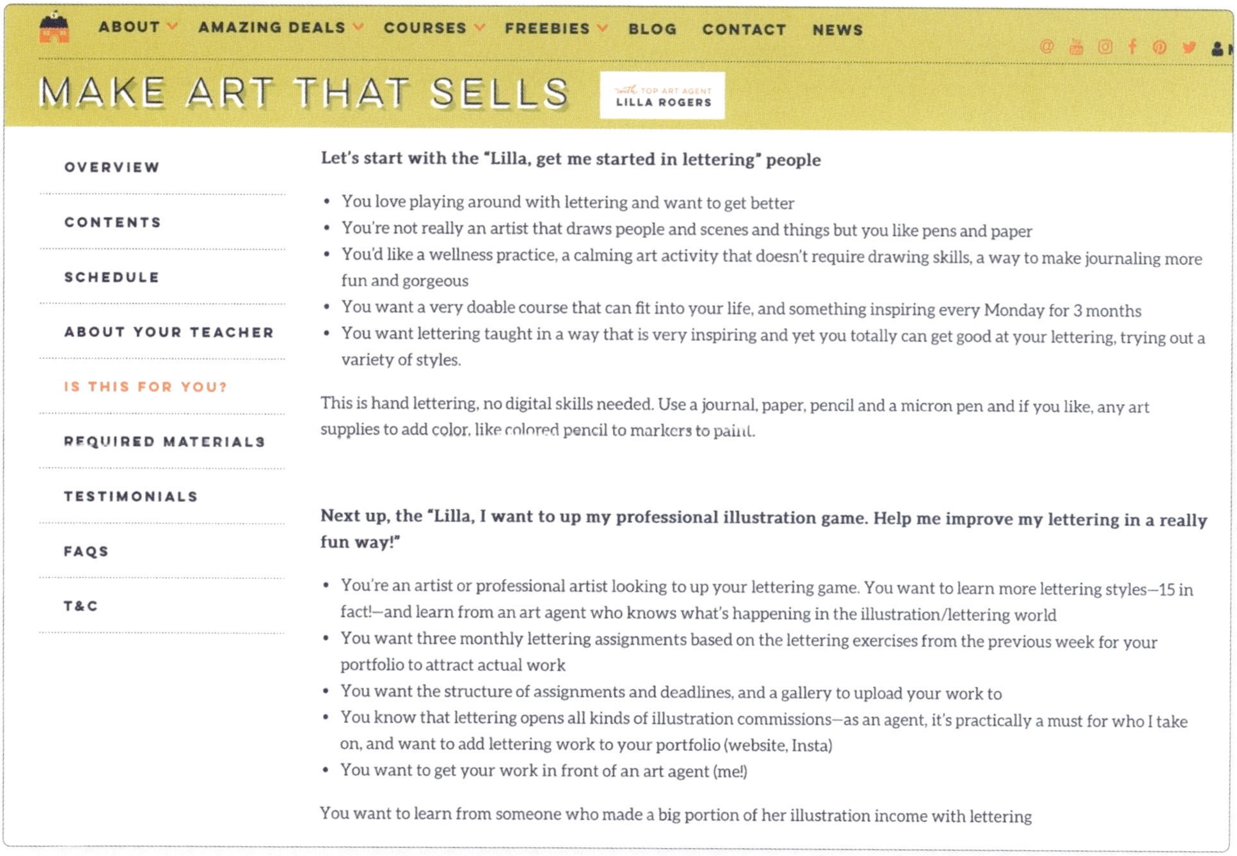

ABOUT AMAZING DEALS COURSES FREEBIES BLOG CONTACT NEWS

MAKE ART THAT SELLS with TOP ART AGENT LILLA ROGERS

OVERVIEW
CONTENTS
SCHEDULE
ABOUT YOUR TEACHER
IS THIS FOR YOU?
REQUIRED MATERIALS
TESTIMONIALS
FAQS
T&C

Let's start with the "Lilla, get me started in lettering" people

- You love playing around with lettering and want to get better
- You're not really an artist that draws people and scenes and things but you like pens and paper
- You'd like a wellness practice, a calming art activity that doesn't require drawing skills, a way to make journaling more fun and gorgeous
- You want a very doable course that can fit into your life, and something inspiring every Monday for 3 months
- You want lettering taught in a way that is very inspiring and yet you totally can get good at your lettering, trying out a variety of styles.

This is hand lettering, no digital skills needed. Use a journal, paper, pencil and a micron pen and if you like, any art supplies to add color, like colored pencil to markers to paint.

Next up, the "Lilla, I want to up my professional illustration game. Help me improve my lettering in a really fun way!"

- You're an artist or professional artist looking to up your lettering game. You want to learn more lettering styles—15 in fact!—and learn from an art agent who knows what's happening in the illustration/lettering world
- You want three monthly lettering assignments based on the lettering exercises from the previous week for your portfolio to attract actual work
- You want the structure of assignments and deadlines, and a gallery to upload your work to
- You know that lettering opens all kinds of illustration commissions—as an agent, it's practically a must for who I take on, and want to add lettering work to your portfolio (website, Insta)
- You want to get your work in front of an art agent (me!)

You want to learn from someone who made a big portion of her illustration income with lettering

Common mistake: Thinking that you only have one type of client

Most successful businesses have different client groups, usually around five to eight, but sometimes many more! While each group will have things in common, they also have distinct motivations and learning needs.

For example, at The Design Trust I work with a broad range of professional creatives who all want to start and/or grow their creative businesses. Within that general group we have very clear subgroups, each with specific goals, purposes, needs and wants:

- **Recent graduates and new creative business owners** often have limited time and money, and a part-time job. They are interested in typical starter topics such as costing and pricing, identifying who they and their clients are, starting to sell online, or the legal and financial requirements to set up a business.

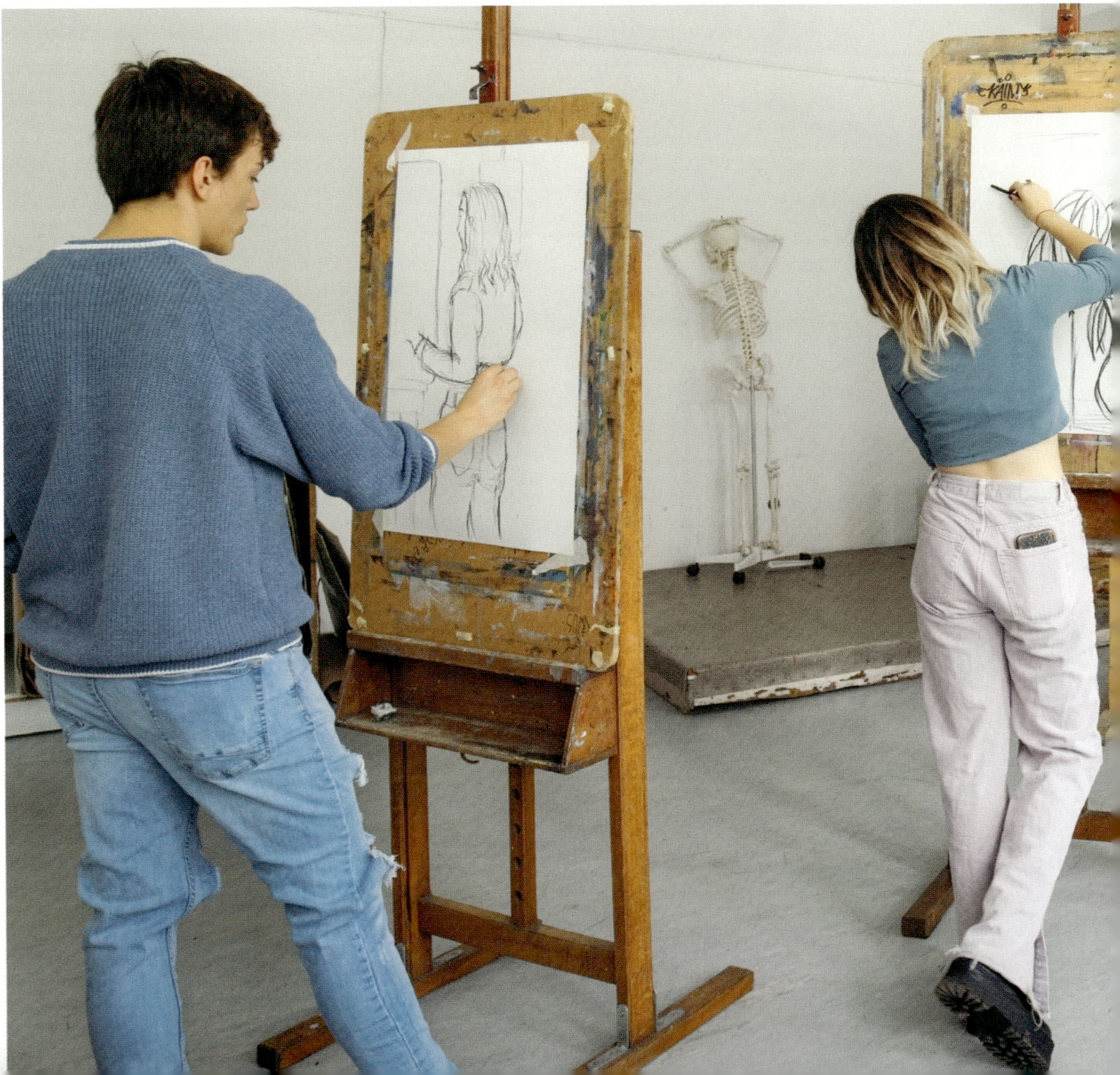

- **Creatives with two to five years' experience** are more interested in growth topics such as how to sell more online, selling to galleries, and how to use social media and email marketing better. They are often very busy in their lives and work too, but are prepared to pay for the right solution.
- **Creative clients who have been in business for more than 20 years** often want advice about getting sales away from galleries. Some are well-known and highly reputable, but sales have dropped and they want confidential advice about increasing their salaries and profit, rather than just sales.
- **High-growth creative businesses** – those that turn over more than six figures a year – have more money to spend but very limited time. They often want private confidential advice on financial management, investment, and managing growth with larger teams and projects.

So, although they all want to start and run their businesses, each group has specific areas of interest, and different needs in terms of time, money and delivery.

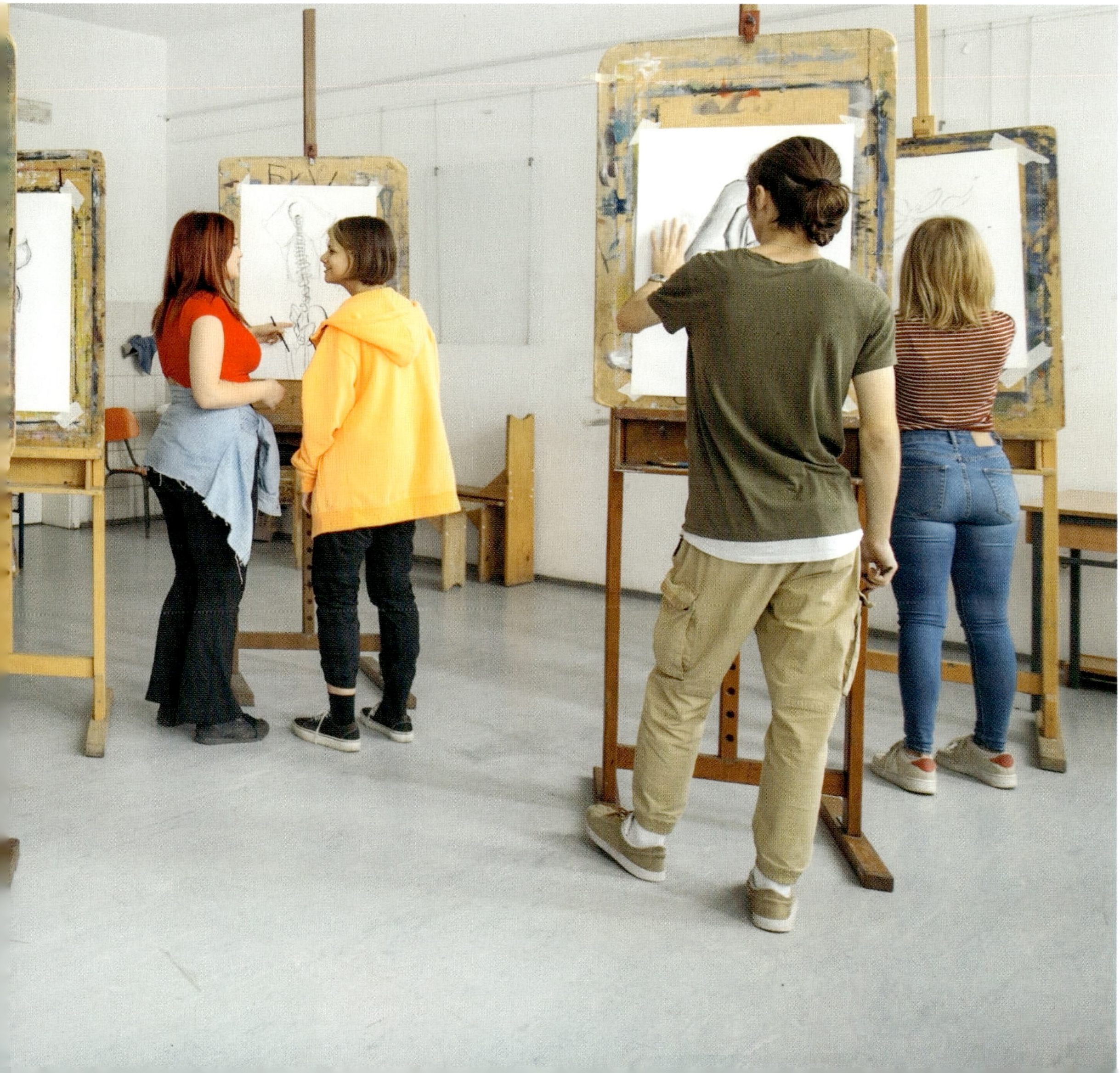

Conduct a potential student survey

One of the best ways to get to know your ideal clients is doing a customer survey. They are one of my favourite marketing tools because they help me identify early specific people who are interested in doing my training in the future.

When I'm creating a new online course or workshop for The Design Trust, I often use a survey (see p.41) to see if there is enough interest, so that I don't spend loads of time creating something nobody wants. The answers give me valuable insights into my ideal students' challenges, and what they really want to learn.

Very often, we think we know what people want, but you might be surprised what their true knowledge and skill gaps are, or what stops them from signing up. Maybe your students or customers love the topic, but they are not planning to attend your six-week evening course because they are not local, or have family commitments in the evening. Instead, they would prefer a weekend course to celebrate their anniversary with their partner.

A survey can give you more ideas for formats, topics and teaching approaches.

If you want to learn more about practical market research and how to create reliable client surveys, I highly recommend the following two books: *The Mom Test: How to Talk to Customers & Learn if Your Business is a Good Idea When Everyone is Lying to You* by Rob Fitzpatrick, and *Testing Business Ideas: A Field Guide for Rapid Experimentation* by David J. Bland and Alex Osterwalder.

Now it's your turn. Put together a short survey and send it out to your targeted ideal students or existing clients.

Use the sample questions on p.41 or download the *Sample Survey Questions* from the Teach Your Creative Workshop Toolkit.

A student survey like this takes between one and two hours to prepare and send, and then another hour or so to review. Take some time to reflect on the responses and, if necessary, adapt and clarify your training ideas. Remember that these are opinions, so don't take things too personally! Be careful to look at what's not quite right yet, rather than focusing on what you want to hear. This feedback can save you a lot of time, money and energy later on. Write your insights and actions in your notebook – the more specific, the better – thinking about these questions:

- What did you learn from your survey research?
- What insights did you get about your ideal students and their motivations?
- What might you need to tweak about your training topic, format and length?

Top Tip

Ask respondents to leave their names and email addresses in the survey in return for a special 'thank you' discount if you launch. This will boost your email list with hot prospects instantly.

Top Tip

Survey DOs and DO NOTs

Surveys are notoriously tricky to create and to get reliable data from. You will need to get a large enough sample of respondents, and ask people who are your ideal students for that topic. Don't ask your mum or best friend for input as they won't give you reliable or useful feedback. They (hopefully) love what you do anyway!

DO:

- **Create a broad but specific survey.** Focus on what your ideal students want to learn about, why they want to learn this, and their preferred learning methods. Ask them what difference the training will make to them. Try to identify their specific challenges, questions or worries in relation to your topic ideas, and what's stopping them.
- **Send your survey to at least 50 potential students.** Make sure that you target people who match your ideal student profile closely so that the feedback is useful. Send it to previous students, or if you have never taught before, ask your current database to identify those who are interested, and then send your survey.
- **Make it easy and short,** with different question formats such as multiple choice and open-ended answers. Start with easier questions, such as their location or skill level.
- **Use software designed for surveys,** such a Google Forms or Typeform, to create free online surveys. They are very easy to set up, and they look professional.
- **Aim to get at least half of the surveys back within a 10-day period.** A good response is a sign that people are interested in your training ideas. If you get a low response rate, then this is not necessarily a bad thing, as you might have saved yourself a lot of time, money and energy by finding out early in the development stage.

DO NOT:

- **Use leading questions,** e.g., 'Would you sign up for this course?', 'How much would you pay for workshop [x]?', or 'Are my courses cheap/ affordable/expensive?' As we will see in Part 2, your pricing needs to be put into context. Avoid asking pricing questions in your survey.
- **Take individual feedback personally.** Responders want to please you, and don't always tell the truth. For the feedback to be statistically relevant, you would need to receive thousands of responses.

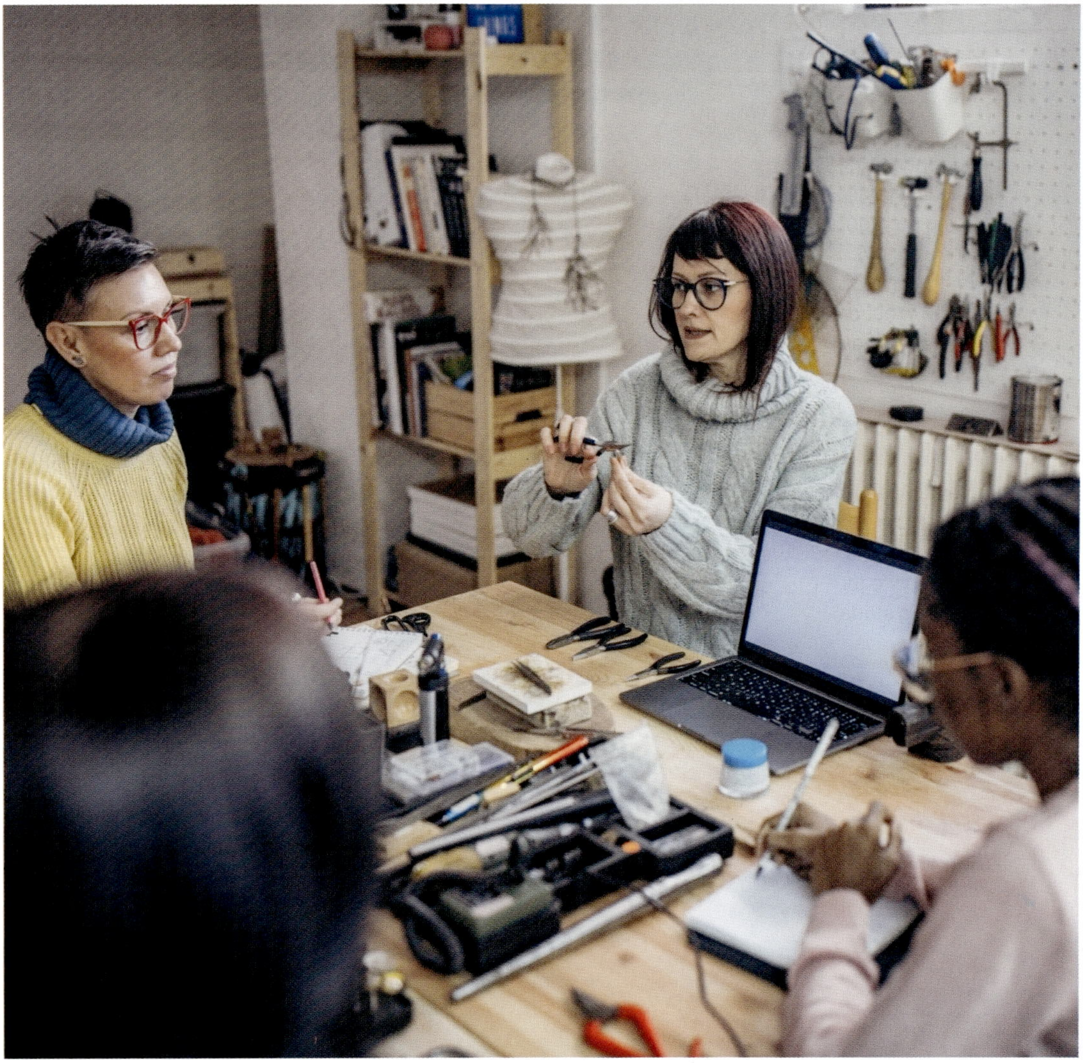

Opposite Use the questions in this real-life student survey for The Design Trust's *Teach Your Creative Skills Online* 2020 course to inspire you.

If you teach in real life, what is your biggest challenge or question around content/topic, time management and running on time, managing your students, dealing with difficult people, finding the right venues or partners to work with, overwhelm and burnout? What would you like to learn more about? What do you worry about? What stops you from teaching in person?

If you teach online what's your biggest challenge or question? Around equipment and software, content/topic, adapting life topics to online teaching, engaging students over a longer time, different ways of teaching online? What would you like to learn more about? What stops you from teaching online?

If you teach online or in real life, how do you currently promote your courses, workshops, demonstrations, talks, memberships? What are your top three marketing tools that you use to get ticket sales?

What questions have you got specifically around marketing your creative training (online or in person)? What would you want to learn or know more about? What are your specific marketing questions or challenges that I should address in my book?

How do you cost and price your creative skills training at the moment? Do you pick a number out of thin air, look at competitors, check how many hours you do, online vs in real life, or does it depend on partners and venue? Be honest, please!

What money questions have you got specifically around costing and pricing your creative training? Are you charging enough? Do you need to increase your prices? How do you deal with last minute cancellations? Is your training profitable and making you money? Do you know?
What would you want to learn or know more about? What are the specific money and finance-specific questions or challenges that we could address in our book?

How have you learnt to teach? What have you done to become a more confident and creative teacher?
We are really looking for any recommendations in this area (books, courses, blogs, experts, podcasts, etc.)! What has helped you to become a better and more confident teacher?
Because being a fabulous creative does not necessarily mean that you are a brilliant teacher.

When it comes to managing yourself and your students, what do you find difficult or challenging? What questions have you got? Think about time management, planning, being organised, overwhelm, public speaking anxieties, burnout, or group dynamics, seating plans, keeping online students engaged over a longer period, etc.

Putting it together: What's your niche?

What do you want to be known for? What is special or great about you? And who is interested in that, and will pay for access to you? **The answers to these questions will define your niche.**

- **It's much easier for niche businesses to stand out** and become known in highly competitive markets.
- **People love learning from experts!**
- **You can get to know your ideal students really well** because you teach them regularly. When you truly understand your students and their worries and challenges, then you can create training that's perfect for them. Your topic, activities, venue and marketing will all line up beautifully.
- **A clear niche will often increase your confidence too.** When you know your stuff, your students will see it. Your credibility and profile will improve, and you will be less overwhelmed and inclined to jump on the latest teaching or digital trend.
- **Niche businesses often create truly authentic experiences** that are more memorable and meaningful for everybody involved. Your students will love what you do and be eager to come back and bring their friends!

Time to pause

Get your notebook and look back at your notes so far. Make time to define your niche:

- **What do you want to be known for, and by whom?** Describe in 50–100 words what and who you want to teach. Identify your motivations, talents and values (as a teacher and artist), and your ideal students. Be specific, but succinct. For example, if you are a knitter, do you focus on specific techniques or projects, knit with recycled materials or create community yarn bombing projects?
- **Reflect on how having a clear niche could help you specifically.** Think about your teaching topics and formats, but also your marketing and branding. We will return to your niche throughout this book.

I am a big fan of niche creative businesses. Why? Because it makes a lot of business sense for small creative businesses to have a focus.

As we are getting to the end of this chapter, start to put your training ideas together, and to sum up what and who you want to teach.

Creative Exercise

Start to create your teaching plan

This is a key exercise that will really help you turn your ideas into reality.

To make it easier, you can download the *Your Teaching Plan* worksheet from our Teach Your Creative Workshop Toolkit.

Go back through your notes, and focus on the top three topics you wrote down in Chapter 2 (the exercise on p.24). Match your training ideas with the specific client groups you identified.

Top Tip

Keep it simple, especially if this is your first in-person or online course. It's easy to become overwhelmed with big courses, so set yourself boundaries. Limit the delivery time for each training idea to a maximum of four hours. If you are considering online training, limit it to two hours.

For each of your training ideas, identify:

- **A working title:** keep it to around five to eight words. Be clear on what you will teach and who it is for. Review your competitor research, or do some now to avoid duplication.
- **The overall purpose:** why is the student doing your training? Is it for a fun day out, to start or boost a hobby, professional development or transformation?
- **The training goal(s):** What are the skills, techniques or projects you are planning to teach? What will students take away, literally or figuratively?
- **Your ideal student:** include their current skill level, motivation and what's important to them, and where they live.
- **Your role:** are you a tutor, coach or facilitator? Will you teach alone, or have guest teachers or an assistant?
- **Format and length:** will it be a three-week online course, a half-day masterclass or a five-day retreat in a gorgeous location?
- **Timing:** are there quieter and busier times in your business that you might want to take into account?
- **Location:** will you teach online, use your own space or hire a venue?
- **Teaching methods:** do you have specific methods or activities in mind, such as demonstrations, activities, discussions or reflective questions?
- **Group size:** how many can you teach?

Starting your teaching plan now will help you to get more focus and clarity, and feel less overwhelmed. Think it through and put down some specific ideas if you can. You can add detail to it later.

Your teaching plan will be the foundation for your lesson plan and filming and content plan (for online teaching), which you will develop throughout Part 1.

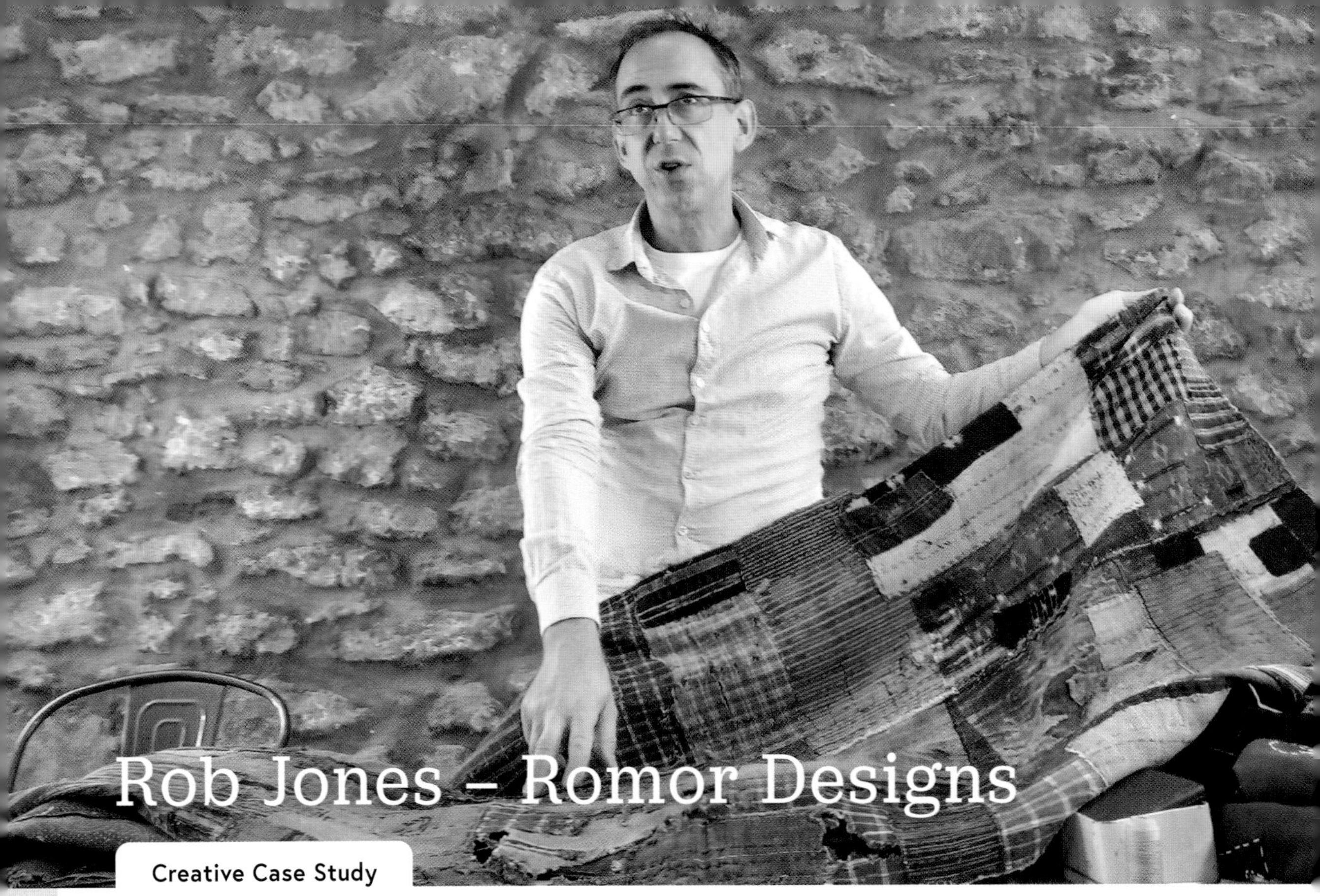

Rob Jones – Romor Designs

Creative Case Study

Rob Jones is a specialist in Japanese textiles. He learnt *shibori* at West Dean College and in Japan with his sensei, international textile artist Bryan Whitehead. Since then, he has become an artist and teacher in different Japanese textile crafts, including *shibori* dyeing, *katagami* stencilling, and *sashiko* and *kogin* embroidery.

He has dyed outfits for the rapper Tinie Tempah for Levi's. His *sashiko* and *boro* work was featured on the semi-final of *The Great British Sewing Bee* in 2022, and he has exhibited at the Japanese Embassy in London.

You can find out more about Rob and his work at www.romordesigns.com

Above Rob Jones with makiage *shibori* indigo-dyed fabric at Clayhill Arts in Somerset.

When did you start teaching?

I started teaching early in my career, as I recognised that it's hard to make a living just selling products. I approached a friend who ran a knitting shop in north London, who was already offering textile courses. Then I approached sewing schools, and at one point I was teaching in six or seven places across London. Japanese textiles were something completely different for them, and nobody else was offering it at the time.

Why do you teach?

I love teaching people who are interested. I love sharing my passion for Japanese textiles, and inspiring people to take up the crafts that I teach.

What do you teach?

I teach various Japanese textile crafts, including *shibori* resist work with indigo dyeing, *sashiko* and *kogin* embroidery and *katagami* stencilling. I run small classes from my studio in north London, and I teach courses at West Dean College. I also offer live two-hour online courses, and I get invited to teach at venues too.

Who are your ideal students?

They tend to be middle-aged to mature women. I will often get people who are teachers or artists themselves who want to learn something new. Men very rarely attend; often they only come with their partners. Occasionally, I'll get a guy to come along and then they end up becoming one of my super fans!

How do you plan your courses?

At the start of the year, I review the previous year. I check when my major selling events are and put workshops in around those. I work out roughly what income I need to derive from the different income streams and set financial goals for the year. If there are quieter months, I will build more teaching into those months.

I schedule online classes in January and February as it's too cold for workshops in my studio. I have been teaching a summer school for a week at West Dean for the last few years and at several other venues around the UK. In the run-up to Christmas I need to prepare for the craft shows, so I do less teaching then.

I have developed content that fits into a three-hour class, grouping together techniques that sit well alongside each other. They can be run as a two-hour online class, or a three-hour in-person class that includes dyeing.

From these three-hour modules I can create one-day or longer courses. Recently a museum picked two modules for me to teach, one with *shibori* and indigo work, and another with *sashiko* embroidery and *boro*-inspired mending.

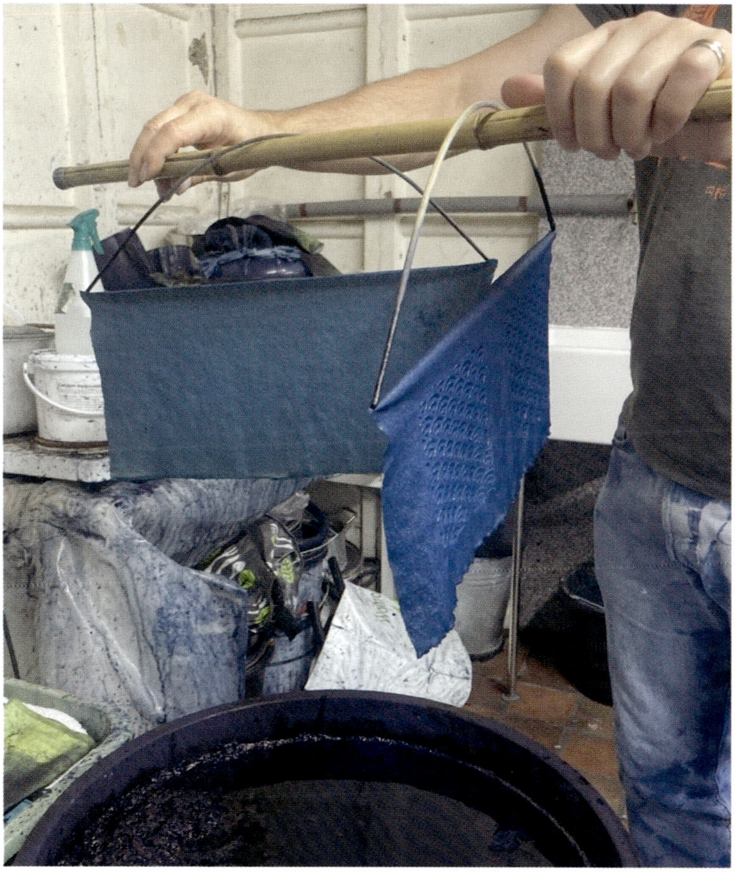

Right Several dips in indigo dye are needed to achieve the right level of colour.

Preparation and drying times often determine how the workshop runs. For example, my *katagami* stencilling workshop is broken down into different stages.

Students start off by cutting a stencil for an hour or so, based on a design they prepared in advance. Then we prepare the rice paste that needs to go in a steamer for a few hours. And they often spend a bit more time cutting, while I share stories of my travels to Japan and talk about its history.

In the afternoon, we apply the rice paste through the stencils onto fabric, which is dried and then dyed in the indigo vat. The indigo dyeing process is magical, as the dye changes colour rapidly when it comes out and we often need to give it a few dips.

I show students how to pattern-match for continuous patterns, and we can be more playful, layering various stencils on top of each other to create interest.

What are your students really learning?

Apart from the craft techniques themselves I want to share a bit of wonder of the skill of professional Japanese craftspeople. For example, a *katagami* stencil cutter undertakes a 10-year apprenticeship to qualify as a professional. There is something about that long-term commitment mindset that I want to share.

> *'I've been doing* shibori *for 12 years, and I've reached a level of competency that I feel confident in, but I would never claim to be a master of the craft. There's still so much that I can learn and improve in my practice. I find that exciting rather than limiting. And I want to share that Japanese mindset with my students.'*

What about your online teaching?

When COVID-19 hit, I did The Design Trust's *Teach Your Creative Skills* course. I already had a lot of teaching content, so I did a sample session on Zoom with some past students to get feedback and work out how to compress it into a two-hour class.

What works really well online is my two-camera set up. One is face-to-face, so students can see me when I speak, and the other is my phone in a selfie-holder on a tripod. This means the camera is reversed over the top of my table, and people can see my hands as if they were their hands. The camera is also great for showing close ups, which is ideal especially when doing a particular stitch.

What doesn't work so well is when students need to show their work in progress to their camera. It's harder because ability levels vary a lot, and people use a broad range of technologies; they might not have fast internet connection, or their lighting isn't great. I am thinking about creating WhatsApp groups for my classes so that they can share photographs of their work as they go.

How have you become a better teacher?

As I did a lot of courses myself, I looked at the behaviours of teachers and decided what I liked about being taught by them. For me, it's about sharing my passion and knowledge – providing inspiration. I have been to Japan, and I understand the history and the background of the crafts I teach. It's so important for me to have credibility as a teacher.

In the beginning, I was overambitious about what I thought I could teach people in the time available. I've since cut a lot of stuff out, and I'm also quicker to get people started now. Nobody wants to sit there and listen to you talk for half an hour. Now, I wait till they have done all the prep work and they're doing the indigo dyeing in the last hour before I start talking about my journey.

At West Dean College I used to be available all the time. You are there during breakfast, lunch and dinner, and you are still a teacher in that context. But I have pulled away from that. You need time for yourself. Teaching residential courses can be so intense, and I get really exhausted. I need a walk or to go to my room to switch off. It's so important to remember that when you are teaching residential courses.

Below Rob spreads rice paste over a traditional *katagami* stencil during a workshop in his studio.

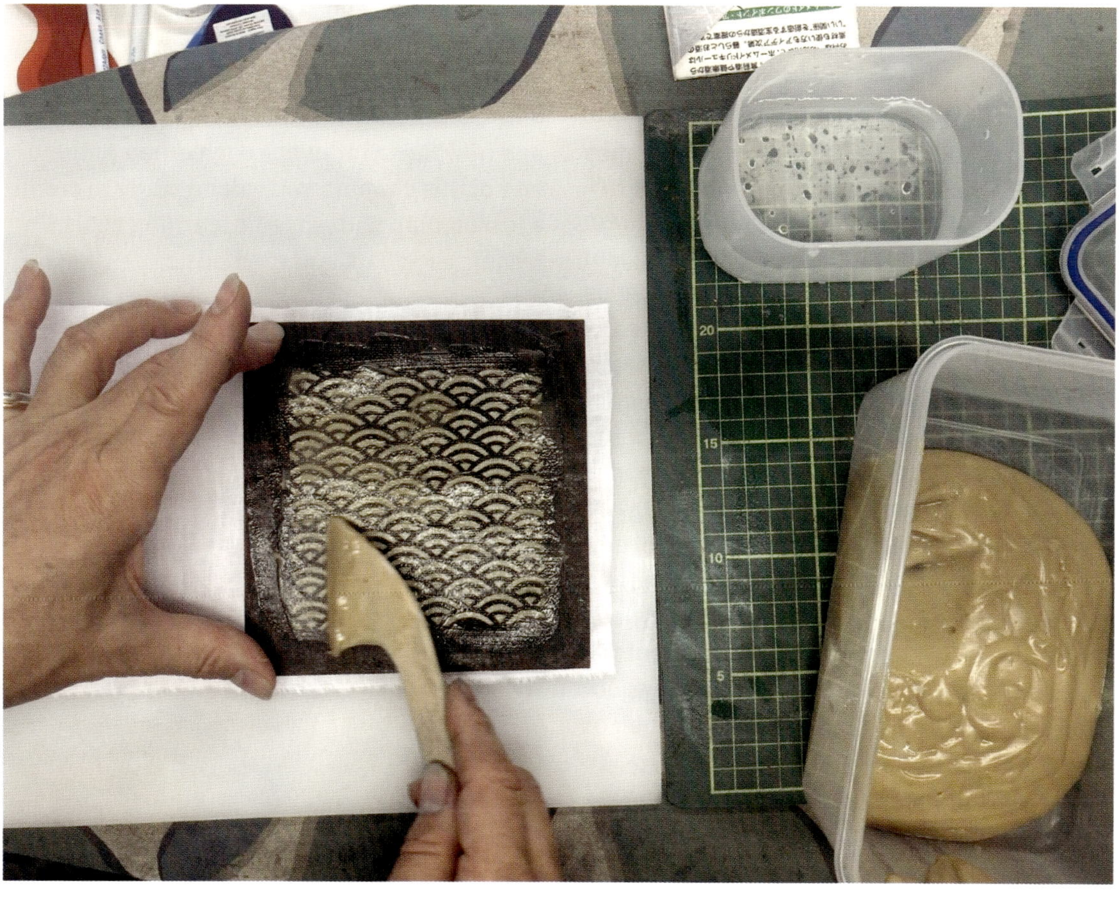

A mentor is often a few years ahead of the mentee, and therefore has insight into teaching creative and professional skills, but also sharing connections, and the attitude and behaviour that's required to reach this level. The mentor is often unpaid, and the relationship between them is usually personal and mutually beneficial, and can last for many years.

Coach: focuses on performance and encourages coachees to evaluate their own progress. A coach doesn't need to have knowledge of the subject at hand, but is an expert in making progress, building confidence and dealing with setbacks. Coaching involves asking reflective questions that lead to action, and listening for what is missing or stopping progress.

Facilitator: Like a coach they are not necessarily an expert, but a 'guide on the side' who facilitates the learning process of a group, and moderates to ensure all voices and points of view are heard. They ask questions, encourage participation and engage a group through different learning activities, with a strong focus on self-learning and collaborative decision-making.

Top Tip

It's up to you to decide what role and relationship you want with your student(s), the process of engagement, and how best to support them. **This is one of the great advantages of teaching in the informal sector.** Many creatives who teach in formal higher and further education leave the profession because of the structural limitations. Make full use of this flexibility and independence!

Below Embroider Hanny Newton at work.

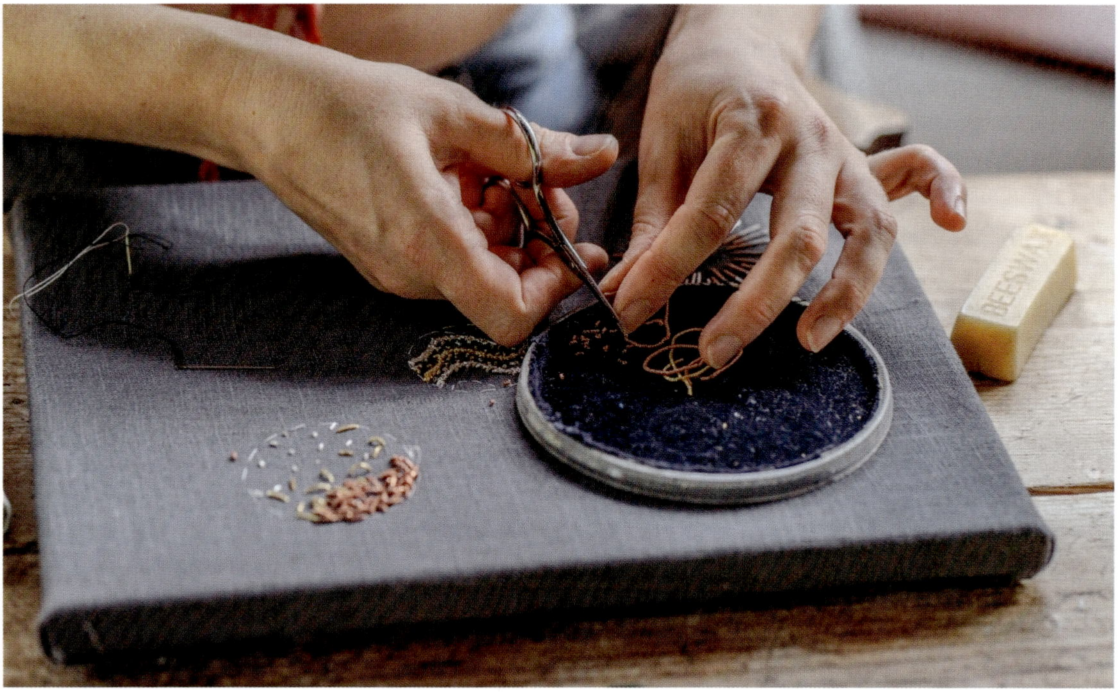

'I don't feel comfortable being "the boss", or the one that knows everything. I'm only just beginning to know what I'm trying to say about myself as an artist! I create and teach in a more democratic way, so I don't teach any solutions or give answers, and always explain that I share just one possible way.'

Hanny Newton, embroiderer

Time to pause

Get your notebook and make time to reflect on the following questions:

- **What role(s) do you want to play** in supporting the development of a creative skill? Do you want to be a 'sage on the stage' or a 'guide on the side'? Why have you chosen that role?
- **What skills do you currently have** that relate to these roles?
- **Which skills do you want or need to improve**, and how could you do that?

Common teaching formats for in-person and online training

As we have seen, there are many different and creative ways that you can teach and share your skills, knowledge and experience. We will now dive deeper into the different teaching formats that would work best for you, your existing skills and preferred roles. Being aware of the different teaching formats and methods will enable more variety in how you want to teach.

Common teaching formats for in-person training include:

- **Talks or demonstrations:** often at an event, a conference or trade show;
- **Workshops:** a practical and interactive group-learning format, often limited in time;
- **Short courses** (often weekend or evening): provide longer periods of in-depth learning, often with homework in between to improve learning e.g., a six-week evening course;
- **Retreats:** multiple-day, transformational experiences, often focusing on well-being or creativity;
- **One-to-one teaching,** coaching or mentoring: very effective for expert skill-sharing and professional development;
- **Formal courses** with certification: take place over a longer period, often based around a curriculum with specific learning goals and targets, and proof is required that the student has achieved a certain level.

Common teaching formats for online training include:

- **Presentations:** a slightly formal format where information flows one way through lectures, demonstrations, slide presentations or screencast workflows, often delivered by an expert;
- **Interviews:** Two or more speakers are visible, discussing a topic or answering questions, often in a talking head format;
- **Online workshops:** a more interactive form of online teaching where students will often practise along with the teacher;
- **Podcasts:** audio-only interviews featuring two or more people;
- **Q&A:** an opportunity for participants to ask questions. Often used as a promotional tool by teachers;

- **Online courses:** teaching on a specific topic or project over a few sessions, delivered live, pre-recorded or a combination of both;
- **One-to-one or group coaching,** advice or mentoring: can be a stand-alone offering, or as an upgrade after students have done an in-person or online training;
- **Memberships:** pay a regular fee to access live or pre-recorded training, often with access to an online forum and networking opportunities with other members. This could be as simple as a private Facebook group or a regular newsletter featuring advice and tips, or teaching content exclusively for members. This is a great way to build relationships and stay in touch with previous students;
- **A library or 'vault' of content:** people pay to access pre-recorded content and can dip in and out of a variety of videos, workbooks and cheat sheets.

Time to pause

Get your notebook and make time to reflect on the following questions:

- **What teaching format(s) do you currently use?** And which ones are you considering for your next training?
- **Did the lists on pp.51–52 include any formats you hadn't considered?** Do some research and read the Creative Case Studies for inspiration. Then, add more detail about your teaching formats to your teaching plan.

We will look in more detail at in-person and online teaching and each of these formats in Chapter 5 (p.84).

Below Jessica Rose of the Jewellers Academy hosts a regular podcast attracting many new students to their online Jewellery School.

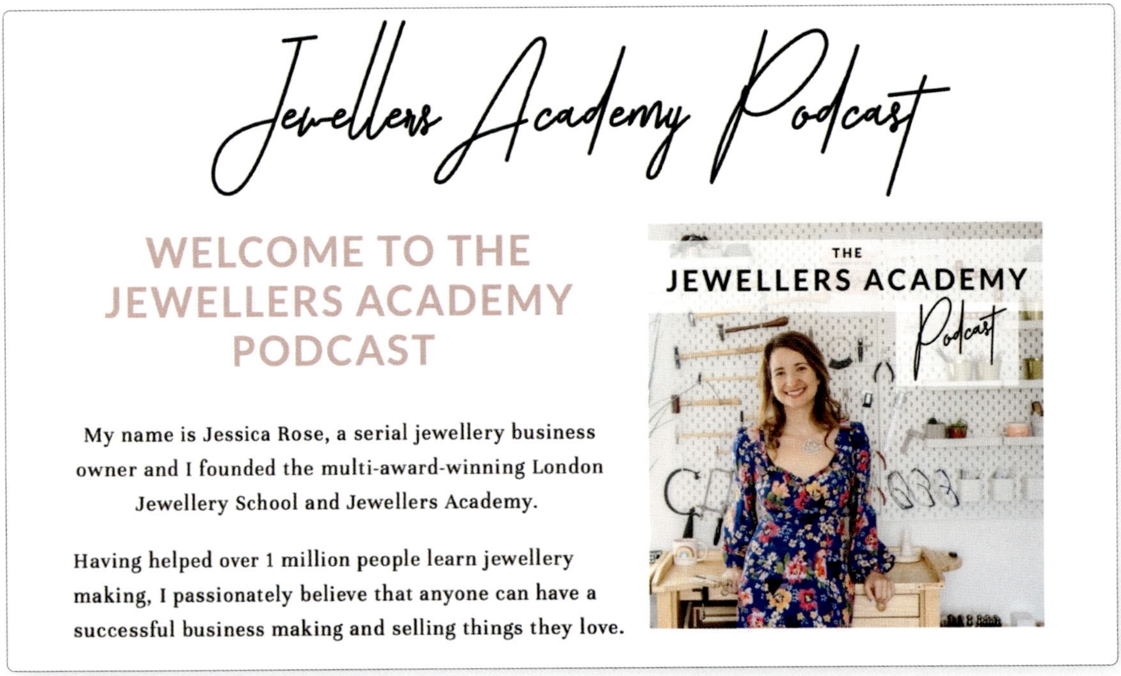

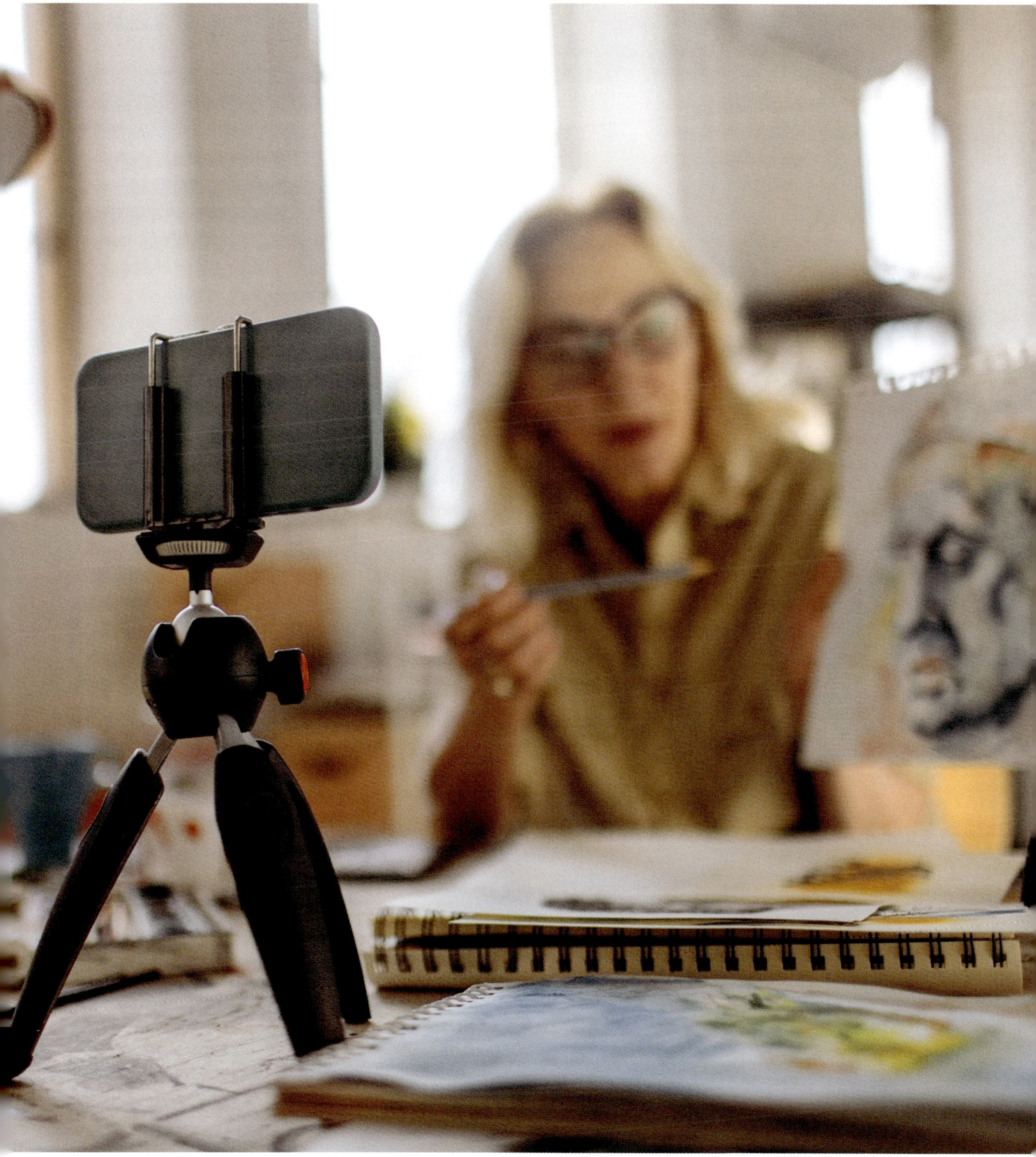

Common teaching methods for in-person and online training

How will you teach? Do you know? Very often, creatives are not aware of the various methods or activities they can use, as often they seem obvious choices.

Explanation:

- What's the best way to **verbally or visually show or explain your techniques or processes**? Break actions down into easy-to-follow steps, or use a more formal tutoring approach, e.g., a PowerPoint presentation where students take notes or fill in a worksheet.
- Do you **show examples of work in progress,** and add visual aids such as diagrams or illustrations?

Demonstration:

- Do you **demonstrate live,** or have you prepared examples of each stage or technique in advance to speed up the real-time process (especially for online teaching)?
- **How will your students observe** and understand the process?
- **Can everybody see you properly?**
- **Demonstrating online presents different challenges** and opportunities to demonstrating in person. For example, when online you might be able to zoom in on detail, but it's harder to talk, demonstrate and film at the same time.

Hands-on practice by students:

- **It's the best way to learn a creative skill!** Practical experience is often what your students come for.
- Do you **provide enough time for your students to experiment** and improve their skills and confidence? Experts recommend that 80 per cent of teaching time is spent on practical application by students.

Personal attention and feedback:

- While your students are practising, do **walk around and offer tailored advice**, ask and answer questions, connect with individual students, and encourage your students based on their individual needs and experience?
- **How will your students share their progress** or get personal feedback from you or other students if you are teaching online, either live or pre-recorded?

Reflection:

This is one of the most powerful but undervalued tools a teacher can use. Reflection helps your students to step away and process their learning; it encourages critical thinking and connects what they have learnt to their situation, which is essential for storing new knowledge in their long-term memory. How will you set aside enough time for reflection during your teaching?

- **Ask open-ended questions** about what they are really learning, what they enjoy the most, their challenges and discoveries.
- Do you **pause to share work in progress** and highlight the different interpretations or results together? Observing different interpretations for different levels is creatively very powerful.
- Do you **give the group the opportunity to identify difficulties** and problem solve together, rather than relying on you as the expert all the time?

- What about **using reflective writing exercises for students**, so that they can document their own progress?

Collaboration and teamwork:

- How will you **encourage students to work together**, learn from each other, share ideas and provide constructive feedback to each other?
- Can you include a **joint creative project** or brief to encourage teamwork?
- Could you **add a 'game' element**, timed activities or even a bit of friendly competition?
- **Critiques:** this technique, where students present their ideas or projects to others for constructive feedback, is very common in formal education, but less so in informal learning. It can work well in longer, more advanced courses as a way to analyse and discuss work in progress, and to foster a deeper understanding of techniques, concepts and design skills.

Additional resources and research:

- Do you **provide examples**, inspiring visuals, additional videos, books, online resources, worksheets, cheat sheets or checklists during or after your training?
- Do you **encourage research?** Include field trips to local museums or outdoors, or invite guest speakers.

Homework:

Another underrated teaching method to deepen learning or prepare students.

- **If you run a course**, what do students need to do before or between sessions?
- **If the training is a one-off workshop**, what could they do afterwards, by themselves, to continue practising and developing their skills?

Time to pause

Take your notebook and make time to reflect on the variety of teaching methods and activities in this list. **Review your teaching plan and add more detail:**

- **Do any of these methods particularly appeal to you**, or do you use any of these already?
- **Which of these methods do you think would work well** with your current teaching ideas?
- **Are you using the best method each time?** Especially with online training, you can provide additional resources and add exercises or discussions, rather than just providing video recordings.

This exercise will help you to become more aware of different activities, and be more creative in how you teach. Your answers will help you to align your teaching with your values, making it more distinguishably 'you'.

We will look much more at teaching methodology when you put together your lesson plan at the end of this chapter.

Before we move on to some fundamental pedagogic theory, I encourage you to read the next Creative Case Study.

Embroiderer Hanny Newton has developed a truly unique way of teaching over the years.

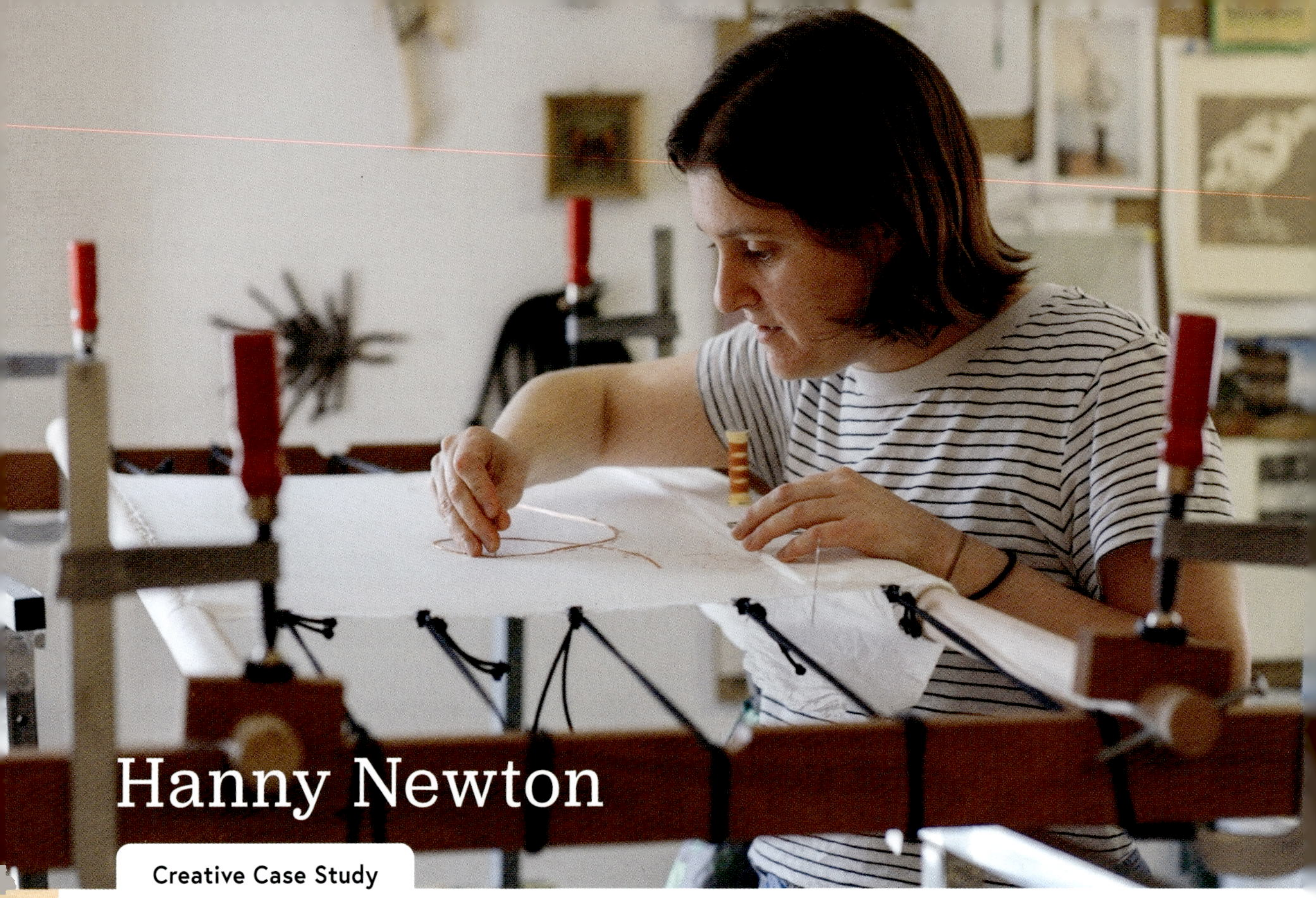

Hanny Newton

Creative Case Study

Hanny Newton is an embroiderer who focuses on metal thread embroidery.

She works from her studio on the Shropshire/Powys border. In 2023 she received a Queen Elizabeth Scholarship Trust (QEST) scholarship to explore the inclusion of natural, sustainable materials into her work. Her creative practice includes working to commission with interior designers and art consultants creating bespoke projects for hotels, restaurants and private residences in the UK and abroad.

In 2023 she launched her first creative goldwork online course. She regularly teaches in person, and has been a guest tutor at West Dean College and with Hand & Lock in London.

You can find out more about Hanny at www.hannynewton.co.uk

Above Hanny Newton at work.

Why do you teach?

I started teaching soon after graduating, as it's an obvious way of making money as an artist. In 2015 I got asked to give a talk to my grandma's embroidery group. That went well and they asked me to do a workshop. From the start, I wanted to do it in my own, creative way. My focus is not the technical stuff for its own sake, but as a vehicle to self-expression.

I have always felt that teaching is a big part of my practice – a way of better understanding what I'm doing as an artist. Goldwork is a very traditional craft, and I want to create a space where other people can respond to these centuries-old skills.

What do you really teach?

I want people to question and feel, rather than being told what to do. When you strip the skills back to their purest form they are quite simple, and that is empowering. The repetitive rhythm of stitching taps into the creative process itself. When you're making, you're on a never-ending journey, constantly discovering, questioning and failing.

I embrace failure because in conventional embroidery classes there are too often very clear rules, and the teacher shows you exactly what to do. My courses are about trying, about starting people on their own creative journey.

I like to break it down to the core. It can be a lot simpler than it appears to be. So, I teach just one stitch over a couple of days. For me, there is so much in this one stitch. You don't need to keep moving on, you just need to keep going back. Question everything. Don't just accept what someone tells you.

Below Hanny Newton stitching a large design.

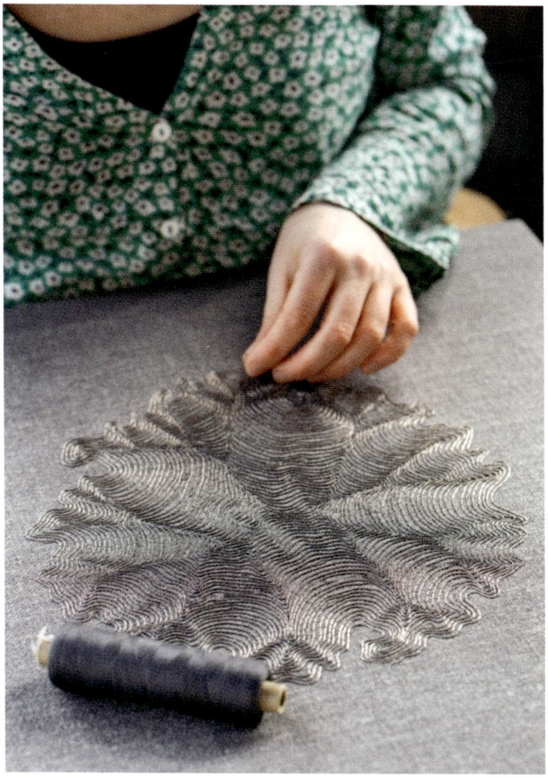

What kind of teacher do you want to be?

For a long time, I tried to work out what an embroidery teacher would look like, what the values of an embroidery teacher should be, and it was killing me. I've had to unlearn so much.

I don't feel comfortable being 'the boss', or the one that knows everything. I create and teach in a more democratic way. I don't give answers – I share just one possible way of doing things. I encourage my students to question, 'Why it is done this way? How else could it be done?'

For years I felt ashamed of how intense I can be, and I tried to dial it down. Then I realised that I should do exactly the opposite. Embroidery is about digging deeper and deeper, and the more I do that, the less I worry. I don't think people would get the same experiences anywhere else.

How do you teach?

I take away a lot of their options. As Anni Albers said, 'Great freedom can be a hindrance because of the bewildering choices it leaves to us. While limitations, when approached open-mindedly, can spur the imagination to make the best use of them and possibly even to overcome them.'[2]

I'll give them one thread, so they're just thinking about that thread, not about the colours or anything else. I'll teach pretty much all the techniques you need in the first 20–30 minutes, and I really take my time. I always say, 'If you're new to this, this is just the introduction.

We are going to pick this apart all day and play with it, and you'll have so much time to put your own spin on this. For now, just be with this one stitch.'

They start with a straight line, and then I'll just let people play. They don't get any control over the threads or the colours. They're listening to the thread, listening to themselves. They're not trying to create a pattern or trying to be 'good'. They are just meandering, taking a thread for a walk.

After an hour or so I'll ask what people have discovered, and we start to crowdsource. I'll write down what we found out. Somebody might have stitched with two threads, and I will ask, 'Has anybody tried with three?'

It's about hyperfocus, and maybe that's my ADHD [attention deficit and hyperactivity disorder], but I've never had complaints. People often ask me, 'Is this all we're doing today?' after an hour or so, and by the end of the day they sign up for the next course.

How do you plan your courses?

It takes me a week to prepare for a week-long course at West Dean College. To get my lesson plan together I have to shut the world out. I have to have a strategic plan, but within that it shifts depending on where everyone is at on the day.

As a teacher with ADHD, I need to strip back so I can stay on track, and not get overwhelmed, or overwhelm others. I need very clear parameters defining what I'm sharing and what I'm not.

What about your one-day workshops?

For my one-day course I have created a kit, digitally printed on fabric. People can choose from four different abstract designs based on paintings I did. People build it up in their own way, throughout the day. It's inspired by my work, but I hope it gives people space to find their own style rather than copying mine.

Tell me about your latest online courses

In 2023 I created my first pre-recorded course, which I hosted on my website. I wanted a way to share my creative approach to goldwork with a growing international audience and I needed a structure that supports the time and space it takes to nurture a creative practice, as opposed to the more intensive, time-limited in-person workshops.

My online courses are a balance of technique and experimentation. We always begin with the foundations of stitching with metal threads, and use this as a jumping-off point for play, taking away the idea there is a right and a wrong way to use these threads in your own work.
I also share systems and methods for generating ideas and pushing your creativity without it becoming overwhelming.

I really love teaching online. It gives me control over how and when I teach, and it works really well with my style of teaching. My courses are creative and open-ended, so being able

'That's what an ADHD person needs to focus on. Take away everything. Just focus on one important choice, focus on that one thing. For me it's like you turn off what feels like seven radios being on at the same time. And you just leave on the one that you choose to listen to.'

to spread my courses over a month gives everyone a good chunk of time to respond to the materials, while being able to ask for feedback any time.

The platform that I've created can keep growing and evolving as an income stream alongside my art practice – one that allows me to connect with stitchers all over the world.

Starting to teach online is one of the best investments of time and money I've made in my business!

Below On Hanny Newton's one-day embroidery courses, participants choose from four different abstract designs.

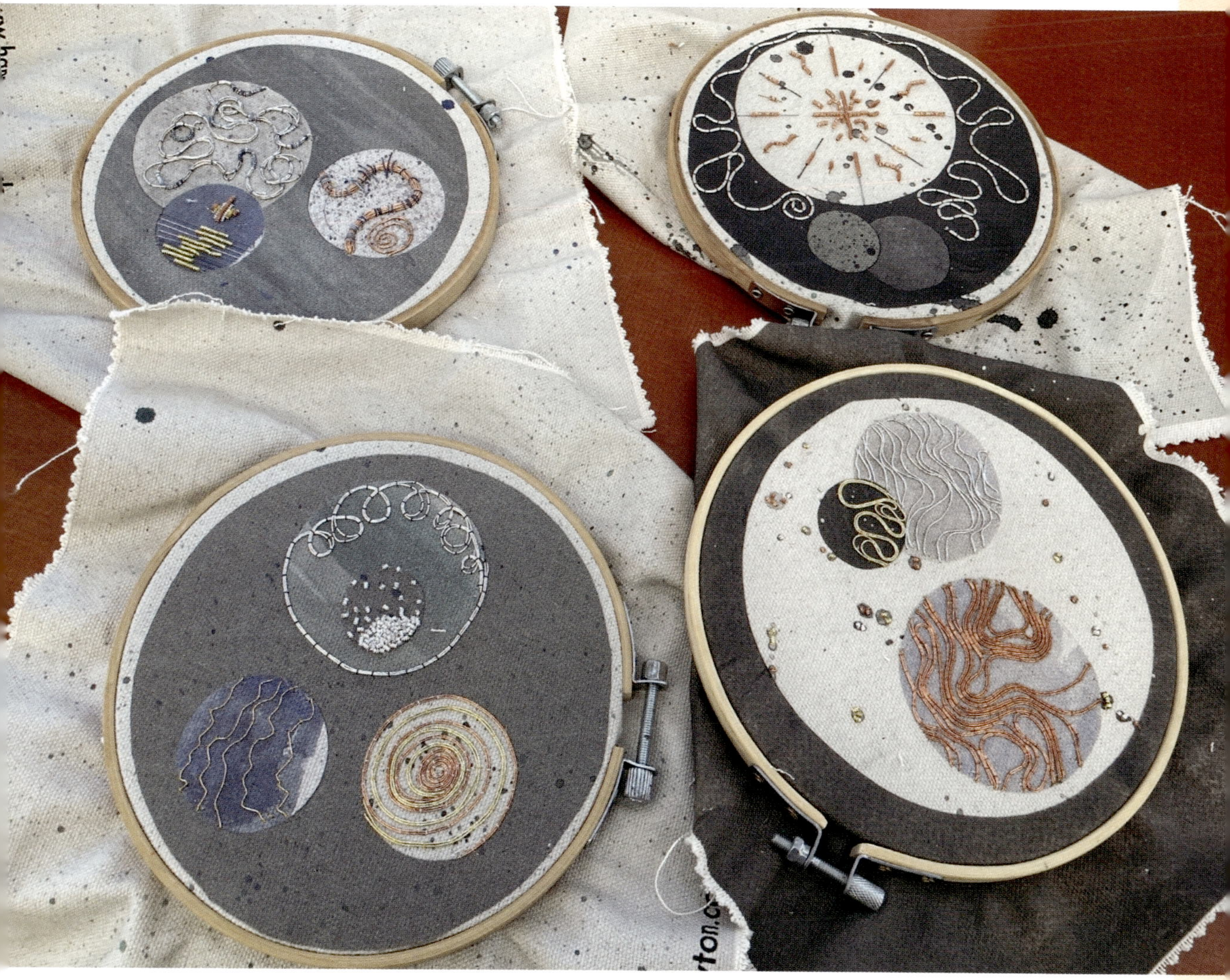

Fundamental pedagogic theory

Many creatives who start teaching in the informal sector lack fundamental pedagogic knowledge on how to teach.

When I started to teach online at The Design Trust in 2013, I found it really useful to get some basic knowledge – and I want to share that with you here. Investing a bit of time (and money) really helped me to become a better, more confident and creative teacher.

Learning styles

In the last few years, awareness of different learning styles and neurodiversity has, thankfully, increased, and with it the understanding of how important it is to use different approaches and activities with individual students.

As you are teaching creative skills, it's only natural that many of your students will be visual learners, but you may also meet auditory or kinaesthetic learners. These learning styles are derived from Howard Gardner's *Theory of Multiple Intelligences*.[3]

Here is a quick overview of some typical learning style characteristics:

Visual learners

- focus on seeing;
- like to make lists, draw and use coloured highlighters while learning;
- visualise words or concepts easily;
- remember people's faces;
- are good at reading and following instructions;
- prefer to sit at the front of a classroom to see everything.

Auditory learners

- focus on listening and talking;
- enjoy listening to lectures, podcasts and music;
- talk to themselves while studying;
- repeat words or names aloud to remember them;
- like to talk it through with someone else;
- might prefer a quiet environment, as they get distracted by noise.

Kinaesthetic (tactile) learners

- focus on variety of activities;
- like to move when learning, and tend to fidget;
- take a lot of notes;
- love mind maps and doodling;
- want to figure it out for themselves, rather than listen to somebody explain;
- like to use their hands or other senses to explore and learn;
- remember feelings better than key concepts.

Some learning style theories add even more to this core list, including verbal learning, social/interpersonal learning, solitary/intrapersonal learning, logical/analytical learning and naturalistic learning.

The impact of implementing teaching in accordance with these learning styles is a topic of debate, but most teachers and students agree that all learners benefit from a broader range of teaching techniques and activities, especially as awareness around neurodiversity is improving.

When you start to create your lesson plan later in this chapter, I will encourage you to include different activities for different learning styles.

Time to pause

Get your notebook and make time to reflect on the following questions:

- **What's your preferred learning style?** How do you like to learn and memorise? How does this preference manifest?
- **What is your preferred teaching style?** You might notice that your learning and teaching styles are similar. Which teaching formats or methods/activities seem most natural to you? Which ones have you selected so far for your teaching plan? Are you a visual, auditory or kinaesthetic learner and teacher? Search 'teaching style quiz' online if you're unsure, or check the pedagogic book recommendations at the end of this book.
- **Stretch exercise:** return to your teaching plan and for your favourite training idea identify a visual, auditorial and kinaesthetic activity. What about for neurodiverse students? Make notes on your teaching plan. This will be very useful when you start to create your lesson plan later in this chapter.

'[Because I have ADHD I am] more aware that there are loads of different learning styles, and that makes me want to leave more space for other people.

I will check in and ask my students, "How is everybody's brain space? How much more can you take in? Do you want silence? More information? Examples? Discuss? How are your energy levels and your capacity to take stuff in now, after two days of this?" I think that's ADHD. The acknowledgement that we're not machines.'
Hanny Newton, embroiderer.

Understanding your students: Kolb's learning styles

Over the last few decades, theories around learning styles have evolved. One theory that I have found especially useful for improving my own teaching is David Kolb's experiential learning theory, which identifies four distinct learning styles.[4] According to Kolb, we make two decisions when we are learning:

First, how we **react** to new information. Do you feel or think first?

- **Feelers love to be immersed in an experience,** focusing internally, relying on their own experience and intuition. They want to get personally involved, love to hear and share stories, enjoying dialogue and group activities.
- **Thinkers look for information externally.** They prefer to read, research or learn from an expert. They enjoy well-structured, well-organised presentations with concrete data and clear concepts.

Second, how we **process** and make sense of new information. Do you watch first, or jump in and do?

- **Watchers prefer to reflect before moving into action.** They want to understand first, before deciding what to do with new information. They often ask clarifying questions.
- **Doers jump into action!** They want to get started quickly, sometimes disregarding any instructions. They also tend to finish quickly, and aren't interested in content that isn't practical.

What are your learning preferences: Are you a feeler or a thinker? A watcher or a doer? Find out on the next page.

	Do	Watch
Feel	**Concrete experience (CE)** • Dynamic, hands-on learners; • Favourite question: 'What would happen if I tried this in a different way?'; • Like to make things happen; • Spontaneous and curious; • Instinctive rather than logical; • Seek hidden possibilities, innovate, take risks; • Learn by trial and error and self-discovery; • Enjoy variety, flexibility and change; • Struggle with rigid schedules or agendas; • Don't like it if one person is dominating the discussion; • Enjoy teachers who allow for creative adaptations and refinements.	**Reflective observation (RO)** • Imaginative, sensitive learners; • Favourite question: 'Why is this important to me?'; • Seek meaning and connection; • Need to be personally involved; • Learn by listening and sharing ideas; • Look at things from different perspectives; • Love brainstorming, stories and discussions; • Interested in people; • Ideas-led, innovative and imaginative; • Struggle with unresolved conflicts, lack of trust in group, and impact of decisions on others; • Want individualised feedback; • Enjoy teachers who are authentic and personal.
Think	**Abstract conceptualisation (AC)** • Common-sense, solution-oriented learners; • Favourite question: 'How does it work in real life?'; • Love the practical application of ideas; • Hands-on learning; • Love problem solving; • Often prefer solitary activities to save time and reduce frustration with others; • Struggle with getting off track, and teachers who don't move into action; • Enjoy teachers who focus on real-world skills.	**Active experimentation (AE)** • Analytical, logical learners: • Favourite questions: 'What information is available?' 'What do the experts think?'; • Want clear explanations, facts and details; • Love to research and collect data; • Like to evaluate information; • Enjoy well-structured lectures, schedules and agendas; • Thorough and industrious; intellectual; • Enjoy more traditional teaching in a classroom setting; • Need time to think things through; • Struggle with teachers who don't see the big picture, and if there is no written agenda or time to prepare; • Enjoy teachers who are knowledgeable, organised and structured.

Above Kolb's four distinct learning styles.

Do you recognise your own or your students' preferred learning style? This awareness can help you understand why you find learning or teaching easy or intuitive in one situation, but not another.

Identifying learning styles is not about labelling people. **It's about raising awareness and offering a more diverse and creative approach** to your teaching formats and methods. Everyone needs and responds to different stimuli to some extent, and sometimes a specific situation calls for a specific approach.

Top Tip

Add 'flipped' learning to your teaching format. Flipped learning has become popular in recent years, and aims to shift the focus from passive learning from a tutor to active student engagement.

In a flipped learning environment, students get instructional materials (e.g., a video lecture or reading materials) to read or watch by themselves.

The time in class (in person or online) is then focused on doing and learning as a group, often resolving real-world challenges with collaborative activities and discussions.

This approach helps students to apply their knowledge, collaborate with peers and get guidance from the teacher.

Time to pause

Get your notebook and make time to reflect on the following questions:

- **What is your preferred Kolb teaching style?** How do you know? It's very likely your own learning style!
- **Which of the four teaching styles is a challenge for you?**
- **Can you think of a moment, as a teacher or student, when a student really annoyed you?** It's very likely that their learning style was different to yours! What insights can you get about this teacher or student and your response?
- **How can you use Kolb's framework to make your own teaching more diverse and creative?** Make more notes in your training plan or notebook now so that you can refer to it when you create your own lesson plan.
- **Go through this book and look at how I use different learning styles.** Which exercises do you like to do, and which questions have you avoided so far? Reflect on those insights for a moment and make notes. What do you need to do to make the most of this book? What do you need to stop doing?

You can download a useful checklist, entitled *How to Make Your Teaching More Diverse and Accessible*, from the Teach Your Creative Workshop Toolkit. Use it to give you inspiration for ways to incorporate different learning styles into your teaching practice.

If you're interested in finding out more about Kolb's learning styles, I recommend the late educational specialist Jeanine O'Neill-Blackwell's brilliant book *Engage: The Trainer's Guide to Learning Styles*. In it, she introduces her 4MAT® learning styles, and includes many appropriate activities and questions. You can use the 4MAT® Learning Style Quiz online if you are unsure about your own.

Levelling up your teaching: Bloom's Taxonomy

At what level do you want to teach? Do you want to keep it simple and straightforward, working with beginners who want to have a fun day, or do you want to push your students outside their comfort zones? That's what we will explore in this next practical pedagogic theory: Bloom's Taxonomy.

Many creative workshops are aimed at basic skills. The teacher demonstrates a technique, and the student follows and replicates it. Of course, that's how most learning starts; students need to learn

Below Teaching creative skills is often very visual and tactile; Ruby Taylor of Native Hands making a grass basket.

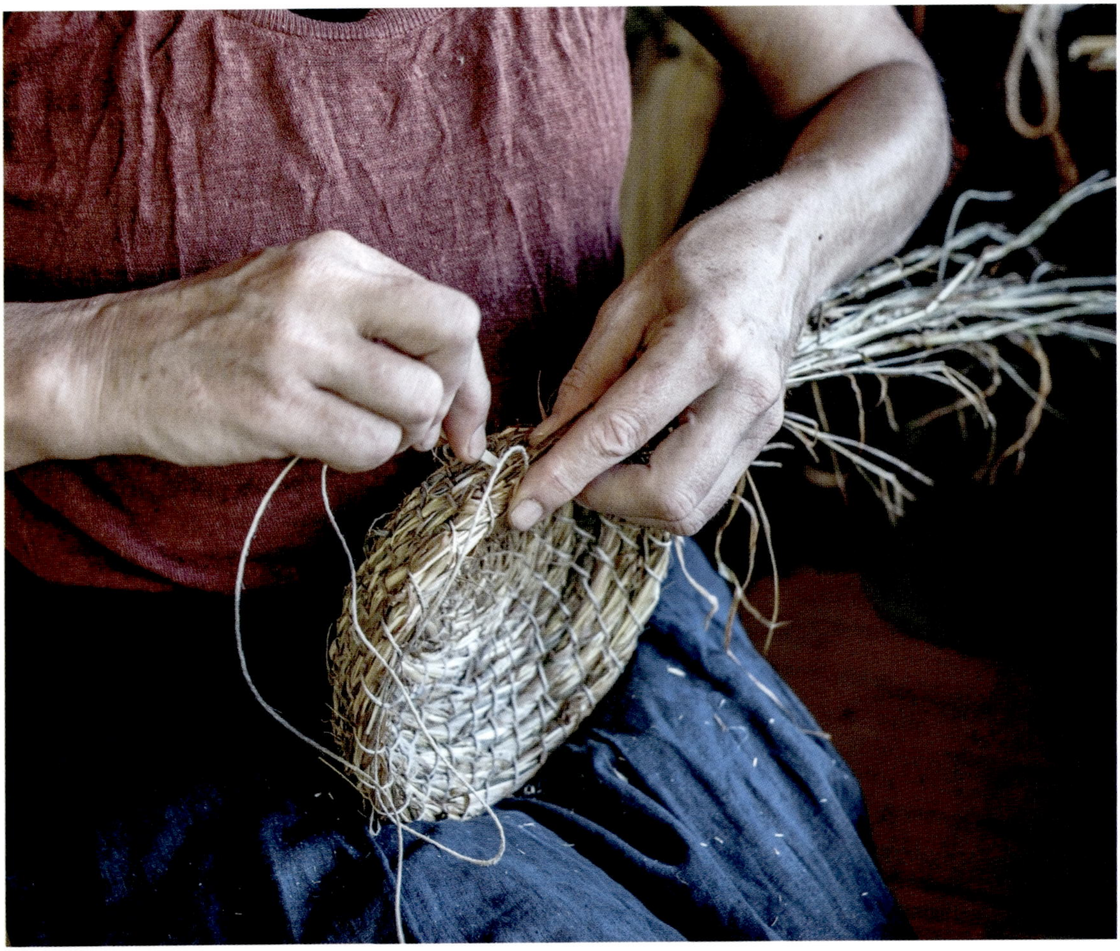

the basics first. With some crafts, such as basketry, you will need to follow the rules otherwise your basket will simply fall apart!

But, what if you want to encourage your students to become more **innovative and experiment independently**? Or if you want to teach higher-level skills, such as creativity or transformation?

When I came across Bloom's Taxonomy of Learning for the first time, after having been a teacher for a few years, I found that this framework helped me make more sense of the learning journey from beginner to mastery. It gave me a practical and detailed insight into how to include these higher-level thinking and learning skills and activities for a diverse range of students.

Bloom's Taxonomy is based on six levels of thinking skills, ranging from the basic (remembering, understanding, applying) to the advanced (analysing, evaluating, creating).

The basic levels in Bloom's Taxonomy focus on understanding concepts and ideas, and remembering facts. These stages encompass learning a basic technique or skill, getting to know materials, and understanding the rules of good design. Examples of these basic types of creative skills are:

- knowing which brush to use for which effect;
- knowing how to hold a tool safely;
- knowing what a certain technique is called.

The advanced levels encompass working towards mastery, and creating new products, ideas or perspectives. The student becomes more independent and experimental, making their own creative decisions. Examples of how to use these higher skill levels are:

- designing a chair;
- creating a reduction linocut featuring an animal in an environment;
- creating a storyboard for a three-minute film.

Right Bloom's Taxonomy with six levels from beginner to mastery.

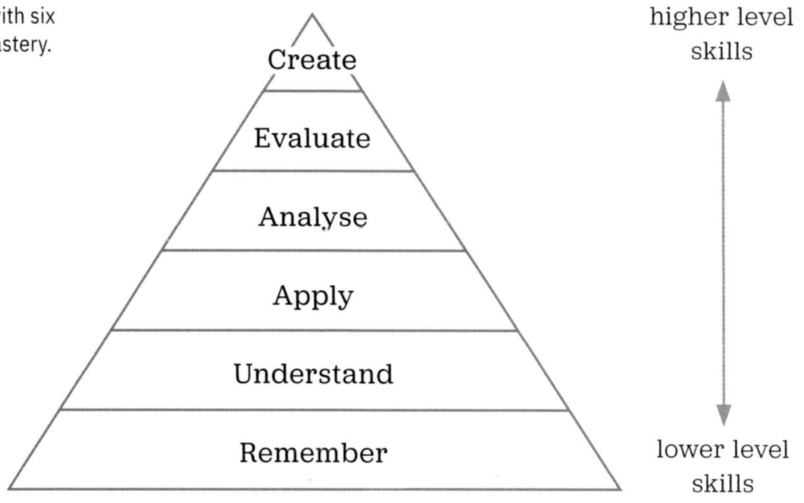

As our knowledge about how people learn has evolved over the last few decades, we have become more aware that **learning isn't a linear process**, and that students' beliefs and emotions play a critical role in the learning process, which is not accounted for in Bloom's Taxonomy.

However, it still provides a basic, practical pedagogic framework for teachers to help their students develop more advanced thinking and skills, and **to identify appropriate actions and activities at different levels**. It also clarifies that without understanding basic principles of design, composition or colour theory, your students will be unable to make the jump to more complex, conceptual ideas.

How can Bloom's Taxonomy help you?

I've used Bloom's Taxonomy to identify, differentiate and improve the different levels of difficulty when I am preparing lesson plans and activities. It gently reminds me about what it takes to learn, and that learning is a journey full of challenges. What might be easy for us as experts is really hard to comprehend, let alone do, as a beginner.

We often forget what we didn't know when we started out; these are the exact challenges your students will be facing!

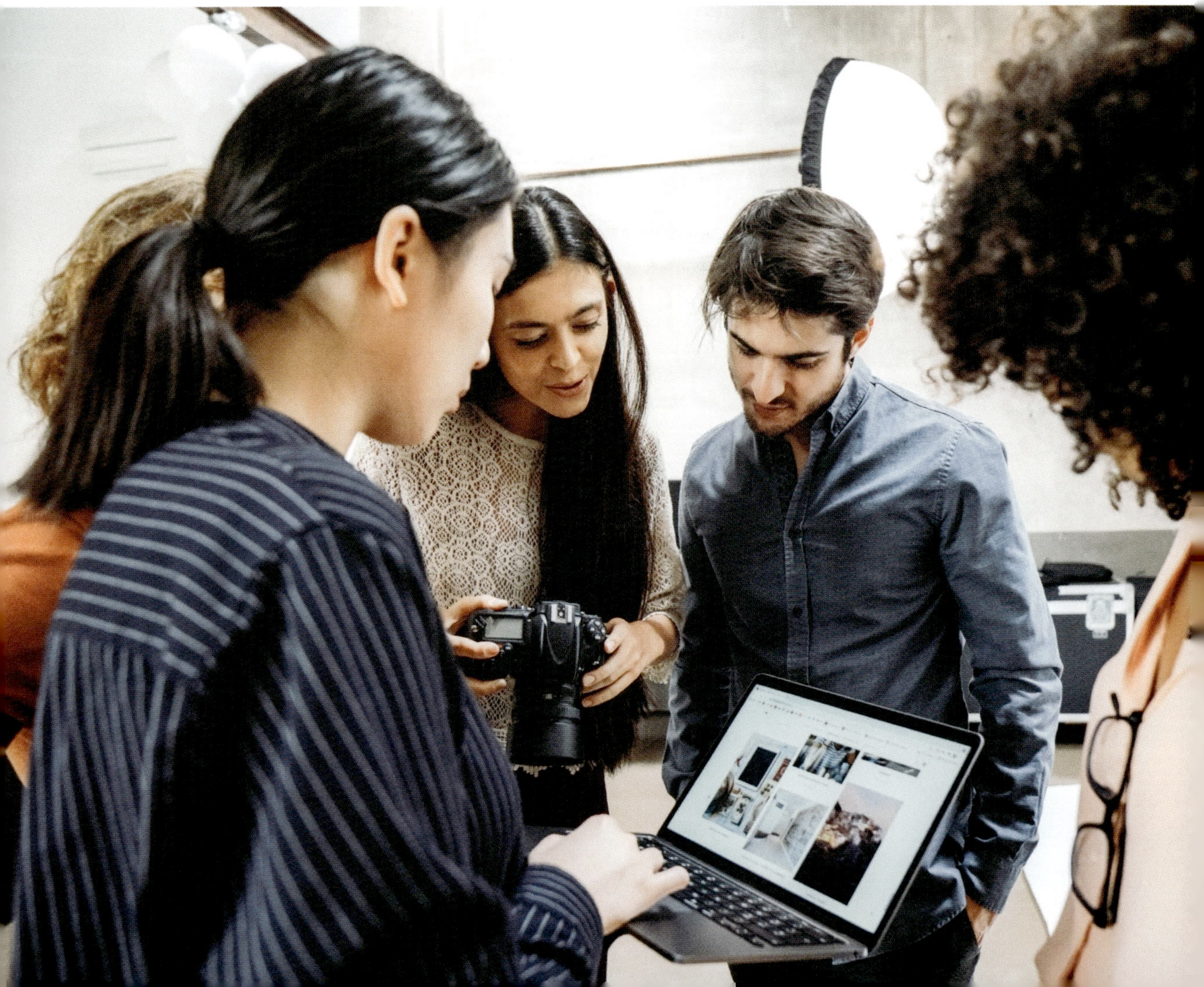

Awareness of this pedagogic framework can help you become a better, more creative teacher by:

- **making you more aware** and realistic about what beginners can achieve;
- **challenging you to take your students beyond basic creative skills** and copying your steps, and supporting them to become more independent and innovative;
- **enabling you to offer different levels of learning** within the same course. This is especially useful for online courses, where the skill base is often broader;
- **encouraging you to add more variety to your teaching methods** and activities, to cater for different learning styles and levels;
- **helping you to define what your students will do more specifically,** e.g., will they learn which brush to use for a specific technique (remembering), copy the style of a painter like Cézanne (applying), or create an artwork with contrasting colour schemes (creating)?

I really hope that by sharing these pedagogic theories I have inspired you to make your training more creative, diverse and student-focused in a way that allows you to bring your own uniqueness and creativity to your teaching.

Time to pause

Get your notebook and make time to reflect on the following questions:

- **Find out more information about Bloom's Taxonomy online.** Look particularly at creative resources that mention specific verbs, activities or reflective questions at each of the six levels. Google 'Bloom's Taxonomy teacher planning kit' for more details.
- **How can understanding Bloom's Taxonomy specifically help you** to create better and more diverse training? Reflect on how this pedagogic knowledge can impact on how you teach, and how you can add more diversity and different skill levels to your training.
- **Stretch exercise:** return to your teaching plan and the Bloom's Taxonomy skill level for your favourite training idea. Use Bloom's Taxonomy to identify specific activities and verbs for the appropriate level, and make notes in your teaching plan. This will also help you later on when writing your marketing materials.

Our next Creative Case Study is a great example of how using your personal skills and experiences can lead to creating truly unique and transformational experiences for participants.

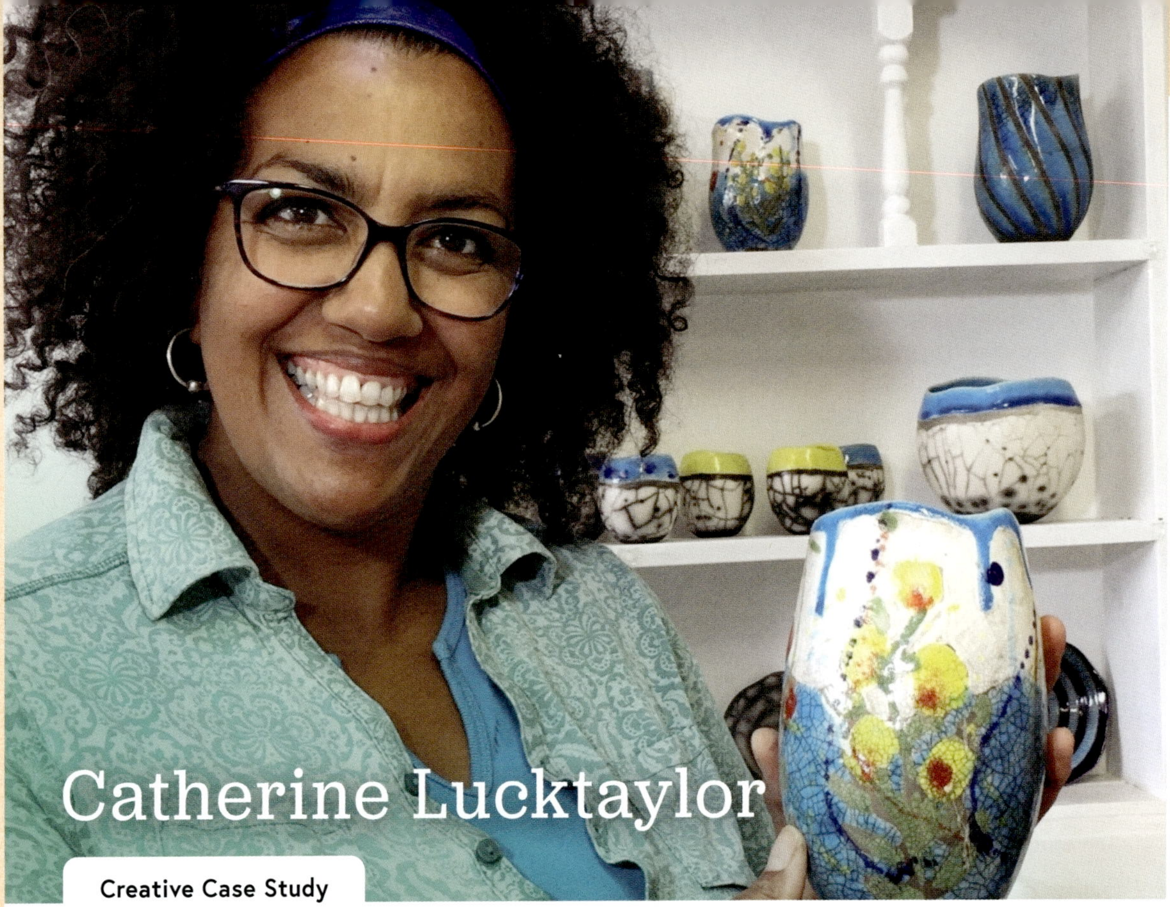

Catherine Lucktaylor

Creative Case Study

Catherine Lucktaylor's contemporary hand-formed raku ceramics beautifully blend her African ancestry with the wild landscape of Cornwall where she lives and works.

After studying art and design and ceramics, Catherine moved to Brighton where she had a studio at the Phoenix Gallery for many years. In 1999, she received a Travelling Fellowship from the Winston Churchill Memorial Trust, which took her on an exciting journey through West Africa and Brazil, researching traditional religion and sacred art. The expedition facilitated a profound connection with her Ghanaian heritage and led her to reunite with her Ghanaian father.

Only after moving to Cornwall in 2009 did she start focusing on her career as a ceramic artist. She established her large rural studio near Penzance and began offering raku courses, nurturing aspiring artists while showcasing her ceramics at galleries and on her website. Recently, Catherine has incorporated her training in ancestral lineage healing into her practice, and hosts healing arts retreats and grief rituals interwoven with creativity and ceramics.

You can find out more about Catherine at www.lucktaylorceramics.co.uk

Why do you teach?

When I set up my ceramics business, I worked from a little shed in my garden, so didn't have the space to teach. Then a client asked if I could teach her, and that's how it started. I was selling to a few galleries, a little on Etsy, and I thought it would be a good income stream.

Above Ceramicist Catherine Lucktaylor with a colourful Wild Cornwall Pot.

Opposite Catherine with raku kilns outside of her studio.

I really wanted to share my knowledge because I had been doing raku for a long time and not a lot of people were doing it back then. I found it easier to promote and sell my courses than my own work.

How do you manage to create and teach?

It's been challenging over the years to find a balance. I've tried different ways of running courses. At one point, I had too much going on in my personal life and stopped teaching. Now my son is a bit older, I have more time and capacity. I don't want to be teaching all the time because it takes a lot of energy away from my own work, so, when I started teaching again, I looked at it quite analytically. How many one- or two-day courses can I run? What can I charge? How will this cover my overheads? I spread courses out more over the year now.

What do you teach?

I now run three one-day courses and three two-day courses per quarter. For the two-day workshop, we do the making on one Saturday and the firing on the following Saturday, so the pots can dry in between. For the one-day courses people either bring their own biscuit-fired pots or I make or buy them, and they do the raku firing on the day.

Recently, I added the Raku Experience, which is really popular as it's a two-and-a-half-hour session with Cornish cream tea. Participants glaze the pots, and while it's in the raku fire they have cream tea, and then they clean their pots and take them home. That's been really good fun, as people often have something to celebrate.

I think I offer something different. If they go to a pottery night-class, they are not likely to do raku as they won't have the facilities. At my studio, I've got the kilns and loads of outside space for the firings. Some of my students have gone on to create their own raku set up. I now also teach the safety aspects of how to set up your own raku kiln. At least three of my students have gone on to specialise in raku and sell their work.

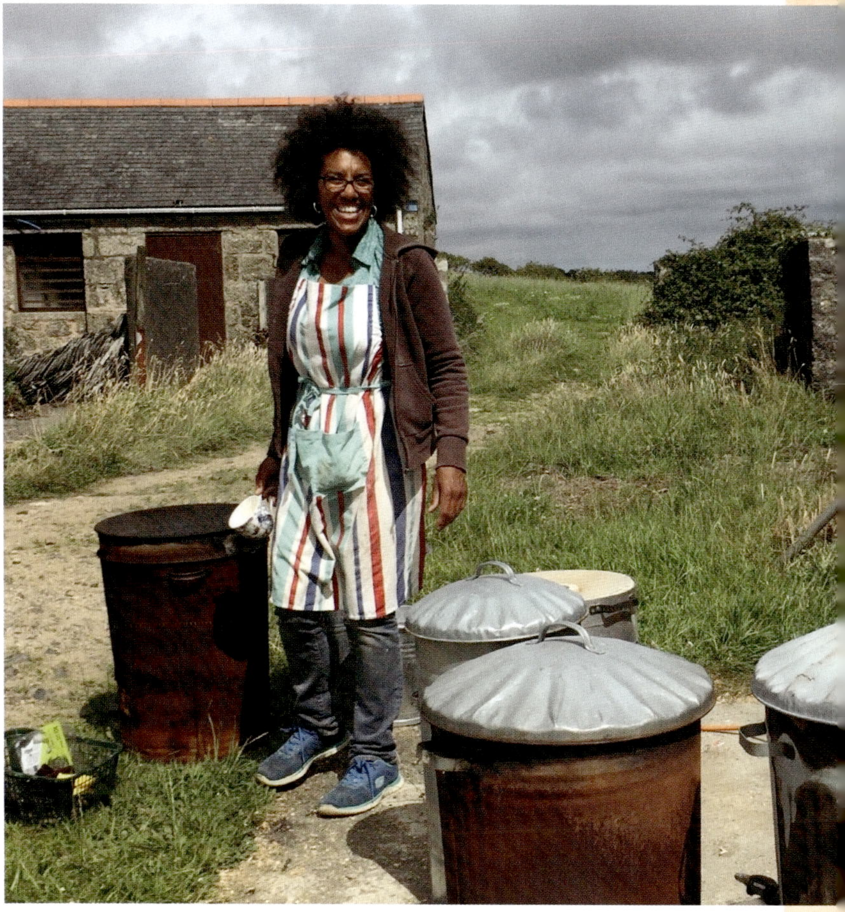

Talk us through a typical course day

The one-day courses normally run from 10.30 a.m. to 4.30 p.m. I always include lunch, and there's loads of tea, coffee, cake – all the bells and whistles. We have between three and eight people on each course.

On the day, I start by showing them my work and examples of the glazes and different masking techniques. I demonstrate and talk them through the process of glazing the inside, and drying and closing the outside. There are certain steps that they need to follow, and I let them get on with it. It's all really informal. When they do the glazing, I will go around and check that they are doing OK, as they are often at different levels.

Then we do the raku firing. I try to do five firings in a day and have two kilns going, so that's quite intense. The first firing takes a bit longer – around 30–40 minutes, and then you've got clean-up time.

At the end of the day, they leave with lots of lovely pots. They look great because raku is like that. It very rarely goes wrong, even if it doesn't come out how you expected.

Can you tell me about your grief ritual workshops?

I'd always had this dream, ever since I moved to Cornwall, of running healing art retreats. Now, 10 years later, I'm ready. I combine creativity, rituals and grief in a whole package.

In 2022, I received funding from the Arts Council to develop my own creative practice. I took part in a grief ritual with Sobonfu Somé – a member of the Dagara tribe of Burkina Faso – who have grief rituals as part of their culture. I always felt that it was something I really wanted to do. Then some friends contacted me and asked me to conduct one.

I did my first Grief Ritual Weekend last year to see if I could hold the space. I decided not to use raku, but work with clay instead, creating what I call 'spirit rattles'. We write notes of things we want to release and wrap them around balls of clay. We then do a traditional pit-firing directly in the ground, drawing on my African heritage, using local seaweed, and bringing all these different elements together.

Only a handful of people came but they were really into it. It's so special being in a beautiful location in Cornwall, which has loads of magical places, stone circles and sacred sites. That atmosphere is really nurturing. It really boosted people's confidence and creativity.

For me, it was about creating a safe space where people were looked after, and where they could share what they were going through with other people. It wasn't heavy at all. There were deep emotions, but then there was a sense of relief.

I wasn't sure how I would handle it. I had a good friend on standby to support me. But I just felt amazing – really empowered. I felt fully able to hold that space with people and they really bonded as a group. They all left feeling lighter.

What's next?

I am now doing an ancestral lineage healing course, and it is such a beautiful process. Now that I've done my training, I will be able to run Ancestral Healing Circles and bring in creativity and clay. I am thinking about creating two-day retreats, or maybe even a week on a friend's farm, where they are creating a healing art space.

Opposite Students cleaning raku pots.

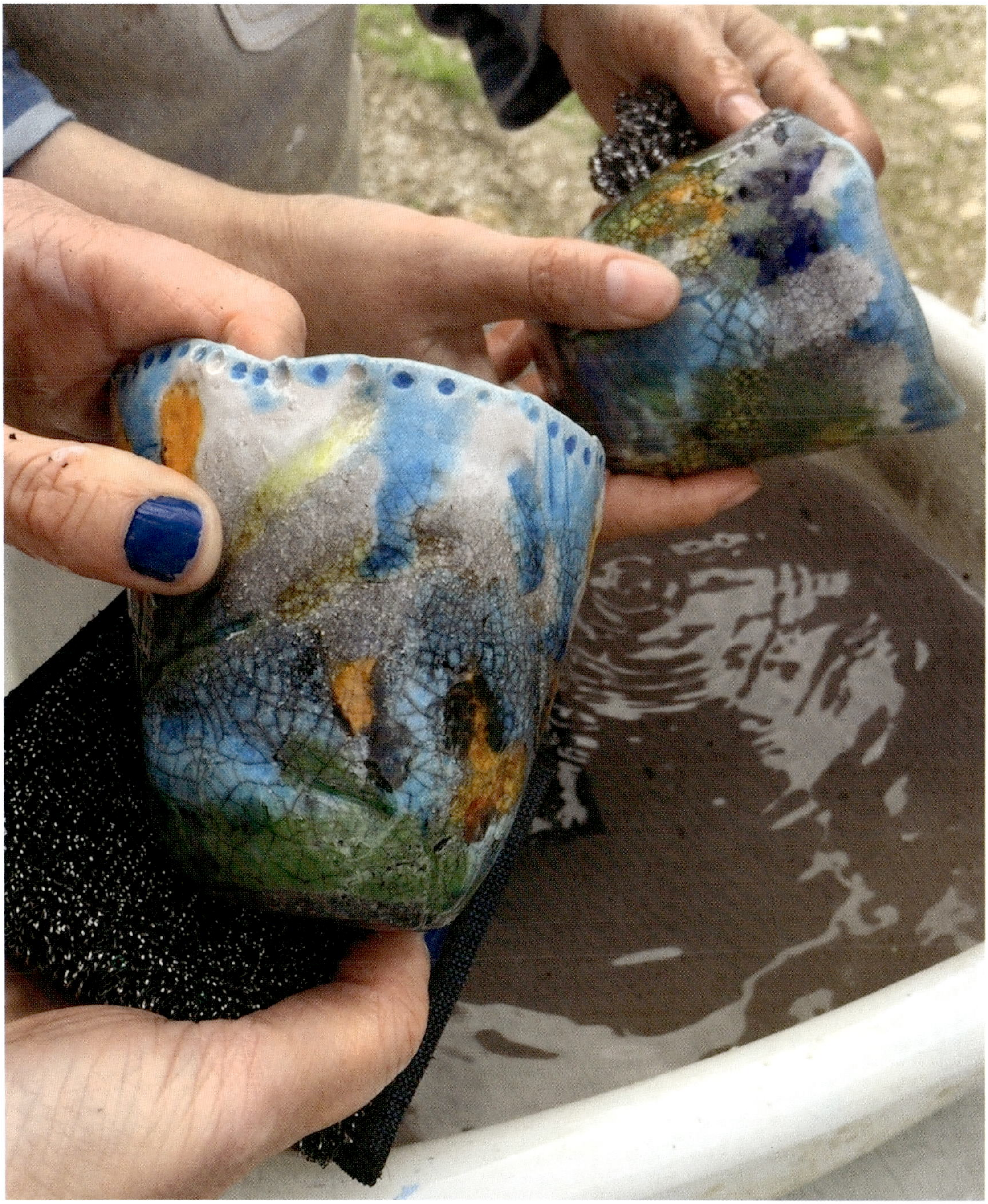

‘When people are making and working with their hands, they often have really deep conversations. The retreat was based on grief, but we don’t often talk about that loss. What the retreat did was give people a place where they could have those conversations.’

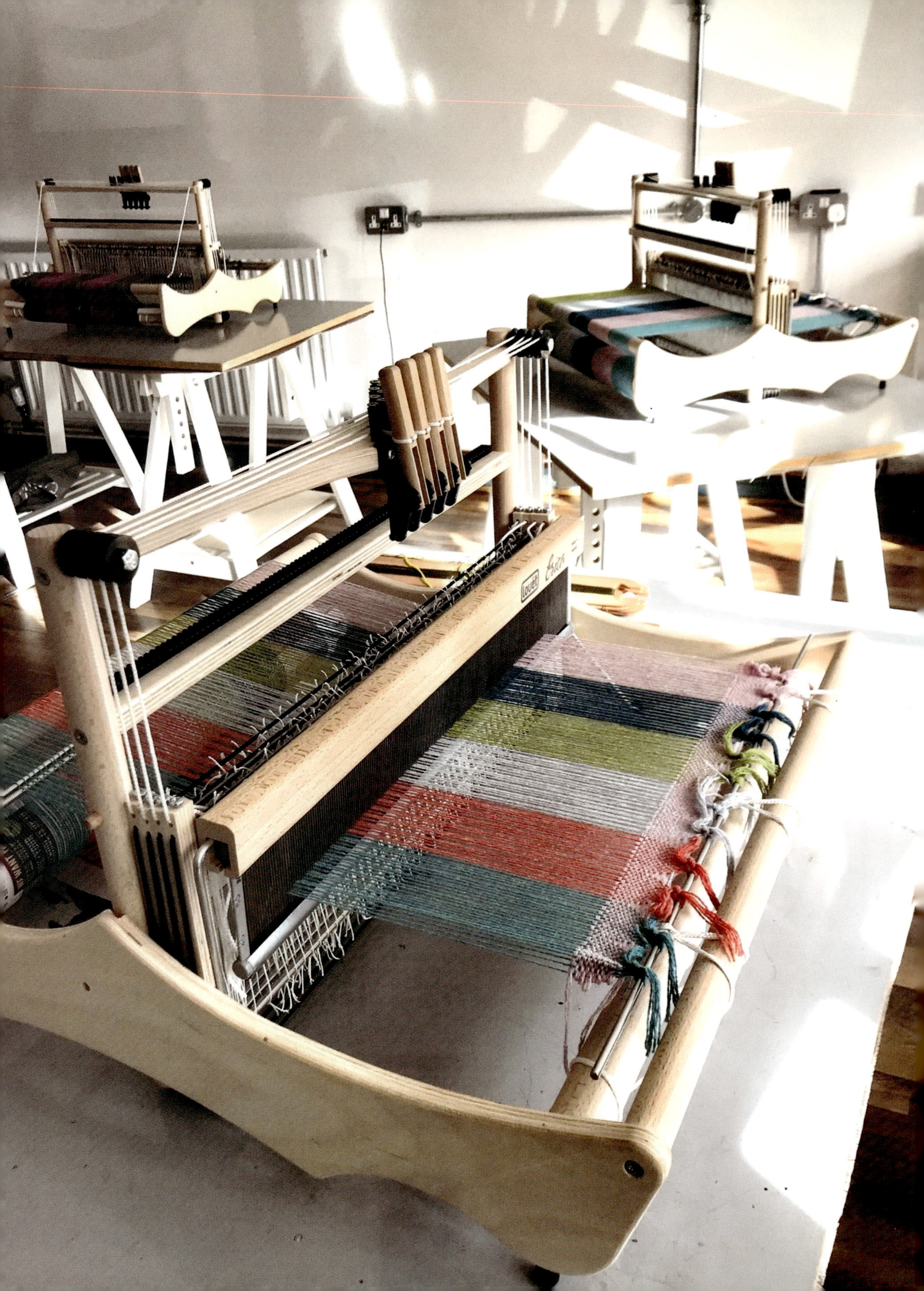
louët

Create your lesson plan

So far, you have explored different topic ideas, formats, methods and activities, and looked at different learning and teaching styles. You have made lots of notes in your notebook and worked on your teaching plan for your three ideas.

Now we are getting to the end of this chapter, we will bring this all together in a key creative exercise: A lesson plan for your training.

Why create a lesson plan?

A lesson plan will provide you and your students with an overview of what you will teach and what the students will do and learn. So, why is this so important?

- **It provides structure.** Often, the planning itself is more important than the actual plan! Thinking it through and making decisions will give you clarity.
- **It helps you focus** on the purpose and goal, and the exact steps and activities you need to get there. This is the time to get creative and brainstorm, and then to decide what to include and what needs to go.
- **It will get you into action.** Creating and delivering training (especially online) can become overwhelming. Planning helps you to visualise the process and break it down into smaller goals and activities. If you are doing pre-recorded online training, you will need a lesson plan to create a filming plan (which we will do in the next chapter).
- **It will give your marketing materials clarity** and transparency. Training courses are intangible, so you need to be really clear about the content and delivery to attract the right students and manage their expectations.
- **It will help you stay on track** during the training. It's important to plan out what activities you will deliver and time how long each will take, but you also need to factor in some flexibility. If live training overruns you may need to cut out content, which is stressful for you and frustrating for students. When creating pre-recorded video training, you need to keep to a tight filming schedule, especially if you are working with professionals.
- **It will keep your students motivated.** Having a clear goal and structure will help students know what's coming up, how different parts of your training fit together, and what they are aiming to achieve.

‘My own best teachers would tell us at the start of each lesson what the lesson was going to be about, so, I start by saying “I'm going to talk for 10 minutes and I will run through the entire process.”

I demonstrate the weaving process, making sure everybody can see, and then I just get them going. I go around individually to get everybody started. Once everybody's 10 minutes in I'll pop the kettle on and start getting the drinks. Then we weave and talk.

Once they've got the hang of the plain weave after about an hour, I will show some of them examples of a more complicated twill weave. For people with no experience of weaving, that's just like alchemy and it's so exciting to see them have a go.

The participants generally weave at different speeds which is ideal. For the last 40 minutes I'm really busy transforming their weaving into a cushion one-by-one as they finish, for them to take home.’

Angie Parker, textile artist

Opposite Angie Parker workshop set-up with looms.

Write your lesson plan

Creating a lesson plan for your best teaching idea is one of the key creative exercises in this book, and it follows on from your teaching plan in Chapter 3.

We will start with the format of a lesson plan and how it looks, and then I will take you through the three natural steps to organise your own lesson plan.

Format of a lesson plan

On the opposite page you can see an example of an in-person lesson plan for the start of a one-day weaving workshop, based on a similar one run by Angie Parker. The day is split into blocks of time, and each block has a goal/purpose, specific activities, necessary equipment and materials, and extra notes.

You can also download the *Lesson Plan* template from the Toolkit on The Design Trust website (p.11).

Organising your ideas into a lesson plan

Now let's move on to organising your ideas and creating your own lesson plan.

Choose your favourite teaching idea from the ones you identified in your teaching plan (see p.43). I recommended earlier that you limit yourself to a four-hour session if you are planning to teach in person, or a two-hour session for online training. Keeping it simple makes it more doable and less overwhelming.

To organise your lesson plan there are three steps:

1 Choose your start and end time, then identify overall learning goals and time blocks

- **How much teaching time will you have?** Identify the arrival and start time (two different times), breaks, departure time and lengths of teaching sessions.
- **'Start with the end in mind':** what do you want your students to know or achieve by the end of your training? Take their current skill level into account, and what they can realistically and comfortably achieve in the given time. Be generous with your time allocation.
- **What are the natural teaching time blocks?** Let's say that you start at 10 a.m. and finish at 4 p.m. Your day will need at least three breaks for refreshments. Plan a break of around 15–30 minutes mid-morning, 45–60 minutes at lunch, and another 30 minutes mid-afternoon. That will split up your day into three teaching sections of about one or two hours each. As energy levels are higher in the morning, include a longer teaching session then, and allow for longer breaks in the afternoon. Plan generous breaks so that you can shorten them if you are running out of time (although this is not ideal).
- **Does your creative process require non-making time,** e.g., ceramics that need to be fired before you can glaze them? How will you plan that in? What could you do instead in those hours – research, invite guest speakers, go outdoors?

TRAINING TITLE: Weave a Cushion in a Day

DATE AND TIME: One-day workshop, Fri 10 a.m. – 4 p.m.

STUDENT TYPE: Beginners, friends, fun day out, start of a hobby

HOMEWORK, OR WHAT THEY NEED TO BRING:

LEARNING GOALS:

- How to use a table loom
- Introduction to different weaving techniques

Time	Purpose / Teaching method	What to do? Specific activities	Materials needed	Notes
9.30 – 10 a.m. (30 mins)	Arrival.	Meet and greet upon arrival. Registration and hot drinks.	Welcome packs. Name badges. Hot and cold drinks.	Room set up with two chairs per table.
10 a.m. (10 mins)	Introductions.	Short intro about me and the venue. Health and safety. 5 min intro in pairs. Discuss the format of the day.	Agenda on whiteboard and handouts.	Check to see if anyone has any health concerns (e.g., back, eye sight, hearing, left handers, colour blindness).
10.10 a.m. (10 mins)	Demonstrate.	Show the cushion we will make by end of today and various examples of colours and weaving techniques. Demonstrate how to use the loom.	Examples of various woven cushions and some examples of different weaving techniques.	Tell them that they can choose their own colours and techniques to make it their own.
10.20 a.m. (40 mins)	Get them started to practise.	Each participant to choose a loom, then colours. Get them started.	Loom set up for each participant. Plenty of wool.	Remind them that it doesn't matter which one they will choose as the weft colours will dominate.
11 a.m.	Coffee and tea break for those who want to.		Put kettle on. Dairy and non-dairy milk. Cookies.	Ask them if they'd like some music on, and if the temperature is OK for everyone.

Above Example of a finished lesson plan (morning).

2 Break your themes and learning goals down into specific activities

- **What are the key themes,** learning goals, skills or steps for each block of teaching time? Identify the 'must know', 'should know' and 'nice to know'.
- **What are the best teaching methods** (e.g., demonstration, practice, reflection) for these goals? Include enough time for practice and reflection.
- **How can you make your training more creative and diverse?** Think about stories, quotes, case studies, metaphors or samples.
- **Return to your notes** around your teaching methods, learning styles and Bloom's Taxonomy (pp.64–67) for inspiration.

When I am at the planning stage, I often create a mind map, flowchart or sketch (as you can see from the lesson plan sketch opposite) to put down my ideas. I start by writing down the big goals and then chunk that down into smaller steps and activities.

I often use a circular mind map for connecting ideas, or a linear one for planning a journey from A to B.

I often use sticky notes to get all my ideas out there, with one activity per sticky note, and then move them around or put them aside. Many of my clients use kanban boards to plan their course outlines.

Take your time on this step. Be creative and add ideas, but also think about what to cut out – it's a fine balancing act.

Keep it simple. I really mean this – it is probably the most important lesson in this entire book, which is why I keep repeating it.

You will **need to cut some of your content**. But don't worry, this is not a waste of your time. Keep your notes, and you can use the 'should know' and 'nice to know' content ideas to create other levels of training, or e-books, blog posts or free promotional content.

Top Tip

If you are struggling to come up with activities, return to your competitor research or look at online courses with similar content. Did you do the survey on pp.38–41 to identify what your students want to learn?

For an example of the running order for a typical teaching session, check out the download entitled *Get Ready to Deliver Your In-Person Training* in the Toolkit.

Opposite A first stage lesson plan sketch of my own one-day online workshop for The Design Trust with key topics, timings and content ideas.

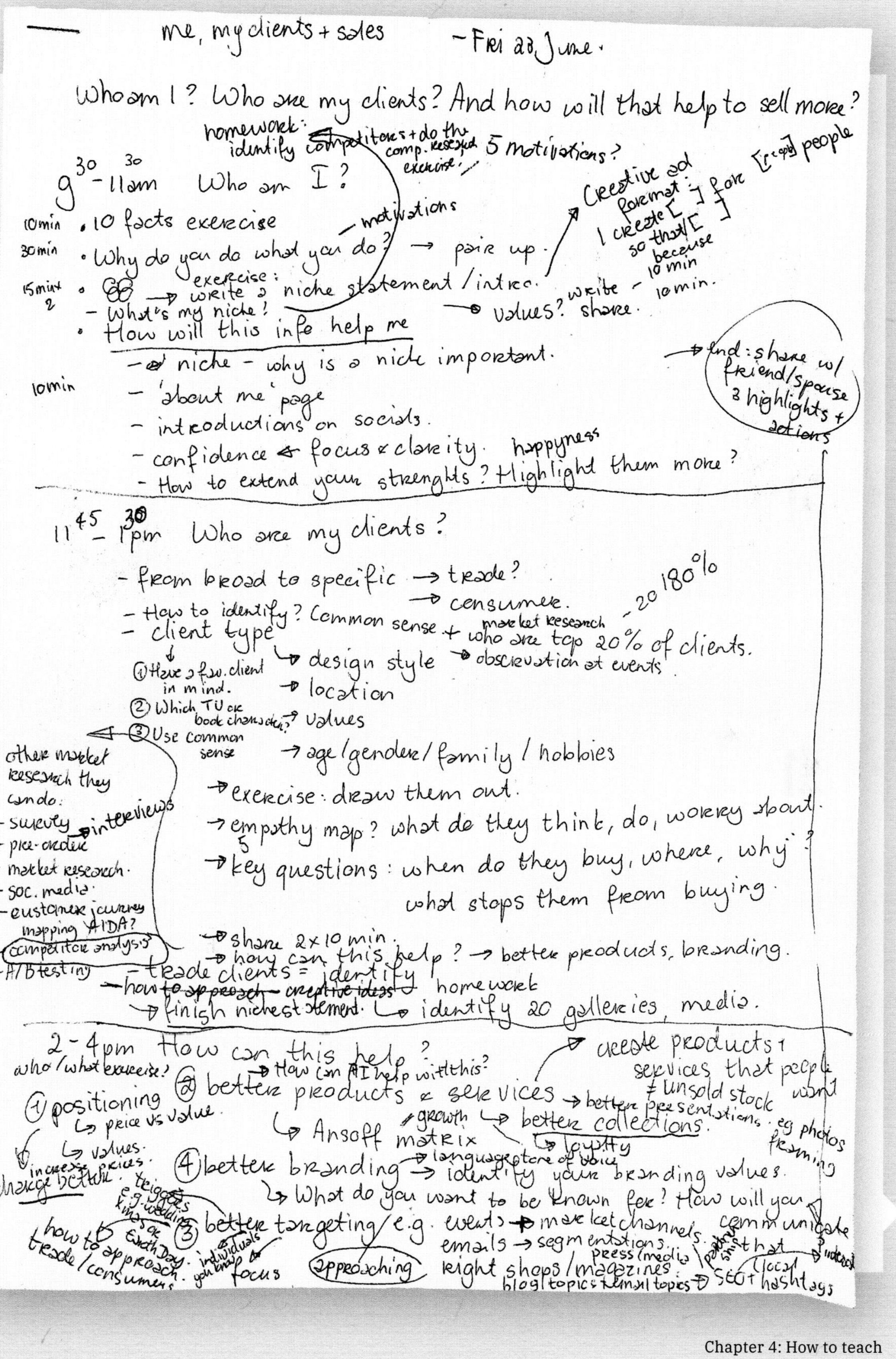
me, my clients + sales — Fri 28 June.

Who am I? Who are my clients? And how will that help to sell more?

homework: identify competitors + do the comp. research exercise — 5 motivations?

9 30 – 11 30 am Who am I?

- 10min • 10 facts exercise — motivations
- 30min • Why do you do what you do? → pair up. → Creative ad format: I create [ ] for [recipe] people so that [ ] because — 10 min
- 15min 2 • 88 → exercise: write a niche statement / intro. — write – 10min.
  - What's my niche? → values? share.
- • How will this info help me
  - niche – why is a niche important. → end: share w/ friend/spouse 3 highlights + actions
  - 10min – 'about me' page
  - introductions on socials.
  - confidence ← focus & clarity. happyness
  - How to extend your strenghts? Highlight them more?

11 45 – 1 30 pm Who are my clients?

- from broad to specific → trade? → consumer. — 20/80%
- How to identify? Common sense + market research who are top 20% of clients.
- client type
  - ① Have a fav. client in mind. ② Which TV or book characters? ③ Use common sense
  - → design style → observation at events
  - → location
  - → values
  - → age / gender / family / hobbies
- → exercise: draw them out.
- → empathy map? what do they think, do, worry about.
- → 5 key questions: when do they buy, where, why? what stops them from buying.
- → share 2×10 min.
- → how can this help? → better products, branding.

other market research they can do:
- survey → interviews
- pre-order
- market research.
- soc. media
- customer journey mapping AIDA?
- competitor analysis
- A/B testing

- trade clients = identify
- how to approach – creative ideas
- → finish niche statement. → homework identify 20 galleries, media.

2 – 4pm How can this help?

who / what exercise?

① positioning → price vs value → values. increase prices. charge better.

② better products & services → How can AI help with this? → create products + services that people want ≠ unsold stock → better presentations. eg photos framing → Ansoff matrix growth → better collections. → loyalty

④ better branding → language tone of voice → identify your branding values. → What do you want to be known for? How will you communicate

③ better targeting / e.g. events → market channels. triggers e.g. wedding, kings or Earth Day. individuals you know focus; emails → segmentations. right shops / magazines. press (media) partnership that interest; blog topics + email topics → SEO + (local) hashtags

how to approach trade / consumers. — approaching

3 **Review.** Now is the time to decide what is a 'must include' and what is 'nice to have' and needs to be cut.

- **How will you deal with different skill levels** or faster/slower students?
- **What key questions do your students have**, and how will they get the answers? Will you tell them, or will you encourage them to find the answers themselves? The latter is a much more effective way of learning and discovering.
- **How will you manage their energy?** Are you offering a variety of teaching methods? Does your training flow? Have you broken down the activities into clear steps? Provide plenty of time for the students to practise, and to reflect. Include individual and group activities for different learning styles.
- **Can some of the teaching be delivered more effectively** by sharing resources before or after the session? Could you include homework in advance? Or you provide a worksheet explaining which tool to use to create a specific outcome?
- **How will you make your students feel welcome?** Think about the atmosphere of the space, registration procedures, and how and when you will introduce yourself.
- **How will you use 'mistakes' by your students?** Will you share the most common mistakes and highlight them in advance so they can be avoided? Or will you let students have a go first and then reflect on what works and what doesn't? Take care not to make them feel bad if things aren't entirely right.

Now it's your turn to create your lesson plan. Download the *Lesson Plan* template from the Toolkit, and make sure you have your updated teaching plan to hand.

Refer back to the three steps while you work, and use the suggested brainstorming techniques to capture all your ideas and move them around.

Keep editing and adding to your lesson plan until it looks and feels right. Don't worry if it's not perfect or 'finished'. You will continue to work on it throughout this book, so keep it close.

Creating the first draft of your lesson plan is a big job, and it's likely to take you a few hours. If you put in the work in previous chapters, you will find it easier now. Congratulations if you did it ... this is a crucial step towards creating and launching your next creative skills training!

In the next chapter, we will look at teaching in-person and online, as well as hybrid models, which will give you further insight and inspiration for ideas to include in your lesson plan. If you are planning to create pre-recorded online training, your lesson plan will be an essential tool for creating your filming plan.

But first another Creative Case Study. In this one Sam Marshall talks about how she runs her online workshops live on Sunday afternoons, and her reason for this.

Opposite Real-life example of a final lesson plan for *FLOW*, Hanny Newton's online embroidery course.

CONTENT for videos (8 videos / workbook sections over 2 modules)

FLOW: playful goldwork couching

1) Intro to couching – straight line. Really take my time in going over the foundations – this can be used for future courses!
- Materials needed.
- How to couch in a traditional way.
- Plunging and tying back.
- This is very much a starting point – unlike a traditional goldwork class, this introduction to technique is intended to be a jumping-off point – take your time to understand the technique. We will be delving and questioning as we go along, and the demo I give you here is *one way* to do it – not *the* way! Keep that in mind as you try it.

2) Taking a line for a walk – taking time to instinctually play and explore – don't rush this bit, just be with it! This is such an important part of this process – put on some music, your favourite podcast (could have a section for suggested stitch listening!). If you just did this, and nothing else, I believe you would get lots out of this – the rest of this course builds on this.

3) Short video – As you stitch, start to ask yourself – what else could I do with this? Can write in the workbook provided or in your sketchbooks (create a 'What happens if?' sheet! Include an example). Important to include this before sharing technique – want you to think for yourself – this isn't about me being the expert.

4) Introduce couching variations:
- Separating two threads
- Overlapping two threads
- Jagged
- Looping
- One thread
- Combining two different threads

5) Drawing exercise:
- Draw two lines / markers – or use whole page.
- As quickly as you can, how can you travel from one side to the other? Do at least ten ways. Not about getting it right – especially if you haven't drawn lots before, you need to warm into it. Just see what happens – you don't need to like them! Just keep going. Pause this video and do it now!
- Now look over those lines – What do you like? What don't you like? Why?
- Now do another series, and take your time with these – craft a line, capture that feeling you had from the stitching earlier – take your pen/pencil for a walk.
- Prompt words to use now you are honing: quiet/angry/scared/bold/sad – or use your own.
- You may like to put these drawings away for a while and come back to them – sometimes it's easy to be too close up to something – there's a different feel to the making and the viewing of something!
- Choose one of your lines, and think how you could refine and change this. Think about using different pens, thicknesses and scales – how big and small could you go? Colour if you like.
- None of this is intended to be a box-ticking exercise – dip in and out – put it away and come back – for me, making isn't a linear thing – I often discover drawings I did five years ago and realise that's what I want to be doing now

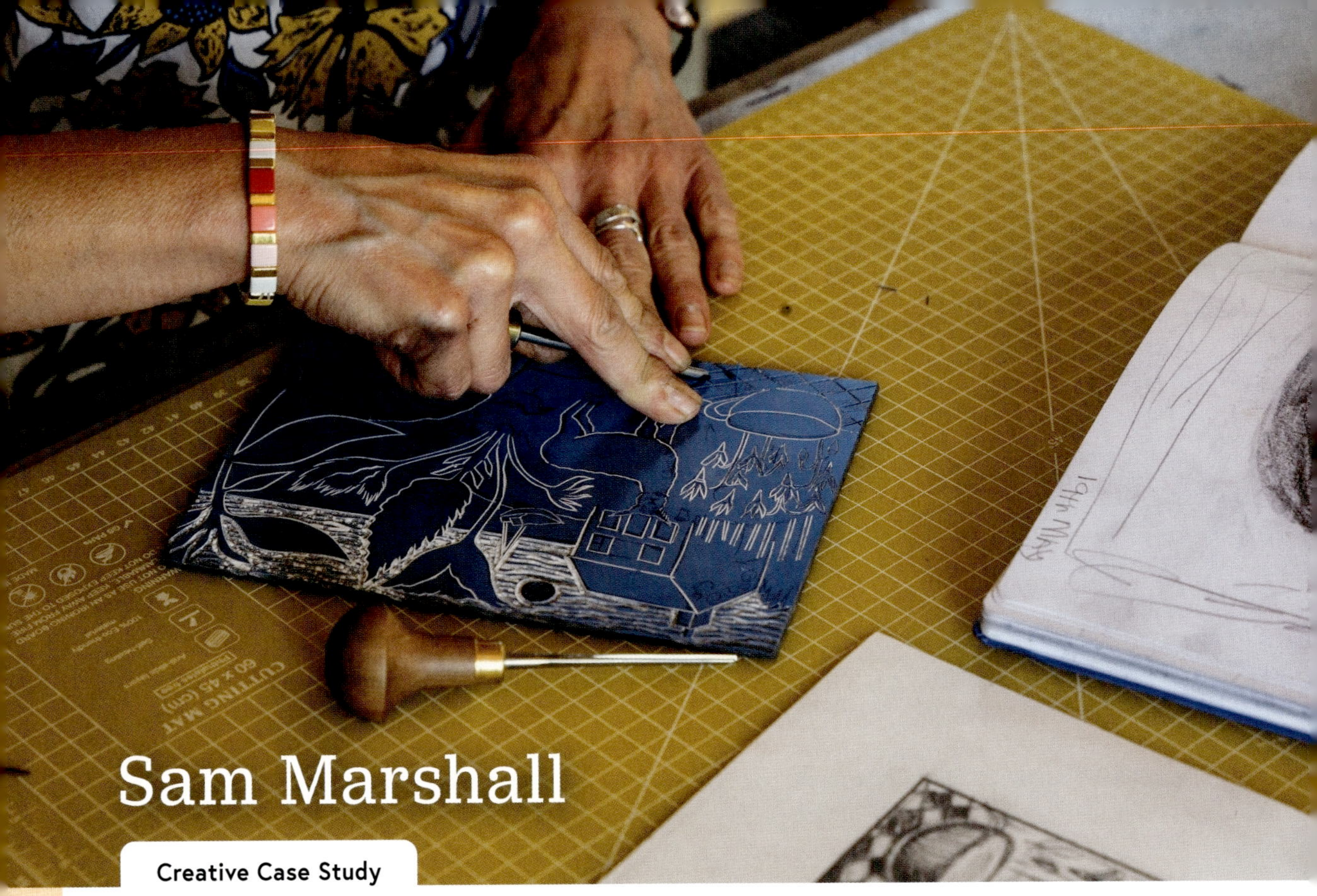

Sam Marshall

Creative Case Study

Sam Marshall is an artist specialising in drawing and printmaking. Her work tells stories about her life, travels, garden and miniature dachshund, Miss Marple.

She runs live online workshops, provides creative coaching and teaches at The Royal Drawing School. After 20 years in London, she relocated to rural Northamptonshire to focus on her own artwork.

She works from two beautifully organised and colourful studios in her garden. Living in the middle of the countryside provides all the inspiration she needs. Her book, *Linocut: A Creative Guide to Making Beautiful Prints*, was published in 2023.

You can find out more about Sam at www.sammarshallart.com

Above and opposite Printmaker Sam Marshall at work.

When did you start teaching?

I started teaching after I left The Royal Drawing School in my mid-30s. The School organised after-school clubs for kids who were interested in art, and I really got into that. I took a PGCE for artists, and went on to teach part-time at The BRIT School in Croydon, and at The Foundation Year, run by The Royal Drawing School, and fitted my own work around that.

Why do you teach?

When I was young, I had a friend who struggled to get things and I remember really enjoying helping her understand. I remember thinking, 'Oh, I'm quite good at this', so when I had the opportunity to teach, I jumped at it.

For me, there's always been a bit of guilt around making, because art is sometimes so insular. I love to share my passion and inspire people. Seeing that light in their eyes and helping them overcome their obstacles is what it is about for me.

What do you really teach?

I offer a variety of live online workshops on linocut and drawing. I like going back to basics, back to pencil and paper, and seeing what happens. That's where it all begins. I always encourage my students to draw – no tracing anybody else's work! It's about trying to find your true unique creative voice through drawing.

If you don't think you can draw, I don't care, go out and try because you will create marks that are unique to you. That's how I teach – find your style by doing the work and trusting yourself to create an image that you can then transfer to linocut, rather than copying somebody else's work.

My students come to me to get a confidence boost. I am absolutely not going to tell them exactly what to do. I suggest that they do things and that they're able to do it by themselves.

There are so many people who think they aren't creative, and have been told they aren't creative. It's my passion to make people believe that everybody's got something that they can create. It's not about the end result, it's about the actual process.

How do you plan and structure your teaching?

I run workshops in spring, autumn and winter, roughly every other weekend, depending on how much time I have. I run the same sessions every quarter or every other quarter. The titles and content come naturally to me because they are based on specific techniques.

I run my creative coaching sessions in the morning and towards the end of the day, so I have the rest of the day for me and my work. I do online teaching mostly on weekends. It's very organic, and it changes from week to week.

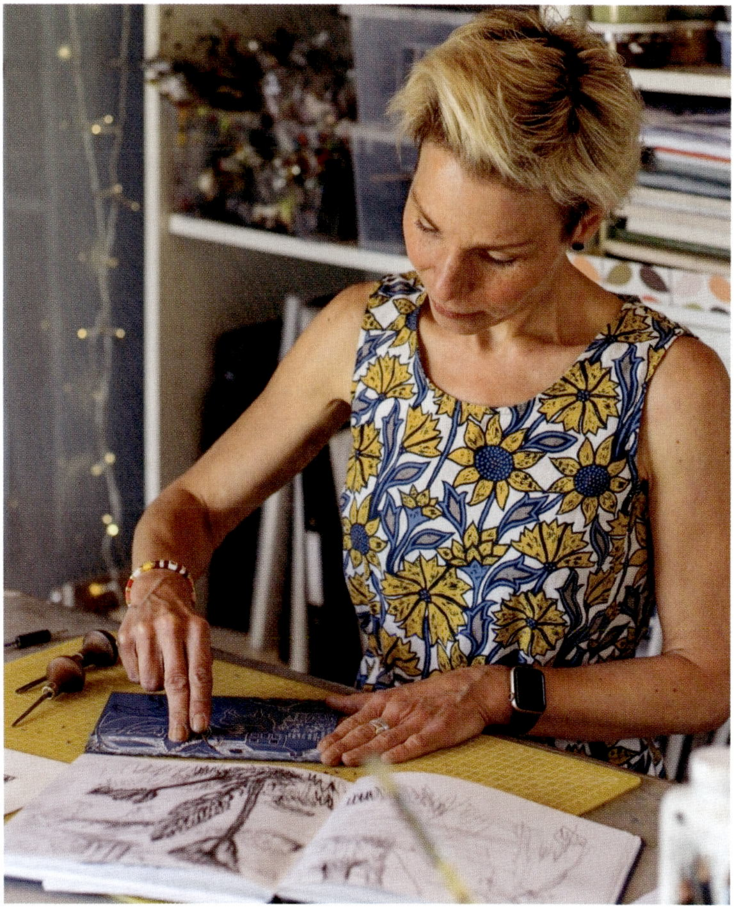

The sessions are live because I don't feel comfortable recording. I am not demonstrating what to do; it's more about discussing ideas. I like the live sessions as it punctuates my weekend.

'I live by myself in the middle of nowhere, and it's quite nice to hang out with some people from four to seven on a weekend evening.'

Each workshop is limited to 10 people, so that I can get to know them. At the start, when we're all coming together, that's a really special time to have some fun. We are just playing. I take the pressure off, I tell them that they're not going to get a mark at the end of it.

My sessions are very structured. Each session is three hours long. From my teaching experience I know that students can concentrate for that amount of time. Anything longer, especially online, is too taxing. We never run over and there's a break halfway through.

Sessions have a very clear trajectory, I'm confident in my teaching methods. I have a clear plan for how much time we're going to spend on each part. I'm very good at timekeeping, pacing and structuring because of my teaching experience.

Do you prefer online or in-person workshops?

Interestingly, my online workshops have a higher 'success' rate than my physical workshops, because students have to buy their own materials and print in their own space. It makes it a reality for them. If they come to my workshop they get access to my equipment and materials, and they then believe that to make a linocut they have to have everything I have.

'Teaching online encourages more independence.'

Online students can't become too reliant on the teacher, and it requires more self-discipline than actually being in a class.

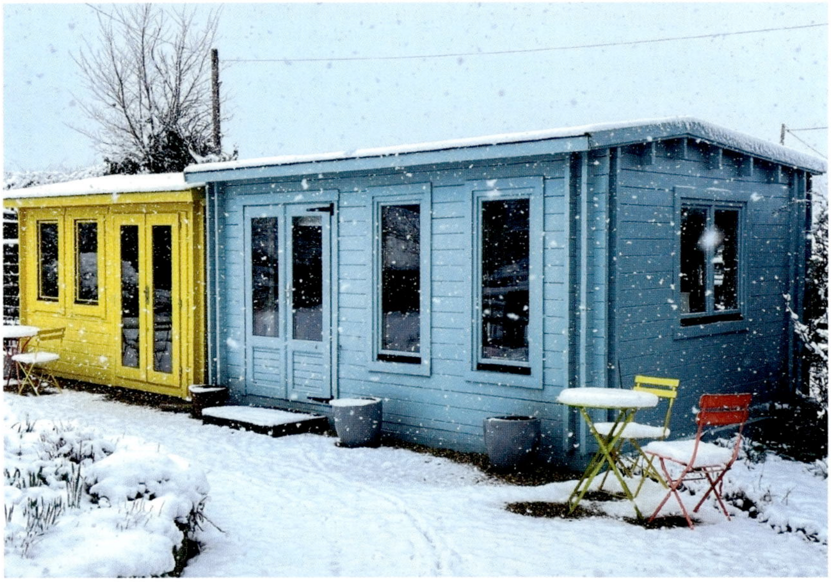

Opposite Sam Marshall's making materials in her studio.

Left Sam's studio.

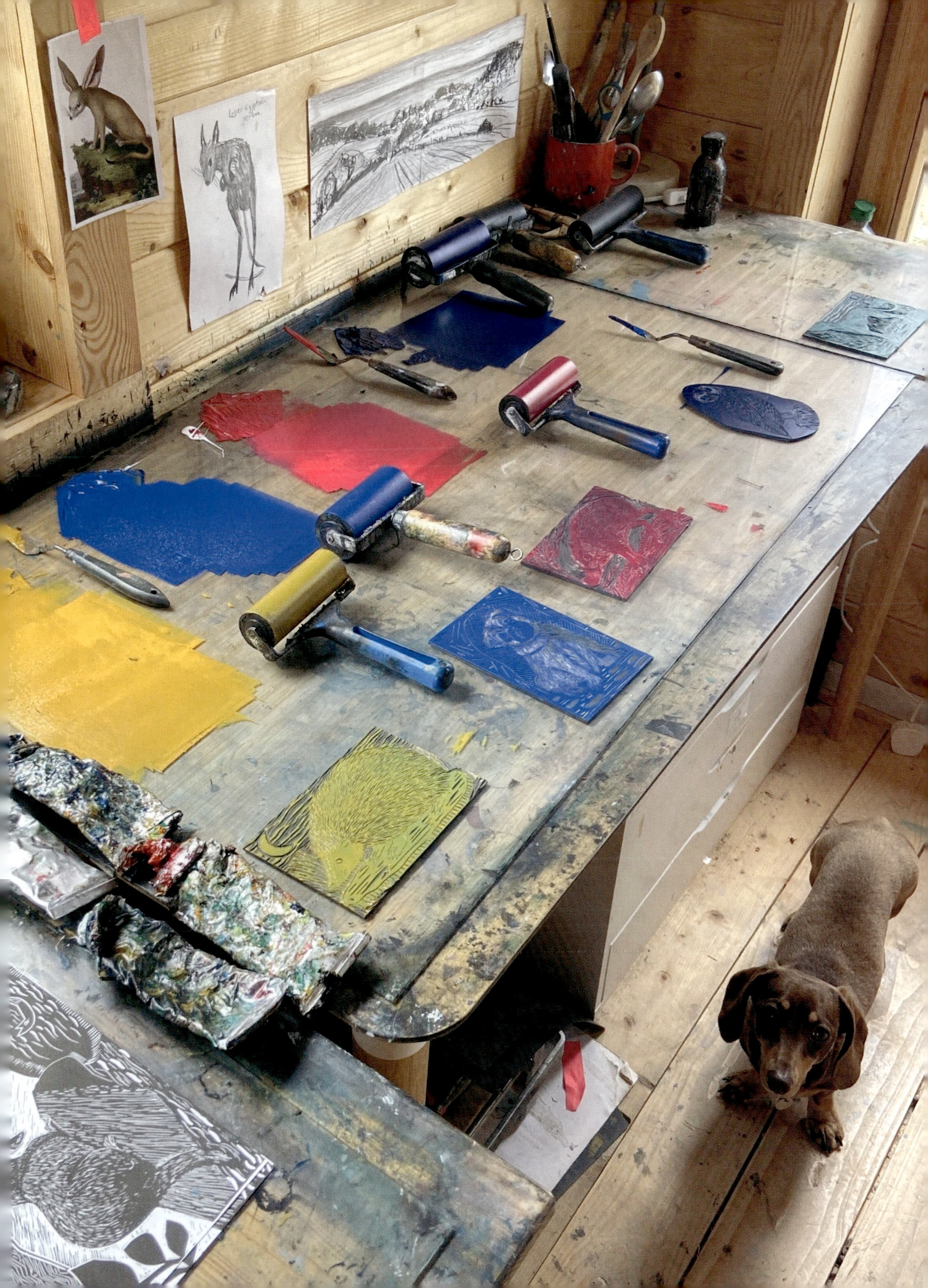

CHAPTER 5

Where to teach – in person, online, or both?

This chapter is slightly different as we will look at three options – teaching in person, online or combining both. If you are already certain which path is best for you, then you can go straight to the relevant part and skip what doesn't relate to you. If you are unsure, or curious about how you can expand your training opportunities, then I invite you to read this chapter in full.

We will start by looking at the **advantages and disadvantages** of both in-person and online teaching, before dealing first with teaching in person, and second with teaching online.

In the **in-person section** we will look at finding the right space or partners to work with, and how to create the right learning environment for your students and training. We will dive into preparing to deliver in-person training, and I will share some very handy (downloadable) checklists with you.

In the **section on online teaching**, we will look at common formats and methods, and things to consider when deciding whether to teach live, to pre-record your lessons, or to offer a mixture of both. We will also look at the **three main challenges when teaching online**: how to motivate your students to finish your online training; competing in a very crowded market; and managing your time to avoid overwhelm.

I will also show you how to **turn your lesson plan into a filming and content plan**, give you some really practical information on software and equipment, and share some expertise from photographer and film-maker, Yeshen Venema.

At the end of this chapter, we will bring in-person and online training back together in a hybrid model, as they can complement each other very well. We will finish this chapter with **two real-life challenges** – creating a short educational or promotional film and doing a test run of your training idea.

It's by applying your knowledge that you will get the most of this book. The more you put in, the more you will get out – and the closer you will get to launching your own training. Are you ready?

Teaching in person and online: Advantages and disadvantages

Teaching in person and teaching online are two very different beasts. It's like reading a novel or watching the film adaptation. You can't simply pluck existing content and assume that it will work online. It just doesn't work like that.

Below Yeshen Venema's team on location with Ehrman Tapestry at the studio of Janet Haigh.

During the COVID-19 lockdowns, many in-person educators quickly moved online, often using content developed for their in-person classes. They (and their students) quickly realised that this really doesn't work. It is no surprise that the reputation of online learning suffered. The online teaching industry is still battling against this.

As you will see on the next page, both formats have challenges, but they also offer great creative opportunities in terms of how, what and who you teach, and to make your training a financial success. They can also complement each other very well, which we will look at the end of this chapter.

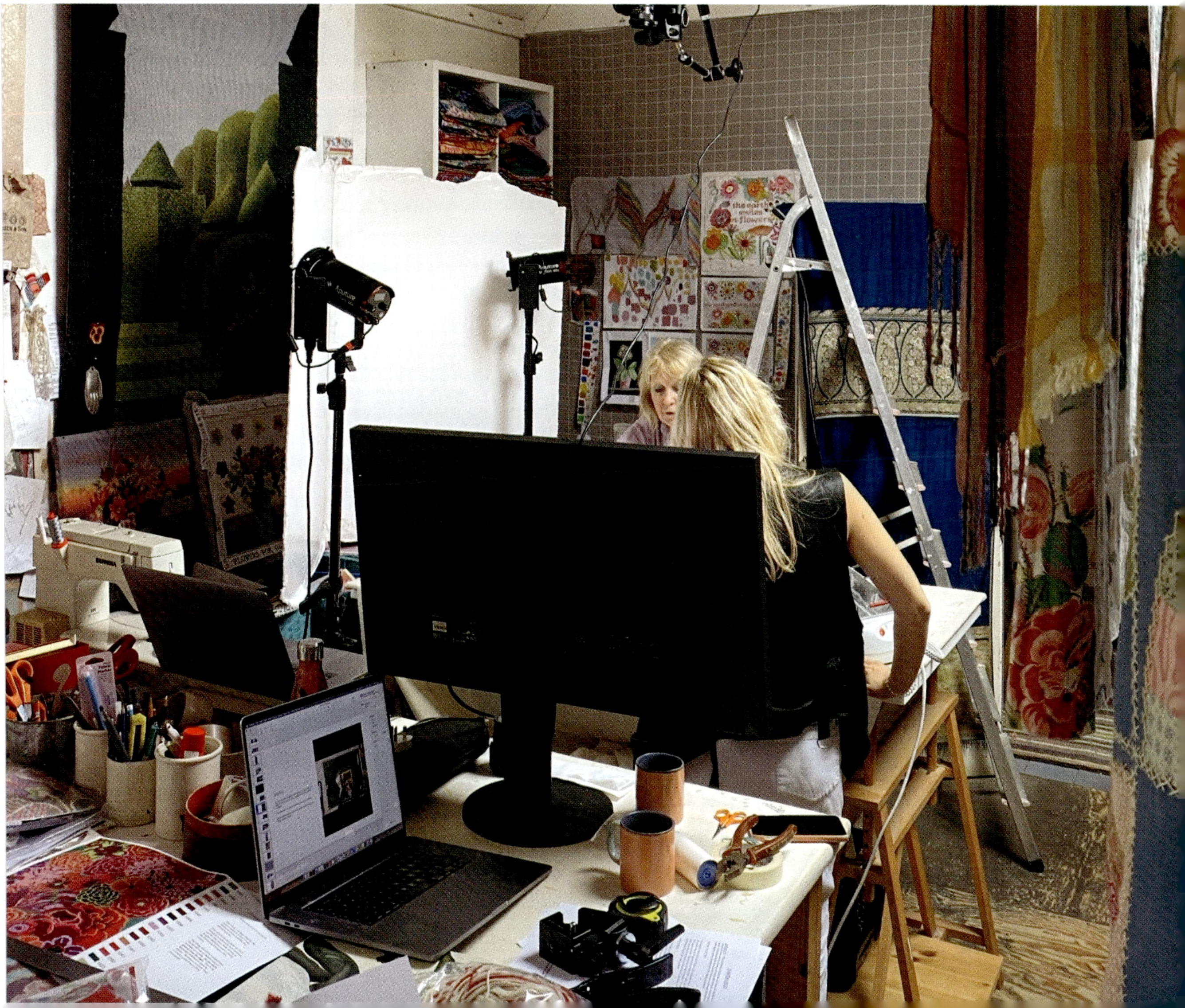

Where will you teach?

In-person workshops and courses can be hosted in many different venues and locations, depending on space and equipment requirements, and your budget.

Many artists run workshops in local community centres, church halls, schools or art colleges, or in galleries or museums. Increasingly, craft events host creative workshops too. Some artists teach in their home studio or studio space. You can even teach outdoors.

Working with venues and partners

Will you be responsible for finding the right teaching venue, or will you work with venues who hire you to teach? These two approaches are very different.

When you choose the venue, you are responsible for the hire, payment, admin and everything else. If you sell enough tickets to cover your costs, you will make a profit.

If you are approached by a venue to provide training for them, you will usually be paid a standard day rate, although this is often negotiable. Alternatively, you can approach venues who run creative training already and pitch your training to them.

Working with a venue or delivery partner means a lot less risk and work for you, because they take care of the venue and other costs, most of the marketing and the administration. It can also increase your profile and credibility, but make sure that they have the right facilities, and check their cancellation policy in case not enough tickets are sold.

How to find the right venue

The easiest ways to find venues are:

- **Researching where other creatives teach already,** especially people working in your field. Research online, especially at websites such as craftcourses.com or Eventbrite;
- **Searching locally** for suitable venues including craft studios, community halls, museums and craft events.

When researching venues, take the following into consideration:

- **Space:** the layout, cleanliness, display opportunities, storage, furniture and equipment.
- **Location and venue:** road and public transport links, accessibility, ambience and local amenities.
- **Finance:** cost of venue and equipment hire, catering, insurance, and payment and cancellation terms.
- **Availability:** is it likely to get booked up?
- **Catering:** will you provide food (through venue), or will participants bring their own? Are there hot drinks available?
- **Insurance:** what are the requirements?
- **Administration and marketing:** who is responsible for marketing, admin, signage, etc.?
- **Health and safety:** first aid provisions and security.

You can download an extensive checklist entitled *How to Choose The Right Venue* from the Teach Your Creative Workshop Toolkit.

Top Tip

Look at your competitors' websites, social media or newsletters for details of potential venues or partners.

Eventbrite is a very useful research tool too. It is also useful to look at listings in creative or local magazines.

'Thanks to the money that I earned running online courses during COVID-19, I was able to save up enough to buy a flat-pack log cabin, which we built ourselves in the garden.

It's a lovely light space with big windows. I can easily fit eight students now. Because it's separated from the house, I can run the art sessions without it affecting our home life. I also create my own art here, away from distractions.

The cabin really has made my business grow. I keep pinching myself that I have it!'

Sally Goodden, animal artist

Below Sally Goodden's cabin, where she teaches and works.

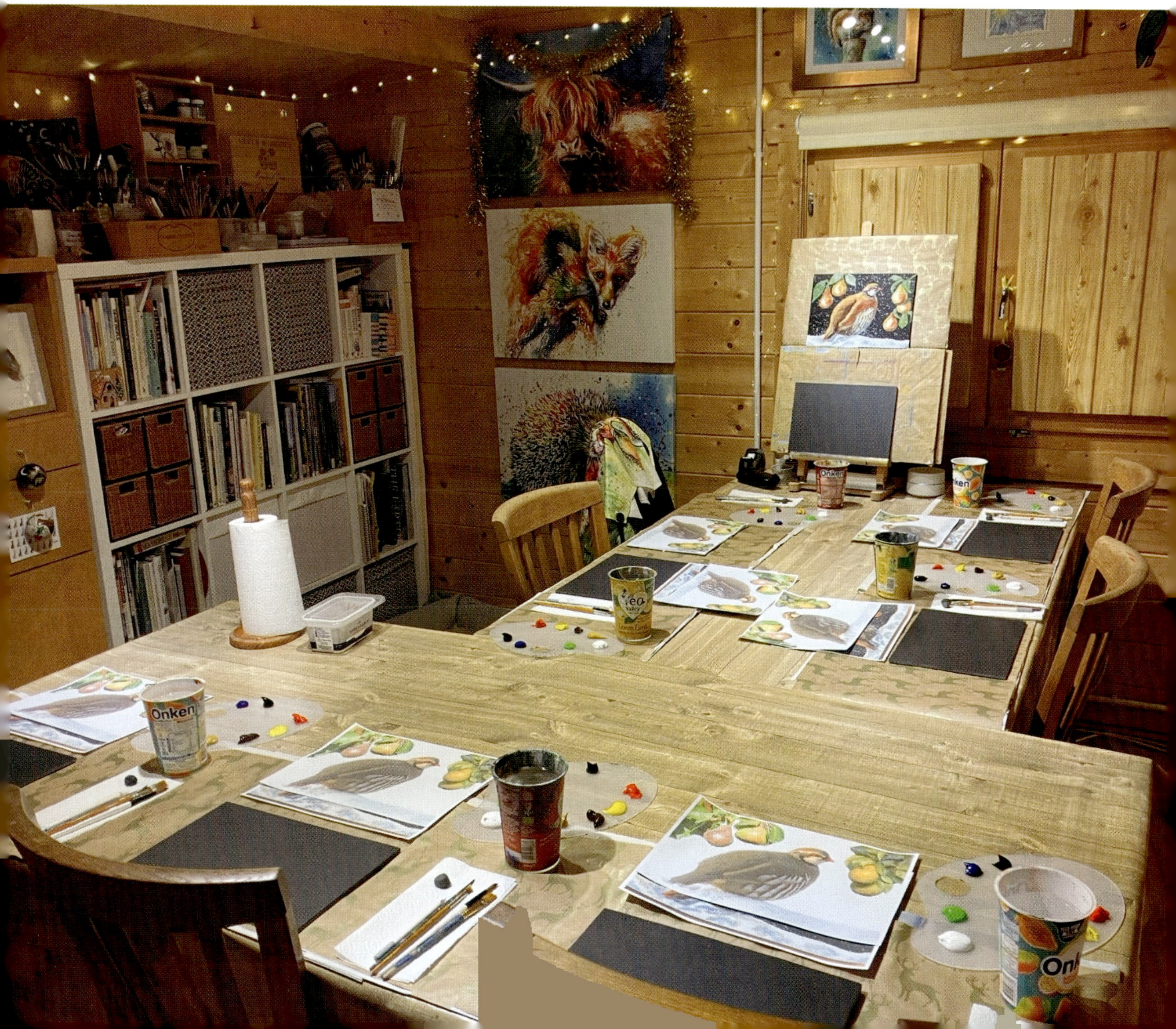

Teaching in your own studio or home: A warning

Many creatives start by teaching in their own home or studio space. It's simple, as the costs are lower, and you have easy access to your materials and equipment. It's a great starting point, especially if you want to work with individuals or a small group, or you are just starting out.

There are some important considerations:

- You might need to do a good clear up before you can start to teach (depending on how messy you are!).
- You might not feel comfortable with students seeing projects in progress, or using your tools and equipment.
- Your own space may be small, which limits the number of students you can work with, which can really impact your profitability.

There are also **some really important legal considerations** when teaching in your own home or studio:

- Many councils in the UK will not allow you to teach in your own home, especially if you have students regularly coming and going, or causing parking issues for neighbours. Find out about these restrictions or if you are required to notify your local council.
- Are there any specific health and safety issues, depending on which materials or equipment you use?
- Your household insurance might not cover loss or damage to stock, tools or equipment if you have students in your home or workspace. You may have to add these to your policy.
- You must have good public liability insurance in place that covers your home and/or studio. It's very important to check if your insurance covers teaching from your home or workspace.
- If you are working and teaching in an official studio or workspace then ensure that your landlord allows for this use.

Creating your teaching space

Designing a space for teaching involves careful planning to ensure a safe and inspiring learning environment.

You might find it useful to draw out a floor plan in advance. This will help you prepare, and will make setting up the room easier.

Always configure the space to make it as welcoming as possible for your students. Consider the following:

- **Workstation layout:** what equipment and furniture do you need? How many students will you teach? Will students work alone or in pairs? Does each student have enough space to work individually and/or collaboratively? Does everyone have access to light, power and water? Is there natural light?
- **Your demonstration area:** what equipment will you need? Can everyone see you?
- **Safety:** check for hazards like uneven flooring or electricity cables on the floor, and keep the emergency exits clear.
- **Tools, materials and supplies:** is everything labelled and readily available?
- **Storage space:** allocate space for personal belongings, materials and tools.
- **Display or showcase area:** will you provide textbooks or samples for reference? Will you display students' work?
- **Accessibility:** can students access and move around their workspace easily? What about students with special needs or disabilities?

- **Breakout area:** for a quiet moment or some fresh air – for you or your students.
- **Food and drinks:** what refreshments will be available?
- **Does your space reflect your training goals, values and niche?** Your workspace environment is a big part of how your students will experience and feel about your training.

You can download a more extensive checklist, entitled *Creating the Best Teaching Space* from the Toolkit.

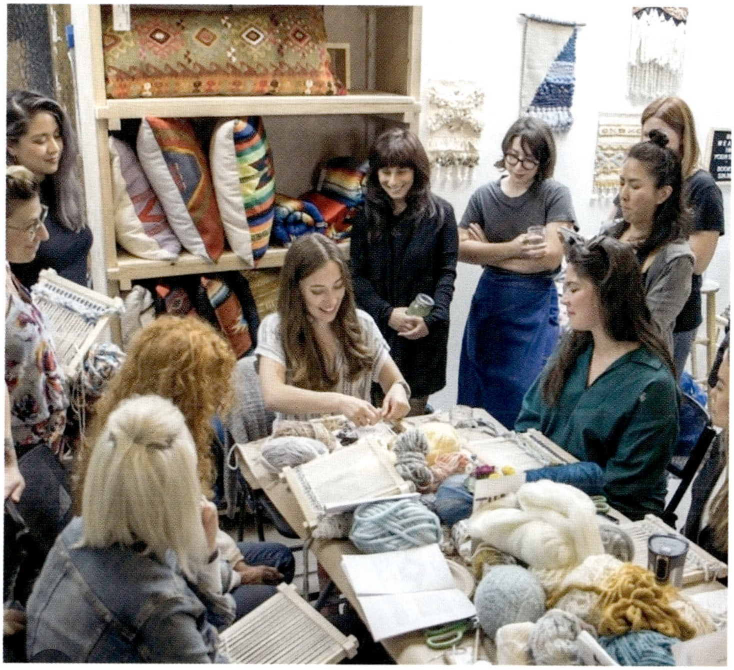

Above Lindsey Campbell of Hello Hydrangea teaching an in-person class.

Time to pause

Get your notebook and make time to reflect on how to find and select the best venue, and create the right learning space for your in-person training:

- **Where do you want to run your training?** What criteria have you set for your ideal venue, delivery partner and location? Start to research and identify suitable venues. This practical action is an important step towards launching your in-person training. It can be inspiring and help make your training idea much more real.
- **Do you want to teach at home or in your studio space?** Be aware of the legal and health and safety issues discussed on p.90.
- **How will you create the right learning space for your ideal students?** Make notes on what space and equipment requirements you have. Get creative with making the space part of the experience. How can you create a more welcoming space for all your students? How can you create an environment that highlights your values and motivations for why you teach? This is a very juicy and creative exercise.

Get ready to deliver your in-person training

Teaching in person can be one of the most exciting and inspiring aspects of your career and creative practice, but it is also scary, overwhelming and exhausting.

We are now going to jump ahead to the day that you will deliver your in-person training. Of course, before you are ready to deliver your training you will need to cost, price, market and launch your course or workshop, which we will cover in detail in Part 2.

One of the most useful things you can do to prepare and plan for your in-person training is to use checklists, even if you have been teaching for years. It's very easy to forget essential steps or equipment when you are busy.

Here are some useful checklists to help you get ready for your workshop.

You can download an extended version entitled *Get Ready to Deliver Your In-Person Training* from the Toolkit.

Checklists

1 What to bring, including:

☐ all your equipment, tools and materials;
☐ student information and welcome packs;
☐ any stationery, books and handouts;
☐ your lesson plan;
☐ any signage;
☐ refreshments for you;
☐ feedback forms.

2 What to do one or two days before the training. This could include:

☐ finalising timings with the venue, especially access and catering times;
☐ making sure you have everything packed;
☐ running through your lesson plan and checking your timings.

3 What to do on the day of the training:

☐ arrival at the venue and meeting staff;
☐ space and workstation set up;
☐ venue checks, e.g., parking, accessibility, emergency exits, first aid, catering, etc.

4 Running order, to include:

☐ arrival and meeting and greeting;
☐ setting the ambience;
☐ introductions;
☐ housekeeping announcements;
☐ what you will do during each session;
☐ how you will end the day.

5 To make the process run more smoothly for you and your students on the day:

☐ **be prepared:** a well-run but flexible workshop often involves a lot of preparation.
☐ **walk the room:** check in with their progress, make yourself available to answer questions and give specific feedback. Share discoveries and highlight excellence. Observing your students while they are learning is a crucial tool for identifying areas to improve on.

□ **go around and help:** don't do the work for them, unless they specifically ask; rather, demonstrate on a sample piece so they can copy you.

□ **keep on track:** It's easy to run over or get distracted with long conversations about a side issue. Avoid rushing through or cutting down the breaks if you fall behind. These relaxation periods are essential – for you and your participants.

□ **check the energy in the room regularly:** do students need more time or are they ready to move on? The best teachers read the room, anticipate and are responsive to their students' needs in real time.

□ **think about how you use your voice:** can you adapt your speed, volume or tone? Play with your voice to create different experiences, and use it to your advantage to share your passion and enthusiasm.

□ **reflect and debrief at the end of an exercise:** ask the group for feedback before sharing your own. Encourage them to look at each other's work, and highlight their diversity and creativity. Ask questions, such as 'What did you enjoy about this activity?', 'What went well?', and 'What could you do differently?'.

□ **don't go on to the next step until everyone has completed the previous task.** You need to build into your lesson plan alternatives for students who are faster or more experienced.

□ **look after yourself during the training:** teaching is very intense, and it's essential to take regular breaks.

□ **make notes for future reference:** what questions did your students have? What worked well and what didn't, or what's missing? It's especially important to note how long activities really take.

Time to pause

Get your notebook and make time to reflect on the following questions:

- **How can you better prepare to deliver your in-person teaching?** Review the checklists or download the checklist from the Toolkit. Add your own notes.
- **What questions, challenges or worries do you have about teaching in person?**
- **What do you need to learn, do, research or create to be even more ready to teach in person?** What do you need to stop doing? Make a list and find specific solutions. Can you discuss these with a more experienced teacher?
- **Review your Teaching Plan** and Lesson Plan, and add more detail.

In Chapter 6 we will look at how to become a more confident teacher in more detail.

Do you want to teach online as well as in person? The next section is full of ideas and tips to help you teach online. Keep reading, pausing and writing down your actions.

If you are not interested in online teaching (yet), you can skip to the end of this chapter, and start making your training ideas real with some juicy and creative exercises: creating a short film, and doing a test run of your training.

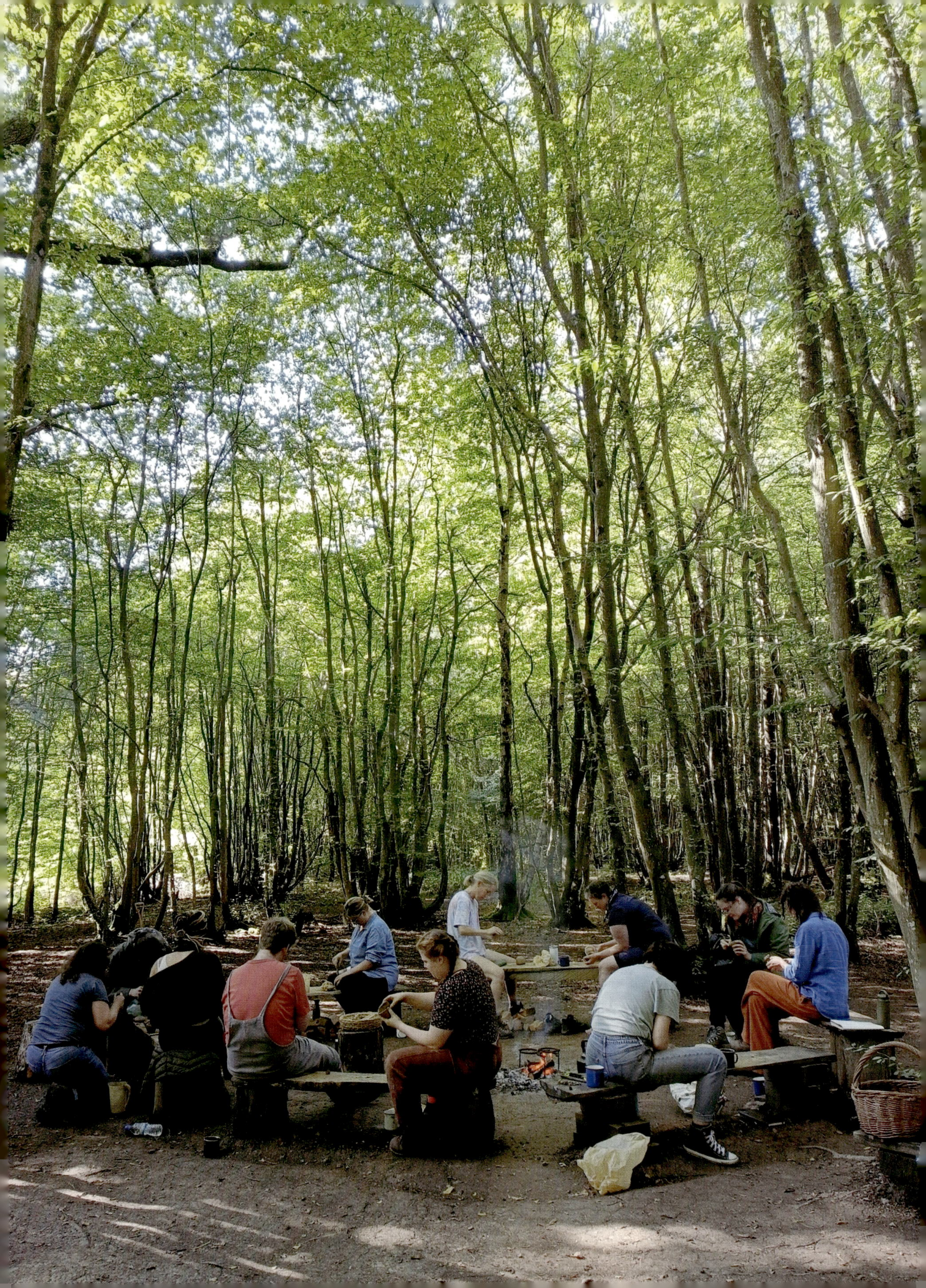

What does a workshop day look like?

During my teacher training, the importance of teaching plans was drummed into us. I still do them, even for courses that I've taught before.

I make an overview of the sequence of events for each time block, with notes on what needs to be emphasised. Most of what I teach is very process-oriented, and certain steps need to be completed before doing the next thing.

Whatever the weather, we'll be in the woods. We start the day with a silent walk to the woodland teaching area. Then we light our campfire together and do a spot of guided mindfulness. Activities at the start of a day that support spaciousness can make learning easier for people.

We use the fire to cook lunch and boil the kettle for teas throughout the day. We have very little infrastructure in the teaching area. I deliberately keep it simple, as I want us to have a small footprint.

I always start a teaching session by offering some inspiration. I give everyone baskets, pots and plants to handle, to show how amazing they are. Then I offer an overview of what they're making. You can't go straight into anything technical or start with the details.

We often then go and meet the plants we're working with, or the clay we're digging. We usually go into processing the material and then begin the making itself with demonstrations. I aim to break down the process into bite-size chunks, and support people one-to-one as needed. When appropriate, I encourage the group to support themselves and each other. Peer-to-peer learning can be more effective than teacher-to-student learning.

Opposite Ruby Taylor's Native Hands woodland teaching space.

Above Harvesting and preparation of natural materials is part of the process in Ruby's workshops.

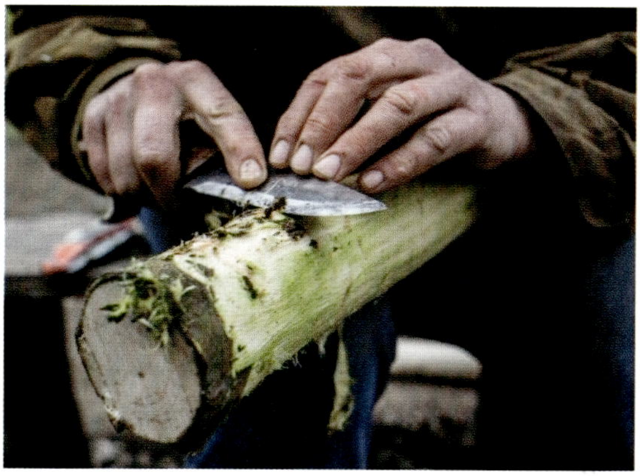

As the day progresses, I'll keep an eye on how each person is doing, how they're responding to any challenges, and observing their learning styles. People need different kinds of inputs, and a lot of what I teach is quite technical, so I have to respond creatively to support the learning. A relaxed atmosphere is essential. It's lovely to hear the group laughing and chatting over lunch.

How do you look after yourself as a teacher?

I make sure I'm learning outside of my teaching time, so that I get inspired and nourished, and so that I'm regularly reminded of what it feels like to be in a learning situation. I make sure I get enough physical rest, because my teaching is physically demanding.

I have a helper who supports all the practical aspects of the day, and during a teaching day, I aim to take myself away for 20 minutes at lunch. I'm careful about what I eat and how I hydrate.

I have supervision, someone professional who I can talk to about work issues on a regular basis, like challenging interactions or things that have gone pear-shaped. We unpick them and explore new ways of managing situations. That's invaluable.

2: Teaching online

In the last few years, online teaching has massively increased in popularity. According to Statista, the online education market is projected to reach US$185 billion in 2024. Domestika, one of the most successful creative learning platforms, offers more than 2,000 courses, created by 1,300 creatives, to more than 8 million members.

Do you already teach online, or are you thinking about it? Remember that teaching is a broad concept. Even recording a few Instagram Reels or hosting a Zoom meeting counts as online teaching. In this section we will focus on the unique opportunities, challenges and practicalities of this training format.

> *'There are some real advantages to online teaching, especially with jewellery. We can go really up-close so you can see a lot more detail. We can get the exact angle, which you can't get teaching face-to-face.'*
> **Jessica Rose,** founder of Jewellers Academy

If you are ready to take your online teaching to the next level, read on.

Why do you want to teach online?

As we saw at the start of this chapter, teaching online has many advantages, both for you and your students, in terms of reach, accessibility, time constraints, affordability and profitability.

When I started The Design Trust in 2011, one of the key reasons that I launched it as an online business school was that I could reach many more creative businesses in the UK and beyond. I love online teaching's affordability, accessibility, and wide reach, and how it works well with upgrades, such as one-to-one advice.

We have our Business Club membership, where we regularly invite experts and successful artists to share their knowledge, and we offer four- to six-week online courses on topics such as selling online and creative commissions, with options for extra private coaching and accountability on top. This has been a very successful business model for me over the last decade.

Time to pause

Get your notebook and make time to reflect and answer these questions:

- **Return to your notes from Chapter 1. Why do you want to teach?** It might be a while since you wrote down your answers. Take some time now to review. What is really important to you?
- **Then focus on why you want to teach online, specifically.** Review the advantages and disadvantages of teaching online at the very start of this chapter. What resonates with you?
- **Are you planning to teach live or pre-record your training?** What are the advantages or disadvantages of these two different formats for you?

Online training formats and methods: A creative recap

As we saw at the start of Chapter 4 (pp.51–52), there are some common teaching formats for online training:

- **Talking heads:** live talks, interviews or Q&As.
- **Presentations:** often accompanied with PowerPoint slides, focusing on a specific topic.
- **Online meetings and discussions:** speaker-led and interactive.
- **YouTube or other social media videos:** short, often free online tips or advice.
- **Tasters:** free introductions to courses or programmes.
- **Online workshops or courses:** full-length live or pre-recorded training.
- **Online conferences:** one- or two-day events, with a wide range of speakers.
- **Memberships:** often combining live and recorded video or audio content, with membership community tools such as directories, forums or online community groups, e.g. a Facebook group.
- **Vaults or libraries:** secure, restricted areas where useful content is shared, e.g., recordings, downloadable resources.
- **Online one-to-one advice or mentoring:** offered as a stand-alone, or as an upgrade to training or membership.

In Part 3 we will dig deeper into some of these creative online learning opportunities to grow your creative business significantly.

Many online training programmes often offer more than live or pre-recorded video training. The best and most in-depth courses and memberships **offer broader and more creative learning methods**, such as:

- **step-by-step instructional guides** to support the video training;
- **forums** for posting questions, homework or work in progress for feedback;
- **downloadable** workbooks, checklists, cheat sheets, and templates;
- **quizzes, polls, or point-earning systems** to increase engagement and to gamify students' progress;
- **additional resources,** e.g., art supply lists, recommended books and videos;
- **membership** networking opportunities, including membership directories, forums, Q&A sessions and member meetups;
- **special offers** and affiliate deals, especially around materials and resources.

Time to pause

Get your notebook and take time to reflect:

- **What are your favourite online training formats?** Why do you like them?
- **What training content and additional resources could you provide** beyond video to increase value for your students or to make your teaching more appropriate or creative? Identify between three and five different ideas and add these to your teaching plan.

Taking a thread for a walk

See Video 1.4

Getting started:

- Before put any stitches down, use your fingers to talk to your thread, smoothing and gently moving, rearranging your metal, enjoying the shapes, curves and flow the thread allows for - notice what you find pleasing - what shapes are you drawn to?
- Now your couching stitch becomes a tool to take a 'snapshot' of shapes that you wish to capture. You do not have to work your stitches in order here, focus more on adding stitches in places that will hold a shape you wish to capture in place.
- As we are working on such small scale, it shouldn't pull your fabric too much, so feel free to jump around with your stitches - they dont always have to be in succession!
- This exercise is so much about BEING in the moment with your stitching - its not necessarily about thinking about the bigger picture and where is it going (will we open up more design possibilities in the next module) - For now, its much more about thinking about what shapes you can create - right NOW that make you say "ohhh thats pleasing!'

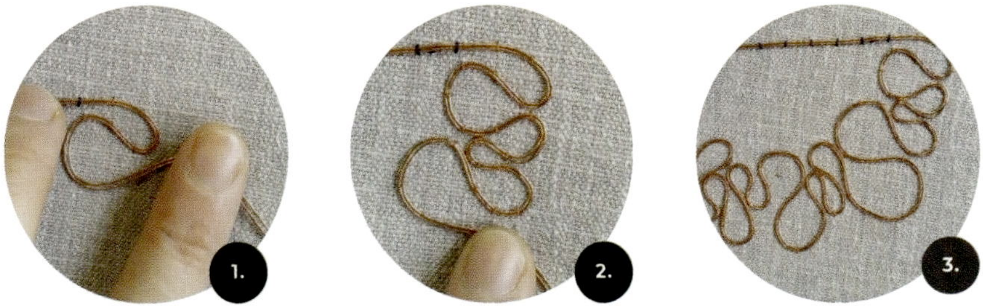

Things to consider

- Do you find yourself being drawn to stitching particular shapes: larger, swooping curves? perfectly even circles? tight, intricate loops? squiggles?
- How could you vary your stitching to explore shapes you hadn't considered before - use the suggested promts above to get the ideas flowing
- How big can you go before your shape looses its 'flow'
- How small and tight will your threads allow you to go?
- What makes a 'perfect' shape for you?

Whats next?

- You may like to really take you time with this exercise, allowing your threads to grow and meander around a larger hoop or canvas, enjoying all the possible shapes - the longer you do this, the more you will discover! It will also become an interesting 'stitch dictionary' of sorts which can inspire ideas in the next module. In fact... if you decided to stay with this exercise alone, you would produce some beautuful work!

 P9.

Above Hanny Newton provides a detailed PDF book with instructions for FLOW, her online embroidery course.

Online teaching: Live, recorded or both?

One of the big questions with online teaching is whether you want your training to be live, pre-recorded or a combination of both.

The big advantage of live online teaching is that it's **easy to set up and cheap to get started.** Also, if training is live at a particular day and time, it's much more likely that your student will turn up and participate with fellow students.

Many new creative tutors visualise a professionally created recorded and edited course, as these are very popular on online marketplaces such as Skillshare, Domestika or CreativeLive. **However, pre-recorded training is much more complicated to create,** and often needs input from experts for the filming, lighting, audio, branding and editing. Pre-recorded training needs much more preparation, and a highly structured lesson plan, often combining video content with written texts and homework assignments.

Many new online teachers underestimate the skills and, especially, the time and money involved in creating pre-recorded training.

Top Tip

If you are new to teaching online, start with some live rather than pre-recorded sessions. It's easier and cheaper to get started, and you can build up an audience. You will likely be nervous about making mistakes, but it's a good way to improve your teaching skills and confidence.

Often, **the best online training solution is hybrid teaching, combining live training with recordings.** Adding a live element to your training will give students a reason or deadline to stay on track. It builds in accountability and allows for more personal interaction, thereby increasing the chance that they will finish the course. Some examples combining live and recorded online training include:

- **training delivered live,** with a recording made available to participants in case they missed it or want to watch it again. Extended access can increase the value, and students are more likely to sign up.
- **a series of pre-recorded sessions** that students watch in advance, so that live group sessions can focus on collaboration and feedback on work in progress. This is the 'flipped teaching' model.
- **access to a library or vault of pre-recorded sessions** with basic techniques. This adds value for students, as it offers extra training, and saves you time and minimises frustration for both parties.

In the Toolkit you can download a full overview of the formats, methods, advantages and disadvantages of live, recorded and hybrid online training.

Want to do pre-recorded training? A warning about VAT MOSS for UK and EU businesses

VAT MOSS stands for Mini One Stop Shop, and refers to the VAT tax regulations related to pure digital services to consumers in the EU, which is relevant if you sell downloadable content such as e-books or knitting patterns, but also if you provide pre-recorded training without any live support.

Although this tax was introduced across the EU, very few small businesses are aware of it, or assume that as they are not VAT registered it does not apply to them. This is not correct, and even if you are not based in the EU, VAT MOSS applies to your small business.

To avoid VAT MOSS:

- Do not provide 'pure' digital services without any human interaction. If you add an element of live interaction in a group or on an individual basis then this doesn't apply.
- Use specialist digital marketplace Gumroad or an online marketplace (such as Etsy or Domestika) who are legally required by the EU to charge and administer this EU VAT on behalf of their suppliers. Your student will be charged more, but the marketplace will pay the VAT on your behalf. Note that Etsy doesn't allow you to sell services unless you provide something tangible, like a PDF course book with links to your training.
- If you are already VAT registered then talk to your accountant or tax adviser about this to get personalised advice.

You can find out the latest information about VAT MOSS on the gov.uk or europa.eu websites.

Time to pause

Get your notebook and make time to reflect and answer these questions:

- **Read more about the opportunities and challenges of online recorded teaching** in the Creative Case Studies of Jessica Rose of the Jewellers Academy (p.234), David A. Smith (p.113), Kara Leigh Ford (p.162) and Lindsey Campbell of Hello Hydrangea (p.178). What did you learn from them?
- **Review some of your favourite online courses and teachers.** Identify what different teaching methods they use. Analyse their online training – not just their live or recordings, but additional training methods. What can you learn from them?
- **Review the advantages and disadvantages of live, recorded or hybrid online teaching on p.99 and 101.** Which format are you considering? Why did you choose that option? Update your teaching and lesson plans accordingly.
- **Combining live and recorded online training in a hybrid model** can be very creative and more effective. Review your lesson plan and note whether sessions will be live or recorded. This will be useful when you start to create your filming and content plan later in this chapter.
- **If you are planning to create pre-recorded online training,** you will need to invest more time and money. Do you have the skills to film and edit high-quality films, or do you know somebody who can help you? What do you need to learn? Reach out to film-makers and editors now to discuss your content ideas to avoid disappointment later on.
- **Is VAT MOSS relevant to you?** If so, then spend time researching the legislation and resolve this issue.

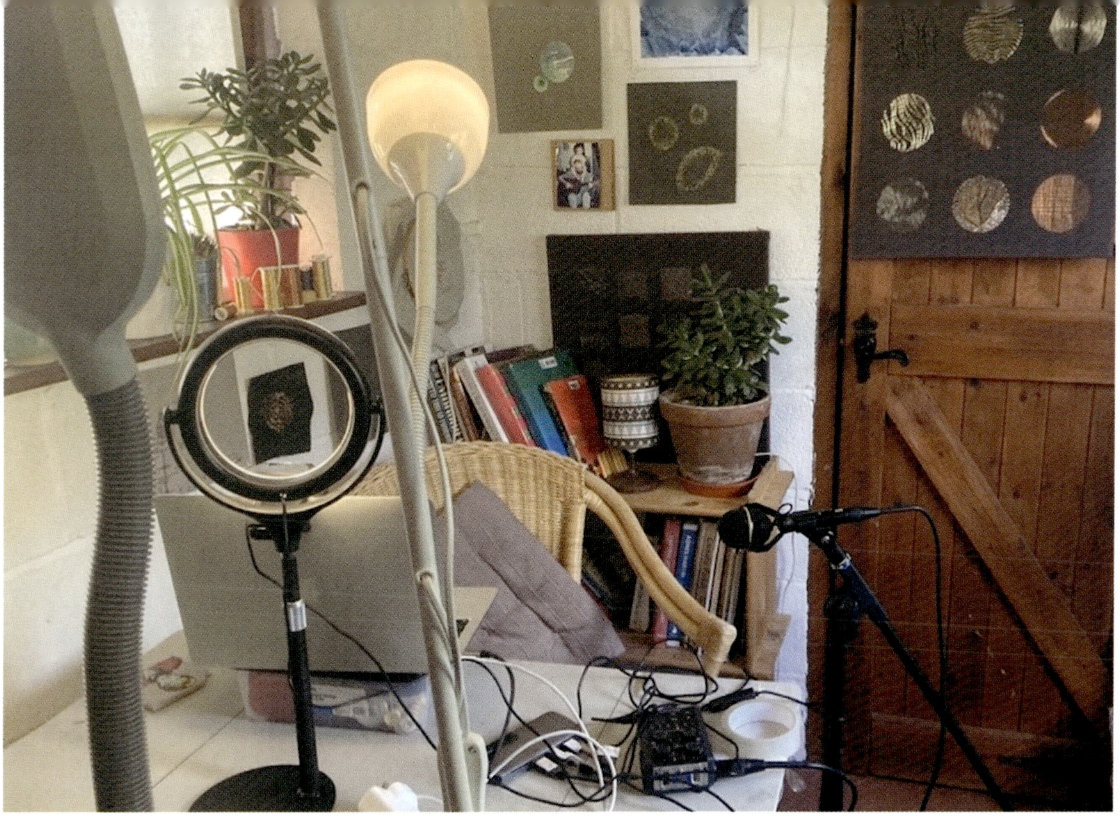

Above Hanny Newton's behind-the-scenes recording set-up.

The three big challenges of online learning

Challenge 1: Motivating your students to finish your training

> *'The industry average for online course completion is 3 per cent. 97 per cent of people buy a course, and don't do what they set out to do.'*
> **Dr. Carrie Rose,** *The Completed Course*[5]

I find that a rather shocking statistic, don't you? **What stops people from finishing online training?**

- **Do they have the time** and are they really committed? Online learning is often a solo activity, and students need to be more self-motivated to finish an online course than with in-person training. Be transparent about how much time they will need to invest.
- **Did they sign up on a whim?** Online training is generally cheaper and more accessible than in-person courses, encouraging impulsive purchases.
- **Do they have access to the materials and equipment they need for the course?** This can be a major challenge.
- **Have they got the technical ability and computer equipment?** Many parts of the world have limited or inconsistent broadband or Wi-Fi connections, which might make live online training harder.

How can you **overcome these challenges**? By taking extra care before and during the training to motivate and attract the ideal students for your course.

Before: Motivating students before the training starts

- **Keep your training short** and simple! Break a larger course down into smaller ones.
- **Be very clear on your website** and promotional material about what and how you will teach, who it is and isn't suitable for, and how long the whole course and the practice will take.
- **Focus on a niche technique** or project, rather than a generic skill.
- **Do market research in advance:** use the survey (pp.38–41) or do a pilot run to get their input, test your teaching ideas and approach, and check how long it takes students to finish.
- **Run a free Q&A session** to introduce yourself and your training. Potential students can ask questions to see if it's suitable for them.
- **Think about how you can help students** to get back on track if they fall behind. People are often too optimistic about their motivation and what they can achieve. Life happens! Don't make them feel like a failure. Let them know that this is a common challenge. Give them helpful tips on resuming.
- **Increase the price of your course!** This might surprise you, but if students pay more, they are likely to be more committed to do the required work.

During: Maximising engagement during the training

- **Use engagement tools:** share work in progress, create breakout rooms for small group discussions, encourage sharing via chat, or get students to create work alongside a teacher in a live group.
- **Create a private online community** for additional support and accountability: encourage peer-to-peer learning or create a buddy system or accountability partners.
- **Make it interactive:** offer different activities for different learning styles, e.g., reflective written work and verbal group discussions, or ask previous students to participate in a Q&A on how they achieved success.
- **Host live review or Q&A sessions:** sessions on specific dates and times will provide accountability, group support, inspiration and encourage attendance.
- **Limit time access to your course** and give deadlines to complete homework exercises: many people need a deadline to encourage them to get into action.
- **Use gamification techniques** to keep your students motivated: think about how you can reward them along the way, e.g. include quizzes to check their progress; creative incentives for attending; run a competition for the best work; give certificates for finishing a course successfully.
- **Be aware when or where they might get stuck:** check your software to see how students progress and make a note of any bottlenecks; answer their questions quickly so they feel seen and heard. When students get stuck, they can become demotivated and stop, so responding quickly is vital.
- **How can you help them** to get back on track if they fall behind? Offer the option to upgrade to individual support, e.g., coaching or advice sessions, or a review of work. Personal feedback gives students the incentive to do the work, especially if there is a deadline.

Time to pause

Get your notebook and make time to reflect on the following:

- **Clarify what 'completion' of your training would mean.** Should they watch every video recording, do all the homework and download and fill in every worksheet? Is it necessary for them to perfect each step to get something useful out of your course? You can have low completion and engagement, and still effect a major transformation for your student.
- **Identify three specific actions you can take before your training starts,** and three that you can take during the training to engage your potential online students. Update your teaching plan and lesson plan as necessary.

Challenge 2: Standing out in a competitive market

In the last few years, online teaching has become very popular, partly due to COVID-19, which gave people an opportunity to learn new creative skills, while in-person training disappeared overnight. Technical developments have also made it much easier, and many creative professionals have realised that teaching can be a much-needed additional income stream.

Therefore, as we discussed in Chapter 3, it's **really important that you have a clear niche** as this will help you to stand out in an increasingly competitive market.

There is also **a lot of free training available** on YouTube and social media, and you might ask, 'Why would people sign up for my paid-for course?' The quality of much of this free training varies, much of it being very simplistic. You might be surprised how helpful it is for your students to be able to find everything in one place. Similar content might be available for free online, but it takes time to find, and isn't as good as yours.

It is very likely that similar training to yours is available, but it's unlikely to be exactly the same. Throughout this book, I have encouraged you to check what's out there in the market already, but also to make your training distinctly yours in terms of what, how, who and where you teach.

Below The Jewellers Academy runs many free short courses.

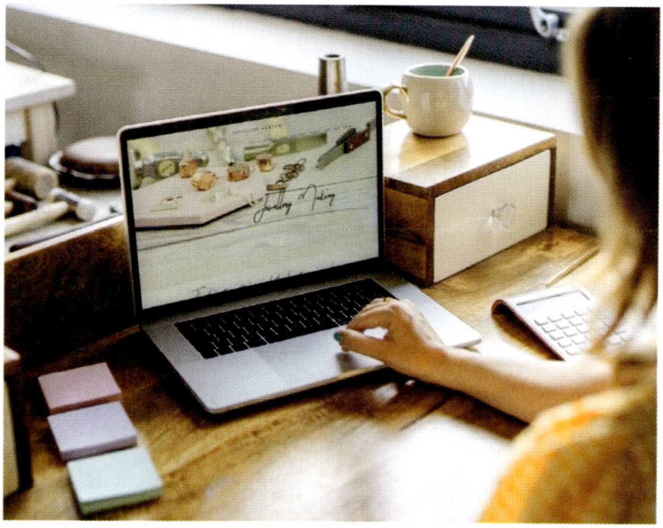

Challenge 3: Time management and overwhelm

Planning and creating online training can be overwhelming, especially if it is pre-recorded. Often, new teachers want to teach far too much at once and underestimate the variety of skills involved in creating professional-looking training – script writing, filming while demonstrating, editing, adding voice-over, etc.

Pre-recorded training often combines various teaching formats and methods, of which the recordings are only one part. Often you will need to add text or images on the course pages to introduce the videos, explain details or provide additional resources. Putting this all together can turn into a complicated jigsaw. It can be useful to ask advice from people who have created pre-recorded training, including other creative teachers, freelance film-makers or video editors. A filming plan is an essential tool to manage this.

If you decide to outsource some of these specialist tasks, you will need to work with a team of experts, including a film crew and editors. To make this process go as smoothly as possible, you will need to be extremely well-prepared, so you know exactly what to say and do during filming, and how the different parts fit together.

If you are planning a pre-recorded course, you could start with a few short, free promotional videos. This can help you to focus your training, make things real, give you practical experience with filming and editing, and warm up your potential audience. It's never too early to start promoting your training and to get sign-ups.

Later in this section, I will challenge you to make a short film about your number one training idea.

How to select the right film format for your online training

So, what equipment or software do you need to start filming? Before we get to that FAQ, it's useful to note that the filming format is often dictated by your teaching format (what and how you want to teach):

Talking heads: a person speaks on screen

☐ Very common for online meetings, discussions, guest interviews or sharing quick tips on live social media.

☐ Quick and cheap to get started.

☐ It is a static approach, with little variation in camera angles. Audio and camera quality might be low.

☐ Recommended software: Zoom, MS Teams, Crowdcast, Facebook or Instagram Live.

Physical demonstrations

☐ Very common for creative skills teaching to show the skills and steps involved.

☐ Harder to do live, because speaking while doing can be tricky and slow in real time. This format is often pre-recorded to show key steps and the end result, using bite-sized segments instead of continuous footage.

☐ Usually requires more than one camera to show different angles, and to zoom in on details.

Slide presentations

☐ Very common and useful for teaching and explaining step-by-step instructions.

☐ You, as the presenter, are less visible as the presentation takes up most space.

☐ Can be boring, especially if the presenter reads from a script, if there are no images, photographs, diagrams or quotes, or if the audience has no opportunity to engage.
☐ Recommended software: Powerpoint, Keynote, PDF, Prezi for creating the slides; Zoom, Go to Webinar, Crowdcast for sharing them. Many online training platforms, such as Thinkific and Ruzuku, have their own built-in webinar software.

Screencast workflow: you share your computer screen
☐ Very useful for teaching digital applications or for behind-the-scenes website or app instructions.
☐ Recommended software: Camtasia, Vimeo.

Podcasts: usually audio-based, often following a theme or featuring interviews
☐ Very popular online medium, but it's not visual – more discussion, opinion and concept-based.
☐ Many marketing opportunities to appear as a guest on other podcasts.
☐ Recommended software: Adobe Audition, Audacity, Riverside.

Broadcasting live events: e.g., conferences or live talks at events
☐ Can be recording a presentation, interview or panel discussion. For example, CreativeLive teaches creative courses with a presenter and a live audience, using 'hot seats' to discuss and resolve specific creative challenges.
☐ Requires serious investment in professional studio equipment and experts to ensure good image and sound quality.

FAQ: What filming and broadcasting equipment do I need?

So, as we just saw, your teaching format often dictates which software is best to record your training. Most online skills training uses screensharing technology, the camera of your computer or additional plug-in cameras.

For physical demonstrations, you will need to invest in professional film equipment and software, although it's amazing what you can achieve with two smartphones!

Besides filming and recording equipment and software, you also need to think about:

- **Filming:** A digital camera, either on your phone or stand-alone. Using a tripod reduces shakiness.
- **Audio:** A separate microphone will improve audio quality. Use a clip-on lapel mic, especially if you don't like headsets or are demonstrating and talking at the same time.
- **Lighting:** The quality and professionalism of your videos will be improved by using softboxes or LED lights in the background. Daylight is preferable, but be aware of changes in natural light.
- **Editing software:** This is particularly important for pre-recorded training, and for trimming your live recordings. Options include Adobe Premiere Pro and Apple Final Cut Pro.

If you are training with a live audience, professional venues often have cameras and microphones built in for static filming. For more professional, TV-like presentations, you will need to hire a film crew.

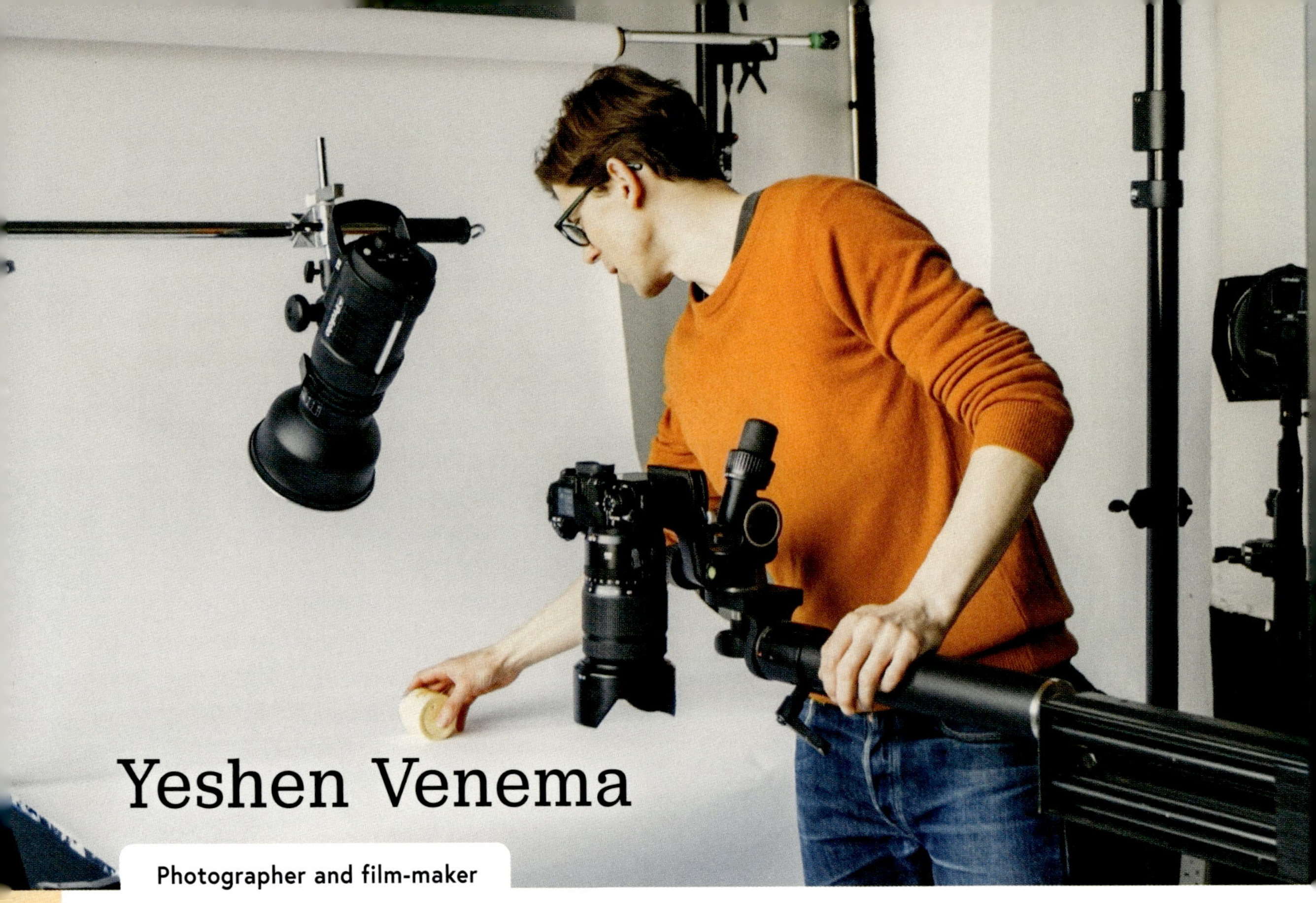

Yeshen Venema

Photographer and film-maker

Expert Tips: Film your pre-recorded online training

Yeshen Venema is a Product and Lifestyle Photographer and Squarespace Specialist who helps artists, designer-makers and micro businesses thrive.

Teaching is a core part of Yeshen's work and in many ways the most satisfying. During photoshoots Yeshen gave his clients DIY photography tips, so it was a natural progression to offer formal workshops and one-to-one online training sessions, and follow-up Squarespace training. Yeshen uses Google Meet as it has screen-sharing and recording functions. He aims to empower his clients to take control of their camera or website and learn how to present their work better. More recently he has launched an online membership for creatives who want to learn about product photography.

You can find out more about him at www.yeshen.uk

Make a plan (and a storyboard)

Creating a storyboard is as simple as sketching out the scenes/shots you need on index cards or sticky notes. You can then edit the shots and change the sequence, if needed. Write out your dialogue or narration in Word and print it out

Above Yeshen Venema at Hackney Downs Studios.

using a large font that is comfortable to read.

Even if you decide to film and record yourself, it will be very helpful to have a friend or colleague on hand to help. If you plan to work with a freelancer for camera and/or sound, send them some images of the space in which you plan to shoot in advance so they can prepare and offer advice on the set up.

Record your voice after your video is edited

Unless you need to talk directly to camera it's more effective to record your voice afterwards once you have edited the film. You can then be sure it fits the edit, and you can record small sections at a time – no need to be a 'one take wonder'!

Most phones have good-quality voice recording apps, and there are paid apps available that allow higher-quality recording, such as MOTIV™. Use an external mini directional microphone placed about 30–40 cm away and pointed at your face. The Rode VideoMicro offers professional-quality sound.

Set-up and lighting

Your shooting area should be free of clutter and styled to reflect your audience. Think 'less is more'.

For lighting, use either natural light – a large window to the left or in front in the morning will work well – or controlled LED lighting. Natural light changes throughout the day so try and shoot at the same time of day if shooting over multiple days.

If you are using LED lighting, block the windows with a large black cloth to make your lighting more consistent. An LED panel light with built-in diffusion and a large white foam board to bounce light back in on the opposite side will improve the lighting quality.

Shoot multiple takes from multiple angles

It's never a bad thing to have a few options for each section of your film when it comes to editing. Even if you are recording the dialogue/voice-over separately, you may wish to switch between camera views or prefer a slower transition between scenes. When you are recording, this may seem boring, but you have gone to the effort of setting everything up, so use the time efficiently to get multiple shots.

The Cam Link adaptor will allow you to record through your webcam and an additional camera via HDMI into Google Meet or Zoom.

Back up, then back up again

Digital content (in this case video and audio) does not really exist unless it's in three separate places. Ideally, have a copy on the camera's memory card or your phone, on an external hard drive and in a cloud storage solution like Google Drive or Dropbox. For an extra backup, save to an additional hard drive and keep this in a different location.

To make it easier to locate your footage, rename the files in plain English, e.g., 'How to do a cross stitch angle 1' or 'Mixing the colour part 3', and save in sub-folders. Edit copies of the original material in case you make a mistake and accidentally delete important footage.

Edit and upload

Keep the content free of any online platform's brand names, as this will enable you to upload your videos to multiple platforms. You can always record separate intros for each platform and edit those into the start of the film.

Creative Exercise

Create a filming and content plan

To help you get organised and ready to film your training, especially if you are planning a pre-recorded or hybrid training, then creating a filming and content plan is essential. It will give you clarity on the content, the priorities, and the length of each film, as well as other content to create your online course. Your lesson plan, which you started in Chapter 4, will be the filming and content plan.

Opposite is an example of a filming and content plan for a pre-recorded giftware course that I was part of, to inspire you to create your own.

1 Start with adding more detail to your existing lesson plan

Answer the following questions:

- Have you **identified your learning goals** and the steps and activities required to reach them?
- **Which parts will you teach using video?** Will this be live or recorded? Will you do a demonstration, a slide presentation, talk to the camera, or invite a guest speaker?
- **What other teaching methods** will you be using, e.g., explanatory texts or images in your course pages, downloadable workbooks, additional resources, quizzes to check knowledge?

Opposite Filming and content plan for a pre-recorded giftware course.

Download the *Filming and Content Plan* template from the Toolkit.

2 Create a filming plan to give you clarity on the different steps or modules, what each of the recordings is about, rough timeframes for each recording, and any other teaching methods that your online course will use.

Start to fill in the details:

- What are **the main segments?** What are the different parts and steps? What are the activities or what will you demonstrate?
- What is **the content?** What will you demonstrate or talk about? What teaching method will you use for each element, e.g., essential reading, video recording, practical homework, research? What is video and what's written down?
- Include your **visual ideas**. What filming format will you use? What will you show on screen?
- What **materials or samples** will you need?
- **How long will the recording be?** How many words of text?

This process will encourage you to focus and cut out any unnecessary detail in advance. It will also help you to stay on track during the filming and editing of your training.

Chap	Title	Written/ video	Notes	Words/ duration
1	Introduction	W	Introduction to the course – what you will learn/how it works Introduce module Aimed at both new jewellers & textile designers and more established Understanding the giftware market and its potential	200 words
2	Meet the tutor	V	Visual ideas: head shot sitting in chair + images of website Introduce Patricia • How did you get into what you do? • What's your expertise? • What's the favourite part of your job?	5 mins
3	Meet the tutor	W	Written introduction to tutor. Use standardised questionnaire.	200 words
4	Introducing the giftware market	V	Visual ideas: Graphics with main questions/key points Why turn your creative products into giftware? Share key statistics e.g. CC report, any data from the GA about annual sales of jewellery? Visual ideas: Gifts in shops and online – people looking at them/buying. • What is different about gift than non-gifts? • Obvious but the customer is somebody else – wider appeal, more 'neutral products needed, return policies, more nervousness about buying. • Time and price limit – for a special date, time pressure. • Make it giftable e.g. packaging • What makes a gift & who buys them? Intro to popular gift categories e.g. wedding, baby, pets. • Also think about gift experiences e.g. workshops Visual ideas: Shots of categories explored Action: Ask question + show on screen • Where do you fit? Identify your category and style and link to potential client group. • Identify your gift buyer: Who are they? What motivated them? Importance of market research. Visual ideas: buyers (high street/fair)	10 mins

3 Review your filming and content plan

Making time now to review, delete and really focus on how your pre-recorded training will come to life is essential. It will save you a lot of time, energy and potentially costs (especially if you are working with a film and editing team). Use the following questions:

- Does the **order make sense**?
- Is it **doable** for your students and for you? Be ruthless and cut everything that's not essential.
- Is it **interactive and varied**? Does it strike the right balance between watching videos, practical exercises and reading? Do you cater for different learning styles?

Time to pause

Read the Creative Case Studies with Jessica Rose of the Jewellers Academy (p.234), artist Esté MacLeod (p.218), embroiderer Hanny Newton (p.56) and ceramicist Linda Bloomfield (p.28). Find out how long it took them to create their pre-recorded training.

What were their specific challenges? What was especially time-consuming? What did you learn reading their case studies?

4 Planning and time management

- Use your filming and content plan to **identify how long it will take you to create the video for each element,** including the preparation, filming and editing. Do the same for additional non-video content, e.g., workbooks, additional resources, etc. This will give you an overview of how long it might take you to create the course.
- **Keep it simple!** If you look at the list and feel overwhelmed already, that's a clear sign that you need to cut some content out and simplify it. Remember that I suggested that your first online course should not be longer than two hours. Can you replace some of the pre-recorded video with live training? Do you have existing resources that you can include?
- **Set a start date and launch deadline.** This will help you to focus and provide external accountability. You might even find that you want to launch before you are ready (more about this later).
- Remember that **things don't need to be perfect for your launch.** You can always make changes to an online course afterwards.

I hope the next Creative Case Study with David Smith will inspire you to teach your creative skills online too!

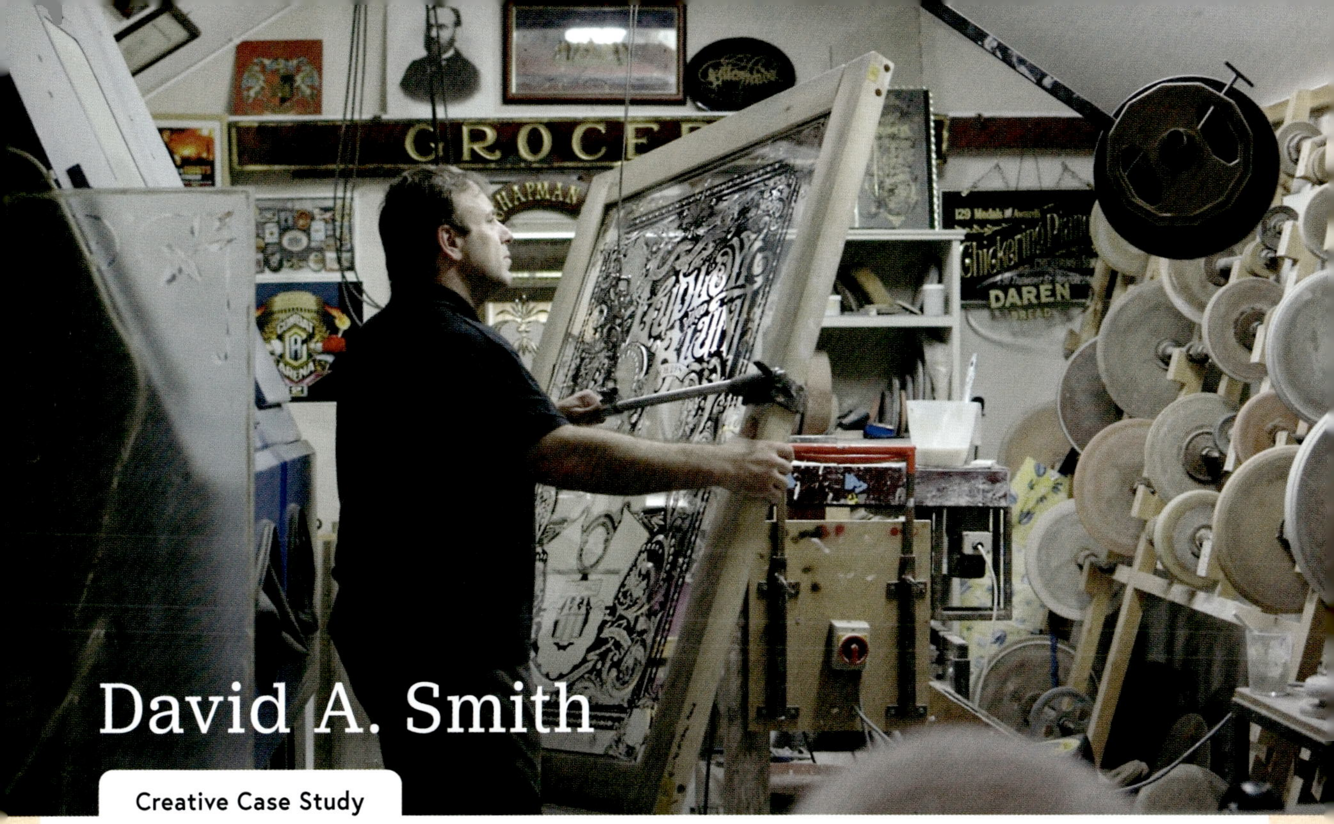

David A. Smith

Creative Case Study

David A. Smith MBE is a master craftsman in the traditional skill of glass gilding and signwriting. In 2019 he received an MBE for Artistry in Reverse Glass processes and for keeping the craft alive around the world.

David started his signwriting career at 16 and was apprenticed for five years with a traditional sign-painting company. In the 1990s he became self-employed and took on additional staff, but times changed when computers were introduced. He sold his business in 2003 to focus on traditional sign painting, reverse glass gold leaf work and album cover design. David also creates hand-drawn digital fonts, scrolls and designs that he licences to iStockphoto and Getty Images.

He has been teaching small group workshops for nearly 30 years from his studio in Devon, and has launched two highly successful online courses in the last two years.

You can find more about David A. Smith on his website davidadriansmith.com

How did you get started with teaching?

I started teaching small classes in 1995, and I still teach today. I teach gold leaf reverse glass gilding, like you see on old pub windows and mirrors. In the beginning, people would write to me to ask if I could teach them sign painting or lettering. They would work with me for a few days in my studio and we would create a glass piece or reverse glass sign with old ephemera, using traditional techniques. I have taught over 3,500 people in this way.

‘It’s nice to think that people around the world are gilding glass using some of the processes that I’ve taught them. It keeps the craft alive and stops this unique traditional craft from dying out.’

Above David Smith in his studio.

Why do you teach?

I just love teaching. I like to talk about the craft, and I get to meet some really lovely people. I really enjoy it. It feels right to pass these skills on to other generations.

Sometimes you meet students, and you think, 'This person has got it.' There have been quite a few like that. You keep in touch and some of the work they do now is just incredible. I also learn from them. In every course I teach I learn something.

What and how do you teach?

A few times a year I teach gold leaf gilding and sign writing workshops from my studio in Torquay. I run a three-day course that is suitable for beginners up to advanced artists. We look into design and typography, how to generate your own ideas and colour schemes, and I show a lot of Victorian techniques.

These workshops are extremely rewarding. They are limited to only four people, which is more intimate, and lets me give each student individual support. We start at 9 a.m. and often don't finish until late in the evening. I like to give them a really good time. I always make a lot of friends and they stay in touch. Because it's kind of an 'olde worlde' craft, sometimes the students expect me to be old-fashioned and quite strict. I like to make the learning fun.

The course is taught in my studio, so I can teach techniques using equipment that people normally wouldn't have access to, like brilliant glass cutting using stone wheels.

What about your online courses?

I launched my first online course, *An Introduction to Glass Gilding Techniques*, in early 2023. It's a 52-hour, in-depth online course where students create 12 beautiful gilded letters using lots of different techniques.

I show them how to apply gold leaf to glass using 18 different methods, including water and oil gilding, which give very different finishes. After that, I take them through the process of handling and controlling a brush to get straight lines and circles. They will make a sign, and once they have finished that they will make 12 gilded letters, starting off with basic techniques and working their way up to something more elaborate.

I decided to start teaching online because I have a long waiting list for my in-person workshops. It had nothing to do with COVID-19. I wanted to share my skills online with people who couldn't afford my live course.

We do provide online students with a list of materials and tools that they can purchase anywhere in the world to make it really easy to do at home. They get lifetime access and if they make a mistake they can watch the recording again. If they are not sure about something, they can always email me, but I only get about one email per week!

It took my daughter Lauren and me two years to put the first online course together. I wanted it to be thorough and to make it feel like I am with them in the room, talking directly to the camera. I talk while I paint and share tips when they pop into my head. I dropped a brush once and my daughter said that she would edit that out, but I said, 'Let's keep it in and show them how to clean the brush.' It's important for me to be myself.

When we started, I thought we would do three letters and a sign, but it changed as we went along. I started with a project that took 15 hours but it was too complicated, so we added the techniques at the start to explain the details. Then I came up with other techniques that I wanted to include. My daughter kept telling me to put it in another class, but I am glad I did it this way, because I know they really treasure the course. I want to give them value for money and not devalue the craft by offering one of those cheap online courses.

How do you keep your online students motivated and engaged over 52 hours?

I think that they keep going because they want to get their money's worth. They know it's a challenge and that they have signed up for something special, so they are really keen and committed. There aren't a lot of similar in-depth courses around. A lot of my students have always wanted to do this. Many of them log on very regularly.

And throughout we encourage them to share their progress and finished pieces on social media. I really celebrate their steps and achievements with them.

What's next?

I want to try and create my own posters. I want to be able to replicate old-fashioned, high-calibre lithography of the 1900s, and learn and explore things myself. I'd like to put some time aside to learn from someone who really knows their stuff.

I don't need to retire, as this is my job and my hobby. I can just pick and choose what I love to do.

I will always teach and share this beautiful craft. It's been a large part of my life.

Below Still from David's film showing the making of a gilded sign for Ludlow Blunt in Brooklyn, New York, a commission that took nearly two years.

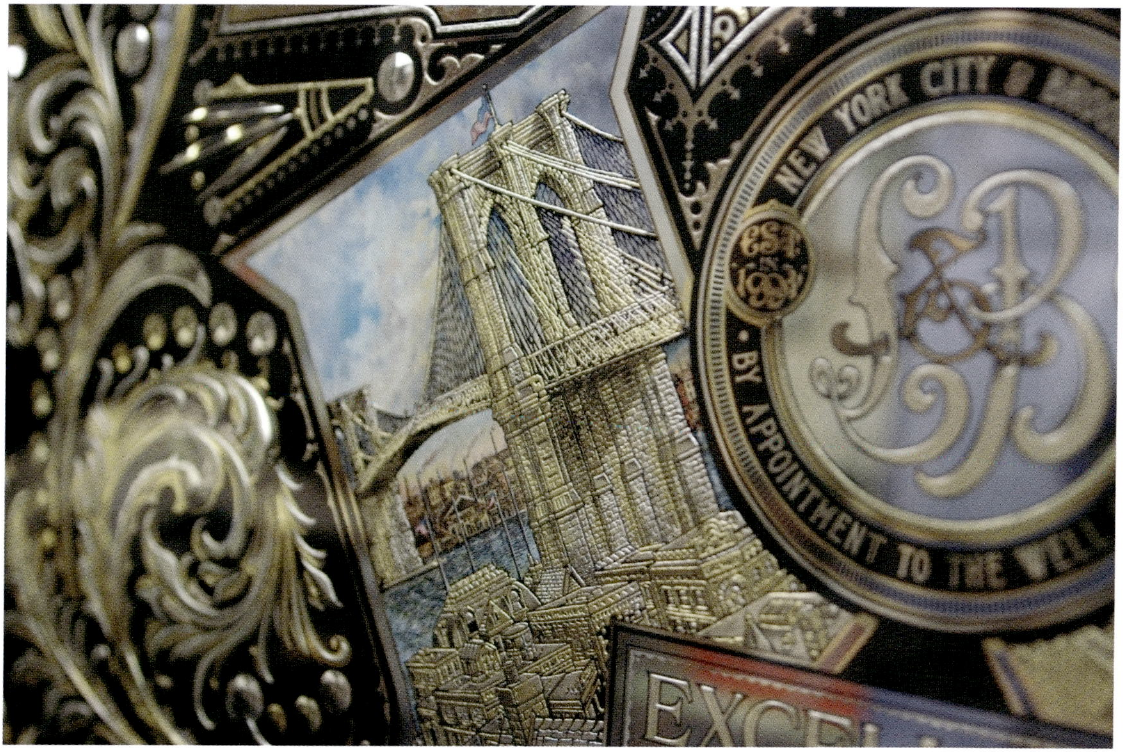

3. Combining in-person and online training

Combining both in a hybrid model can overcome some of the challenges and problems we have seen when it comes to getting enough bums on seats, extending the in-person experience, standing out in a competitive teaching market, encouraging and motivating your students throughout their learning, and managing your own and your students' expectations.

The use of social media, online communities and digital tools can make it **easier to get student feedback, build supportive communities, and provide cost-effective ways to offer additional motivation,** support and advice, for which you can charge more.

In terms of marketing, **online and in-person training support each other very effectively,** helping you to build your profile and credibility with potential students to building longer-term, beneficial relationships using free content. We will return to this in Chapter 8.

Examples of creative integrated in-person and online training:

Offer online resources before or after your in-person training:

- give access to course materials;
- offer discounts on kits or books you sell;
- provide feedback to students, e.g., a virtual 'office hour' or Q&A session a few weeks after the in-person training.
- create a 'flipped classroom' providing reading material in advance online, and use class time for practice and group collaboration.

Use a blended learning approach:

- Combine in-person and online learning materials. Let in-person students watch an online instructional video or let them do research online to mix learning styles up.
- Upgrade to offer online mentoring, advice or coaching after in-person training.

Create an online community:

- Set up a Facebook or WhatsApp group or other online forum for students to connect, share their work and support each other before and after their training.
- Use collaborative tools like Google Docs, Padlet or Trello for group projects and peer feedback during and after training.

Use social media and your website to showcase student work:

- Share images of your workshop and the work your students created. Include their testimonials or even more in-depth case studies about the impact of your training – but don't forget to ask permission first.
- Encourage students to share their work with their own followers.

Time to pause

Get your notebook and write your answers to the following questions:

- How can you combine in-person and online training? Identify three specific, unique actions.
- What will you do in the coming week, the next quarter or during the year to combine in-person and online training? Commit to some quick and easy actions and identify some longer-term projects to work on.

Creative Exercise

Do a test run

There is a moment where a student needs to move into action and start to practise. Yes, I am talking to you! There is only so much you can learn from reading and listening. It's like learning to ride a bike – it's not until you get on and try to pedal that you really learn how to do it.

Now is the time to start creating and working on making your training idea real. Coming to the end of this chapter, I invite you to take an important practical step: create a short film about your training idea and do a test run for your favourite in-person or online training idea.

Of course, you can continue to read the next chapters to get the overview first, and then return later to put your learning into practice, but there will be a moment where you just have to take the leap, and have a go at teaching.

Before you deliver any in-person or online training for the first time, I highly recommend that you do a test run with real people, especially if you are new to teaching.

You can offer this trial session for free (online), charge or invite existing clients or students at a significantly reduced price. Ensure that you mimic the real situation as much as possible, and that your participants closely match your ideal students in terms of skill level and motivation.

A pilot workshop will help you to:

- **find out if there is enough interest in your topic** before you spend a lot of time, money and energy on developing training that not enough people are interested in;
- **identify potential challenges,** ensuring smoother execution when you teach. You will worry less about the logistics so you can concentrate on teaching and engaging with your students;
- **fine-tune your pacing,** ensuring you allocate enough time to each lesson block;
- **find out how your students respond to your teaching style,** activities and group dynamics. They can give you additional ideas and great insights into what they want to learn and how they learn. Formal feedback is an essential part of doing this test so that you can identify areas for improvement, and don't forget to get testimonials (see Chapter 9 for more information on evaluation);
- **perfect your lesson plan** that you started at the end of the previous chapter. It's far better to get feedback and adapt your lesson plan now.

Even if you have experience in teaching, a pilot session will be beneficial. Together with the client survey (pp.38–41) this provides a reality check, giving you useful insights on all aspects of planning, delivering, marketing and pricing your training.

Create a short promotional film

I am challenging you to create a short film for your in-person or online training. I want you to have a go and see what you can do to **quickly start promoting** yourself and getting people interested in your training. It's also really useful to get some experience of preparing, filming, presenting and editing.

I want you to **create a film between two and five minutes long** – the right length for a quick introduction. It could be about your creative process, a practical tip related to your course idea, or a teaser for your training idea.

- Try not to spend more than four hours doing this exercise. The recording should be five minutes long at the most.
- The easiest option to film, record and broadcast is to use Facebook or Instagram Live or use webinar software (see p.107 for which equipment to use).
- Promote this free session in advance to your contacts and followers so you have a live audience.

Have a go! Make notes on what you've learnt about your presentation, editing, time-management and marketing skills.

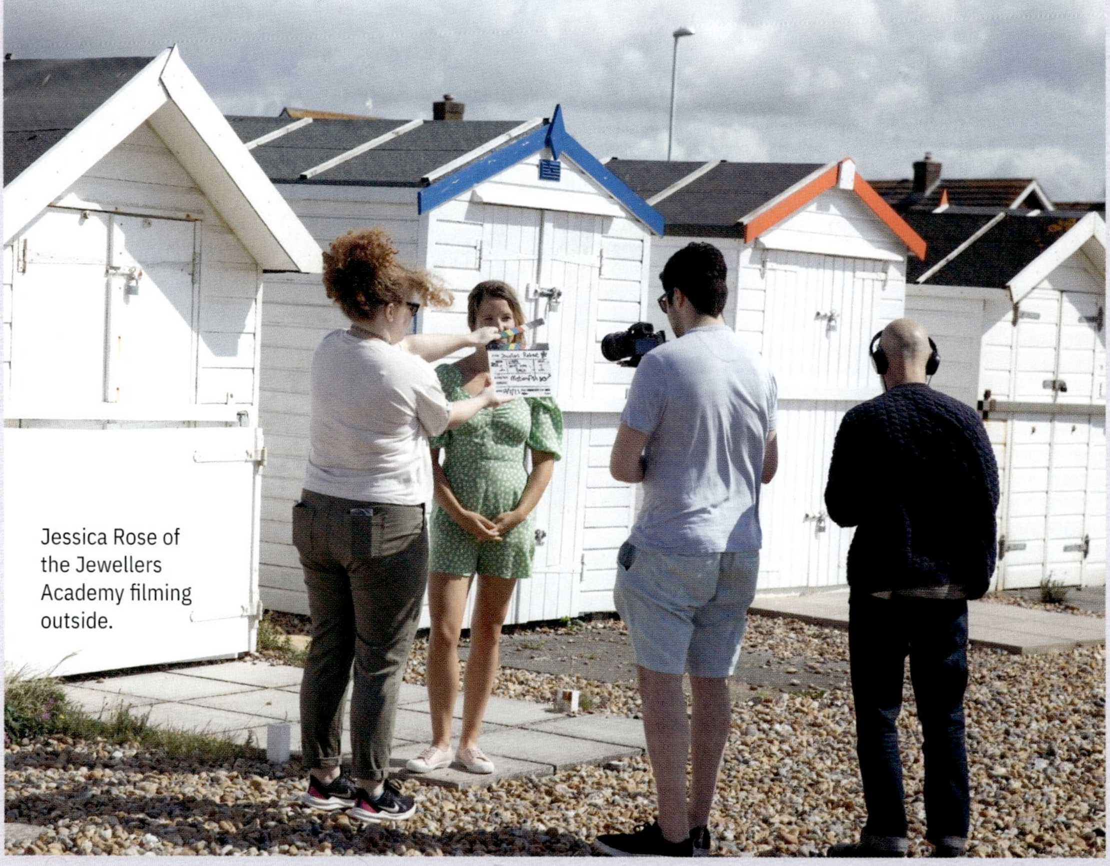

Jessica Rose of the Jewellers Academy filming outside.

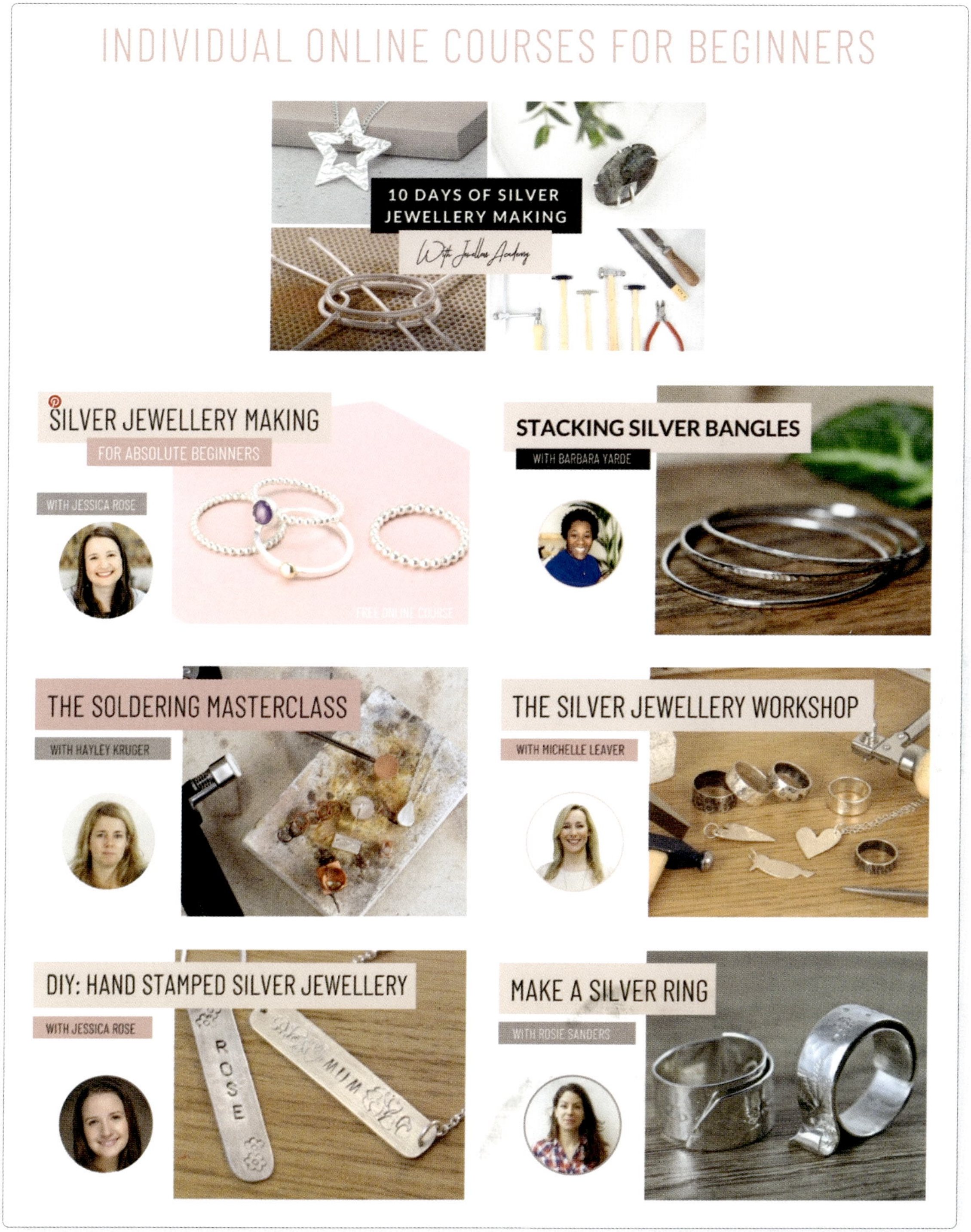

Above The Jewellers Academy offers many short and free online courses on their website to entice new students to sign up for their longer courses and diplomas.

FAQ: How many people can I teach?

Class size depends on several factors:

- **Will you teach online or in person?** Online training can offer far more capacity, but many communication software and training platforms set a class size limit, or increase their prices for larger class sizes.
- **Your ability to interact, answer questions,** give personal feedback and encouragement, and keep students engaged. Be realistic about what you can do alone, and consider whether you need extra support staff.
- **If you teach in person,** how much physical space is available? Venue capacity dictates how many participants you can work with at a time. Teaching from home or your studio doesn't incur extra costs but there might be health and safety issues, and limits on space might impact on the financial viability of your training.
- **How much space and equipment does each student need?** A hot glass workshop will have different needs than a contemporary calligraphy class.
- **What level do you teach?** Beginners need more personal attention, and you'll need to be able to go round to check in with all students regularly. However, many advanced students prefer one-to-one support to ensure confidentiality and individualised advice.
- **What's your teaching format?** Do you want to run an intensive retreat or do a talk in a large conference hall? What would be the best group size to optimise group dynamics? How will you make sure participants have access to you?

So, what's the optimum number? Most creative teachers will say that a beginners' workshop group is ideally between four and eight participants. For larger groups (12 and more) you will need to adapt how you teach with more lecturing and demonstrating.

There is a strong connection between student numbers, ticket price, student expectations of the experience and profitability of your training. We will look more into this in Part 2.

Below Jessica of the Jewellers Academy teaching one-to-one.

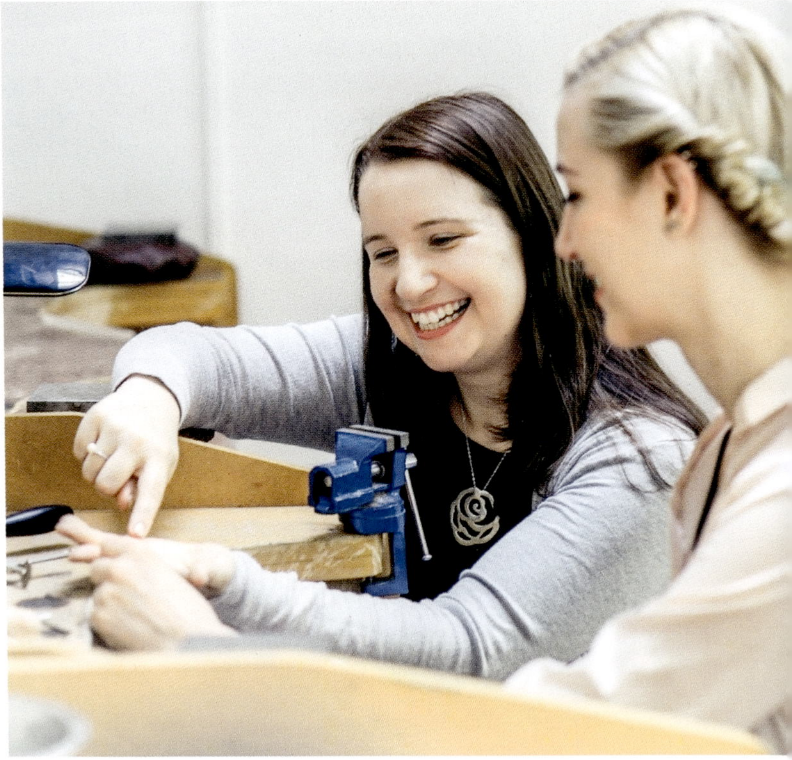

Time to pause

Take your notebook and reflect on **the number one thing you learnt in this chapter** about teaching in person or online. How will this insight help you?

It's very easy to overcomplicate your teaching and to get overwhelmed with too many ideas. I find it useful to have a clear goal and a deadline to help me take action and not get lost in the detail. So, let's look ahead towards the launch of your training, which we will cover in more detail in Chapter 9. Write down some answers to the following questions:

- **When are you planning to launch?** Is this a good time for you, and are your students likely to want to learn then?
- **Working back from that date,** what will you need to do in the next few weeks or months? Be as specific as possible. Think about planning and writing your course, finding venues or software, pricing, launching, delivering. Create a visual plan with deadlines for what you need to do by when.
- **What is stopping you from making progress?** What do you need to do, learn or create for a successful launch? Identify specific actions and break them down into smaller chunks to make them more doable.
- **What decisions do you need to make?** Remember that your launch doesn't need to be perfect and often it's about moving forward imperfectly. Keep it simple and set yourself limits in terms of the length and complexity of your training.
- **Who can help you?** Reach out to creative teachers with more experience or to film-makers who can help you with creating, delivering and launching your training.

In the next chapter we will dive into how to look after yourself when teaching, before we move on to Part 2, and get into the practical business side of your training – finances and marketing.

But first we have a Creative Case Study with illustrator Sally Goodden who teaches children and adults from her own garden cabin.

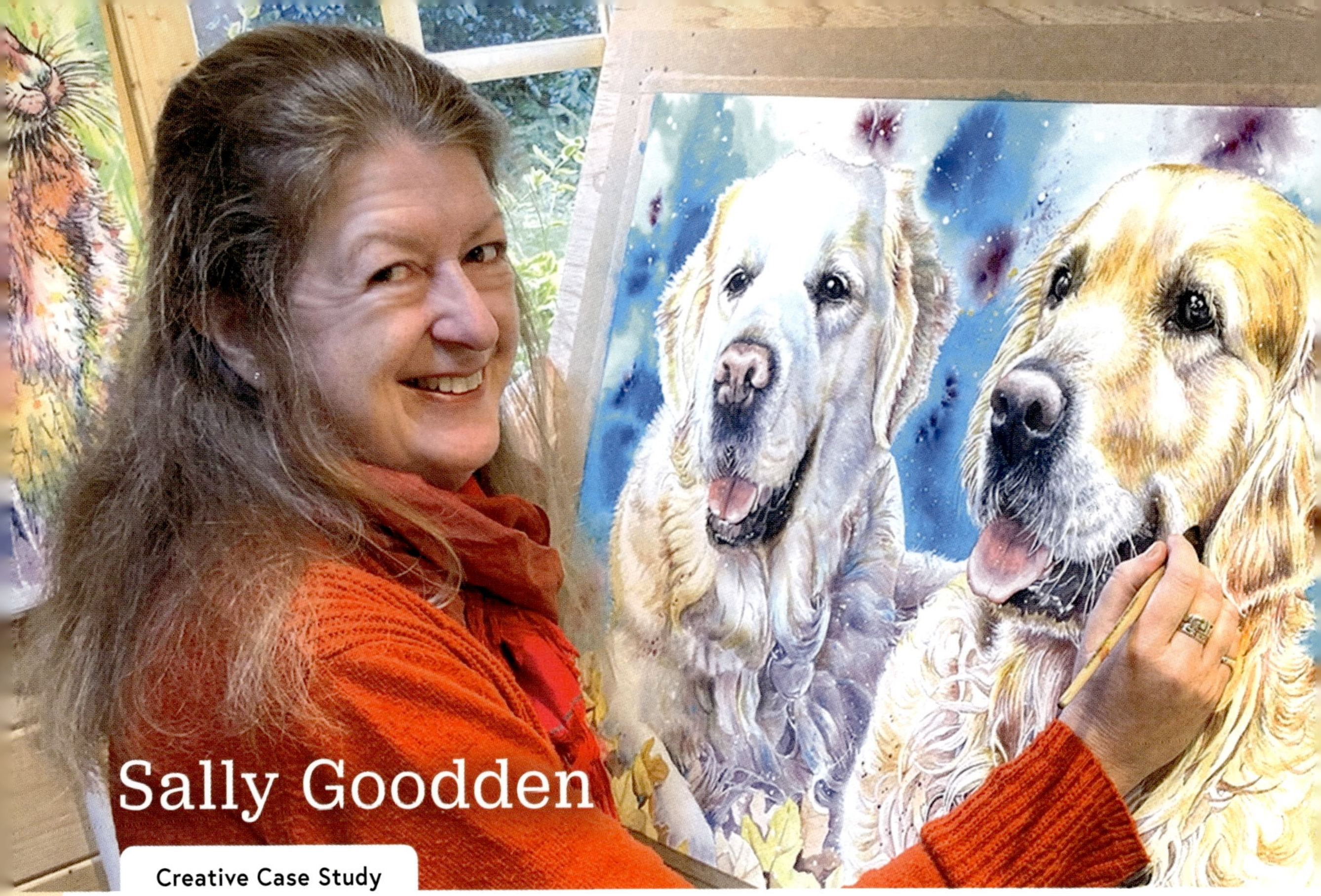

Sally Goodden

Creative Case Study

Sally Goodden trained as a scientific illustrator in the 1990s, and now creates vibrant, energetic animal art for wildlife art exhibitions, commissions and murals.

For the last five years, Sally has been teaching observational visual art techniques to both children and adults. She runs regular after-school classes and relaxing adult art nights from her purpose-built garden studio.

You can find out more about Sally at www.animalartist.biz

Tell me a bit about yourself

I grew up on a butterfly farm. My father was an entomologist, and he would get us very involved with nature. I've always loved to draw and sketch and paint, but it's always been nature that has inspired me.

I graduated with a degree in scientific illustration, and started out illustrating books on science, gardening, and natural history, in publications such as Collins Field Guides.

As my children grew up, fellow parents started asking if I would teach their children art. I get so much joy out of creating art myself, and I wanted to pass that energy on to other people. I started with just one session a week with five children. I now teach 24 children each week.

Above Sally Goodden with her work.

What and how do you teach?

I teach observational art, inspired by nature. We look at the natural subject, and examine the textures and details. That's why the children I teach are from the age of nine upwards, as observational skills start to really kick in at that age.

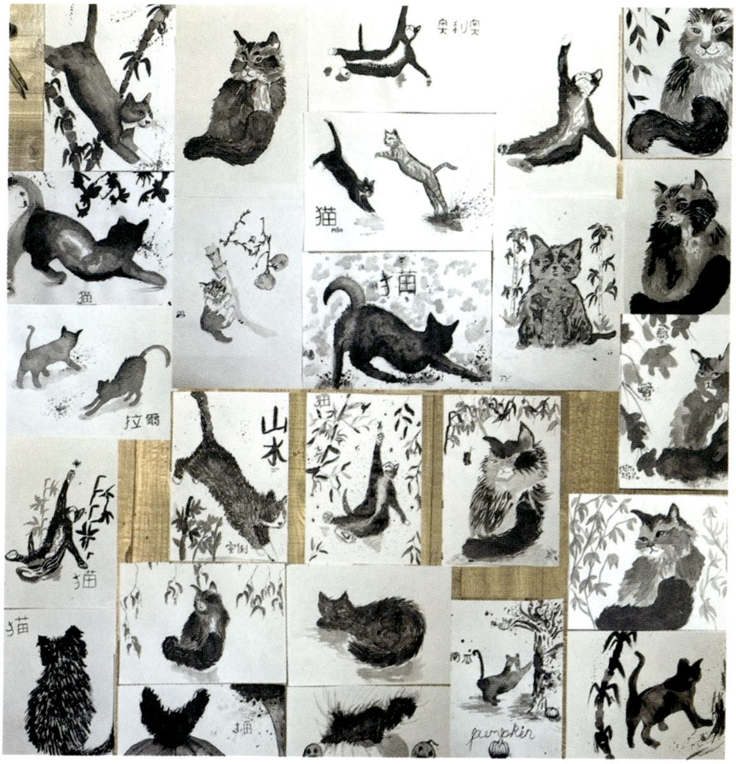

Right Examples of Sally's younger students' work in Chinese ink.

In my after-school classes we use different media each week for six weeks at a time, to fit in with school terms. I challenge them to try lots of different media. Students often start off saying, 'I don't like pastel week, it's so messy', but as they do it regularly they get more confident and enjoy it.

They learn about composition, first drawing the main basic shapes and then going into the details. Then we look at texture, light and shade. They will also learn about the natural subject that they're drawing, and discuss their experiences of that subject. They are learning to become better artists.

They love it when I get something wrong, because they can see that although I'm a professional artist, I still make mistakes! Usually, I can make it work and turn it into something else. That shows my students that if you make a mistake, you just take a deep breath and go with it.

What's the difference between teaching older children and adults?

I have found that adults are less confident than children and like to be led step-by-step. When I've done that with children, they get bored more quickly.

The adults who come to my occasional Friday art nights are there to relax. They don't really want to think too hard, and who can blame them at the end of a busy week? They don't necessarily want to be challenged and pushed in the same way as the children.

The adults want a safe route to create, but this could be due to the more occasional nature of my art nights. My plan, in the future, is to set up some weekly adult classes to see if we can start going into the more creative, challenging realm.

How do you teach?

I sit where everyone can see my easel, so that they can always refer back to the image or my work that's right in front of them. Occasionally I will ask them to stop and watch me to show them specific techniques.

It is really important for me to go around to them individually. Some of them will need help with certain techniques, or extra encouragement. The after-school classes are an hour and a half, so we need to keep going at a certain pace. Right at the end I put all the pieces together for a photograph which I send through to the parents, so that they can see all the different interpretations of that week's subject – this is always fascinating!

What about online teaching?

I started teaching in-person classes in June 2019, and then COVID-19 hit. I ran my regular classes online via Zoom, but there was little social engagement. Everyone was very quiet, which was never the case face-to-face.

I signed up to The Design Trust's *Teach Your Creative Skills Online* course in spring 2020. It was exactly what I needed, because I had so many ideas in my head but didn't know how to focus.

During COVID-19 I ran in-depth pre-recorded courses online, based on the format of my usual classes, and introduced a 10-minute individual accountability session each week for each student. A lot of my students loved that as it made them do the art every week and get personalised feedback. We had a giggle too!

I don't run online courses now and am happy that we've moved on from this. I enjoy the live face-to-face teaching much more, getting that instant gratification of working with someone, picking up a pen, demonstrating something, and seeing them immediately do the same.

How do you promote your courses?

For the after-school classes, I have long waiting lists as most renew each time for the next term. In the holidays I offer half-day workshops to eight children who don't regularly create with me. They choose an animal to paint in watercolour or acrylics. As a result of these sessions, children might either book another holiday workshop or join my after-school waiting lists. Sometimes a parent might even sign up to my adult Friday art night. I get a lot of repeat customers and local word of mouth as I live in quite a tight-knit community.

I do email marketing and have mailing lists now. When I have adult or children's workshops to promote, I'll put them out to the mailing list and often get enough bookings from that straightaway, without needing to use social media.

My website has all the details of the art classes, art nights and private art parties. I think people like the ease of being able to just book on a website rather than having to phone me up and arrange it.

'When I started teaching online, I used to struggle with being able to talk and draw at the same time because you use two different parts of your brain, but that gets better with practice. And when you're trying to explain something online, you can't just do the action, you have to explain in words what you are doing as you go along.

Teaching online has made me come up with different ways to express myself better, and to keep it as simple as possible. They watch, but you really need to explain the process all the time. "Why's that line suddenly darker?" "It's because I'm pressing down harder now."

Realising that difference was so useful for me as a teacher because it made me start to think like someone who had never drawn before. It's made me think much more about what students need to understand, beyond just watching.'

How do you price your workshops?

For the adult workshops, I thought about what I would be happy to pay and also looked at fellow art teachers' prices. I think people like being shut off from the rest of the world in a log cabin, feeling the energy and joy that comes with focusing on creating something beautiful, and they happily pay for that experience.

We're in quite an affluent area, with good schools, so I knew I could price the children's workshops at the upper end of the market. With this budget, I can buy high-quality materials which really transform the students' art.

Also, I want to teach children who really want to learn. If it's too cheap, their parents send them because it's cheap, and it becomes a form of childcare. I am looking for that real hunger to learn art that I had at that age.

From what I have observed, people want experiences for themselves and their children. People are paying for the space without distractions and the overall experience. I make it cosy and have tea and coffee freely available. It's all very relaxed, fun and chatty.

Below Examples of Sally's younger students' work.

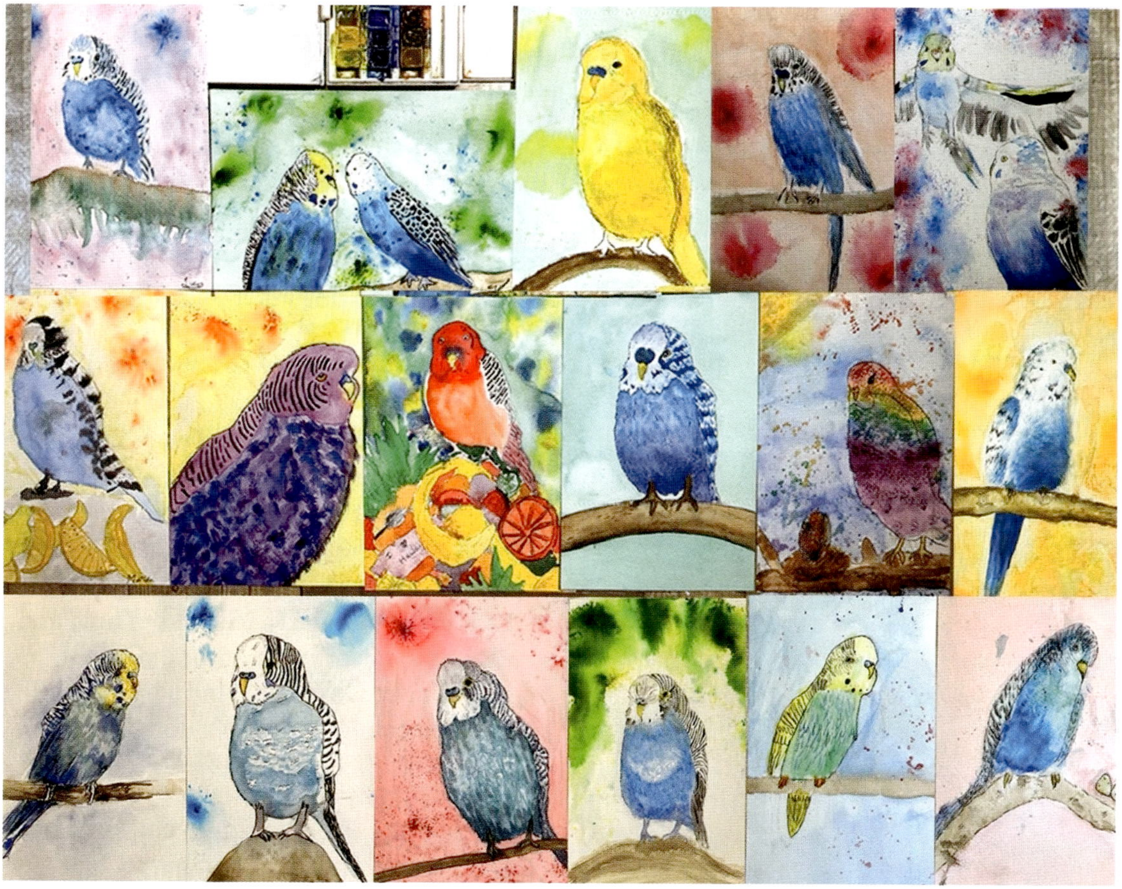

Managing your confidence

> *'The first time I taught at West Dean [a large residential creative college] I filled the whole room with samples because I was bolstering myself – showing how much I knew, how many options there are.*
>
> *Now I realise that was my insecurity. I was trying to prove that I deserved to be there as a teacher. I don't do that anymore.'*
>
> Hanny Newton, embroiderer

For many artists and creative teachers, confidence is a huge challenge. Even though we love what we do, many of us struggle with public speaking and putting ourselves 'out there'. Lack of confidence has many sneaky ways of showing up. Have you ever thought:

- 'I don't have anything interesting to teach.'
- 'I don't know enough yet (about my skill or running training).'
- 'There is so much competition out there. Why would anybody come to my workshop?'
- 'What if I don't sell enough tickets?'
- 'I am busy. And online teaching is so much work and hassle.'
- 'What if somebody steals my ideas?'
- 'I am an introvert. I don't like talking to people or being the centre of attention.'

I will admit that although I have been teaching in person and online for more than 25 years, I still get nervous every time! Sometimes I am not sure if it's nervousness or excitement to share new insights with a group of students. These two are easily confused, as your body will respond in similar ways: faster heartbeat, dry throat, lack of appetite, talking too fast, higher pitched voice, the list goes on.

In my practice as a creative business adviser and coach, confidence is a very frequently discussed topic and over the years I have learnt one thing:

> *You don't have to be confident yet, but you need to work on becoming more confident. Nobody can make you confident, only you can do that, and it's an ongoing job. Confidence is like a muscle that you need to use regularly to strengthen. Only by practising a lot will you become more confident.*

Many of the creative teachers that I interviewed for this book admitted to very similar challenges. But regardless of how they felt, they **had a go and learnt from their experiences**. They practised, planned, prepared and observed, and then they did it some more.

> *'Being expert is hard to pin down. There's no clear moment when you "get there". You're in a perpetual state of becoming, zooming ahead in some areas and lagging behind in others.*
>
> *That's one of the things that characterises true experts. They're always dissatisfied with where they've got to, always aware they could do things better.'*
>
> Roger Kneebone, *Expert: The Path to Mastery*[6]

It's very unlikely that your training will go perfectly to plan, whether you teach online or in person. You will make mistakes! It often will take students longer than you anticipated to do things. You may find a student annoying or disruptive. Not everybody will be giving you rave reviews.

Checklist: Becoming more confident

Improving your confidence is a process that you need to work on: it's becoming confident, not being confident. Use this checklist to ask yourself some deep questions. Take your time, and answer them honestly. You might be surprised at your answers.

☐ **Are you (quietly) excited** about teaching and sharing your skill with others? Does it give you true joy? How can you use that positive energy to support yourself?
☐ **Do you like working with other people?** Do you have empathy for people who are different from you? Use those insights to inspire others to have a go.
☐ **Are you a quiet listener or an extrovert energiser?** Neither is 'good' or 'bad'. It's the ability to observe what the individual and the group needs. Adapting your leadership and teaching style will make a big difference.
☐ **Do you know your strengths and limitations**, as a human being, an artist and a teacher? How can you focus by what, how and whom you teach to celebrate your special talents?
☐ **Do you know your own learning and teaching preferences?** How can you use these more in how you teach, while also still being flexible to accommodate other learning styles (see Chapter 4)?
☐ **Are you organised?** Can you multi-task and think on your feet? Do you ask for help?
☐ **Do you learn from 'mistakes'?** Will you make time to reflect during and after training, and be honest with yourself about things that didn't go so well? Remember that these challenges can be your best learning opportunities.

Most of this doesn't really matter, as long as your patience, passion and enthusiasm shine through. Only you really know what you had planned, so if things go awry, have a laugh and relax. Lower your expectations, of yourself and your students too, and you will resolve many issues.

If you **panic easily** try to learn how to control that. Be overprepared and have alternative solutions for all eventualities, e.g., if the projector doesn't work or half your students arrive late because of an accident on the motorway.

If you **get confused easily** or forget things, fill your lesson plan with really clear instructions to yourself. Likewise, if you find it easy to get off track, make your agenda visible for everyone so that you can refer to it often. Cut what you want to teach in the given time by about half, and you might just get it all done. Learn to set boundaries for students who want to lead you down a rabbit hole.

And if you **don't know the answer to a question**? Admit it. See if somebody else in the room knows. If it's really important, you can get back to them with the answer later on. Write the questions down, find the answer and follow up afterwards. It's fine not to know everything.

Teaching online often has some specific challenges. Technical glitches can happen to anybody, even the most experienced tutors. Make sure that your broadband or Wi-Fi is as good as it can be. Get to know your technology well by practising in advance with smaller groups.

Write a short to-do list of the actions that you need to do to start, record or subtitle your session and put it clearly on your screen. It's easy to forget these actions when you are nervous. Writing your actions on a sticky note and using it to cover your own face on the screen works brilliantly if you don't like looking at yourself (I don't either!).

Always remember: your training is not about you, it's about the students. Your job is to be creative and to combine the best skills and approaches, and dare to be selective about students who are best for you.

> '*I like the Japanese philosophy of* wabi sabi, *which is about finding the joy and beauty in the imperfect or the imprecise. With* shibori *[Japanese dyeing technique] it often doesn't quite go to plan. But you can end up with some quite unexpectedly beautiful things. I love the moment when you unwrap and see what you've created.*'
> **Rob Jones,** Japanese textiles expert

Checklist: To become more confident

To be a more confident teacher, bear the following in mind:

☐ **Being a bit nervous is often a good sign.** You can use that energy to perform better. It's not about being perfect; your students will love it if you share your mistakes. Your body language and charisma is much more important when it comes to engaging your students.

☐ **Work through the fear and practise, practise, practise.** Reflect on what atmosphere, exercises and teaching methods work for you and your ideal students.

☐ **Keep it simple and start small.** Very often new teachers are too ambitious and try to include too much. I often remind people of my favourite aphorism: 'Don't compare your beginning with somebody else's middle.' Focus on what you can do with your current resources and grow slowly from there.

☐ **Create the right teaching environment** for yourself and your students, in person and online. What do you need around you to feel more confident and professional? It's amazing what difference this can make.

☐ **Have a lesson plan.** Use it as a framework and to make decisions in advance of what to focus on and what to leave out. Be flexible in the execution.

☐ **Prepare and be flexible.** Make a list of all the things that are worrying you, and then brainstorm solutions. Things will probably go differently than you expected, but that might not be a bad thing.

☐ **Invest in learning how to teach.** There are plenty of specialist courses and books out there (see the Resources section on p.252). You can learn a lot about teaching by being a student.

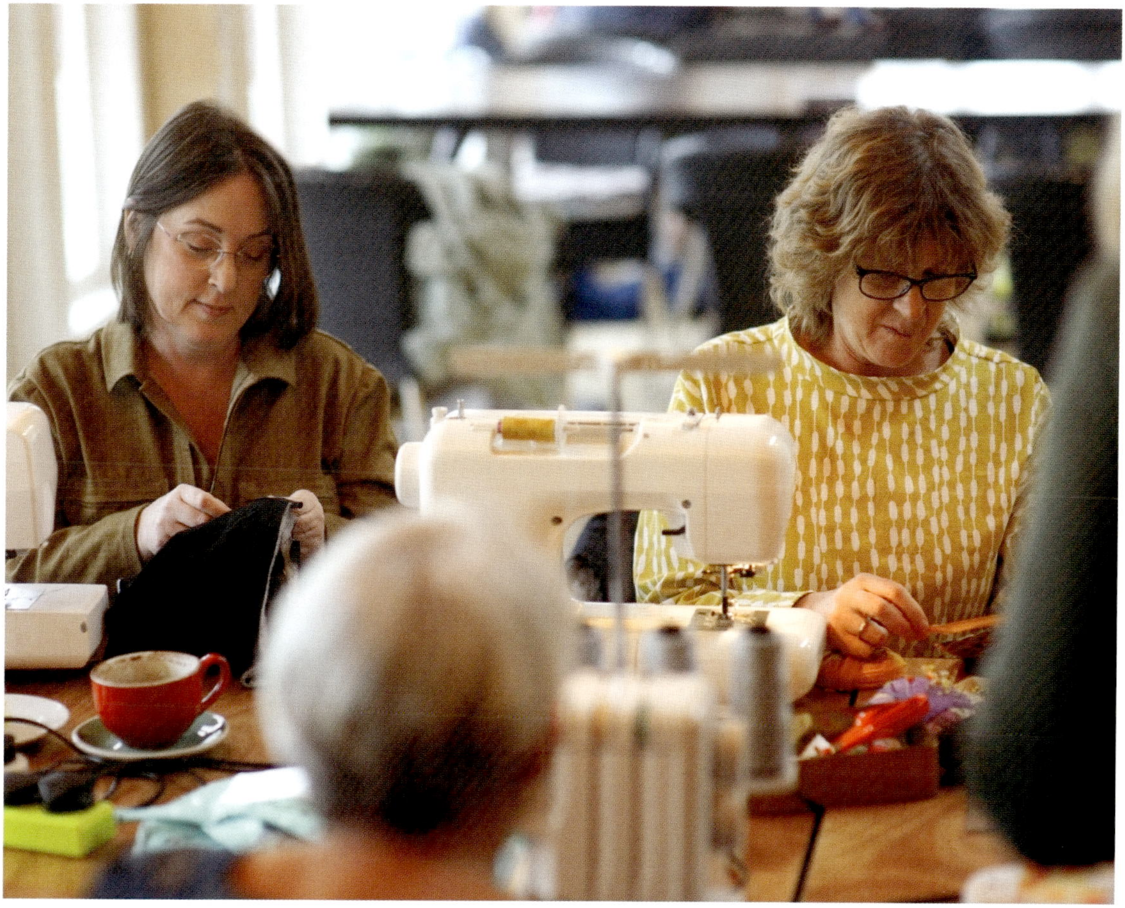

Managing your students

One big advantage of teaching creative skills in an informal setting (rather than in formal education) is that **your students will be eager to learn**. They are there voluntarily and usually very committed to learning and developing new skills (which is regularly not the case in formal education).

Of course, even when your students are eager and committed, there are still many challenges that can disrupt their learning. One of your key roles as a teacher is to encourage and support your students through their learning journey.

'I get a lot of women in their 50s, and confidence is a major barrier. A lot of people arrive and think "I'm not going to be very good." When they start to weave, you just can see their satisfaction. It's really important that people feel surprised and regain their confidence.'
Angie Parker, textile artist

Above Always remember why your students are doing your training. Is it a fun day out, a hobby, creative expression or transformation?

Common challenges for students

Learning a new skill can be daunting. Although most of your students will be really excited, it's surprising how many challenges might come up. Being aware of these will help you to make their learning journey much smoother. Challenges include:

- **Lack of confidence:** this is very common, and it's a big one. Many students will start out fine, but then start to doubt their ability or feel intimidated. Setting achievable goals, taking small steps, and providing regular specific and constructive feedback is essential. This is easier with in-person than online training, so don't forget to build this into your online training.
- **Fear of failure:** students might be afraid to make mistakes, worry that they will get in a muddle or be slower than others, which can quickly demotivate. Make your process as easy as possible – take into account different skill levels, and slower or faster students. Encourage experimentation.
- **Overwhelm:** the amount of information or complexity of new techniques can be a lot to take in. Break down the learning process into manageable steps, providing a clear roadmap for progress, and keep it simple!
- **Comparing themselves to others:** this is a major challenge for students when working in any group, at any stage. Perfectionism also plays a big role here. Be aware, and emphasise the value of individual progress. Create a supportive, non-judgemental learning environment by highlighting the diversity of skills and experience within the group.
- **Feeling vulnerable and emotional:** being creative and expressive is what you are helping your students to do, so it's not surprising that they might feel emotional. Some participants might have very busy or complicated lives, and are not used to having me-time or brain space. Many of the creative teachers that I interviewed mentioned that when people in a group are creating something by hand, conversations can often become rather deep and personal. Be prepared for and allow for some tears or deeper emotional connections. There's no need to avoid or fix it, but acknowledge and share, and try to keep things light and inspiring.

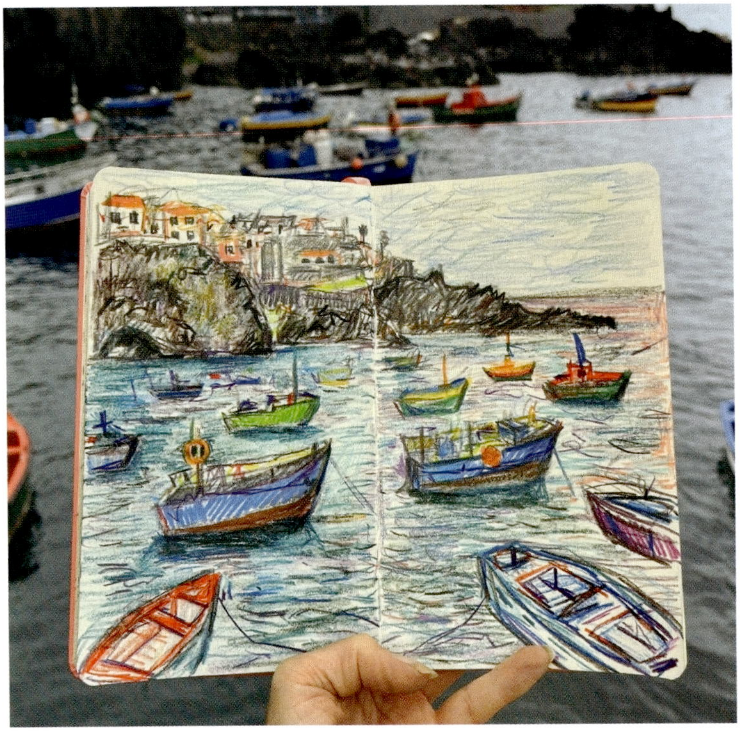

Left Boat study in Sam's Marshall's sketchbook.

- **Lack of or too much inspiration:** Give students inspiration in advance of the training and, if possible, let them bring several designs to work on. Show examples at different skill levels and ask them to choose what they want to learn on the day.
- **Lack of time:** how will you deal with slower students? Don't do things for them, as they can feel discouraged or pressured when they just wanted a day of fun. With online teaching, your students might be easily distracted. How can you help them to plan better, commit properly and make the time required?
- **Lack of technical knowledge:** beginners will of course be unfamiliar with technical jargon, and online students might struggle with software or equipment. Provide clear instructions, demonstrations, worksheets and resources. What might be obvious to you might be an absolute mystery for your students.
- **Additional needs:** find out in advance if any participants have specific requirements in order to access the training. Ask them how you can support them specifically during the training, and be very careful not to make any assumptions about what they can or can't do.
- **Limited resources:** people may not have access to the equipment or tools required, especially for online training. Provide a detailed material list or send a kit with the right materials in advance as part of your online offer.

I highly recommend the book *Expert: Understanding the Path to Mastery* by Roger Kneebone, if you want to understand more about the often decades-long practice of becoming a creative master.

Time to pause

Take your notebook and take time to reflect and answer the following:

- **What did you find challenging or particularly hard when you started your creative journey?** Write that down and make it part of what you teach. How can you share that experience with students?
- **Review your notes from Chapter 4 on Kolb's learning and teaching styles** (pp.61–63). Very often we get annoyed with a student who has a different learning style than us. Check in to see if this resonates, and identify how you can work on your own weaknesses and strengths with different types of people.
- **Review your notes from Chapter 4 on Bloom's Taxonomy** (pp.64–67) about the six steps towards mastery. Can you make parts of your training easier or more advanced? How can you add advanced steps for quicker students?
- **Struggling with a new skill is a sign of learning and growing** – how can you celebrate this often frustrating part of the process, especially on longer courses?

FAQ: How do I deal with disruptive students or situations?

Students might respond in surprising ways when something that they want to do for fun turns out to be harder work than they thought. They might get angry with themselves or others, blame you, procrastinate or feign carelessness.

There is a surprising amount that needs to work between the body and hands and the mind to create something. If students find that things are more challenging than they expected – *especially* if they were looking for a fun day out! **They might get frustrated, grumpy, want all the attention, or disengage altogether.**

> *Be aware and observe your students. It might not be the noisiest or most demanding student that is the "problem"; students who have become more withdrawn need looking after too.*

It is your job to handle challenges with individual students and the group with diplomacy and tact. Listen first before you give any advice or solutions, and be gentle and understanding. Most adults are able to handle their own issues quite well, so ask them what they want. Would they prefer to sit in another place? Do they need some extra help? Would they like to do another project? Do they need a break?

Don't take it personally when a student or situation is challenging. It's very likely that the thing that has triggered them has nothing to do with you.

Become more aware of the kind of challenging situations that trigger your own emotions: very often, the challenging behaviour reminds us of something in our past. Is this student difficult, or is something happening inside you that responds badly to them or to the situation? Try to name your emotions and give yourself some space and time to gain the clarity and resilience that you need.

Some common disruptive behaviours include:

1 **Lack of engagement:** a student who is clearly not participating can be very disruptive.

- Create interactive and engaging activities that cater for different learning styles and levels.
- Combine group, pair and individual activities, and include practice, discussions and reflections.
- Ask questions such as, 'Who found this challenging?' to make students feel less alone, or 'What did you discover during this exercise?' to encourage self-awareness.

2 **Showing their superiority:** you might get a student who wants to show how much they know. They often don't realise they are doing this or are actually not very confident and are overcompensating.

- Rather than ignoring this behaviour, redirect attention-seeking behaviour and provide opportunities for the student to share their knowledge or ask them to support slower or less-advanced students.
- Encourage other students to contribute their knowledge and experiences too.

3 Excessive talking or constant interruption: if they are doing your workshop for a fun day out then you should build in time for tea, laughter and conversation. However, sometimes this can upset group dynamics and be annoying for other students.

- Ask for quietness, privately or more publicly;
- Include plenty of breaks;
- Include discussions in pairs or small groups;
- Put some music on during the practical sessions.

4 Resistance to collaboration or group work: some students are more introverted or prefer to work alone, which should be fine.

- Encourage working in pairs or threes, rather than large groups.
- Make it easy to connect with strangers by providing clear discussion prompts.

5 Negative attitude: approach the student privately and express concern for their well-being. Try to understand what's effecting their mood and offer support.

6 Very disorganised or untidy workspace: some people are messy, others incredibly neat, but an untidy workspace can become dangerous or overwhelming.

- Show students how to keep their workspace better organised, and provide dedicated storage space for materials and tools.
- Do a joint clear up as a group to keep the learning environment clean.

7 Dangerous or inappropriate behaviour: health and safety is important within a creative skills environment.

- Make sure you explain the safety rules and what students must or must not do at the start.
- Point out immediately and very clearly to the individual (privately) and to the group as a whole the importance of compliance with certain rules.
- Keep an eye on potential issues with electricity or dangerous materials.
- Clearly communicate expectations for respectful behaviour before and during the training. Use a code of conduct (see next page), if necessary.
- Address inappropriate behaviour promptly and assertively, and remove a student from the training if needs be.

Time to pause

Get your notebook and take time to reflect and answer these questions:

- **Which specific teaching challenges have you noticed when delivering training?**
- **Which student management challenges are you most worried about?**
- **How can you better support a student in these situations?** What about supporting yourself?
- **What practical solutions could you provide?**

Protecting yourself: Code of conduct and terms and conditions

As we've just seen, setting expectations is key to a smooth journey for your students, and peace of mind for yourself. **A code of conduct can help you to formalise how you want your students to behave and set clear boundaries in advance.** It doesn't need to be heavy-handed, but it can definitely help avoid difficult situations.

A code of conduct can also help you to manage any potential health and safety issues that might affect your training, e.g., hazardous materials, work outdoors, external venues, or teach from home.

You can make your code of conduct part of your T&Cs, which students will need to sign or agree to prior to attending your training. **Your T&Cs are legally binding**, and breaching them can have consequences, such as exclusion from your training with no reimbursement.

A code of conduct provides behavioural guidelines, but these are not legally binding. You can share it online, link to it in emails, or briefly address some of the main issues at the start of your training.

You can include the following in your code of conduct:

Checklist: What to include in a code of conduct

☐ **Health and safety:** what are your rules around use of equipment and materials – hazardous or otherwise? Does your insurance company have specific requirements?
☐ **Use of mobiles:** can participants use their phones at any time, or do you set limits? This can be related to taking pictures as well as taking calls.
☐ **Photography and recording:** is it OK to photograph, film or (audio) record you, fellow students or any work created? It's very easy to record you online and transcribe your words with AI tools.
☐ **AI tools:** be aware of specific intellectual property issues around taking and sharing images.
☐ **Food, drinks and smoking:** can students eat or drink at their workstations or in designated areas only? What about alcohol or drugs, especially during a longer residential or outdoor course?
☐ **Copyright:** this is a big topic, and we will look more at this in the next section.
☐ **Confidentiality:** both for you and your students, especially if they have access to your studio and projects you are working on.
☐ **Damage:** what about potential damage to your work, property or tools? Would breakages need to be replaced? How will you address compensation?
☐ **Dangerous or inappropriate behaviour:** what are the consequences? What happens if they disrupt or hinder other students' learning or practice? How will you encourage an inclusive environment and deal with any discrimination based on race, age, disability, religious beliefs, actual or perceived sex, gender identity or sexual orientation?

FAQ: What should I include in my T&Cs?

Your T&Cs are an essential part of a professional training business, and will protect you in case of legal issues such as cancellations and payment delays. It will also help you to avoid problems with your students or clients.

While it is not a legal requirement to have a set of written T&Cs, in the event of a dispute you will be in a much stronger position.

If you are working with a venue/training provider, you might need to sign their T&Cs as part of a larger contract.

Most training providers will include the following in their T&Cs:

Checklist: What to include in your T&Cs

☐ **Payment terms:** generally this is either 14 or 30 days, but be specific.

☐ **Cancellations and rescheduling:** students should be informed of their options in a timely manner.

☐ **Refunds:** what your terms are should you or your students need to cancel.

☐ **Privacy policy:** explain how participants' personal information is protected. You can find an example of this on Information Commissioners' Office (ICO) website (ico.org.uk). If USA-based, you can find more information on this at dpcld.defense.gov under 'Privacy'. Or if in the EU at commission.europa.eu under 'Data protection in the EU', or in Australia at www.oaic.gov.au under 'Handling personal information'.

☐ **Copyright notice:** The copyright of any materials used in the workshop should be specified.

☐ **Disclaimer:** this should be included to protect you as the organiser from any liability.

☐ **Code of conduct:** a set of behavioural guidelines to ensure a respectful and professional teaching environment.

☐ **Age or level requirements:** specify if a student needs to meet any specified age or skill requirements.

☐ **Termination:** specify when does this contract becomes invalid.

You will need to display your T&Cs clearly on your website (this is often a legal requirement), and link directly to them on your sales page, the confirmation email, and in any future correspondence.

You will find more information about cancellations and refunds at the end of Chapter 7.

Protecting yourself: Intellectual property and copyright

Is copying an issue for you? When I was interviewing creative teachers for the case studies in this book, copying was a hot topic, and they had very different opinions.

> *'I am worried about copying. I'm doing something unique with the craft, and people increasingly come to me because they want to make my work. I still feel uncomfortable when people ask, "What thread did you use? What fabric is this?" I'm still navigating that.*
>
> *But I also feel like I'm getting deeper and deeper in my own practice, and some things I'm making now, I won't teach. I'm selective with what I teach, showing students the methodology to make their own work. I'm also selective about the samples and images I share. I'm learning that it's OK to have boundaries around what I choose to share and what I want to hold back for my own personal practice.'*
>
> **Hanny Newton,** embroiderer

> *'I'm not at all worried about copying. That might be naive, but I don't think it is. The world of silversmithing is unusual. I depend incredibly heavily on my network of silversmithing buddies, mentors, teachers, students because we collectively hold this skill base between us. We all have a responsibility to teach each other. Being a silversmith is about taking part in a collective experience. I get as much from it as I give.'*
>
> **Rauni Higson,** silversmith

Time to pause

Take your notebook and take time to reflect and answer these questions:

- **How do you feel about students copying your work or downloading illegally?** Is this an issue for you?
- **Are there ways to protect your intellectual property or do you need to educate your students to avoid problems?**
- **Can you use Bloom's Taxonomy to move your students away from copying** (one of the more basic skills) towards more innovative creative skills?

FAQ How to protect yourself from students who copy you?

Students copying you can be a big issue, especially in these two situations:

1 Students copy your work to sell themselves

You might need to be a bit more careful with what you teach, especially if you are sharing processes or techniques that are part of your own individual style and brand. If you sell product that uses the same techniques, do you want others to know exactly how to replicate and potentially sell it too? That might confuse your clients, reduce the market value of your own work and create competition for yourself.

To avoid this situation:

- **don't teach what's unique to you** and what you are specifically known for;
- **don't share specific recipes,** designs or patterns;
- **raise the issue of copying,** and what is and isn't allowable. You can include an intellectual property statement in your T&Cs or code of conduct. I also recommend that you discuss during the training how your students can use recipes, designs or patterns. State that they can use it for personal but not commercial use.

Please note: it's extremely difficult to protect a course or your style of teaching, as these are not protectable by law. It will be very difficult to prove that someone has copied your teaching style or methods. You could protect certain teaching concepts by trademarking them, but you will need to pay for that protection, so that is only suitable if you are planning to commercially exploit your teaching methods through licensing.

2 Students share online recordings with others who haven't paid

This is really hard to detect and avoid, but you can prevent your students from downloading videos on hosting sites such as YouTube or Vimeo by clicking the right permission buttons. Also keep an eye on viewing stats to see if there are any irregularities, but it's often impossible to identify a specific student if you do notice anything.

I recommend that you include your approach to intellectual property on your website and sales page and remind students during onboarding that they can only use the recording for themselves. At The Design Trust, we mention this in our FAQs and T&Cs for each course. State your rights and, more importantly, explain your copyright.

There is a lot of confusion and misunderstanding around intellectual property, so make sure you understand your own rights as an artist and teacher. You can find some intellectual property resources in the Resources section at the end of this book.

This is the end of Part 1, where we looked at why, what, who and where to teach. Before we move on to Part 2, there is one final reflective exercise to complete.

Time to pause

Take time to reflect on and answer the following:

- **At the start of Chapter 4,** on p.49 we looked at different teaching roles and what makes a great teacher. Reflect on what role(s) you want and what is great and special about you as a teacher.
- **Right now, how would you score yourself out of 10 as a teacher?** What score do you want to get in three months' time, or in a year? What would you need to do, have or learn to give yourself that higher score? How do you want to feel? Be as specific as possible. Identify some specific actions to improve your teaching based on your own success criteria.

Are you ready for marketing, launching and getting paid for your creative skills training? First, let's hear from Ekta Kaul, who has adapted her teaching business over many years.

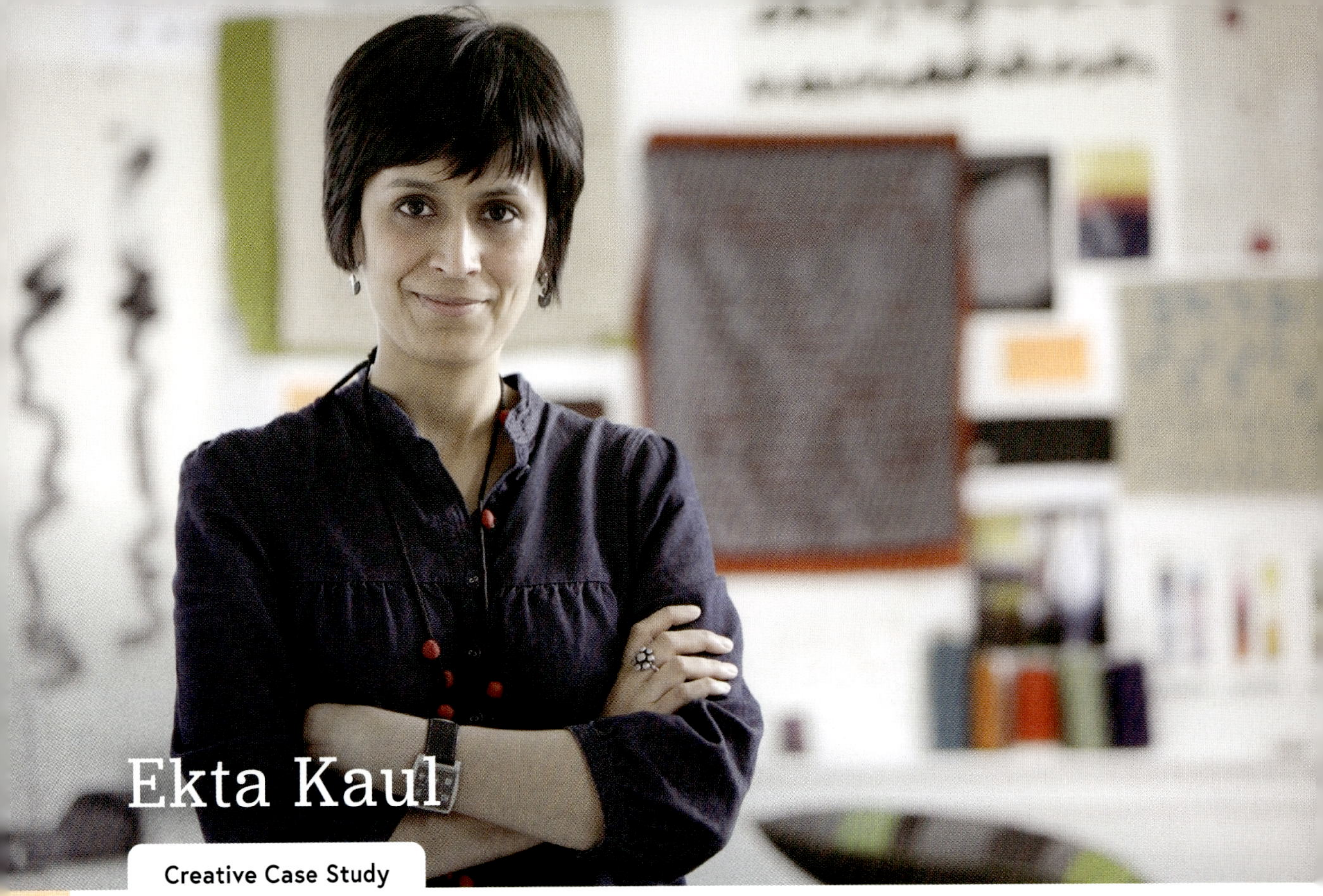

Ekta Kaul

Creative Case Study

Ekta Kaul's creative practice focuses on narrative maps that explore a sense of place, history and belonging. Her pared down aesthetic, coupled with a highly considered use of graphic marks and lines, form the core elements of her art.

Ekta was born in India, and honed her design skills at the National Institute of Design in Ahmedabad. In 2005, she moved to the UK to pursue a Master's degree in Textiles at Heriot-Watt University in Edinburgh has an awardee of two British Council scholarships.

Over the past 17 years, Ekta has cultivated a thriving art practice that seamlessly integrates artmaking, education and exhibitions. She lives and works in London. Ekta is the author of *Kantha: Sustainable Textiles and Mindful Making*, published in 2024.

You can find out more about Ekta Kaul at www.ektakaul.com

Above Embroiderer Ekta Kaul in her London studio.

When did you start teaching?

I began my teaching career shortly after completing my MA. I was awarded the Crafts Council's Next Move business development award, which included an artist residency at the School of Textiles at Bath Spa University. During this residency, I occasionally taught BA students, and discovered a deep passion for teaching. Soon after, I joined the Art & Design Foundation programme at a local college in Bath as a lecturer.

When I moved to London, I began teaching at a college. This role, although fulfilling, left me with little time for my art practice. The birth of my first child allowed me to take a step back and re-evaluate my priorities. I started teaching at my own studio, creating a schedule that prioritised my artmaking and family.

Why and how do you teach?

Both of my parents were university professors, and their generosity in sharing their knowledge left an indelible impression on me.

Teaching is a profound learning experience in itself. It requires stepping outside of one's ego, embracing empathy and seeing things from the student's perspective. It's a dynamic and creative exchange where I constantly find myself enriched by what my students bring to the table.

> *'Through teaching, I continue to evolve and expand as an artist.'*

I noticed a stark contrast between my parents' scientific world where knowledge was openly shared, and the art world, where processes and experiences often remained behind closed studio doors. This sparked a desire in me to shift the narrative. I wanted to be open about my artistic journey, to share not only the techniques of creation but also the pitfalls and learnings. My aim is to foster a more collaborative and open artistic community, where we can learn from each other's experiences and grow together.

How do you combine being an artist with being an educator, and now also an author?

I view my roles as artist, educator and author as interconnected parts of a Venn diagram, with their overlapping sections representing the core of my practice. This intersection is where I find the most energy and dynamism. Being an artist is at the heart of everything I do.

My teaching and artistic practices are symbiotic. For example, in 2018, I delved into Kantha – a traditional Indian quilting stitch – to investigate the running stitch and to connect with my Indian heritage more deeply. This exploration was not just about learning a technique; it was a deep dive into personal and historical layers, connecting with the memories of my grandmother and mother. And that has resulted in writing my book.

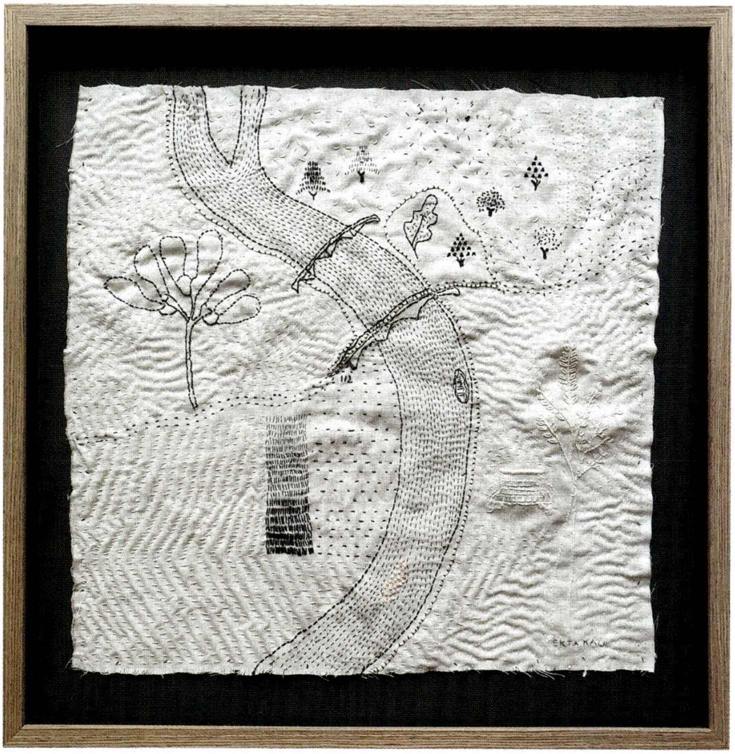

Right *Riverside Walk* by Ekta Kaul.

What's your approach to teaching embroidery?

I strive to create an environment that embraces imperfection. I've noticed that in the traditional world of embroidery, there's often an emphasis on perfection, to the point where many students feel discouraged.

My role as a mentor is to shift this perspective. I encourage my students to understand that it's okay to have stitches that aren't flawless. Embroidery doesn't demand impeccable stitches, rather it is a medium for personal expression. A wonky stitch line can evoke emotions and the maker's unique style, like their handwriting.

How did you get into teaching online?

I hadn't considered online teaching until the pandemic hit, and suddenly, all in-person teaching and exhibitions came to a halt. My journey into digital teaching began with a simple suggestion from my husband, who introduced me to Zoom.

During the first lockdown, while friends were sewing scrubs for the NHS, I was contemplating what I could offer while caring for my two young children. I realised that sharing the gift of creativity could be significant. So, I took to Instagram and announced that I'd be hosting a stitching session on Zoom, focusing on uplifting words through poetry and quotes.

The response was overwhelming; I received over 100 messages within half an hour. It turned into a weekly Friday gathering, which I conducted for free, finding joy and solace in connecting with others and facilitating meaningful dialogues around different themes.

As the pandemic eased, I started offering short online courses, which attracted hundreds of participants worldwide. By then, I had become adept at using the right camera equipment, demonstrating techniques effectively and creating impactful learning experiences. Though 2020 was a challenging year globally, it unexpectedly became a pivotal year for my business growth and impact.

What and how do you teach online?

The courses are topic-specific, focusing on subjects that I am interested in as an artist. My methodology is derived from my own approach to artmaking, ensuring a unique and personal learning experience.

My online membership is tailored to those who are eager to deepen their creative practice and cultivate their own unique voice. It's ideal for individuals seeking a more extended commitment, offering an environment where they can develop their creativity in textiles and learn to create art independently. This approach is about nurturing exploration and growth, guided by ideas, themes and principles.

The sense of community and ongoing personal development has been pivotal in maintaining a strong membership base, with some members continuing their journey with us since the programme began in 2021.

Are you still teaching in person?

At the onset of COVID-19, I paused my in-person workshops. I'm now considering carefully how to make these in-person experiences truly impactful. I'm leaning towards hosting retreats that offer an immersive environment, allowing participants to truly commit to their creative journey, away from daily distractions.

This approach, akin to an art residency, is what I envision for my future in-person teaching. It's about providing an enriching, experiential and transformational experience.

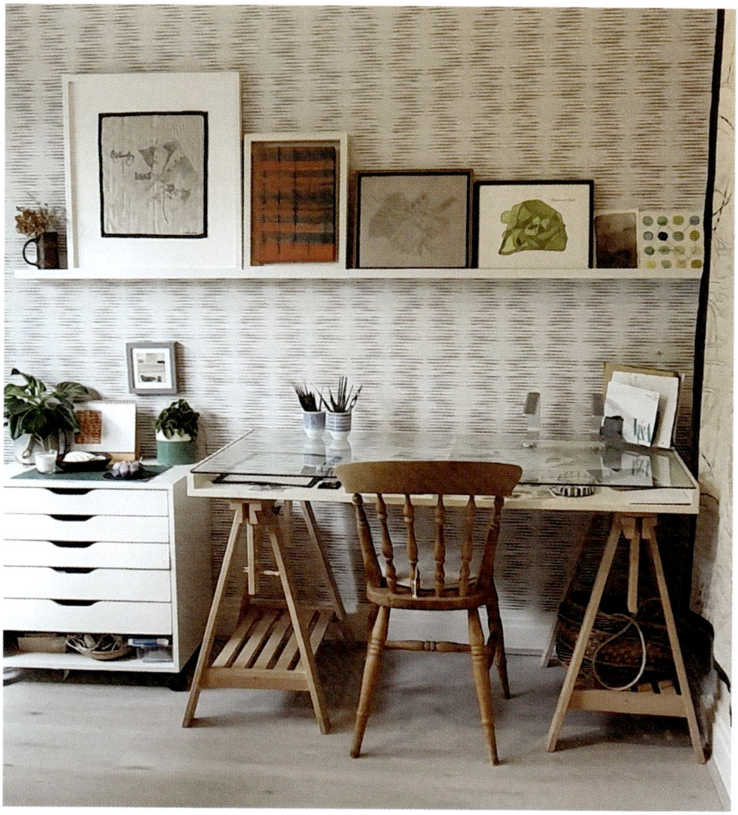

Above Ekta's workspace.

How do you promote your courses?

As creatives, we often view social media as the ultimate marketing tool, but there are more effective strategies, like newsletters and mailing lists. Those who sign up for my mailing list are already showing interest in my teaching and art.

I prioritise nurturing my student and client relationships through regular newsletters. My approach is personal and heartfelt, not sales driven. I share insights into my life, art tips, and resources like podcast recommendations.

> *'I view each newsletter as an act of generosity.'*

Having said that, social media is also important. I use Instagram and have recently started my YouTube channel @ektakaulart.

Collecting testimonials is also crucial. After each course or workshop, I record the testimonials of participants and use them on my website and social media, which adds a layer of social proof to my offerings.

What advice would you give your younger self?

I'd advise her to recognise and embrace the worth of her work. This goes beyond boosting self-esteem; it's about showcasing the potential of creativity and inclusiveness to others.

I would stress the importance of pricing her work appropriately, understanding that her value lies in the years of knowledge and experience she brings.

And learning to say 'no' to opportunities that don't align with her values is crucial, as is seeking out opportunities that do.

2

Part Two:

Making money and marketing

CHAPTER 7

Costing, pricing and getting paid

In this chapter, we focus on making your training pay. Making money is a big motivator for artists who want to add teaching as an extra income stream. However, many creatives undercharge or don't make money from their hard work.

This chapter will give you helpful insights into your numbers, and the psychology around pricing and making sure that you charge the right amount, both for you and your students. I really want to show you how creative costing and pricing can be.

The goal is to make your training affordable but profitable – a conundrum for many creatives. First we will look at costing your training, and I will encourage you to do two really useful creative planning exercises: creating an annual training plan and an annual training budget. Next, we will deal with pricing, and the three most important pricing strategies: cost-based, competitor-based, and on the basis of perceived value.

We will finish this chapter by looking at how to get paid, and dealing with cancellations and refunds.

Costing your training

Before you can set your prices you will need to look at your costs. If you don't know what your costs are, how will you know if you are making a profit – and if all your hard work is worth it?

What are your training costs?

- **Direct costs:** these include the venue, catering, marketing, your travel and accommodation, materials, filming and editing, and software.
- **Overhead costs:** these don't directly relate to training, and are often 'hidden' costs, but they still need to be covered if you want to run a profitable creative business. Examples include your website, insurance and admin costs.
- **Labour costs:** this includes not only teaching time, but also time spent on preparation, marketing and travel. I recommend that you keep time sheets to get a more accurate idea of how much time is involved in creating, delivering and marketing your training.

Your time will very likely be one of the highest costs, but what hourly rate do you use for your calculations? Do you charge a realistic and professional hourly rate? Do you charge the same amount, regardless of the task? Or do you charge less when you are doing the admin or travelling to a venue?

I recommend to professional creatives in the UK who are serious about teaching to charge £25–50 per hour for delivering training, depending on experience and profile. That might sound high, but it is comparable to hourly rates of other professionals. As an artist, you have limited earning hours each week, so your hourly rate needs to be higher than the minimum wage to compensate for that fact.

Common mistake: Not including all your costs

Many creatives 'forget' to include all the time it takes to organise and prepare for their training. They often do not charge a professional daily rate, and rarely include their overhead costs.

> *Teaching can be a very reliable, profitable income stream for creative professionals, as long as you make sure that you charge enough for your time.*

Your clients won't know or appreciate the many, many hours that you spend on perfecting your online presentation, or all the effort that went into editing your pre-recorded training. Keep time sheets to **become more realistic about how long it takes you** to create and deliver a course.

And keep an eye on your perfectionism, as that can cost you a lot of time.

Are you struggling to cover your costs? Think bigger!

> *It's very rare that you can make money with one workshop. It makes much more financial and marketing sense to create, deliver and promote a series of workshops. That way, you can spread the risk and cover your time and costs over more workshops.*

Of course, you'll need to start small, and you might just want to try this out to see if training is the right new income stream for you. But if you want to make money with training, it's crucial to think bigger from the start. Rerunning sessions and repeat business will be key to making your training profitable.

It takes a lot of time to create and promote a single workshop – often as much as promoting several workshops at once. Spreading the preparation and marketing time will significantly lower your total labour costs per workshop. **Being efficient will increase profitability**.

Clients like to have a choice of dates, especially for in-person training as availability is limited. Offering several dates at once, well in advance, will increase the likelihood that people will book.

Students often want to return to do the same or a follow-up course, or recommend your courses to their friends. Doing similar courses will build your profile, credibility and trust. We'll come back to this in Chapter 8.

When you run a similar session more often, you will discover how to make it even better. Learn from your 'mistakes' – from your preparation to your marketing and teaching.

Creative Exercise

Create an annual training plan

Creating a longer term training plan, rather than planning just one workshop or course, will make your organisational and financial planning more efficient and effective. It will also enable you to recoup your start-up and time investment costs over a longer and more realistic time frame than costing and pricing per individual workshop.

Download the *Annual Training Plan* from the Teach Your Creative Workshop Toolkit.

Start creating your 12-month training plan by making a list of all the training you plan to deliver in the next year. Consider:

- **How many courses or workshops do you want to run this year?** How long will each one be?
- **Will they be delivered online or in person?** Pre-recorded or live?
- **How many participants can you teach at each event?**
- **Can you repeat the same workshop or course?**
- **Which months are best for teaching?** Avoid busy times in your creative business or life, and remember that teaching is seasonal so some months might be better to teach than others.
- **Include the launch and delivery date of each workshop.** You might also want to include preparation time in your planning, which is especially important for pre-recorded online training.

Be realistic with your planning. To start with, aim for around 6–10 workshops or courses per year, with some repeats. Return to your original teaching plan to remind yourself of other training ideas you were considering. Can you develop and launch these later this year?

Below Example of an annual training plan for in-person weaving workshops.

Jan	Feb	Mar	Apr	May	Jun
1 × Intro to weaving – 1 day	1 × Intro to weaving – 1 day	1 × Advanced weaving – weekend	1 × Intro to weaving – 1 day	1 × Weave a summer bag – 1 day	
Jul	**Aug**	**Sep**	**Oct**	**Nov**	**Dec**
		1 × Intro to weaving – 1 day	1 × Advanced weaving – weekend	1 × Weave a wall hanging – weekend	

Create an annual training budget

This next exercise is a complementary exercise to your annual training plan, and it will help you to spread your costs and income over a longer period, which is more realistic than costing and pricing per training session.

You can download the *Annual Training Budget* from the Toolkit, and you can see an example on p.150.

1 Start by forecasting your income

Look at your annual training plan and identify how many training sessions you will do, how many students you can get at each session, and roughly what price you can charge for each place.

Are you struggling to set the price? Then do some quick competitor research or guess what you think your ideal students would pay. Choose ballpark figures for now.

Top Tip

When pricing your tickets, assume you will fill only 80 per cent of your places, as this is more realistic. If you sell more, then you have a profit, but you won't be making a loss if you don't sell out.

2 Identify your annual training expenses

What are the direct costs of your training? Include venue(s), catering, materials, etc. What about your travel costs or accommodation? For online training, think about filming and editing costs. Spend some time researching your potential costs; this will give you realistic numbers. **Make a list of all the costs in one year** with their numbers, and add these all up.

As we said before: **your time is the biggest cost**. Have you kept time sheets, or could you find out how long it takes you to create new training? If you are pre-recording training, be realistic about how much time preparation and post-production will take.

Most importantly, what do you charge per hour? What will you charge for the actual teaching time, and what for your admin or marketing time? **Do not charge the minimum wage.** You need to charge a professional fee to compensate for non-billable hours (the hours you work that you don't get paid for) for your training and creative work.

Make a list of the various tasks involved in creating and delivering your training; estimate how long each task will take and what hourly rate you will charge for each.

Top Tip

Research shows that it takes a beginner around eight hours of preparation and marketing time to deliver one hour of training. Even established teachers put in much more work than the students see.

Calculate the overhead costs related to your training. Identify what percentage of your annual workshop income contributes to your overall annual income. I recommend that you then allocate that percentage of your total overheads to your training budget. This allocation will give you a financial buffer to cover the overall costs of your creative business.

3 **Do you make a profit or a loss?** Is your income higher than your expenditure? If not, then play around with your income numbers (quantity of sessions x ticket price x number of students x 80%) and compare to your total costs in the year. Use the downloadable spreadsheet in the Toolkit to make this easier.

Below Annual training budget example.

Income	**£/$/€**
Workshops per year × ticket price × number of students × 80% capacity e.g., 9 live workshops × 120 ticket price × 8 students × 80%	6,912
Expenditure	
Direct costs related to the workshops (venues, catering, marketing, travel, stationery, printing, materials) Average costs for each workshop × number of workshops e.g., 150 × 9	1,350
Labour costs: your time (preparation, marketing, admin, teaching, travel time) Number of events × average hours × hourly rate e.g., 9 workshops × 16 hours × 30 (hourly rate)	4,320
Overhead costs: Annual income from training ÷ projected total annual turnover = % of overheads to allocate to training e.g., 6,912 training income ÷ 30,000 overall income = 23%. If your total overheads are 4,000, allocate 23% of this to training. 4,000 × 0.23 = 920	920
Total expenses e.g., 1,350 + 4,320 + 920	6,590
Profit or loss Income - total expenses	**+ 322**

FAQ: How do I include one-off start-up costs?

When you start teaching professionally, you'll likely have one-off costs, e.g., equipment. When you purchase equipment there are special tax rules that allow you to deduct these costs over several years. **Check these rules with your national tax office**; often they must be spread over three to five years on your tax return.

When creating your annual training budget, identify these one-off costs, divide them over three to five years, and then identify how much you use them solely for training or for other parts of your business too.

For example, you purchase a camera to create online films for £400, and you want to spread this over three years. This amounts to £133 per year. Add this to your overhead budget.

If you use the camera in other parts of your creative business, you can add less, relative to how much time it is used in the teaching/creative part of your business.

Time to pause

Once you've created your annual training plan and annual training budget, get your notebook and make time to reflect:

- **Do your numbers stack up?** Are you forecasting a profit or a loss? At this stage it's OK if you only have a rough idea of your numbers, but I encourage you to research and start identifying realistic costs and income. Play around with the numbers in the downloadable template to see what happens if you increase the number of sessions, student numbers or ticket price, or if you lower your costs or time spent. What do you need to do to make it work financially? Reflect on what you are learning. There will be loads of strategic decisions and potential solutions in the following pages to make your numbers work.
- **Are you currently charging enough for your training?** Do you pay yourself a decent hourly rate? Have you made any of the common costing mistakes in the past, like forgetting to include your preparation time or overheads? Review what you are learning, and what needs to change in your mindset, knowledge and approach to making your training financially successful.
- **How do you feel about charging a higher professional hourly rate?** How confident are you about making your creative training work for you as a business? Your confidence and mindset play a big role in your potential success.

Well done for doing this exercise! It can be an eye-opening and emotional one, but it will give you insights into the financial viability of your current training ideas. **Don't despair if your numbers are not adding up** – yet. We will continue to work on this, and I will show you how to boost your confidence around what you can charge.

Remember that costing your training is only the first step. Pricing and charging are next. Let's go there now.

Pricing your training

Did you realise during the annual training budget exercise that you need to increase the price of your training? Costing is one of the most common pricing strategies, but there are others that will allow you to charge more for what you offer.

Pricing strategy 1: Cost-based pricing

Many creatives base their pricing on cost, which is a good starting point to calculate if you are making a profit or not. But, costs are not the only factor that determines what you can charge!

What else impacts the price other than costs?

- **Your profile.** Well-known and more established creatives or teachers can charge more.
- **Your competition.** If you are an expert in your field and there is limited competition, that increases your value, and therefore the price. What do your competitors charge?
- **Whether you teach live or online.** Most students will pay more for in-person workshops than for online training. There is also a slight price bias towards live versus pre-recorded online training.
- **Length of training.** The longer the training, the more you can charge, but a one-off session is often more expensive to run per hour than a six-week course.
- **The skill level you teach.** If you teach more advanced or transformational skills, you can charge more.
- **Your students' motivation.** If your students want to do a workshop for fun, they will look at alternative classes or compare your prices to other leisure activities (e.g., a massage or nice dinner). If your courses will save a professional student time or make them money, you can charge much more.
- **Group size.** In-person training is often limited by space and how many students you can teach. Teaching from home can therefore limit your earning potential. Students should pay more for exclusive access to you and your expertise.
- **The venue and location.** Do not underestimate the importance of the profile of your venue, the location, and even the quality of the coffee and cakes. These details can make a huge difference to the perceived value of your training.
- **Your confidence!** Are you confident enough to charge what you are worth? Too many creatives undervalue and undercharge for their expertise and hard work. It's up to you to work on this.

Time to pause

Take your notebook and take time to reflect and answer these questions:

- **How can you lower the costs of your training?** Look at how you can be more efficient with your own time, or spread costs over more training sessions.
- **Did you realise during the annual training budget exercise that you need to increase the price of your training?** Referring to the list above, identify specific actions to change the perceived value for your ideal students, and discover more with the upcoming perceived value pricing exercise (p.154).

Pricing strategy 2: Competition-based pricing

Many artists base the price of their own work and training on what others charge. Have you checked what your competitors charge yet? This will give you a good idea of the going rates for similar training.

Top Tip

When doing competitor research it's really important to compare like with like. Many factors influence the price you set, so make sure you compare your training with similar training, e.g., the reputation of the teacher, the format, length, location, size of group, etc.

Time to pause

Get your notebook and reflect:

- **Identify your five closest competitors.** Use Google, Eventbrite and online marketplaces like craftcourses.com, Domestika or Skillshare to find them.
- **Identify what they charge.** Have they set different price levels? What do students get for each level?
- **Reflect on why other creative teachers can charge more for their training.** Try to identify specific differences and opportunities to help you charge the right amount for yours. What do you need, or who do you need to be, to charge different prices?

Pricing strategy 3: Perceived value pricing

This is arguably the most important strategy for setting your prices.

'Perceived value' is the pricing strategy that will help you to charge the right amount for both you and your ideal client.

You might have realised in the last few pages that pricing is about perception rather than the actual cost. It's about what your training is worth to your ideal clients.

Students will look at your entire training offer. This is a student-focused strategy, **strongly connected to their psychology and perception**, who they are and want to become, what they value about you and your training, and the results that they want.

'When I started to do online courses, I learnt that the value of a course doesn't come from the quantity of hours or whatever the product is. The value comes from getting ideas or giving people permission to make time for self-development.

The beauty with online learning is that you can come to the content when you want to, when it works for your life. You watch it again and again.

As an online student myself I'll see things in different ways each time, and that's so massive compared to an in-person workshop, where you get one shot and you're done.'

Hanny Newton, embroiderer

The perceived value pricing exercise

This exercise will show you how flexible and creative pricing and 'training' can be. It takes about an hour in total. Read the following three scenarios, and make notes on each:

Scenario 1: Imagine that you must charge £15 per person for training.

- **What could you deliver to your ideal students that they would pay £15 for?**
- **What teaching format, topic or length would you choose?** Would it be an online Q&A or a downloadable workbook? What would be included in the price? Remember that 'teaching' can be a broad concept. Get creative.
- **Where and when would you do this experience?** Online or in person? What venue or location would you choose?
- **What kind of student would you attract at this price?** How much commitment would you expect, and what do you think their expectations would be?
- **How would this experience feel, for you and for your students?**
- **Where and how would you promote this?**
- **How many students can you deal with in this specific teaching format?**
- **How many students would you need to make this scenario profitable for you?** This might really surprise you as you might get many more students at a lower price, and if your costs are low it can be very profitable.

Scenario 2: Imagine that you must charge £150 per person for training. What would you do then? Answer the same questions as before. What is different?

Scenario 3: Imagine that you must charge £1,500 per person for training.
Answer the same questions. What is different from the previous two scenarios?

If you like, you can even go for a fourth scenario of £15,000 per person!

When you have worked through each of the three scenarios, reflect on these questions:

- **What did you learn from this exercise?** How could you deliver alternative training experiences at different price points?
- **How did working with widely different price points make you feel?** What did you find difficult or challenging? What did you find easy or fun?
- **There are pros and cons to delivering both very cheap and very expensive training experiences.** Reflect on what these pros and cons are for you.
- **Has your attitude to low or high prices changed?** Could you adapt your current teaching idea in light of these new insights? Write down specific improvements to your current idea.
- **What specifically do think your students value about your existing training ideas and you as a teacher and artist?** What might they be willing to pay extra for?

FAQ: How do I keep my workshops affordable but profitable?

Do you worry about how to charge professionally while keeping training accessible and affordable? Your creative training will only be profitable once you have covered all your costs. Make sure that you know your numbers, and what your break-even point is (the point where your sales are higher than your expenses and you start making a profit).

Do you worry that your potential students can't afford their training? Many creatives are anxious about this, often because they themselves are not wealthy. But remember – you are not your student! You will be surprised how much your students might be willing to pay ...

You want to offer affordable training, but it is easy to forget that **when your prices are lower, you need proportionally more bookings**. You might have noticed this when creating an annual training budget (p.149) or doing the perceived value pricing exercise (opposite). For example, if you need to cover costs of £10,000, you can either run six exclusive workshops per year, each with four students paying £416, or 10 workshops, each with 10 students paying £100.

Do you have the marketing skills to either attract higher end clients who pay more, or attract many more students at lower or affordable fees? That's a big aha-moment for many of my students.

Very often, creatives keep their prices low because of competition, which encourages others to keep *their* prices low, and so on.

Time to pause

Take your notebook and take time to reflect on these questions:

- **What do you mean by 'affordable'?** What are you planning to charge?
- **How much do you think your ideal students will pay for your training?** Did they explicitly tell you, or are you making assumptions?
- **Do a quick number-crunching exercise.** Go back to the annual training budget exercise (p.149) and look at your total annual training costs. Now use your 'affordable' price and identify how many workshops or courses you need to run with how many people to cover your costs. Is this feasible? Or could you offer different price levels or offer some scholarships for people who really can't afford it?
- **Write down a list of reasons** why you are not charging properly for your workshops. (Warning: this can be painful!) How much does your mindset about money and what you are worth influence your undercharging?
- **If you are not charging professional rates** for your training (and possibly your own creative work too!), this can have costs in terms of self-esteem, profile and respect, as well as income. What do you need to do? **What do you need to stop doing?**

Why your training isn't profitable: Three reasons

A quick reminder from our annual training budget:

Profit = income – expenses

Income = number of workshops × number of students × ticket price × capacity (e.g. 80%)

Expenses = (total time spent × your hourly rate) + direct costs + per cent of overhead costs

When you created an annual training budget (p.149), did you struggle to cover your costs with your expected sales? We will now dive into the three main reasons for this.

Reason 1: You are not charging enough

- **Review your costing and pricing annually.** Expenses might have gone up. You might need to update your hourly rate.
- **Do you regularly overdeliver but undercharge?** If you charge a low hourly rate or spend much more time than you planned, it's going to be hard to make a profit. You are not the only creative struggling with this challenge. How can you work on your money confidence and set boundaries around your time and perfectionism?
- **Did you do the annual training budget exercise?** Keep an eye on your labour costs in particular, and how much time you actually spend versus what you can afford to spend.
- **Did you forecast based on 80 per cent capacity rather than 100 per cent?** Build in a financial cushion so that you don't have to get a full house each time. It's really useful to know how many participants you need to get to make that session profitable.
- **Could you charge more per ticket?** Have you done some competitor research to see what they charge? Did the perceived value pricing exercise (p.154) give you practical ideas? Are you making incorrect assumptions and holding yourself back?

Be aware that you can sell lots of workshop places, and it might look like your business is doing well, but if you don't charge enough per ticket then you will still make a loss. **Healthy profit margins are really important**.

Top Tip

If your pre-recorded online training costs look very high, it might help you to do a two- or even a three-year forecast to show how your training will become profitable over time.

Reason 2: You are not getting enough sales

You are spending time and money, but you are not selling enough tickets:

- Make sure that you **have a warning system in place** three weeks before each training starts so that you can do targeted marketing or even cancel if you don't have enough students to cover your costs.
- **Do you know what your best-selling training is?** And which are the worst

performers? It's really useful to fact check your bookings and accounts from the last two years:

- What sells and what doesn't do as well? Check which format (one-day or weekend, half- or full-day workshop) sells best.
- Check which days or timings are best and worst for you. Do Fridays or Saturdays sell better, or evening sessions? And which months are best? The success of your training can be very seasonal, and what sells well in one month might do a lot worse in another month.
- How much repeat business do you get? Do you encourage this?

- **Avoid loss-making workshops!** This is a particular issue with in-person workshops, where you need bums on seats to cover your costs. I regularly see creative trainers offer too many workshops and course dates, and then run their sessions with too few students.

Top Tip

It's actually really attractive to have your courses labelled as 'sold out' on your website. Your potential students will realise that your training is popular and limited in spaces, which will encourage them to book sooner.

Reason 3: You are not doing enough or timely marketing

This is a major issue for many creatives and closely related to Problem 2.

- **Do you have great sales pages** on your website and do you drive traffic to it via keywords, email marketing, social media and at events?
- **Do you have a database** to stay in touch with students? You could reach out to them at the last minute to promote your upcoming training.
- **Do you use keywords** in your sales page or blog posts to attract new students?
- **Do you know who your ideal clients are,** why they want to do the training and where to find them?
- **Do you try to encourage your existing clients** to come back, and bring a friend? Your previous students are a lot more likely to sign up for another workshop or course than somebody who doesn't know you. And they often are prepared to pay more next time too.

We will dive into many more marketing activities to make your training profitable in the next chapter.

Time to pause

Get your notebook, and take time to reflect on the following questions:

- **What's the main reason your training is not profitable?** Are your costs too high or your income too low? Or both? What do you need to do or stop doing specifically? Identify three activities.
- **How can you reduce the time you spend** on preparation and administration? And make more time for marketing?

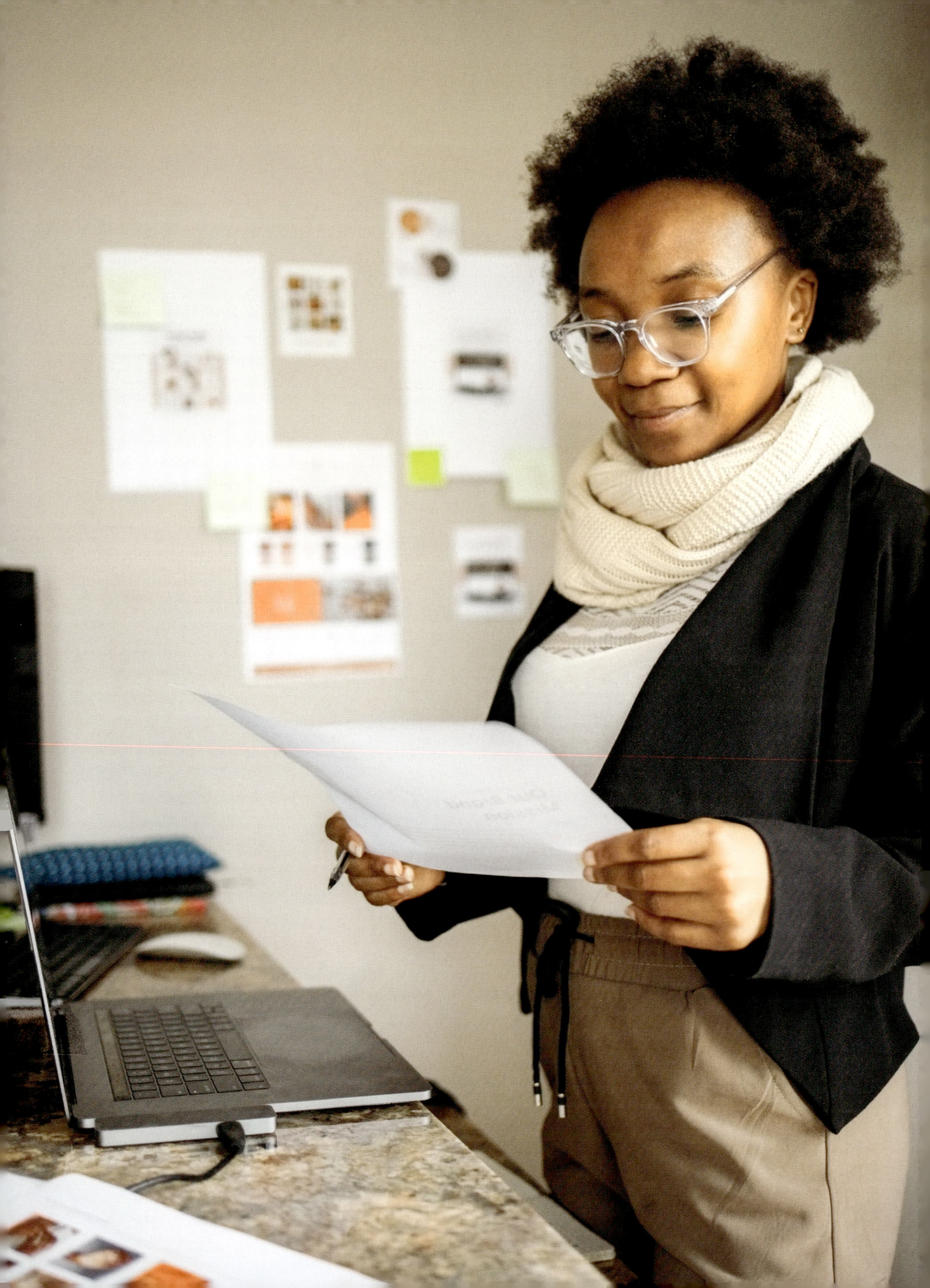

FAQ: How do I confidently increase my prices?

The easiest ways to increase your prices are to use the perceived value pricing strategy and introduce packages at different price levels. As you change what you offer, it's ceases to be comparable with what you offered in the past, which makes it much easier to adjust the price.

If your offer is still very similar, then you could let your previous students know so that they can book before your prices go up. This is good customer care and could generate extra bookings.

If you are struggling with under-pricing yourself (for your training or your products) then I highly recommend the book *Overcoming Underearning: A Five-Step Plan to a Richer Life* by Barbara Stanny.

Remember, you don't need an excuse to increase your prices. If you have realised that you need to increase your prices, then just do so.

Expert Tip

One of the best ways to improve your affordability while increasing your profitability is to add different price points to your training packages. In this way, you can keep your training affordable, but also stretch your ticket prices with valuable bonus content or personal support.

As you could see in the perceived value pricing exercise (p.154), you can get really creative with what your students get at different price points. Creating packages can work really well, e.g., offering training and an upgrade with a private one-to-one online session.

Large online training event organisers regularly provide free access to live sessions on the day, but if clients want access to the recordings afterwards they pay a premium. This 'freemium' pricing model is a common marketing technique that can generate huge profits, because people don't want to miss out.

Top Tip

Remember that your price tells a story. If you charge too little, students do not value what you offer, and often they don't commit as much.

Therefore I charge more for The Design Trust online marketing courses so that it is an investment for the prospective student. By paying a bit more it often means they are more committed and motivated to putting in the hard work. And, of course, it's the hard work that will get them the sales results they are after!

Getting paid: The practicalities

Whether you are offering in-person or online training, **the easiest way to take payments is online,** either on your own website, or through specialist training software or online marketplaces such as Eventbrite and Skillshare.

If you use online payment providers such as PayPal, Stripe, Square, SumUp or GoCardless, you will need to set up a business account with them. They will process the payments and pay them, minus their fees, into your bank account.

Top Tip

If you use PayPal for personal purchases, I highly recommend that you use a separate PayPal business account to process business payments, both income and expenditure. This will make your bookkeeping much easier and more transparent.

An alternative is to **send out an invoice in advance** – something you can do through many payment providers – but this will increase your administrative time.

If you want to take payment on the day for an in-person workshop, I recommend that you **use a card reader.** You can get these from your bank or from various payment providers, and it makes taking payments, invoicing and administration much easier. However, I would always try to get paid in advance to minimise last-minute cancellations.

If you are working with organisations or venues who have commissioned you to run a workshop or course, it's very common that they require you to issue an invoice, often with 30-day payment terms.

Top Tip

People love to pay in instalments, especially if your training is expensive. Many payment platforms offer this option – does yours?

For example, PayPal's Pay in 3 sends you the full amount immediately, while (credit-worthy) students can spread the cost over three months. PayPal manages late or missing payments, which means you don't have to chase them – a huge advantage, as it's never a nice job and can damage your relationship with clients.

'We offer a payment plan for our intensive one-year diplomas.

That's helpful for the students but also for us as we know what our income will be for the year, and can manage our staff and finances accordingly.'

Jessica Rose, founder of Jewellers Academy

FAQ: How do I charge for one-off online sessions?

You can easily create and include a payment link in PayPal for a workshop or course, and then share that payment link in your emails or embed it on your website.

You can also set up a single payment option in your PayPal business account, and send your student a manual invoice.

Many online communication platforms (e.g., Zoom, GoToWebinar) allow you to charge for individual online sessions from within the software.

If you want to lean into DIY, you can email an invoice manually to your student, and when they have paid, you send them a password or a link to a password-protected website page to access the recording directly.

FAQ: How do I deal with cancellations and refunds?

Unfortunately, you, a student or the venue/partnership organisation may need to cancel. This might be for personal or health reasons, a *force majeure*, or you have too few bookings and you want to avoid making a loss.

To avoid problems with your clients, **be as transparent as possible** about your cancellation and refund policy in your promotional material and your T&Cs, e.g., 'I reserve the right to cancel if the minimum student numbers aren't reached one week before the training.'

Note that there may be legal requirements around cancellations and refunds. Check consumer rights organisations or government websites for more information about the law in your country.

There are different options you can offer:

- **Full refund:** in the UK, at the time of writing, participants should be entitled to a full refund if they cancel their registration within 14 days of booking, and at least 14 days before the workshop is scheduled to take place. This is a legal requirement in many countries. You might offer a better deal of, say, 7 days.
- **Partial refund:** participants should be entitled to a partial refund if they cancel their registration less than 14 days before the workshop is scheduled. State clearly what costs you would deduct.
- **Rescheduling:** participants should have the option to reschedule to a later workshop, if one is available, if they are unable to attend the original workshop.
- **Transfers:** participants should be allowed to transfer their registration to another person, provided they notify you within a reasonable time before the workshop is scheduled to take place.
- **Credit:** participants should be given the option of a credit towards a future workshop if they are unable to attend the original workshop.

If you have to cancel, it's good practice to offer a full refund.

Are you ready to get more sales and attract your ideal students? Before we head to the next chapter, let's hear from Kara Leigh Ford, founder of the 'Pottery Club'.

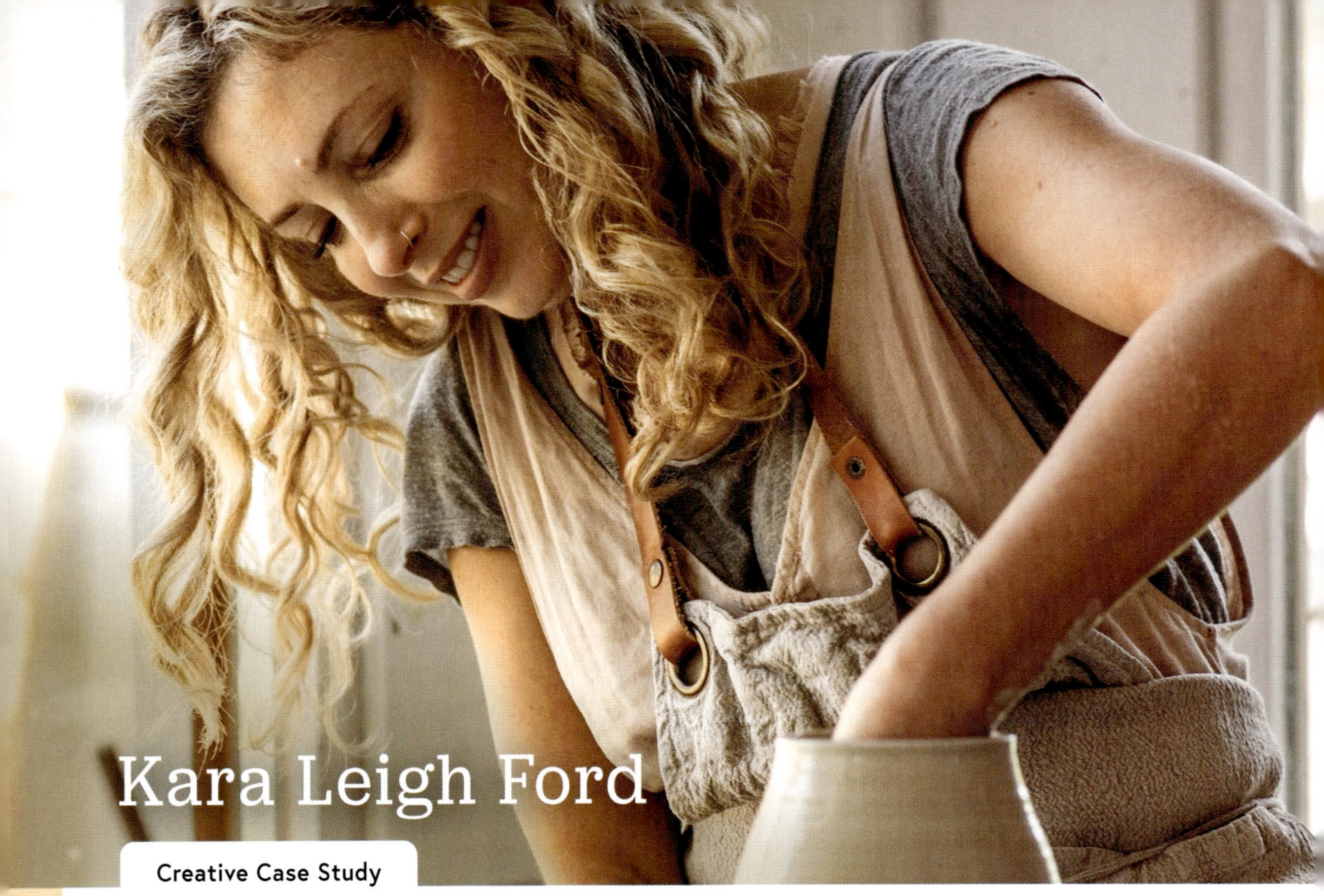

Kara Leigh Ford

Creative Case Study

Kara Leigh Ford studied fine art and theatre studies, first at Plymouth College of Art and Design and then at Bath Spa University.

She began pottery as a hobby to try and keep creative while working in marketing. She quickly became immersed in it, and in 2015 she left her day job to follow her dream. From her studio near Bath, in Somerset, she creates beautiful table and kitchenware inspired by lazy summer days by the ocean.

She has been teaching in person from her studio and online for over a decade now.

In 2021, she wrote her first book, *Pottery for Beginners*.

You can find out more about Kara Leigh Ford at www.karaleighfordceramics.com

Above Kara Leigh Ford throwing a pot.

How did you get started with online teaching?

People were asking me on social media if I could teach them. I was an early adopter. As soon as video was a thing on Instagram, I started filming my making process. They were terrible videos – badly lit, wobbly – but no one else was sharing their processes back then!

It started as a way of educating customers who purchased my tableware, to show how much work went into my pottery, but I got loads of practical questions. 'How do you do that? What tools do you use?' I was getting dozens of questions each day on Instagram. I didn't have the time to answer all these questions and make my own pottery too.

I started thinking how I could make this more accessible, create a helpful resource, and reach people across the world. I selected

Patreon because its paid membership system meant I could answer questions and get remunerated for my time. I wanted to create a really practical video library full of resources responding to questions. If somebody asked me how I centre the clay or how I make handles I would create a video tutorial.

From the start, I offered different membership levels, from 'ask me any question you want but no access to the videos' for just £3 a month, to the highest tier, which included one-on-one online training.

In October 2019, I branded it 'Pottery Club' and it's still hosted on Patreon, although there are more platforms available now. I have around 250 paid members and 400 free members.

There are now more than 120 recordings available in Pottery Club, and I keep adding exclusive videos every month. I want to keep inspiring people, answering questions and sharing my own creative projects and insights. There are video tutorials for beginners, advanced and professionals. There are lots of short 'two-minute tip' videos and the tutorials are about 15–30 minutes long.

How do you keep your members engaged?

It's really hard. You need to keep reaching out and creating a community feel. It helps that in Patreon we can now use group chats where people can share pictures and ask questions.

A lot of people who joined Pottery Club have been there for years. It's really lovely as I've been with them on their pottery journey, and they're with me on my journey. They might not necessarily need the training videos anymore, but they might like the live sessions and community.

But members will move on, outgrow it, find something else, stop doing pottery, or their finances change, and life happens. You're never going to be in control of that. The thing that you can control is the way that you interact with them. Treat them as friends and as VIPs.

How do you plan?

To begin with, I was going to batch things and film everything at once, but that doesn't work for me. What I teach is reflected in what I am doing at that time of the year. People appreciate the seasonality of it. I'm inspired by nature and what's going on outside my studio doors, which comes across in my videos.

I have a list of tutorial ideas that I want to cover in the next few months. I'm always adding to that list and it changes all the time. I might have made something previously, or I need to wait to get the materials, or I get a really interesting question.

I have also introduced guest tutorials with people who have a specific skill. Recently I asked an artist to record a tutorial on throwing porcelain. It's a very specialist material and as I use stoneware it isn't something I have much experience with.

And how long does the filming and editing take?

The monthly videos take a very long time to create. I have to plan out what I am going to make and teach. I have to make all the samples in different stages, so I have a thrown example, one that's ready to trim so I can show that part of the process, an example that's ready to glaze, and the finished item so I can show at the start what we're going to make.

'Filming is the bit that takes the least amount of time. The prep is what takes the time.'

I can throw a mug in three minutes, but it takes up to a whole day to film! I will do a couple of angles, a different focus, a wide and a close up shot, so when I am editing it's more interesting for people to watch.

Then I will write the script. I do this afterwards because I will use the footage to help me write so that I cover what I'm actually seeing in the video. If you write the script first then you might not think of something that comes up during the making process and then you have to go back and rewrite that into the script.

The last thing is adding the voice-over. I record the script and make sure everything lines up. Most of the time it doesn't, because it takes longer to explain something so I have to make or add more footage. Then I add music and the final flourishes like texts and titles.

Tell me about your wholesale pricing course

Wholesale is a difficult area to break into. I wanted to offer my own experience of trying to work it all out by myself.

It's an intensive six-week bootcamp, with recorded and live sessions where students can ask me questions, and a weekly action plan and accountability. It's only open once a year so everybody is working and learning together. By the end of the programme they are ready to approach shops and galleries.

How do you promote your training?

There's not one thing that works, it's a combination. Some people respond really well to me talking on Instagram Reels, other people respond to emails.

For my course I have a weekly marketing plan with exactly what I am going to talk to them about, what I am sending in my emails. It's more focused and within a specific short timescale.

With the Pottery Club it's more fluid and evergreen. I try not to bombard people on social media. I want it to feel more natural. I also often get questions via Instagram and mention the Pottery Club then.

I use Pinterest a lot. I have worked with a VA to create a series of pins promoting all my free YouTube videos and some lead magnets of free downloads on my website. I also write helpful blogs and then mention the membership.

What advice do you wish you had been given?

To relax a bit more! When I first started teaching, I felt I had to prove that I was worthy of that position. I don't have a ceramics degree and felt a bit like an impostor.

It's OK not to know everything and to say to people 'I'll get back to you on that'. No one knows everything, right? Pottery is such an expansive subject. I will always be learning alongside my students and that's all part of the joy.

Opposite Kara getting ready to throw at the potter's wheel.

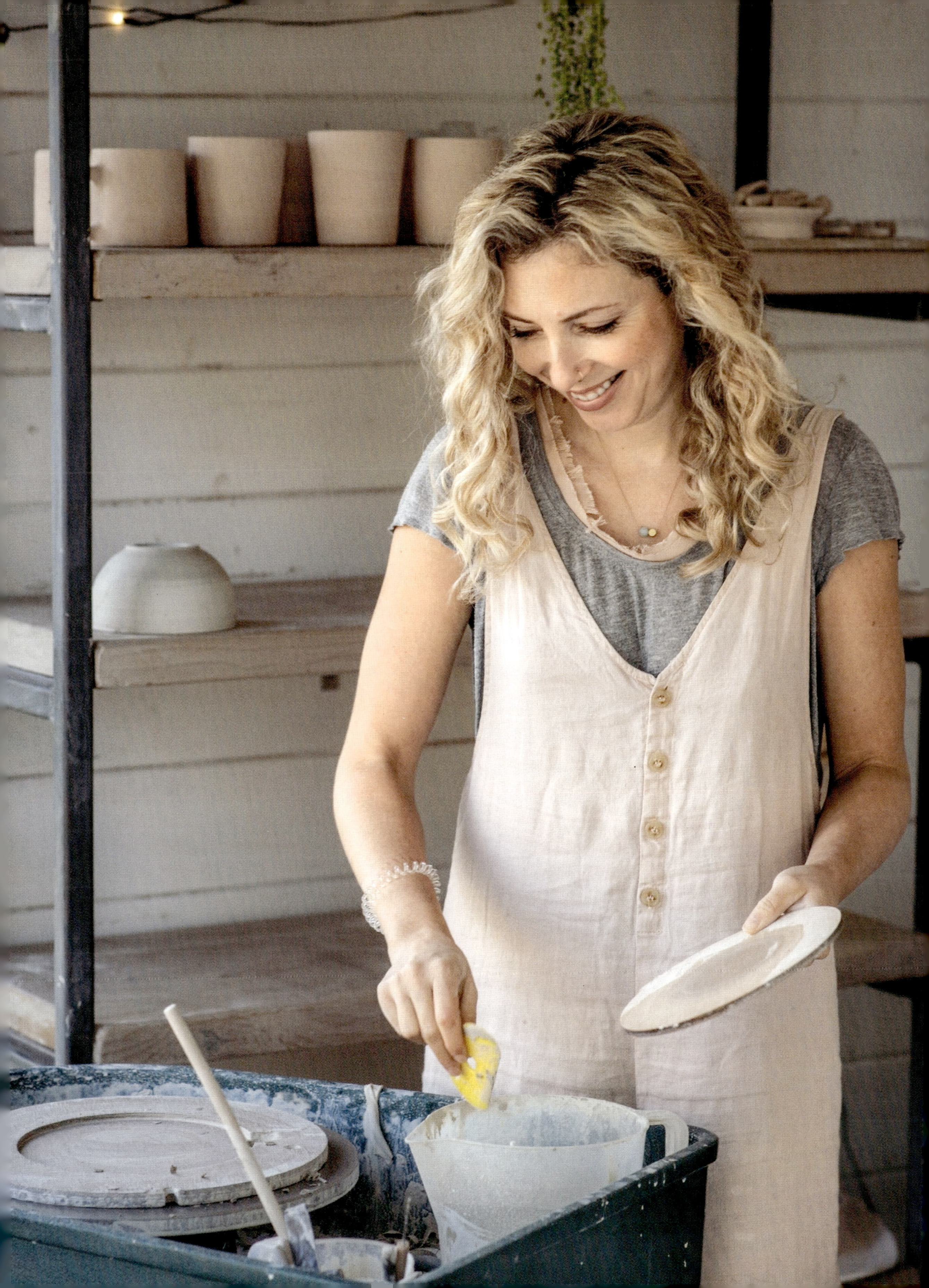

CHAPTER 8

Marketing

Are you ready to start promoting your training? Then let's go! This chapter is split into four parts, covering all aspects of marketing.

We will start with **four fundamental marketing concepts** that will form the basis of your overall marketing strategy:

- **Who are your ideal clients and students?** I will share a great creative exercise to help you really get to know them.
- **How are you unique**, and how can you stand out from the competition?
- **'People only buy from people they know, like and trust.'** How can you build your profile and credibility?
- **How can you turn interest into sales and bookings?**

I will share three of my personal marketing secrets, which have really helped me to build a successful online business school:

- Why repeat business is so important
- How to make your workshops giftable
- How to launch early

Then we will **focus on your website** – the best possible place for you to present yourself and your training, get payments and make admin easier. Once you have created your website, it's time to drive traffic to your website with:

- Search engine optimisation (SEO)
- Email marketing
- Social media
- 'Traditional' marketing

Fundamental marketing concepts

1: Who are your ideal students?

Are you selling directly to individuals, or will you be working with a venue or corporate client? We will start by getting to know your individual students, and then look at identifying and approaching venues or organisations.

The client persona exercise is a great visual exercise that should only take a few hours, but will be very useful long term to really get to know your ideal students, create niche training and will make your marketing more unique and personal too.

Client persona and collages

Remember all the way back in Chapter 3, when we looked at who you wanted to teach? **Return to the *Ideal Student* worksheet in the Teach Your Creative Workshop Toolkit** and review it. You have so much more information now.

You can do this exercise the old-fashioned way and get some large pieces of paper (A1 is ideal) to glue images on, or you can create secret Pinterest boards for each of your ideal students.

Start by identifying between three and five different client types for the 12-month training plan you put together in Chapter 7 (p.148). Write a short descriptive summary of each potential student group, e.g., for an outdoor basketry course, the three client groups might be:

Type 1: loves nature and being outdoors while learning something new;
Type 2: a hobbyist who has done some basketry or outdoor craft courses already;
Type 3: a professional textile artist who wants to expand their creative skills.

Start writing a short biography for each type. Give them a name, age, gender, location, hobbies, occupation, current skill level, and their values related to your topic (e.g., mind-body connection, interest in history and traditional skills).

For each type, answer the following questions.

- **Why do they want to do this training?** How do they want to feel when they book the training, and when they do it?
- **When do they want to do it?** At a specific time of year or for a special occasion?
- **Where will they see or hear about training like yours?** Identify specific websites, media or keywords.
- **What questions do they have about the training?** What might stop them from booking with you?

Visualise your ideal student within each client group. Find images or quotes that reflect them, and the kind of workshop space and experience you want to create. You can draw them, use Pinterest or find magazines that your ideal student reads. It's less about their appearance and more about their motivations to do your training, values and willingness to learn.

Compare your three client types in detail. Focus on their similarities and differences.

When you are finished, reflect in your notebook on what this exercise has taught you about:

- your different ideal student groups;
- improvements you can make to your training (e.g., format, title, content);
- how you will present your brand and your website, sales pages and promotional materials.

FAQ: How should I find and approach potential training venues and partners?

In Chapter 5, in the section on in-person training, we saw that your ideal clients can also be venues; arts or cultural organisations; craft fairs and other event organisers; or universities and adult education providers. **You could hire a room, or they could pay you to run your training,** and help you with organising and marketing too. Working with established or well-known partners can bring a lot of credibility to your training.

Which events, museums, arts or educational organisations would you like to work with? Which venues or organisations provide similar training to yours already? Where are your competitors teaching? Spend some time online to research venues, events or educational places that host similar training to yours. Look at the format too, as they might prefer shorter talks or demonstrations, not just a day or weekend course.

Once you have **made a list of potential training partners,** check if there is information on their websites about how to work with them, or deadlines.

Then approach them – either send a short email or post an information pack to the person responsible for training at that organisation. Refer in your email to similar training that they currently offer, and emphasise the things that differentiate your training.

Build credibility by providing some information about your creative and teaching experience. Include links or flyers to training you have delivered in the past, and some testimonials or images from workshops.

Keep your first email relatively short (500 words at the most) and open-ended, and ask them to reply to you. This is an introductory communication; you can discuss details like fees and logistics at a later date.

> *‘Demonstrating at events can help to bring crafts to life for visitors of all ages and interests.*
>
> *Buyers may gain a deeper appreciation of what goes into crafting a piece, and it can be beneficial for makers who are promoting workshops.*
>
> *And, it’s wonderful to see young visitors captivated by a maker’s processes – discovering a craft for the first time, asking questions, itching to pick up tools.’*
>
> **Deborah Pocock,** CEO of QEST

Top Tip

Working with organisations or venues has the big advantage that you can be more proactive with your marketing because, unlike with individuals, you can identify and approach specific businesses that you want to work with. Especially if you have a clear niche, it’s easy to find venues or organisations that are a good match to your training.

Opposite QEST scholar Wayne Hart demonstrating at ‘Makers in Residence’, Design Centre Chelsea Harbour, 2023.

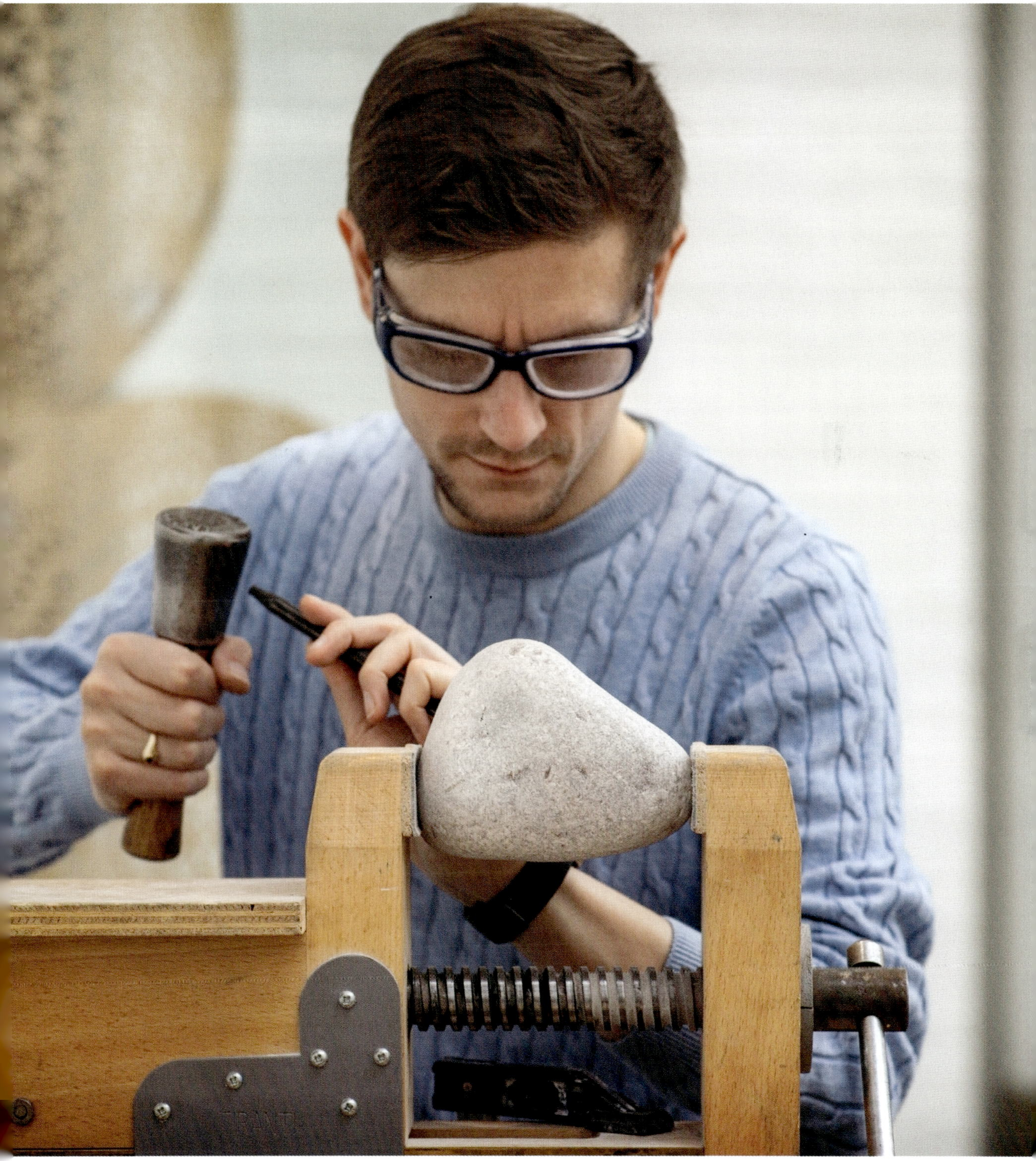

Fundamental marketing concept 2: What makes you stand out?

Teaching creative skills has become very popular in the last few years, so do expect some competition.

In fact, **competitors can be really useful**, as you can learn a lot from them. If you don't have any, there might not be a market for what you want to teach.

In Chapter 2 (p.25) I encouraged you to do some light-touch competitor research for inspiration around your training format and methods, your niche, what to charge, and to identify potential in-person teaching venues.

The competitor research exercise here will go into more depth, and it is one of the best tools to **identify what's special about you** and how you can stand out in a crowded market. It's very useful to do this exercise now, after finding out more about your ideal customer.

This exercise will help you to identify specific gaps and opportunities in your market and to **bring your uniqueness to life** when creating your brand and website later on in this chapter.

Creative Exercise

Competitor research

Download and print off the *Competitor Matrix* and watch the short video in the Toolkit. This exercise will take between two and four hours, but will be very useful and inspirational.

First, identify your five closest competitors and fill them in on the top row in the Competitor Matrix; look for individual creatives who are teaching similar topics to the ones in your annual training plan. Use Google, Eventbrite, craftcourses.com or popular online course marketplaces such Skillshare or Domestika to identify your competitors.

Your training ideas will have developed a lot throughout this book, so **make sure that your competitors are indeed similar to you,** i.e., they teach similar topics in a similar format, at a comparable price point to customers close to your ideal client types.

Second, **look at their websites or social media** to find out more detailed information. For each competitor you identify, fill in the following details in the matrix:

- **What do they teach?** What's the exact title? Is it a project or skills/techniques-based training?
- **What level is their training aimed at?** (E.g., beginner, hobbyist, advanced.)
- **How often and when does it run?** How long is it?

- **What's the format?** Is it an in-person workshop or an online course? If it's online, is it live or recorded? Are there any extra resources or workbooks?
- **Who are their ideal students?** Go beyond age and gender and dig into their motivations and values. Look at your own client personas and compare.
- **How much do they charge?** Are there different price levels with add-ons?
- Check out your competitors' websites and social media. Especially look at the sales pages, and how they promote themselves and attract their ideal clients. **Makes notes on what to include on your own website.**

Finally (and most importantly), fill in the matrix:

- **What are each of your competitors specifically known for?** What do they do really well? This is a tough question.
- **What can you learn from each of your competitors?**
- **Then fill in the matrix for you.** What are the facts about your training? What do you do especially well? Use details from your competitors to identify what makes you different. How can you make yourself stand out from them?
- **Define your niche** (from Chapter 3, p.42). Use your insights from this in depth competitor research to clarify what makes you and your training different and special. This will be crucial when you start working on your branding and website later in this chapter.

Fundamental marketing concept 3: 'People only buy from people they know, like and trust'

At the heart of all the marketing that I do and teach at The Design Trust is this marketing mantra: **'People only buy from people they know, like and trust.'**

This is a fundamental marketing approach if you want to attract customers and get bookings. Unless potential students know who you are and can find you online, that they truly love your topics and teaching style, and trust you as a creative and educational professional, they will not buy, and it will be near impossible to build your teaching business.

So, **how do you build your profile and credibility?** Luckily, you can get really creative in this area. It's often in the detail that the 'real you' can show up confidently and creatively. Here are some ideas to get you started:

- **Focus on your niche and become an expert in your field.** Students love learning from somebody who knows their stuff and is passionate about it. Regularly write and talk about your niche in blog posts, emails or short videos. Get invited as a guest speaker on relevant podcasts or conferences, or approach magazines or blogs with relevant article ideas.
- **Does your website and marketing look professional?** Does it speak to your ideal clients? Start thinking about your branding, the colours, fonts, images and video you use, and the tone of voice of your course titles and descriptions. Creating the right brand is a big part to attract your ideal student. We will find out more about this later in this chapter.

- **Show off your expertise and knowledge.** Where have you studied or exhibited? How long have you been teaching? Where have you taught? Add press coverage and testimonials to your website or LinkedIn profile. Include details on your sales pages, 'About Me' page and your social media bio.
- **Use free training opportunities** so that your potential clients can get to know, like and trust you. For example, write blog posts that answer common questions, or share your opinion about a topic that's relevant in your field, or do a Q&A on Zoom. Promote this free content in your emails and social media to reach even more potential students.
- **Video builds trust very well,** as it's so close to real-life interaction. Record a short video introducing yourself on your 'About Me' page, or record individual videos introducing each course or workshop. Interview a student about their experience of your courses. Short-form social media videos like Instagram Reels or TikTok are very popular, but videos on your website have a far longer lifespan.
- **Offer a collection of shorter, connected workshops,** creating a 'learning path' for your students. Offering recurring training and being consistent in your delivery will build trust and encourage students to return.
- **Work with the right partners or venues.** Can you teach for them, hire a space, leave promotional material or include your workshop in their newsletters? Teaching in and working with the right partners can be a great credibility booster – don't forget to include their names and logos on your website.
- **Let your students blow your trumpet.** Make sure you ask your clients for feedback, and share positive quotes and testimonials on your website and marketing materials.
- **Share happy pictures of your students** and their newly created work on social media – but don't forget to ask their permission.
- **Show images of your venue and catering**. It might surprise you that your future students are looking to learn in beautiful venues, while consuming great coffee and food. These are a very important part of their overall experience.

Top Tip

Most marketing involves actually educating your potential and existing clients, so it's really easy to promote yourself as a teacher.

What questions or worries do your prospective students have? Share some of your solutions and your expertise in clever and creative ways to reach them, and build your profile, credibility and trust in the process.

Opposite Kara Leigh Ford's membership page builds credibility, profile and trust with free tutorials and tips, great images and a personal intro.

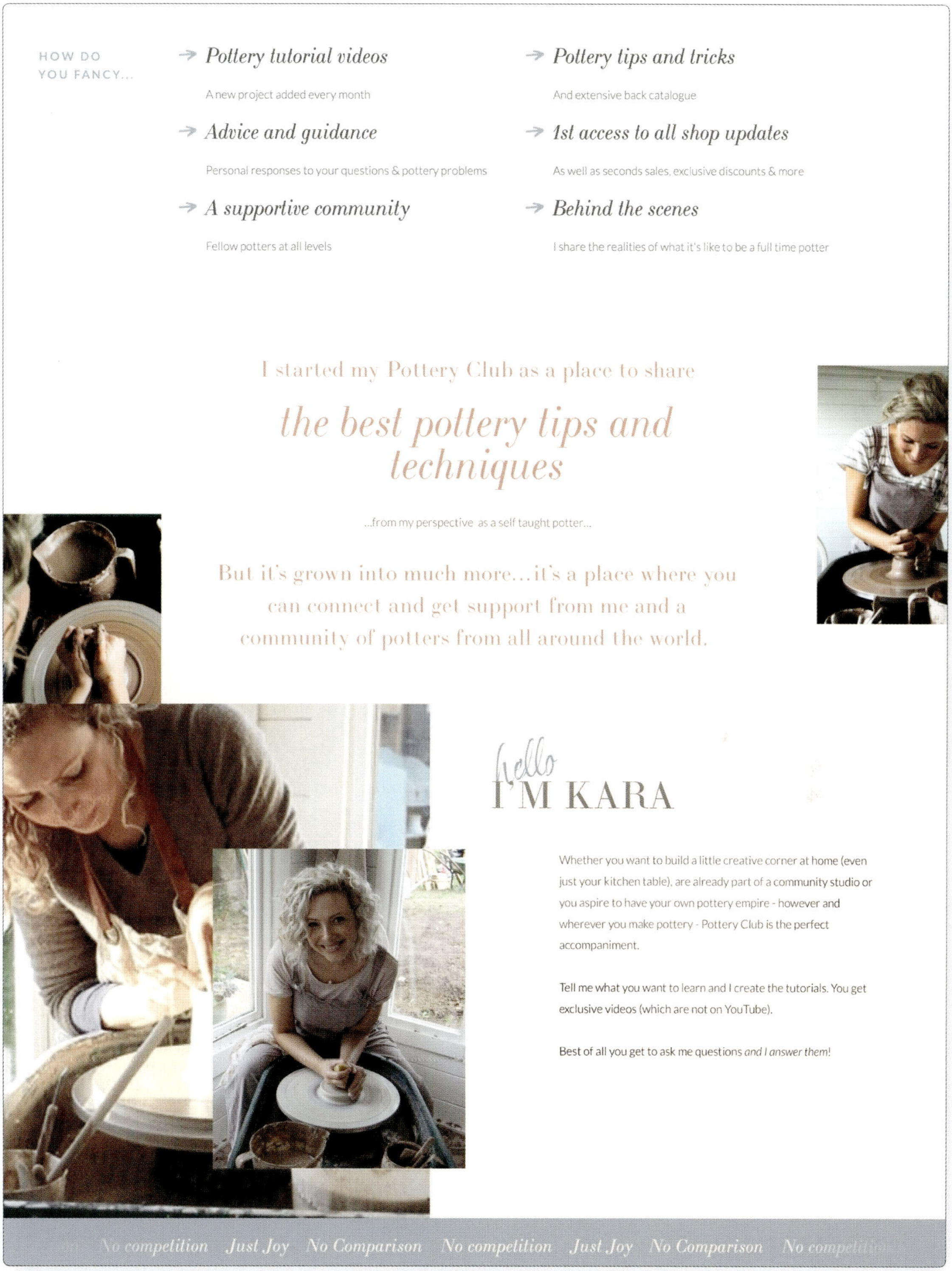
HOW DO YOU FANCY...

- *Pottery tutorial videos*
  A new project added every month
- *Pottery tips and tricks*
  And extensive back catalogue
- *Advice and guidance*
  Personal responses to your questions & pottery problems
- *1st access to all shop updates*
  As well as seconds sales, exclusive discounts & more
- *A supportive community*
  Fellow potters at all levels
- *Behind the scenes*
  I share the realities of what it's like to be a full time potter

I started my Pottery Club as a place to share

the best pottery tips and techniques

...from my perspective as a self taught potter...

But it's grown into much more...it's a place where you can connect and get support from me and a community of potters from all around the world.

hello
I'M KARA

Whether you want to build a little creative corner at home (even just your kitchen table), are already part of a community studio or you aspire to have your own pottery empire - however and wherever you make pottery - Pottery Club is the perfect accompaniment.

Tell me what you want to learn and I create the tutorials. You get exclusive videos (which are not on YouTube).

Best of all you get to ask me questions *and I answer them!*

No competition Just Joy No Comparison No competition Just Joy No Comparison No competition

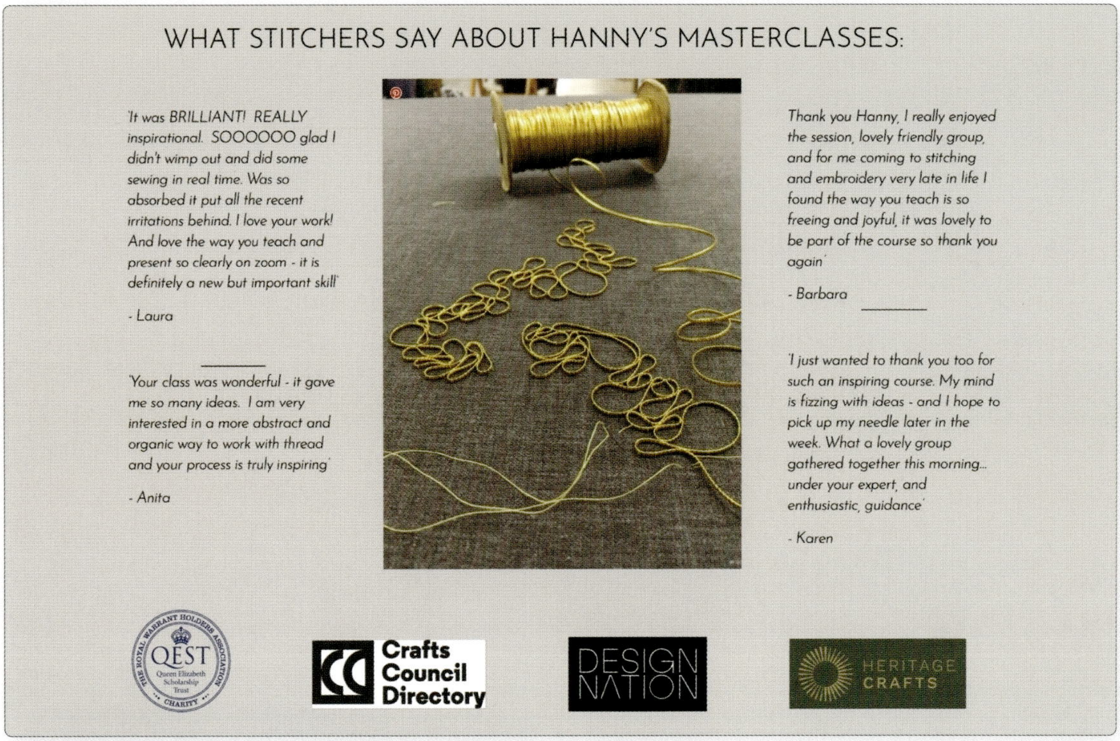

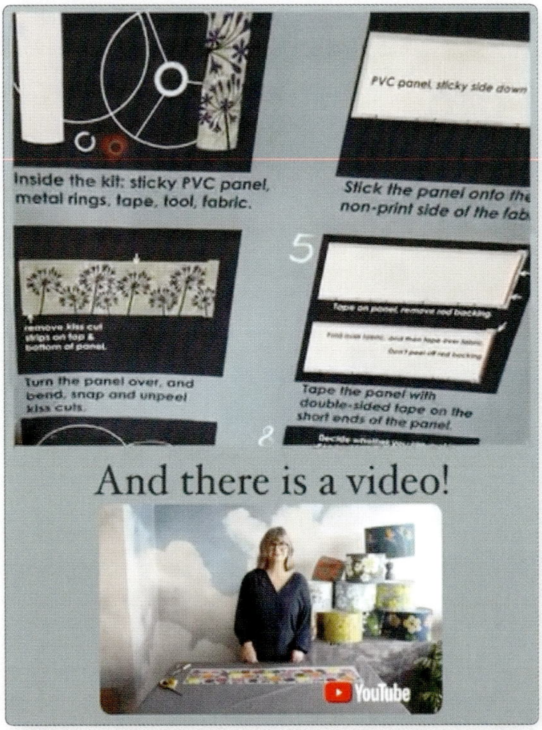

Above Embroiderer Hanny Newton builds the 'know, like and trust' factor by adding student testimonials and partner logos.

Left Alison Bick uses video and shares the extras her students will get as part of her lamp-making course.

Time to pause

Get your notebook and reflect on how you can you build your profile and credibility with your potential ideal students. Identify five specific actions and execute them in the next month. This is a brilliant starting point for any marketing activities that will work.

Fundamental marketing concept 4: AIDA, turning interest into bookings

So you are getting more interest and visitors to your website, but how do you turn that into sales? This is where the four stages of the AIDA funnel framework come in.

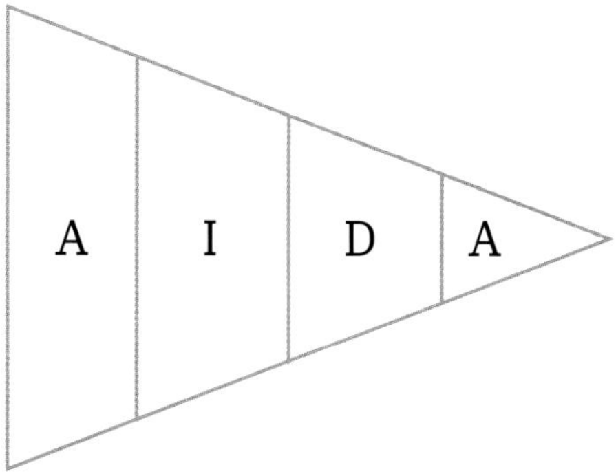

Above The AIDA funnel framework.

When people want to buy something, they go through a series of decisions. This can be a very quick process (impulse buying) or it can take months or years before they commit.

Understanding this buying process will improve your success in converting interest into sales, for both your training and creative work. Before a client decides to purchase, they always have doubts and questions; it's your job as a business owner and marketeer to guide them (patiently, creatively or cheekily) through the four stages of AIDA:

1. **Attention.** 'What is it?' How are you attracting your ideal students to your website (which will be your main point to get sales)? Are you using social media or email to get more traffic? Are your training pages easy to find? Most visitors to your website will just spend a few seconds and if they can't find what they want quickly, they will leave.
2. **Interest.** 'I like it.' How do you get people excited about your course? Are your workshop titles clear? Do your texts and images answer their questions? Can I spend a bit of time on your website to find out more if your training is right for me?
3. **Desire.** 'I want it.' Training is often a very personal, emotional purchase. How can you make that emotional connection with your potential student? Images of happy clients or a great venue, video interviews and client testimonials can add a feeling and emotion to your sales page. It's often this 'special sauce' that will convert your ideal students.
4. **Action.** 'I'll book it.' Do you make it easy for prospective students to sign up and pay? Do you offer a choice of dates, timings, levels or locations? Is your booking and payment system reliable? Can they pay in instalments? Have you displayed your T&Cs clearly?

AIDA is especially important if your course is longer, or more intensive or expensive, because students will have more questions, worries or challenges to overcome.

The real big question that AIDA tackles is, "What stops people booking your training? What do they need to know or believe before they will book?" Get curious about your potential students and the psychology involved in taking part in creative learning.

On the next pages you will see more visual examples of how some of our creative interviewees make it easier for their website visitors to book their training.

Wild Clay Process

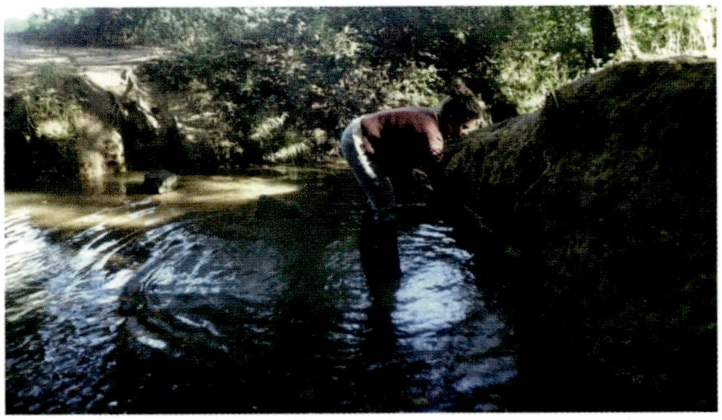

I use wild clay which I dig near my home in Sussex, in the woods. It's Weald Clay here, an iron rich earthenware. This area was known for its medieval potteries and also brick and tile making (still taking place in some areas today).

I dig small amounts of the woodland clay at a time, with minimal impact on the land. I always make offerings before digging: a gesture of reciprocity.

I use 100% wild clay (no commercial clay added) to honour the importance of connecting to place. And because of the rich texture wild clay has when fired. It gives a natural vibrancy, and I leave some surface marks from the making process, traces of the maker's hands.

Pots are fired in the same woods either in an open fire or in a clamp kiln, a temporary kiln structure, leaving no trace when I'm finished. Each piece unique, each connected directly to the land. Echoes of ancient processes.

What does it mean to have an intimate connection to the plants, seasons and land where we find ourselves? There is an embodied process in harvesting and using foraged materials. A rhythm and relationship inherent in the act of making. It's a counterpoint to the pull of our increasingly digitalised and disconnected lifestyles.

> *Know the ways of the ones who take care of you. Introduce yourself. Be accountable as the one who comes asking for life. Ask permission before taking. Abide by the answer. Give thanks for what you have been given. Give a gift, in reciprocity, for what you have taken.*
>
> Robin Wall-Kimmerer from 'Braiding Sweetgrass'

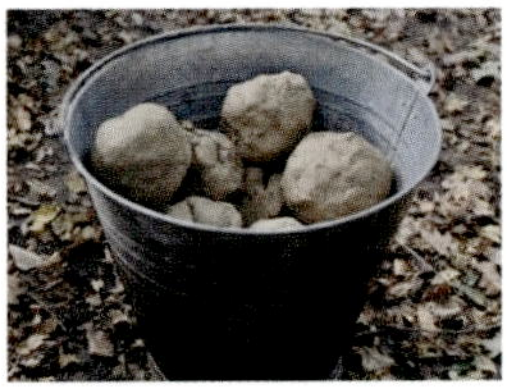

Iron rich clay dug from the Sussex woods.

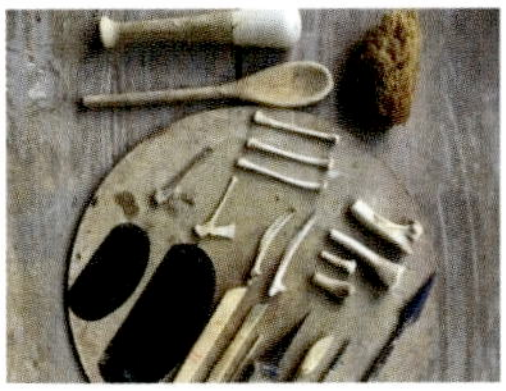

Bone & wood tools. I hand-build all my pieces in the studio (no potters wheel), and evidence of the hand-building process are left visible on the surface of each piece.

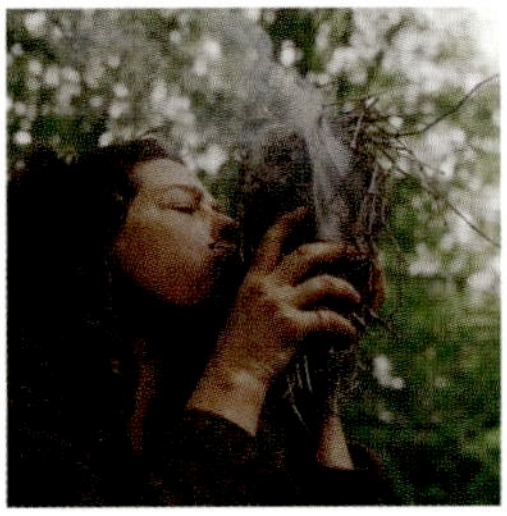

Firings are all done out in the woods, lighting the fire using ancient techniques of flint and steel, catching a small spark on wild clematis bark. Coaxing the fragile ember into a larger blaze, feeding it with local oak wood.

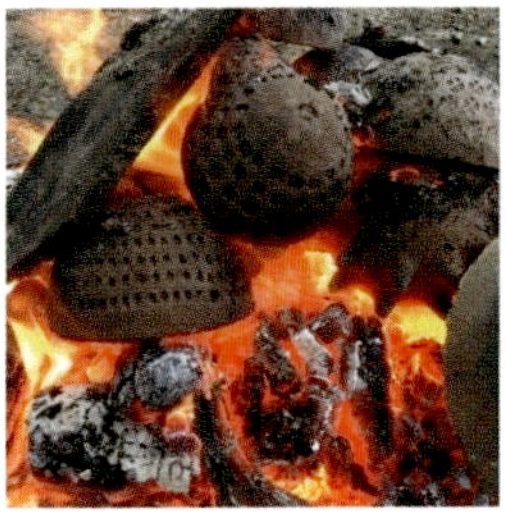

Open firing: a short, fast firing, the original, ancient way. It's alchemy visible as the clay, red hot, transmutes into ceramic.

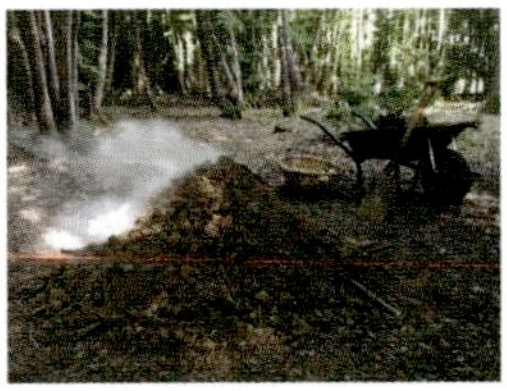

Clamp kiln firing: a temporary structure of wood and earth to insulate the firing. I stay in the woods to watch over it burning for a day and a night.

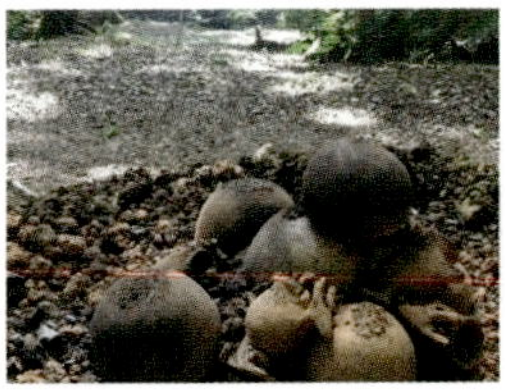

Textures of wild clay, open-fired and clamp kiln-fired. Smoke clouds imprinted on the pot surface from the fire; every pot is unpredictable, every firing a leap of faith.

Above Remember that the best marketing is teaching. Explain your creative processes with beautiful images and text, as shown here on the Native Hands website.

Opposite A strong visual brand with clear categories makes you stand out and makes your website easier to navigate. A great example by Yeshen Venema.

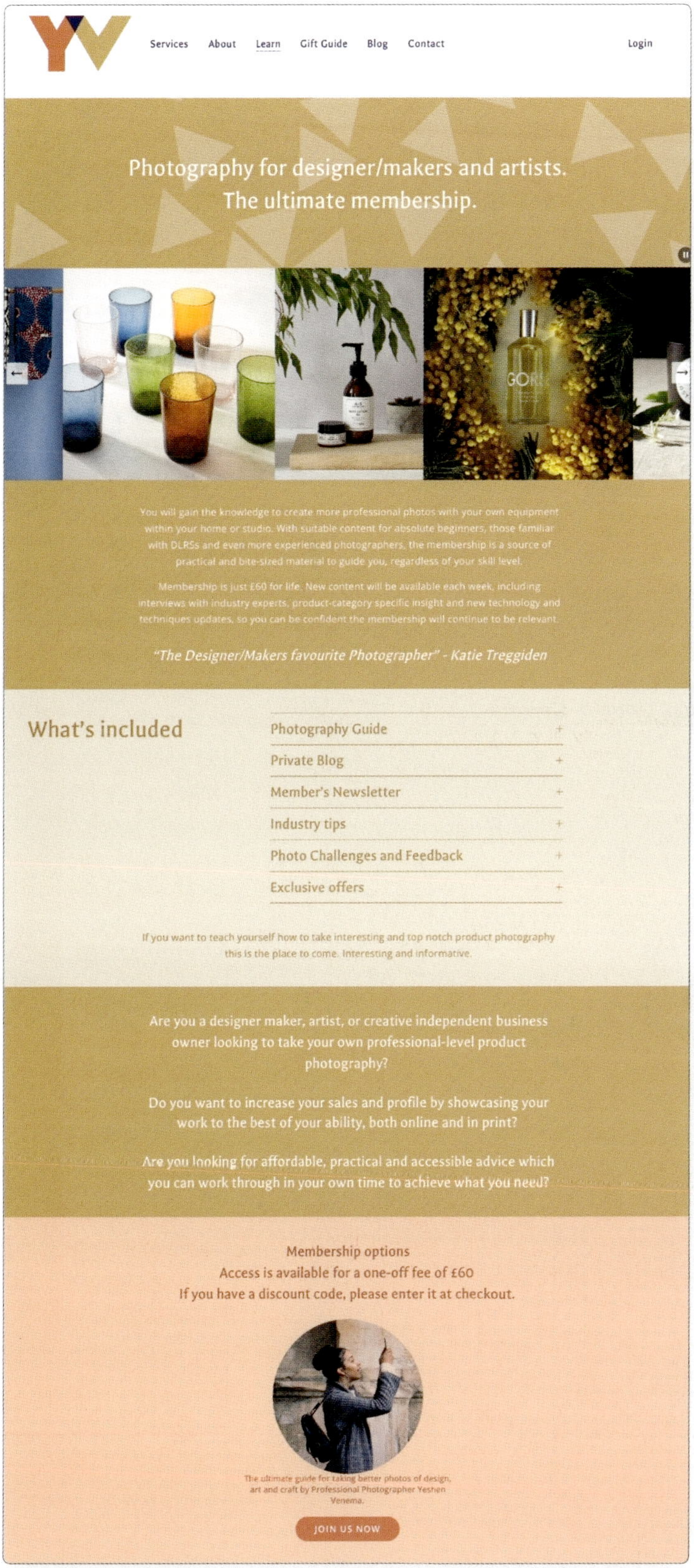

Time to pause

Get your notebook and take time to reflect on the following questions for AIDA:

- **What might stop your potential students from deciding to book your training?**
- **What do you think their specific questions, worries or challenges might be?**
- **What could you include on your website** or in a flyer to make them more confident of your training? Write specific actions down for each stage of AIDA:
  - STAGE 1: Attention. How will your ideal students find you?
  - STAGE 2: Interest. How can you get them excited about your training?
  - STAGE 3: Desire. How can you make a more emotional connection with your potential students?
  - STAGE 4: Action. How can you make it easier to book and pay?
- Look at the actions you identified when you reflected on the 'know, like and trust' factor on p.172, and compare them to your AIDA actions. Do they overlap and support each other?

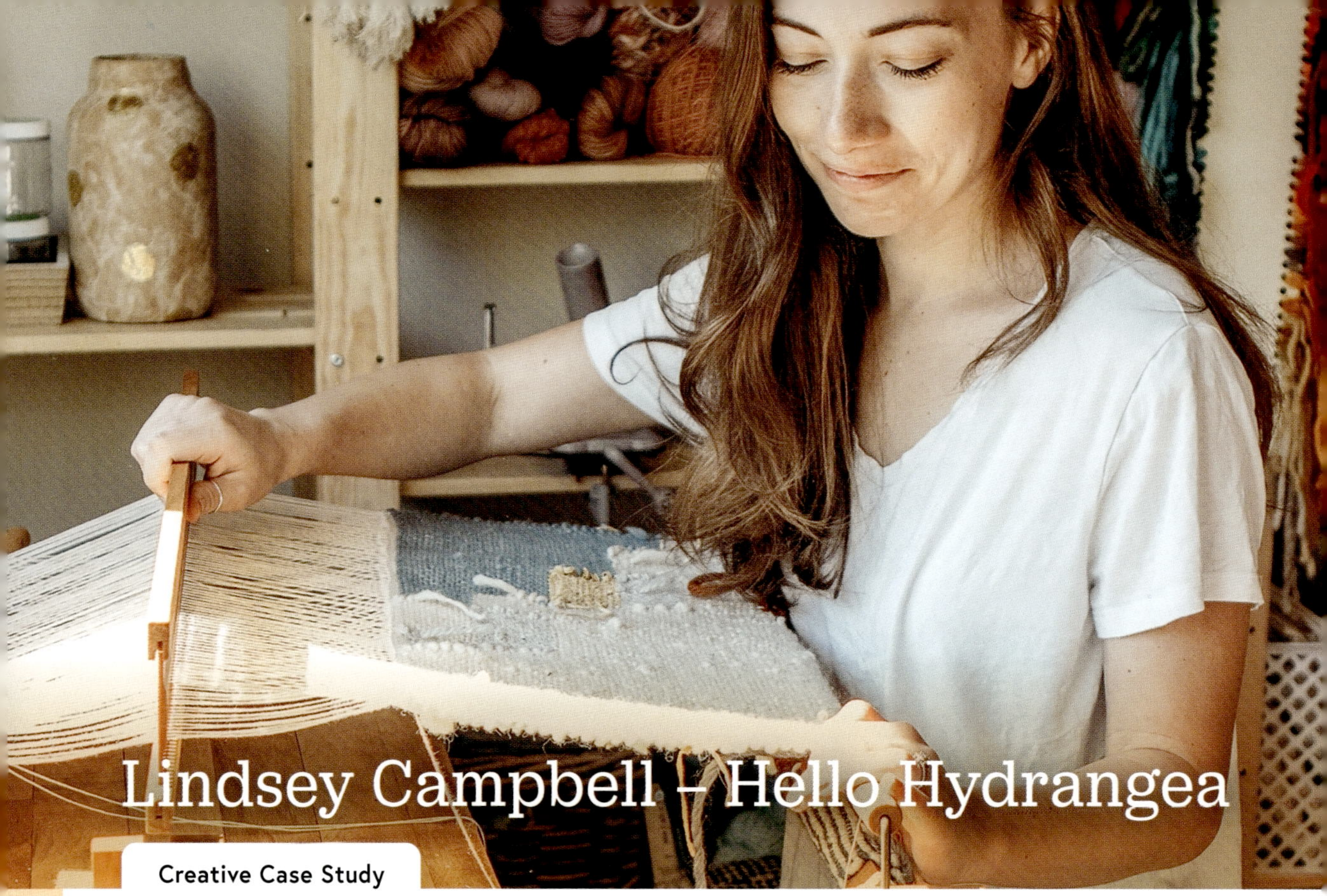

Lindsey Campbell – Hello Hydrangea

Creative Case Study

Lindsey Campbell is the artist and instructor behind Hello Hydrangea, one of the most popular online teachers of weaving and macrame.

She fell in love with weaving as a way to de-stress, and shared her craft projects on her personal blog. Over the years she has created a very successful online training business that focuses on the love of being creative, and makes it as easy as possible for her students to create something beautiful too.

She has worked with brands like Anthropologie, Nordstrom and crafter.com, has written two books on weaving and been featured in many publications. Lindsey lives in the Sonoran Desert in Arizona (USA) with her family and pets.

You can find out more about Lindsey and Hello Hydrangea at www.hellohydrangea.com

How did you get started with weaving?

I started weaving right after college in 2013. I found this old weaving book that looked really cool. I got an old picture frame and I put some thumbtacks in it. I used very cheap crochet yarn and started to weave, and I was literally hooked. I felt like it was magic.

It was the age of blogs and the perfect time to share. I had just got married and moved halfway across the country, and felt a little lost. While I was looking for a job, I threw myself into my blog where I posted photos and craft projects.

After I found a job, I continued to share on my blog as a personal thing. There wasn't a

Above Lindsey at work in her studio.

lot of weaving on the internet back then. I was a young 20-year-old, really interested in this craft, and I couldn't find any modern-looking examples that appealed to the styles and trends that I wanted.

So, I just started experimenting and sharing and I think I was just the right person, at the right place and time. There were only five other weaving accounts on Instagram when I joined, and we found each other across the world. I was invited to join Pinterest. As I had been photographing my work for years for my blog, I now could share all these images on these new social media tools. My images got shared a lot, and it just blew up from there.

I also created a lot. My walls were full of weaving. I opened an Etsy shop because I had so much work! I would put work on Etsy and it would sell within an hour. It was very exciting, but also very tiring, because as an artist, you don't want to recreate your work over and over and become a factory.

In 2016, after my first son was born, we moved back across the country. I left my job, and decided that I wanted to stay at home with him and make my blog full time.

How did you get into teaching?

I always enjoyed sharing what I made with tutorials on my blog with a few tips. It was really natural for me to share the process.

> *'The process to me is as exciting as the final product.'*

I was getting asked for more specific answers. I originally planned to do a short video and take screenshots to share in an e-book, rather than sharing the video itself! By the time I was done, I realised I had created a really cohesive lesson consisting of a PDF e-book with images and links to password-protected videos on Vimeo. But when I put it on Etsy, people were really confused. It was a new concept.

But I was really proud of it, and I had so many more ideas for techniques so I created an intermediate class. And when I shared that, things exploded, I got order after order. It was very exciting and stimulating. I caught this bug of responding to student's questions and creating an online community, and I was making money from it.

> *'That's when I considered myself more a teacher than an artist.'*

I still love making things, but my goal shifted from making things to sell to making things to show people how they can make it themselves. That's what I have been doing since 2017.

I slowly gained confidence to teach in person. I teach in real time at retreats with hundreds of people now. I wrote two books. I just continue to go down this path and I love it.

How has your online teaching evolved?

When I began, I showed six or eight techniques. Then people started asking, 'What can I do with that?'

It's actually really tricky for a beginner to apply a technique, so in 2019 I started my monthly subscription with one project-based tutorial per month. Each project focused on creating a finished product using a different technique or material, learning a different craft skill (weaving, crochet, macrame). People love that!

Online weaving classes have become extremely popular. What makes yours stand out?

My goal with my classes is to make it as easy as possible for students to be creative and playful, so they can jump straight in there to get to the fun part of making. There are so many benefits to creativity: the meditative mindfulness of weaving, the confidence when you finish.

I focus on techniques that beginner weavers probably would never have an opportunity to learn about, like deflected double weave or bordered double twill. You need a really large loom with foot pedals to do that, but I make it bite-size so they can do it on a loom that fits on their lap. I experiment all the time using old techniques in a modern way.

My goal is to make weaving easier for beginners, but in a way that feels professional, with more advanced techniques. I simplify it all, the abbreviations and terms, and make the craft doable; not too long, not overwhelming. My clients are busy; they don't want to spend ages crafting one piece. They want to focus on creating without having to think or research too much.

One of my favourite things with my classes is to see how they then take those techniques and move them up a level. I love weaving and I really truly want to share it with everyone because it brings me so much joy.

What do your online students get?

I have always created e-books because they are so easy to create and so much easier to access for students as they can just save them to their hard drive, so no need to log in. I used to be a graphic designer, so I enjoy making my e-books look beautiful. I want the whole learning process to be enjoyable.

The e-books have the links to the videos, the patterns (if needed), and lots of pictures of the process and the finished piece from the front and back because that helps to understand how to make it. I include a suppliers list with easy-to-find materials so that people across the world can buy them.

Why did you move to a membership format recently?

I created 60 monthly craft projects over the last five years. I recently turned this into a membership vault so they can have access to the entire library.

I changed that partly because it was becoming harder for me to create and publish a project each month. There is so much to do – the editing, script writing, putting together an e-book, doing the marketing. I felt like I was rushing all the time, while so many of my previous projects weren't available for sale anymore.

My new membership will be the best of both worlds – students get immediate access to the entire library of my craft projects so there is much more choice, and I have added other tutorials too, for a monthly fee.

It'll also give me freedom as an artist and busy mum, to decide when I want to put out a new tutorial. It will allow me to work more intuitively, rather than being on a strict schedule.

How do you promote yourself?

I have tried everything, but Instagram and Pinterest are my biggest channels and where I have grown my community [Lindsey has around 163,000 Instagram and 100,000 Pinterest followers].

There's a fine line on social media between being too salesy and being more authentic.

I always get them involved with the creative process through comments and polls. We are doing projects together. I ask for their ideas on what materials to use or how to finish it. When the project is finished, I will put up a more finished Reel and save it as a 'highlight'.

On Pinterest, I have a lot of different boards related to projects, techniques and different ways to use weaving in your home. I don't really have a Pinterest strategy, but I create pins how I like to use Pinterest. It helps that I am often on there, and that I started early on Pinterest.

I have a fairly large email list and send emails every fortnight, as I don't like to bombard people. I see it as a newsletter with inspiration to people who are my friends.

What about your collaborations?

I reached out to crafter.com to ask them if I could create a weaving tutorial for them, and I have now done eight projects with them. I love working with their team, throwing ideas out until we come up with something that works for both of us.

Anthropologie reached out to me in 2015. They wanted to wholesale my actual work, but that just wouldn't have worked for me to deliver those quantities at wholesale prices. It was really hard to say 'no' because I really love their brand and style.

Then they came back and asked if I could design a scarf and they would do all the manufacturing and wholesaling. I went on to do two collections with them. It was a great feeling to walk into one of my favourite stores and see my name on the tags, and to get a design fee. That was very exciting.

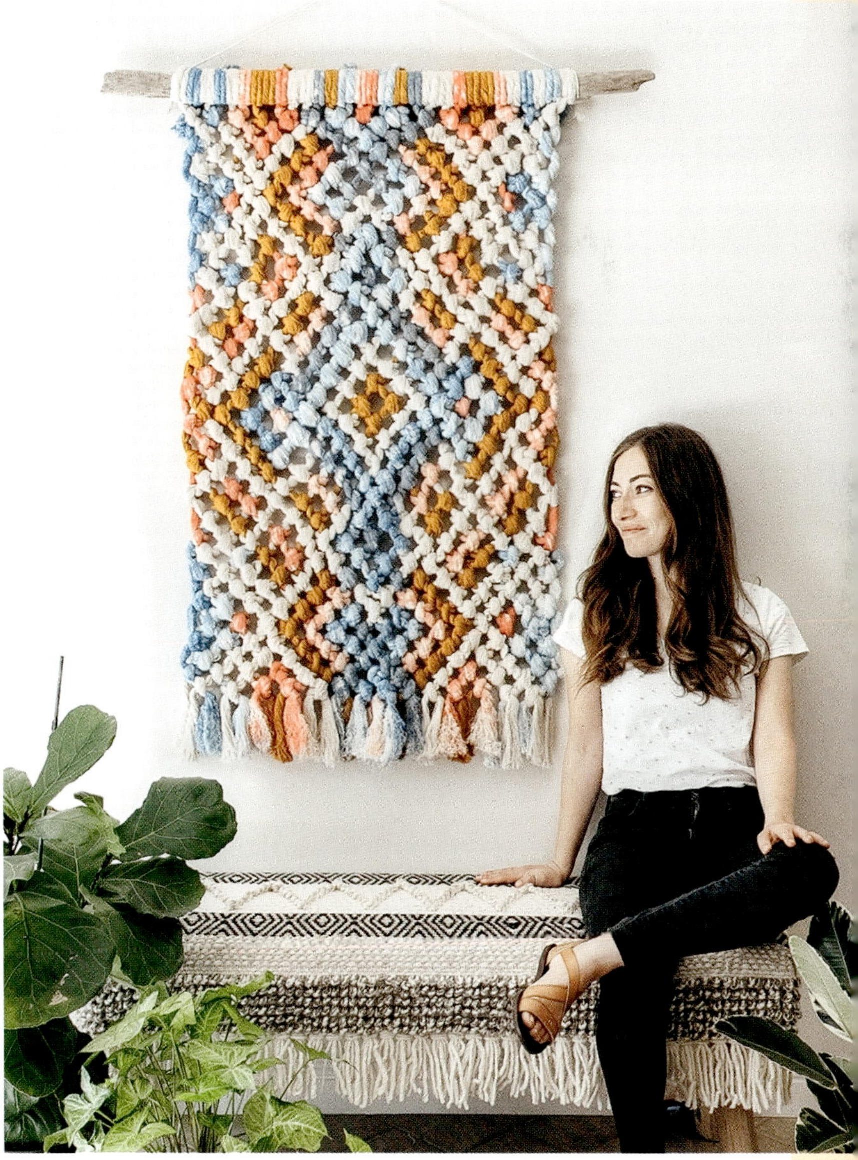

Right Lindsey with one of her larger scale works.

My three personal marketing secrets

I want to share with you three of the most useful marketing approaches that I have used to grow The Design Trust online business school.

1: Get your clients to return: Why repeat business is key

If you want to be financially successful as a creative teacher, **repeat business is essential.** Finding new students takes up a lot of energy, time and, sometimes, money. Getting previous students to come back is often a lot more straightforward.

Why? Because your repeat students already know, like and trust you, and can become your biggest fans. They can do a lot of the marketing for you, as they are more likely to bring friends or recommend you, and they are willing to spend more money too. Also, when students are coming back for more, it's a clear sign that you are doing something right! It's a great compliment and confidence booster too.

I have to admit that when I started The Design Trust, I focused mostly on attracting new clients. I ignored my existing clients and took them for granted ... until I realised that I needed to get to know them, and to find out what else they wanted to learn from me. I started to develop longer-term relationships and stay in touch regularly, especially through email marketing. That was when my training business really started to grow.

My students and their specific questions and challenges are one of the biggest sources of inspiration for new courses, topics and formats. It's they who inspire me to keep improving, and to develop better and more creative training.

Checklist: How to get more repeat business

Do you know about the 80/20 rule also known as the Pareto principle? It's a fascinating phenomenon that states that 80 per cent of outcomes come from 20 per cent of the causes. This means that a healthy business will get 80 per cent of its sales from 20 per cent of its customers. A small group of repeat clients will bring a large chunk of your income.

- ☐ **Look through your sales system** and identify the students who account for the top 20 per cent of your bookings. Segment them as a separate group in your email or client management system, and get to know them better. Do you notice any similarities between them?
- ☐ **Find out what and how your best students want to learn.** Do they want more specialist or advanced courses, or more individual advice and support? What format will work best for them? Do a targeted survey (see Chapter 3) or invite your top students to an online Q&A to find out more about what they want to learn next, and what their specific challenges are.

'I try to introduce a new class every year. It keeps me on my toes, as I need to learn new techniques or improve my skills. But it also gives me new classes to take back to my regular students.'
Rob Jones, textiles expert

Right Japanese textiles expert Rob Jones.

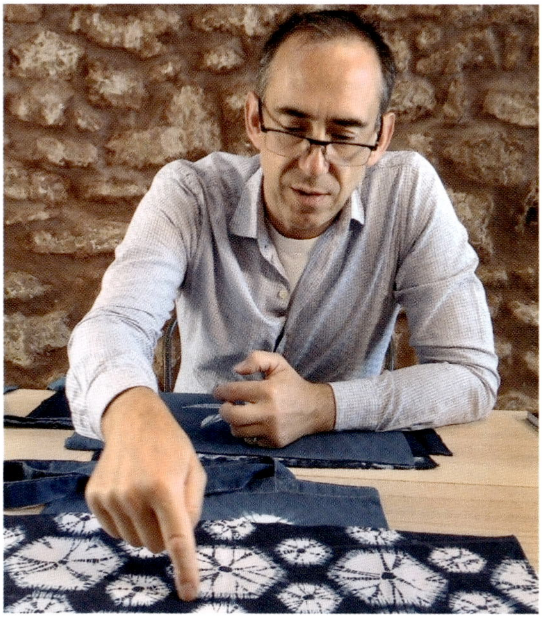

- ☐ **Provide a 'learning pathway'** with a variety of shorter training options that can be purchased individually or as a package. Offering a series of shorter, complementary options is a great way to minimise overwhelm and offer flexibility.
- ☐ **Can you improve the experience for first timers?** They are more likely to return if they enjoy your training and it matches their expectations. Think about your onboarding process, managing expectations and encouraging them throughout the training.
- ☐ **Reward their loyalty.** Think beyond offering discounts – give students exclusive access to you, and promote them in your emails and social media.
- ☐ **Stay in touch to build relationships.** Make sure you send a follow-up email immediately after the training. Add students to your mailing list, and segment them for more personalised follow-up emails. Do you regularly send them useful creative tips or let them know about relevant events? Can they join an online community?

Time to pause

Identify your 'top 20 per cent' clients, then get your notebook and consider the following questions:

- **Who are they?** What are their similarities? Look at their gender, where they live, how much they spend in a year or lifetime and which training they have done with you. You can often use downloadable reports or databases with information about your clients via accountancy or payment software such as Stripe or Shopify.
- **Add them to your email list** and create a segment by giving them a specific tag as an existing or top student.
- **How can you get to know them better** and encourage more repeat business? Identify three specific actions.

2: Make your workshop giftable

People love to receive creative workshops as gifts. Over the last few years, gift experiences have become very popular, and are often easier to sell than your creative products.

However, not all workshops make good gifts. Shorter, half-day or one-day creative workshops aimed at beginners are perfect – they give the student a taster, and are more likely to be at the right price point for gifts. Longer courses are less likely to be gifted, due to price, but you could offer gift vouchers to be redeemed against the higher cost.

Creative workshops are very popular as gifts within families or friend groups, and the gift giver often likes to come too. Is it easy for two or more people to book your workshop at once? Do you offer a discount for pairs or groups? Can you offer private parties for an even more personalised experience?

> ### Top Tip
>
> Giftable workshops are often themed. Think about offering specialist half-day workshops around Valentine's Day, Christmas and family occasions – examples include Christmas wreath-making, or a workshop for couples to make their own wedding rings.

In the run-up to Christmas you could offer gift vouchers for spring workshops. January to March is often a quiet time for product sales, so it's ideal for running courses. Promoting your workshops with downloadable gift vouchers up until Christmas Eve can generate some last-minute Christmas sales.

Below Alison Bick suggests buying her small-group workshops as gifts and encourages self-gifting.

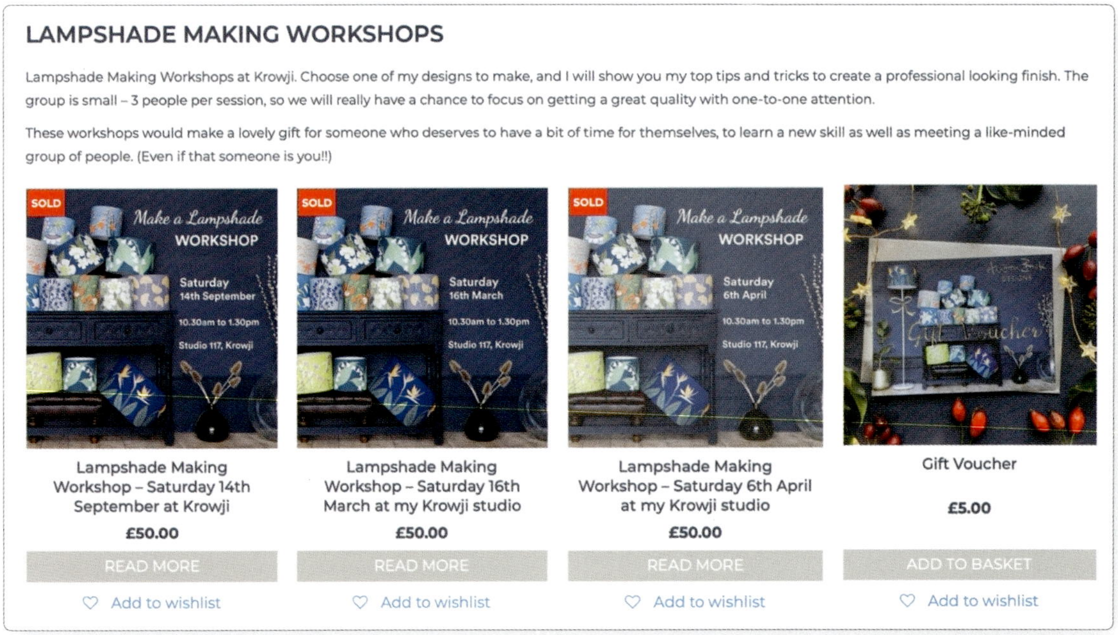

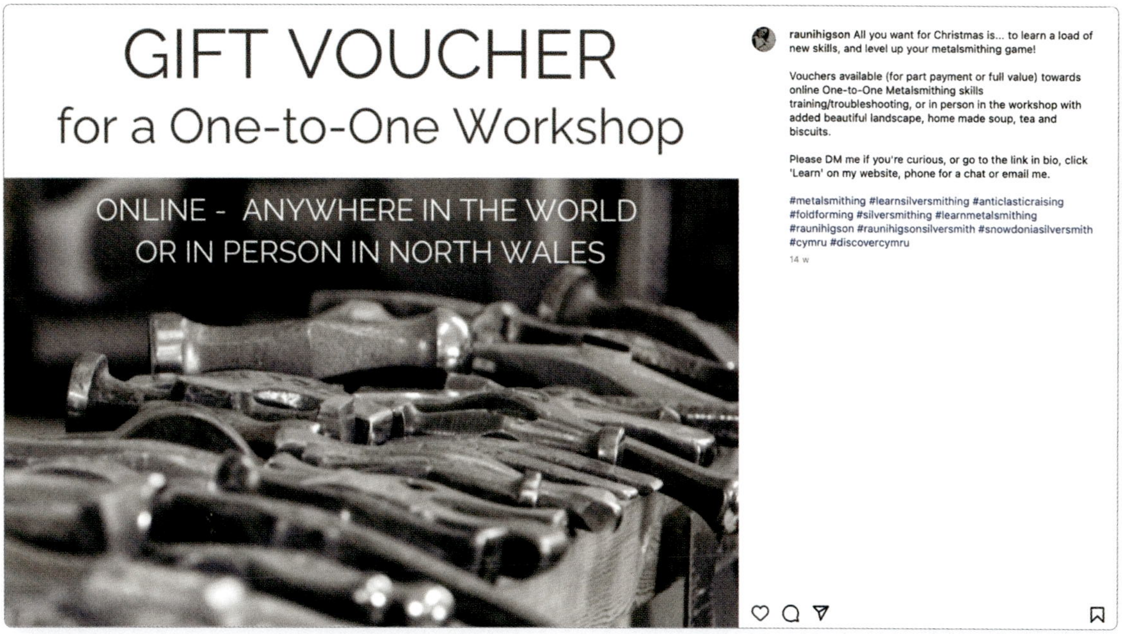

Above Silversmith Rauni Higson promotes gift vouchers on social media.

How to make your training giftable

- **Is it easy to purchase your workshop as a gift?** Does your website software make it easy to buy for someone else? Can you offer gift vouchers? You might need to add some plugins to enable this, depending on which platform you use.
- **Make sure you use gift-related keywords** in your titles and texts (we will look at keywords in more detail later in this chapter). They will boost your search results and ranking, particularly on online marketplaces like Not On The High Street or Etsy.
- **Can you make your gift voucher more unique and tangible?** It can be a bit boring to get an email or printout. Think about sending a leaflet, a small gift, or some course materials or tools with your voucher, especially if your training is more expensive.

Time to pause

Get your notebook and take time to reflect on the following questions:

- **Does your creative training naturally lend itself to gifting?** If not, would you want to make some adjustments? Think about seasonal themes, length, venue or timing of your workshops. How could you encourage two people to join together? Package your training differently. For example, Catherine Lucktaylor talks in her Creative Case Study about offering a 'Raku Experience', which includes two hours of raku firing and Cornish cream tea (p.68).
- **Can you provide gift vouchers online?**
- **Write down three specific actions** to make your training more giftable.

3: Launch early

Launching and selling your training before you have even finished your lesson plan might sound crazy, but I have done this a few times and it works brilliantly at different levels.

In early March 2020, we were ready to start rolling out The Design Trust's spring online course programme. Then COVID-19 hit. Within a week we realised that the existing programme wouldn't be sufficient given the peculiar circumstances, and I decided to create a brand new, three-part online course: *How to Teach Your Creative Skills Online*. I planned the content within a few hours, wrote the sales copy and published it online, without having created any of the content.

It became one of our most successful launches, and one of the most popular online courses I have ever run. For a few of the case studies in this book that was the catalyst to start teaching online. It's also the seed that grew into this book.

The benefits of launching early

- **Seize the moment!** When COVID-19 hit, we created our course as a solution to a big problem faced by many of our clients: they could no longer sell products or in-person training. We received so much feedback from students who told us that this course kept their businesses (and lives) going, because they managed to launch an online offer quickly too.
- **It's a great way to find out if your course idea is viable** before you spend too much time, money and energy on it. Can you get at least 10 people to sign up to your workshop or course before you put in all the effort to create it? Offer your training

Below Alison Bick offers short small-group workshops from her studio in Cornwall.

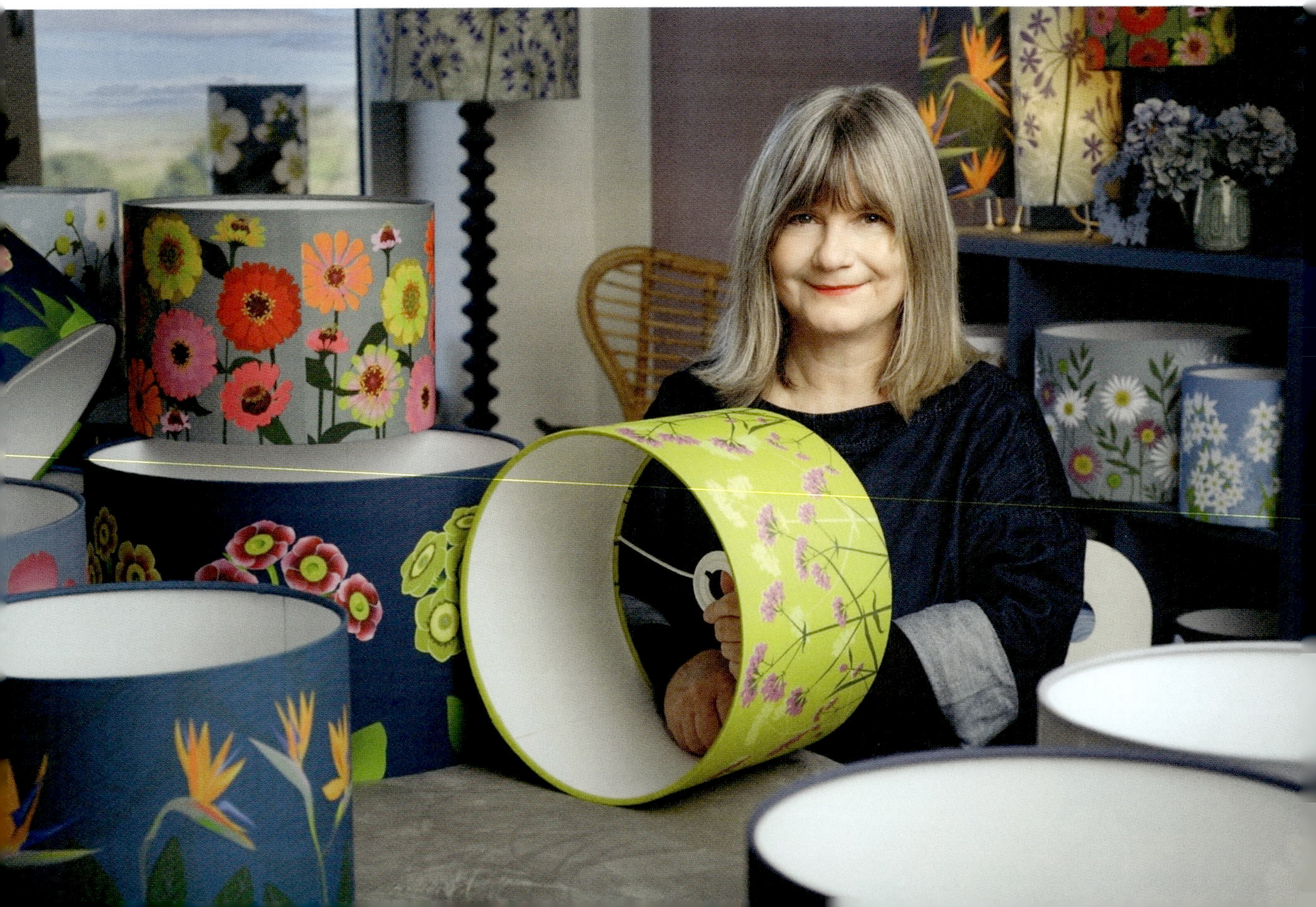

as a pre-order at a highly discounted rate to see if there is enough interest and help your cashflow, or offer a trial run (see p.117).

- **A launch date gives you a deadline** and accountability. Many people need external deadlines to make things happen! Are you a perfectionist and procrastinator? Then launching and getting paid before you are entirely ready might just be the push that you need to make it happen.
- **Creative workshops are often seasonal.** People are more eager to learn new skills in January or September, so these are good months to launch. For example, our creative business planning workshops are especially popular at the start of a new year. If you have a seasonal workshop idea, launch it at the right time or you might need to wait an entire year before the opportunity comes around again.
- **It's better for your cash flow.** Creating online courses especially can take up a lot of time and money, particularly if you hire professionals. By getting participants to commit and pay upfront you can raise the funds that you need to make your training happen.

How to launch early

- **Create a pre-order sales page** that includes key details on your own website or a platform like Eventbrite. Be clear that it's a pilot or pre-order and offer a generous discount. Have a very transparent cancellation policy in case you do not get enough sign-ups. Then start promoting it! This doesn't take up a lot of time, but it will tell you if there is enough interest to make it viable.
- **Launch a minimal viable product.** One of the big mistakes many creative teachers make is to overcomplicate their training and add far too much content. Limit yourself with a short online or in-person workshop and see if you get any bookings, and build an audience before launching longer courses.
- **Create an online 'drip feed' course:** You can often release content over a period of time. This can be done automatically, either scheduled (once a week on Monday) or triggered by an action of the student, such as finishing a task. This allows you to work on content after students have started the training. This can work well for longer online courses, allowing you to create and adapt your content based on your students' experiences in real time.

Time to pause

Get your notebook and take time to reflect:

- **How might launching earlier help you?** Look at the various reasons mentioned here and identify your own.
- **When would you launch?** Why is that a good time, for you and for your students?
- **What are the steps you need to take to launch early?** Write down specific actions in your notebook.

We will look at launching much more extensively in the next chapter.

Before we look at creating or improving your website and sales pages, let's hear from top art agent Lilla Rogers about her online courses.

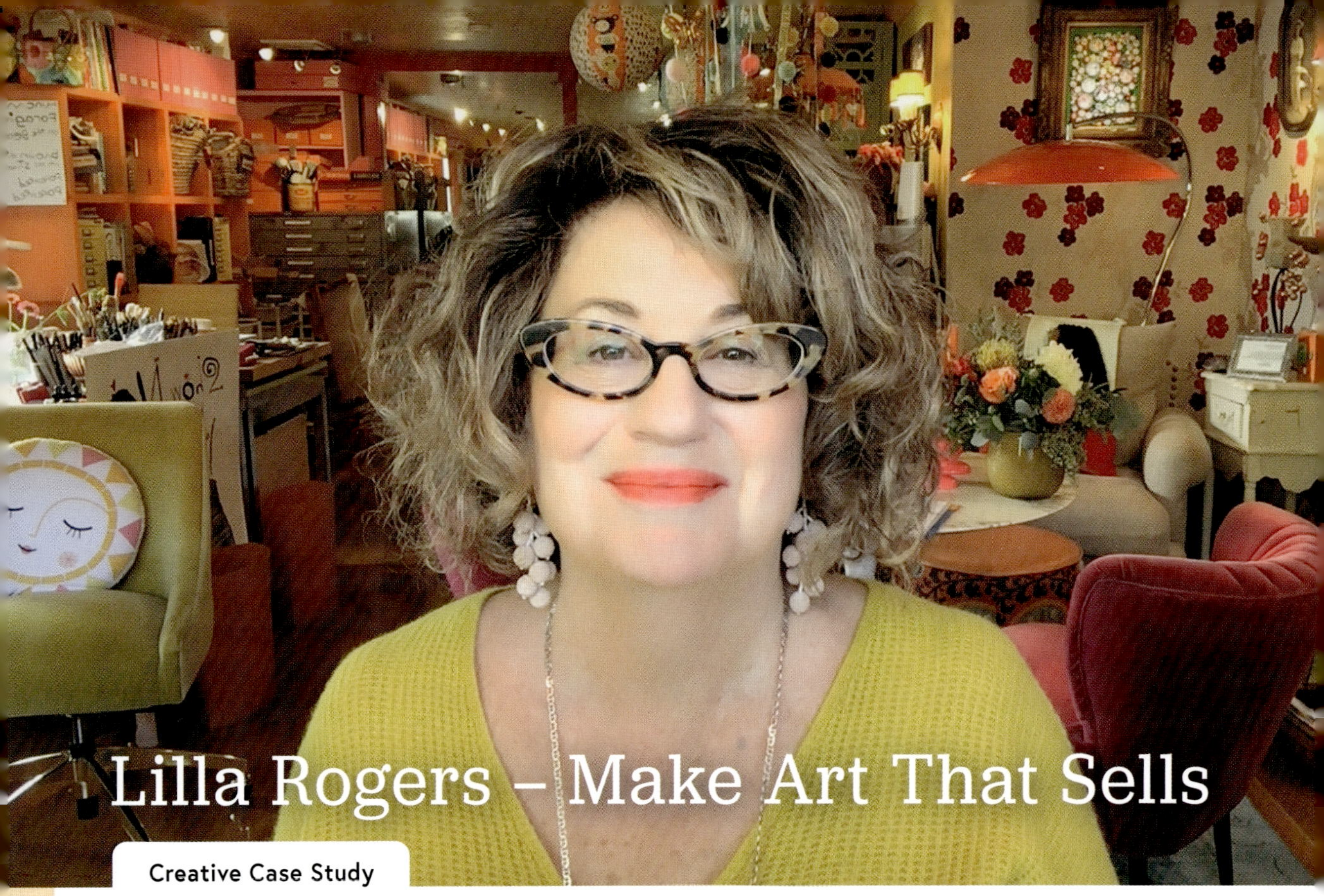

Lilla Rogers – Make Art That Sells

Creative Case Study

Lilla Rogers is a prominent figure in the world of illustration and art licensing. She is a renowned art agent, educator, illustrator, author and advocate for artists. Lilla has established herself as a leader in the industry through her agency, Lilla Rogers Studio, which represents a diverse roster of talented artists worldwide. In addition, Lilla is co-founder of Make Art That Sells (MATS), a leading course site where she helps elevate the creative community with courses ranging from *Money Bad Ass* to *Illustrating Children's Books*.

Aside from her work as an agent, Lilla Rogers is also an accomplished author and speaker. She has written books on art and creativity, sharing insights and advice to aspiring artists. Lilla has conducted workshops and given talks around the globe, inspiring and empowering artists to pursue their passions and build successful creative careers.

Since 2013, Lilla has partnered with best-selling author Beth Kempton as MATS to offer live and pre-recorded online courses for illustrators. MATS offers a wide range of online courses, from toy design to hand-lettering and business skills. To date, MATS has taught over 30,000 students from more than 100 countries and has a 300,000 strong community.

Being an illustrator, a teacher and an agent gives Lilla the unique ability to help artists grow: she fully understands the creative process and how to nurture each artist, but also what is required to make it professionally. You can find more details about Lilla Rogers and MATS on the website makeartthatsells.com

Above Lilla Rogers on camera during one of her online courses.

How did you start teaching?

My first job was in the 1970s, when I had just come out of art school, teaching middle school kids around 10 to 13 years old. I did it for three years, five days a week, seven periods a day, and it was great. Many of them had behavioural problems and didn't want to sit in a classroom. I had to learn to be creative in order to engage them, and I still use that experience in my teaching today.

How did you start teaching online?

Ten years ago, I was approached by Beth to create an 'e-course'. Our first course was called *Make Art That Sells* and it had 500 students right away. In large part, that was because I had personal success as an illustrator and credibility as an agent: for students to get their work seen by an agent, and potentially get signed, is a huge benefit in taking my classes.

I love teaching. I find it intellectually challenging. I love dreaming up a course: I work on it for months, and I often think about how students are going to love these exercises. For me, it's like creating a recipe for a lettering course or a children's book course, but I don't get to bake it. I give the recipe to my students, and then I can't wait to see what they are going to do with it!

My career has always been based on what I'm passionate about and what I love. I have two metrics for my courses: What does my community need to succeed? And what would be really fun for me to create? What do I enjoy sitting down for months for, and love to create content for in unique ways?

What and how do you teach online?

In my teaching, I will always encourage women and marginalised people to honour their own voice, specialness and uniqueness. I always wonder how I can bring that out in them. One thing I always tell them is 'respect your own brain'. I give them techniques and creative challenges, and then I say 'be you with a vengeance!'

We decide 6–12 months in advance which courses I want to teach, so I have plenty of time to luxuriate in creating content, both written and video. Over the last 11 years I've written about 25 courses.

I teach live and recorded online courses that are often one to three months long. The first week of each month always starts with a 'mini assignment', something easy and small that's unintimidating. I give them inspiring, downloadable visuals to work from – maybe oddities from my vintage collection from antique shops. That way, they're not copying current imagery, and they're putting their own unique take on it.

Then they go on to a more complicated assignment for the following week, but the cool part is that the work they've done for the mini assignment has broken the ice. They are already well on their way. I tell them that I trick you into doing your best work.

> *'Deadlines are creatives' best friends. It's a huge benefit for the students to have assignment deadlines and an online gallery for their work. It motivates them to get it done!'*

In many of my courses, I review some of the work from the gallery, selecting the best. I pick the best work because I want the people who work the hardest to be rewarded. I choose the work with my agent hat on and select the pieces that I would feel comfortable sending to my clients, because I want my students to learn what professional work looks like.

As an agent, I get around a thousand portfolio submissions each year, but I found that many don't show the right work to attract paying gigs in illustration markets. I want them to show how their art will look on a mug, or in a picture book, or on a puzzle. I want them to show what they're good at and excited about. I designed my courses so that my students can create work that they can put in their portfolio to help them get real paying jobs.

My students often also have access to pre-recorded lessons with my creative or design advice, or interviews with professional illustrators. After the course ends, they have access for six months for the live courses, and until the end of January the following year for self-paced courses. Reminders are sent before all the classrooms close, so students can keep any 'downloadables' and videos they wish to keep. They may also ask questions on the Facebook groups, which remain open indefinitely.

How do you come up with course ideas?

The genesis of an idea often comes from my students asking me for a course, or what I see the need for in the current climate. What's lucrative for illustrators these days? Who's buying illustration? As an agent, I have daily access to what kind of illustration is being commissioned, including styles that are in demand.

Every morning, I sit in the pink chair in my studio, drinking coffee from the cup my son made, looking at my garden. I journal, write or sketch and, sometimes, a course idea comes up. Today I just actually spent two hours writing a whole plan for a really cool course.

'With anything you do, you have to love it. If you're not excited, it will show and it will be a dud. But you also have to be savvy – it needs to have commercial viability.'

How do you create the courses?

I think deeply about the structure, then I work on a plan. What is the goal? How will the student get there? How will they best succeed? Then I write. I photograph. I make worksheets.

If there is pre-recorded content, I do that, for example if I demonstrate a technique. Lately, I've been doing live art demonstrations, which the students love. One of my students said, 'It's like looking over the teacher's shoulder while they demonstrate!'

I work hard to engage people online. It needs to be like a TV show: very watchable, content-rich, visually engaging. I use a lot of cliffhangers – in other words, I create suspense as to what they will get in the next video, the next download or the next lesson.

I have a brilliant team that helps to put it all together. Jennie Stevenson does newsletters and social media, and gathers testimonials and student success stories. Becky McCarthy is the manager and does a massive amount of organisation and planning. Louise Gale manages the classroom, Facebook groups and customer service. There's website management and a million other things. The team is amazing at what they do, which allows me to create and teach courses.

Each course has mini and monthly assignments with visual worksheets, workbooks and videos, which our amazing graphic designer creates. Our *My Kid Book Pitch* course has a 123-page PDF workbook!

How has your online teaching evolved?

Changes in technology have just been fabulous. It's put more tools in my toolkit.

Live Zoom chat has made it so much easier to interact. I love breakout rooms where students can meet fellow artists and discuss assignments. Lately, for demonstrating, I have a set up for overhead shots for both flat lays and overhead videos where I can use my iPhone!

What advice do you have for somebody starting to teach online?

Make sure that you're really excited about what you want to teach. You will need to sink your teeth into something for many months when you're creating content. So, whenever it gets tough, whether it's a technical issue or how to do a graphic, whatever it might be for you, don't give up. Find a solution, find support, get advice.

Only write content when you're excited. You don't need to be the most knowledgeable in your field. You need to have something you want to teach and the ability to put your heart and soul into it. Then, find a way to make it happen. I wrote my first MATS course at a cafe after my weekly workouts!

Remember what you are excited about teaching and think about how you can help others who are earlier along in the path than you. What would you have loved to know when you started out? Add not just technique but the psychological aspect – teach in a way that is surprising, fresh and visually exciting. Make it yours.

'Make what you love, and there will be people who want it. Don't do something because you think, "Everybody's teaching this, I better get into that". If there's a sense of desperation, that comes through. If there's a sense of joy, that comes through and that's what attracts others to your product.'

What advice have you got for anybody starting to teach?

I became an illustrator at 29, an agent at 39, wrote my book at 57 and started my online business at 59. I am 69 and a half now and will be teaching lettering in France this year.

Take risks. Stay healthy and be open to being inspired!

Below The colourful MATS branding and website really stands out and reflects Lilla and her target audience of illustrators.

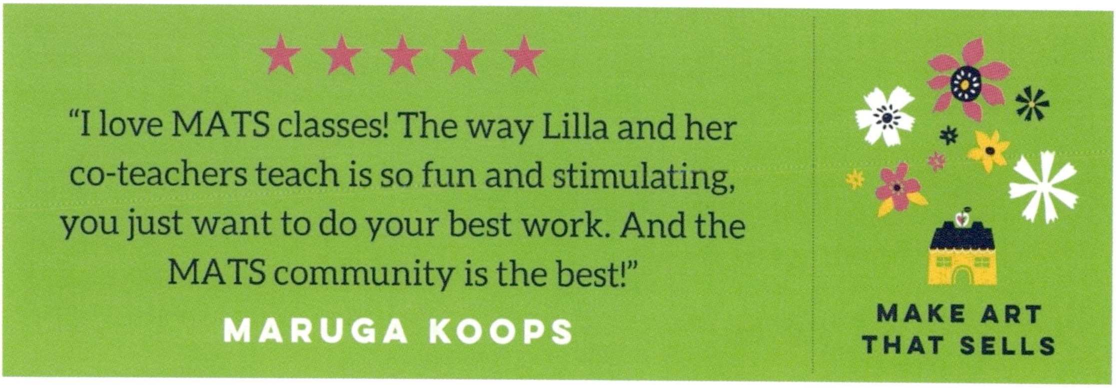

Your website: The hub of your marketing and sales

Fact: as a professional creative trainer, you must have a website.

A website will **make promoting yourself and your training so much easier** and will help you with administration and payments.

It's where your potential students will get to know, like and trust you. If you don't have a website, this will seriously affect your credibility.

In this section, we will go straight into a big, juicy exercise to make your website shine with the right software and branding.

In the next chapter we will look at how to drive traffic to your website.

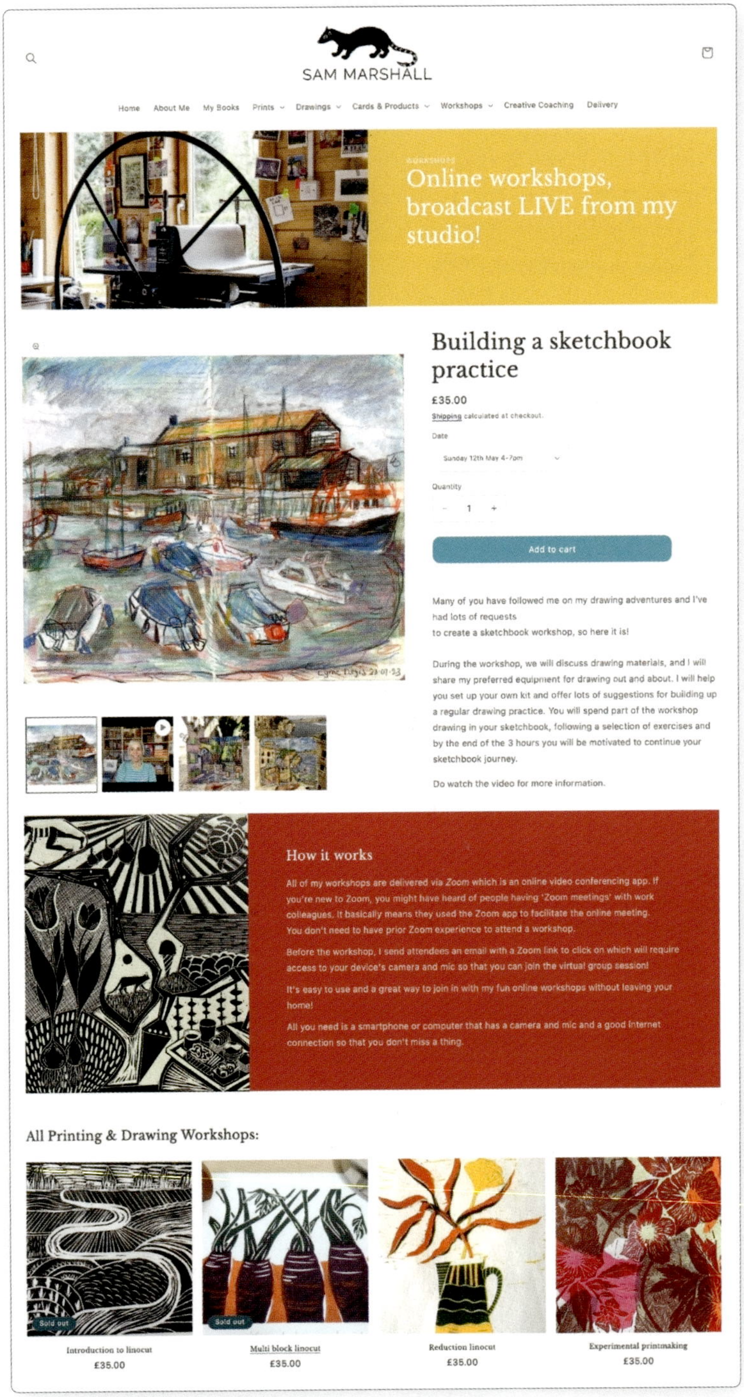

Right Example of a great visual, on-brand and detailed sales page of an online workshop by Sam Marshall.

Creative Exercise

Make your website shine

1 Decide on your website software
Ideally, your training will be hosted on your own website.

There are different website options available:

- At the most basic level: add your training to your website and use platforms such as Eventbrite or craftcourses.com for additional marketing, and the booking and payment process. Or use your existing website software, e.g., Squarespace Courses or Shopify, to present and sell your training. Create password-protected training pages so only your students can access them.
- **Once you become more serious** about teaching online then you might decide to use more specialist online training or membership software, such as Teachable, Ruzuku or Thinkific. If you have a WordPress website, find out which learning management system (LMS) plugins are available, e.g., LifterLMS, MemberPress or WishList Member.
- Once you have established yourself as **an online creative teacher with pre-recorded training,** then you can work with specialist platforms such as Udemy, Skillshare or Domestika who offer commissioning fees to their teachers.

You can find software suggestions in the Resources section at the end of this book.

Below Esté MacLeod's illustrative style is a key part of her course branding.

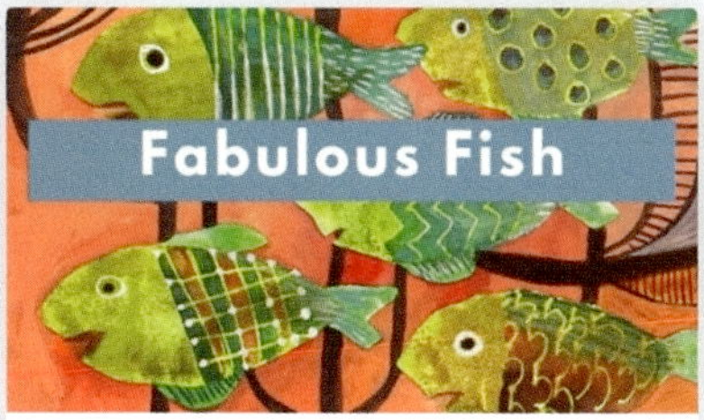

Fabulous Fish

Prepare to be inspired. Fabulous Fish consists of nine projects. Esté will demonstrate ways to help you to create dynamic fish drawings using her Creative Leap method, these will be turned into interesting artworks in watercolour and acrylic inks. Suitable for all levels of experience, this course is just the ticket to get your creative juices flowing.

£47.00 GBP

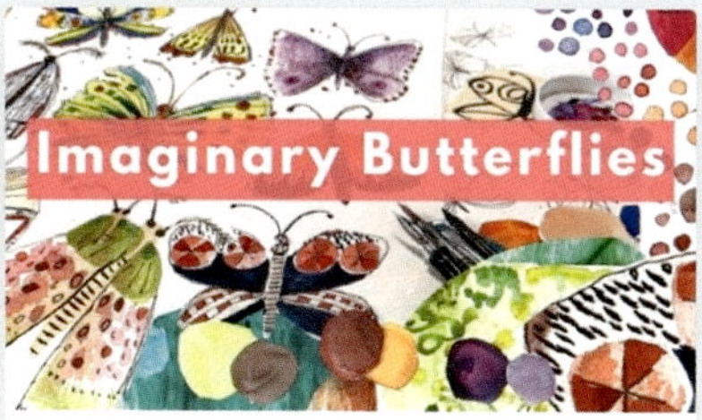

Imaginary Butterflies

This mini-course consists of four video lessons where I will show you how to create interesting layered butterflies with numbers as drawing anchor points and dynamic watercolour techniques using #coloricombo colours as focus.

£47.00 GBP

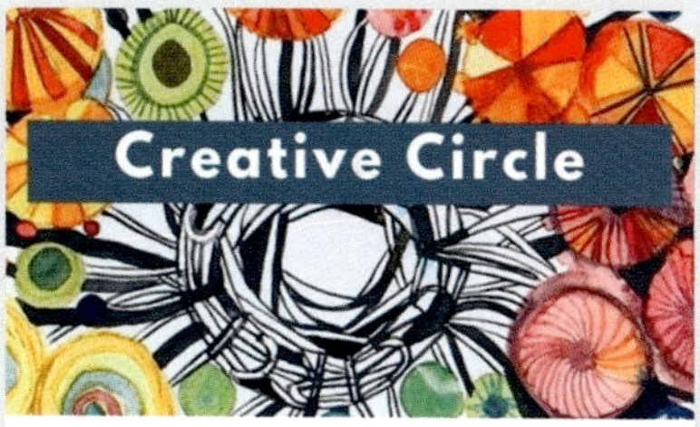

Creative Circle

Make time for art, get your creative juices flowing and enjoy exploring possibilities starting with a simple circle. Over the period of five days I will show you different ways to create your own circular wreath incorporating your unique shapes, drawing style and painted marks.

£47.00 GBP

2 Create a brand

Wikipedia defines branding as 'a name, term, design, symbol or any other feature that distinguishes one seller's goods or service from those of other sellers.'[7]

A good brand creates that all-important first impression, and will attract, engage and emotionally connect with your ideal students. The purpose of branding is to show visually what you want to be known for, who your ideal clients are, and to position you in the market, distinctively different from your competitors.

Develop your brand by focusing on **what you want to be known for** (refer to the niche description you have been creating), and then deliberately choose brand elements that will enhance your brand values, and use them consistently. These elements include:

- **What are the right colours for your brand?** (E.g., earthy tones are often used for sustainable or nature-inspired businesses.) For a fresh and lighter look, use whites, creams or pastels. Take colour symbolism and associations into account too. Choose between three and five brand colours to provide some choice.
- **What are the right typefaces?** (E.g., traditional or contemporary; handwritten or stylised.) I recommend that you choose two or three fonts – one for titles and subheadings, and one for the main copy text. Keep it simple to make your website readable and accessible. There are some excellent online resources for pairing typefaces, E.g., monotype.com or fontjoy.com.

Below Native Hands, who offer outdoor craft courses, have a very strong home page.

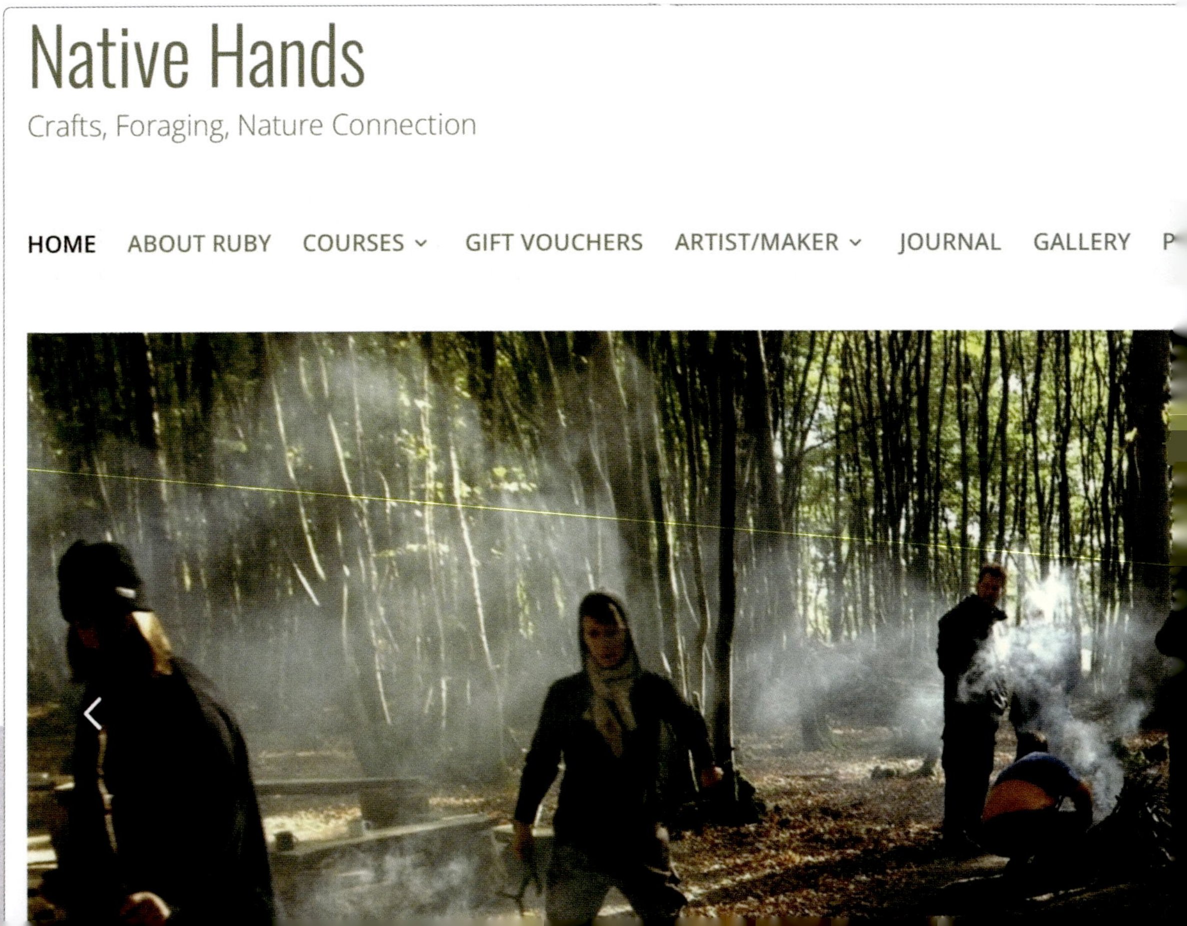

- **Images and video** are a very important visual part of your branding, as they quickly convey the tone and feeling of your site. In your images or video, think about lighting, focus and backgrounds. Show images of you teaching, your students, the venue, works in progress and end results.

Top Tip

Remember that the branding for your creative training needs to sit within the branding you use for your product business.

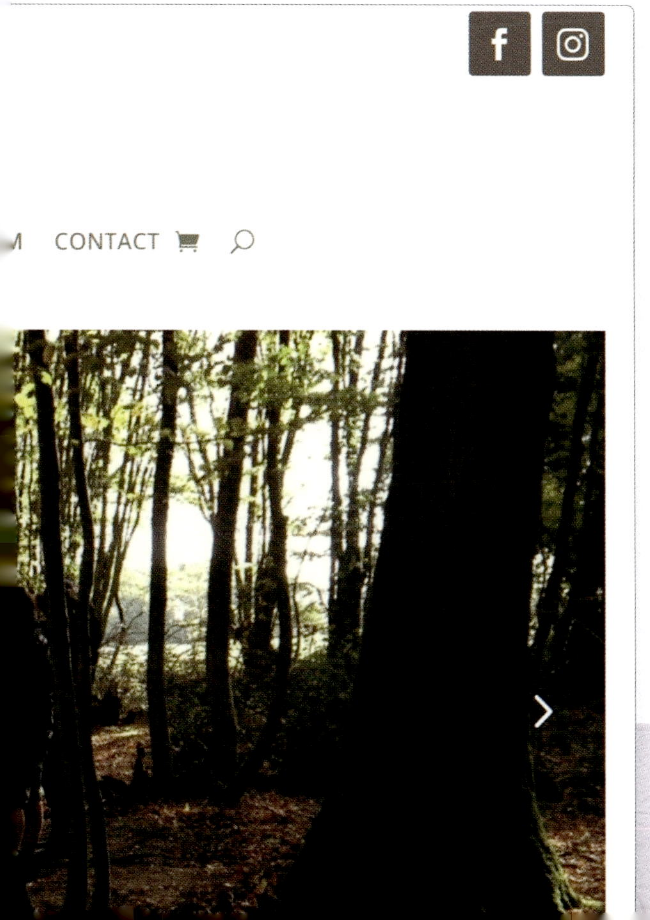

Return to the notes you made about your motivations and values, and your chosen niche. Look at your competitors' websites and branding. Get your notebook and consider the following questions:

- **Start with your niche:** what do you want to be known for and who are your ideal students. What's the first impression you want to create? What's the emotion or feeling you want to convey? A colourful site or something more organised or quiet? Try to pin down the feeling of your site, and then look for the colours, fonts and kind of images that work best with that. Create mood boards and review competitors' websites for creative brand inspiration.
- **Decide if you can do this yourself,** trade services with professionals you know, or if you need to invest in a professional graphic designer, website developer or photographer. This is one of the best investments you can make to take your training business to the next level.
- How can your brand (including colours, images and video) **support the 'know, like and trust' factor** (p.172) and AIDA (p.175)? Identify specific improvements.
- **How can you be more consistent with your branding?** Everything from your website to your social media, flyers, emails and downloadable content should look consistent so that people start to recognise your brand and associate it with your values. Write down specific actions in your notebook and make time to implement them.

3 Design the home page and individual training pages

You will need to have a dedicated space for your training on your website.

This might be one page with all the training details and clickable links (to external sites) to book your training, or a secondary home page leading to individual sales pages for each training you offer.

Use categorisation on your home page to make it easier to find your training.

In your notebook, start to sketch out the structure and layout of your training pages:

- **How many training pages do you need?** Do you want a single training page with links to external payment options? Or will you use images with links to individual sale pages? (See Rob Jones' home page opposite.)
- **Are there subcategories for different levels** or types of clients (e.g., beginners versus advanced, online versus in person) or topics?
- **If you offer a broad range,** will you organise and sort your training by date, topic, location or skill level?
- **What will your training home page look like?** Sketch it in your notebook. What information and images do you need on this page, and on your individual training pages?
- **Where will you include important recurring information,** e.g., information about you, how to book, your T&Cs, payment terms and cancellation policy? Can you make this more user-friendly, e.g., put together an FAQ page?

Look at how other creative trainers have structured and designed their sales pages. Go into detail about what you want or need to incorporate. Start drafting the text and identify some great images to include.

Top Tip

Consider how you name your categories. Using keywords contributes to your SEO, e.g., 'linocut courses' rather than 'training' or 'workshop' will help people to find you. We will look more at SEO and keywords later in this chapter.

Opposite (top) Rob Jones' website is easy to navigate with clear categories and visuals for each Japanese textiles workshop.

Opposite (bottom) Yeshen Venema's website clearly offers different types of training.

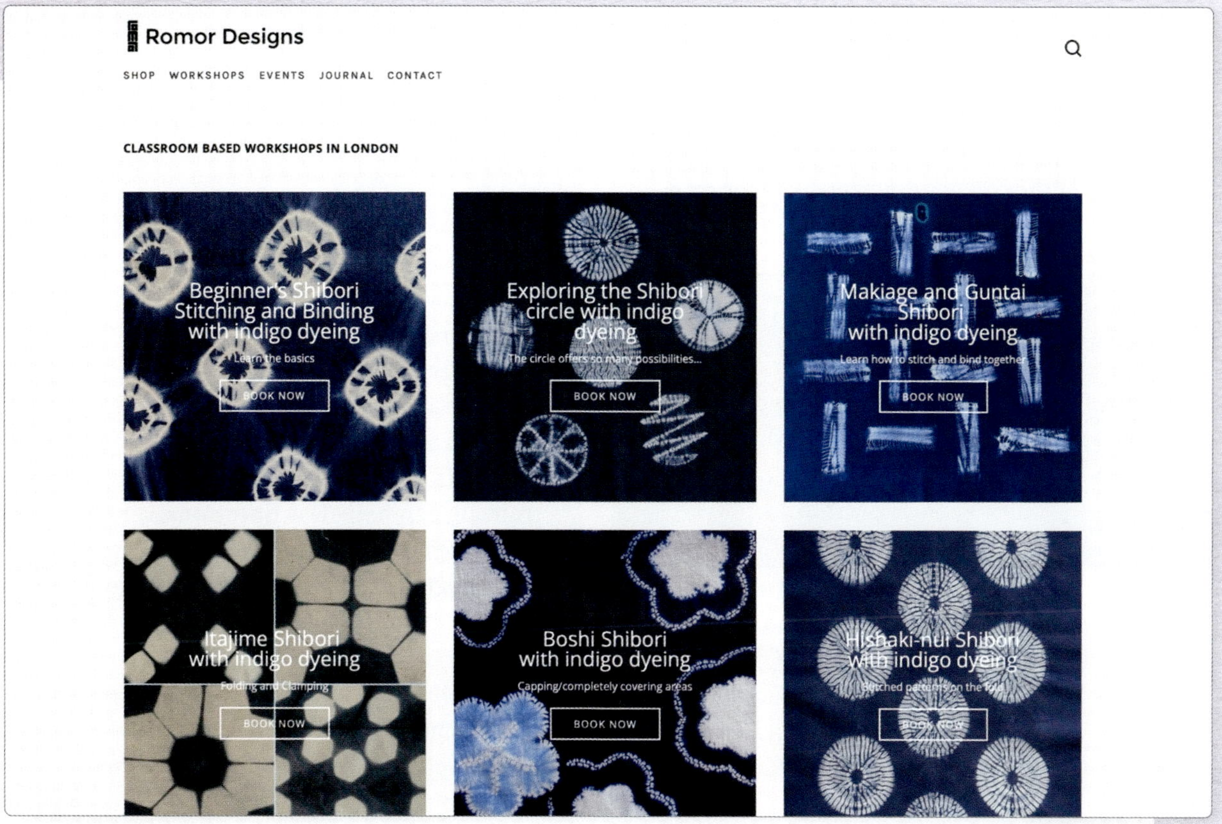
Romor Designs
SHOP WORKSHOPS EVENTS JOURNAL CONTACT
CLASSROOM BASED WORKSHOPS IN LONDON
Beginner's Shibori Stitching and Binding with indigo dyeing
Learn the basics
BOOK NOW
Exploring the Shibori circle with indigo dyeing
The circle offers so many possibilities...
BOOK NOW
Makiage and Guntai Shibori with indigo dyeing
Learn how to stitch and bind together
BOOK NOW
Itajime Shibori with indigo dyeing
Folding and Clamping
BOOK NOW
Boshi Shibori with indigo dyeing
Capping/completely covering areas
BOOK NOW
Hishaki-nui Shibori with indigo dyeing
Stitched patterns on the fold
BOOK NOW

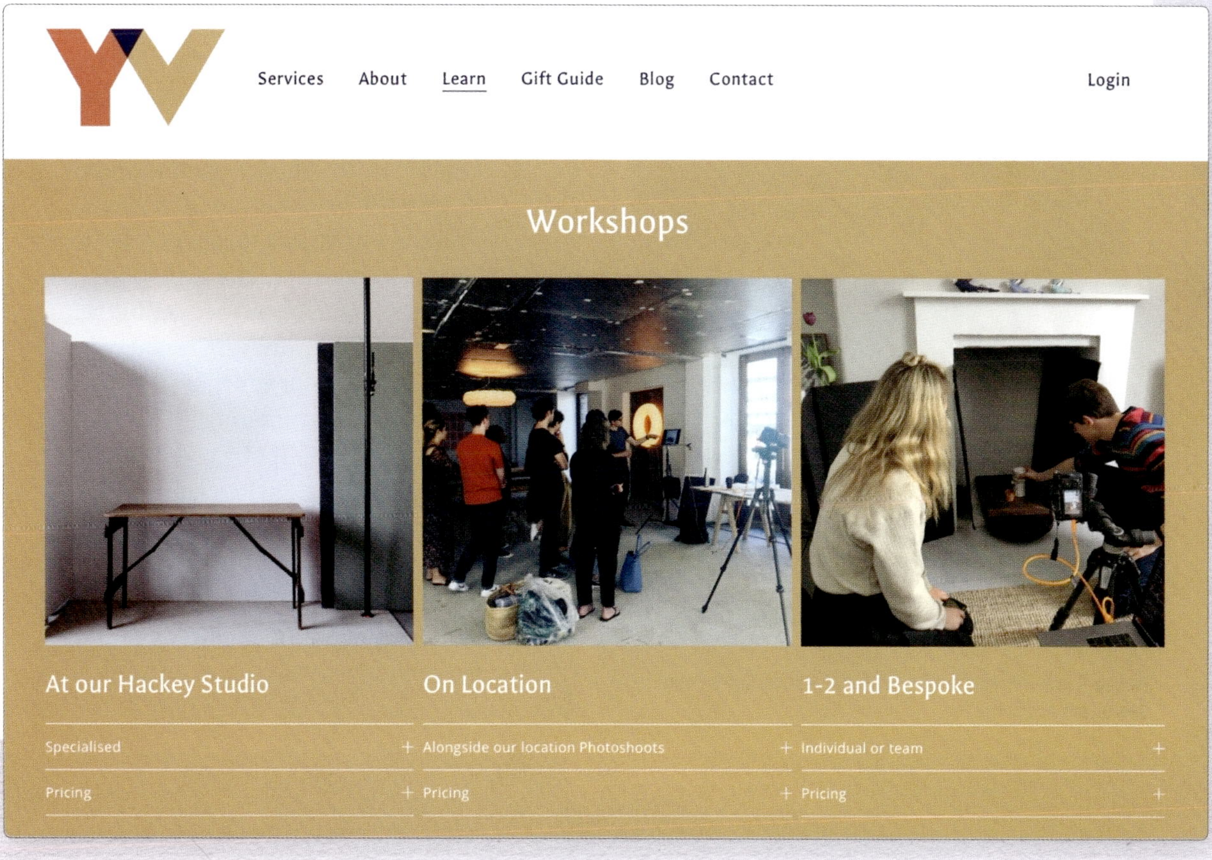
Services About Learn Gift Guide Blog Contact
Login
Workshops
At our Hackey Studio
Specialised
Pricing
On Location
Alongside our location Photoshoots
Pricing
1-2 and Bespoke
Individual or team
Pricing

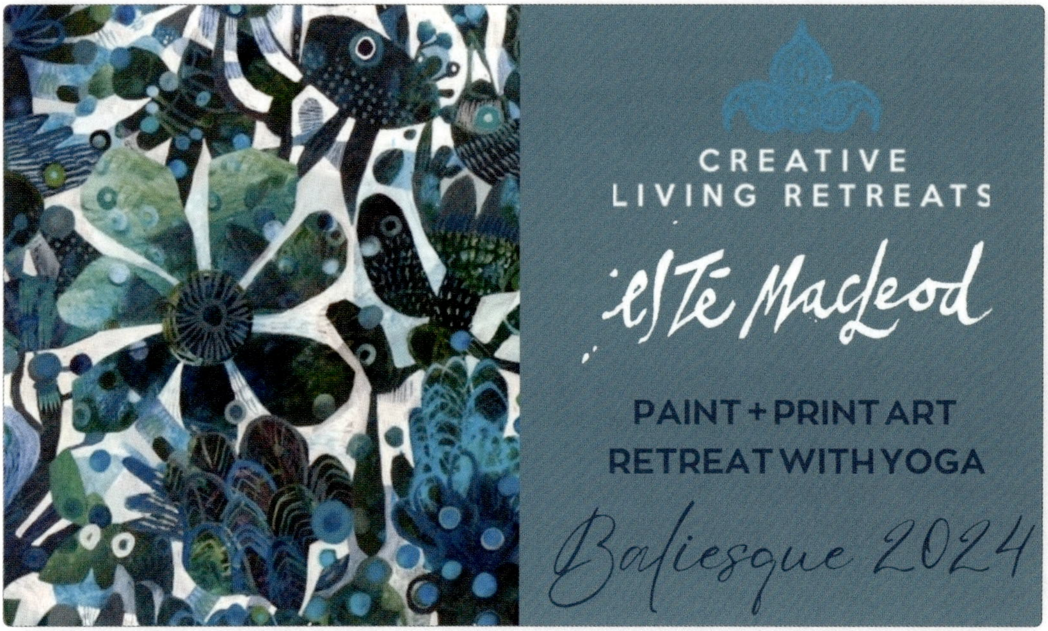

Above Esté MacLeod uses gorgeous brand colours and imagery on her sales pages.

Checklist: Before you publish your sales page

☐ **Check how your page looks** on different devices (e.g., mobile, tablet and computer screens) and browsers (e.g., Chrome or Firefox). You might be surprised how the layout changes, and you might spot some design errors.

☐ **Do a test booking.** Make sure your booking and payment system works, and booking and paying for your training is easy.

- Is it properly integrated with your payment systems?
- Do discount codes work?
- Does your student get an automatic confirmation email and invoice?

We have been using blogging strategically for many years at The Design Trust. It's a long-term, but very effective strategy to get more online visitors who are looking for what you offer.

Over time we have created an archive of more than 100 blog posts, and have included some free video training around popular topics. My regular blog writing encourages consistently high visitor numbers – potential clients find us through search engines, then stay longer for the learning. This helps them to know, like and trust us as a training business.

5 Other website pages to consider

There are two other important pages on your website:

- **Your 'About Me' page:** often this is the most-read page after your home page, and crucial in building the 'know, like and trust' factor. It's best to have one 'About Me' page that covers both your training and your creative products. Include an overview of the topics that you teach and that interest you, highlights of your teaching career so far, any relevant experience or accreditation, and previous venues/partners you have worked with. You can add more specific detail about your training experience on the sales page.
- **Blog posts** are very useful for building your profile and credibility, but also to get found online. Write posts that answer specific student questions and include keywords to increase the chance that potential students will find you.

Below A great example of a blog post on the popular search topic of ceramic books by Kara Leigh Ford.

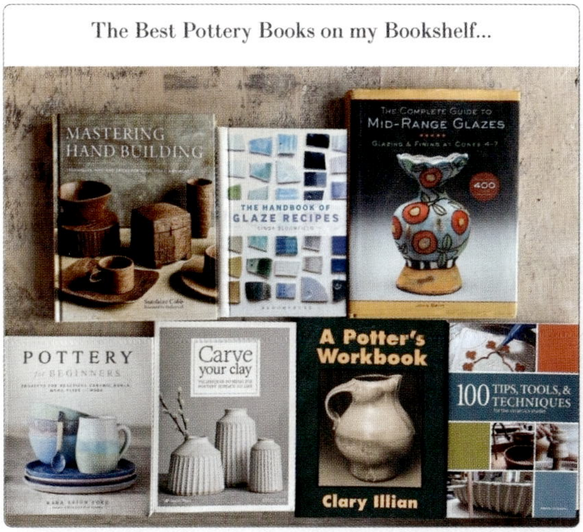

Time to pause

Get your notebook and take time to reflect on the following questions:

- **Does your 'About Me' page reflect both your creative and teaching knowledge and experience?** Is it clear what you want to be known for and who your ideal customers are? Review the 'About Me' pages of other creative teachers and competitors for inspiration.
- **Could you use blogging more strategically** to attract your ideal students? Do you like writing and sharing your expertise, or would you prefer to record videos around relevant topics? You can use different formats and approaches to reflect your interests, values and brand. Review how other creative teachers use blogging creatively and strategically.
- **Start to create a list of your students' questions or worries.** Identify 5–10 specific topics that you can use for blog posts, video content, social media posts or email marketing. Dedicate a page of your notebook to creating a content plan. In the next few pages we will discuss this more.

Now your branding and website are ready to be shared. In the final part of this chapter we will focus on driving traffic to your new or updated website.

Driving traffic to your website

You have been working hard on creating a brand and website that lets your new and existing students know, like and trust you, and make bookings easily. The next step is to **get more of the right visitors to your website** to become students.

In this final part we will focus on the four most important activities to drive traffic to your website: SEO, email marketing, social media and more 'traditional' marketing.

> *'Most of my clients will come through free marketing – Instagram, word of mouth, my newsletter and my website listings. If there are last-minute places available, I'll do a workshop-specific newsletter.*
>
> *Some of my clients come from Eventbrite – people search there for "creative workshop in Bristol", as I've included those keywords. I've also included keywords such as "weaving", "creative colour" and "making cushions", which get results.*
>
> *But the best marketing is actually a poster in the shop window of the space I hire. It's in a lovely location with great footfall and people just spot it. Good old posters still work!'*
>
> **Angie Parker,** textile artist

FAQ: What's the best way to drive traffic?

Many creatives focus on social media to drive traffic, but this isn't necessarily the most effective way to attract visitors and bookings.

So, what works?

- **If you don't have many students or customers yet**, then focus on keywords and SEO, especially on your websites and social media. Also offer free video training.
- **If you have an existing client base already**, then email marketing is by far the most effective way to get bookings, and to stay in touch with your potential and existing students.

Traffic driving tool 1: SEO and keywords

SEO is a very effective marketing tool to drive traffic to your website, especially if you:

- have very few clients and email contacts;
- promote your online courses on marketplaces such as Skillshare, Domestika and Eventbrite;
- need to promote your in-person courses locally;
- use social media to promote your training and include hashtags and keywords to get found, especially Pinterest, LinkedIn and YouTube.

By using keywords in the right places on your website and social media, it will be more likely that **potential students will find your website**.

The first step for many students to find the right training is to search online. Millions of us do this every day – with a little bit of work on your website SEO you can see more organic traffic coming to your website. And you don't have to pay to get results.

Creative Exercise

Find and use the right keywords to boost your SEO

1 Finding the right keywords
Keywords are the words that people put into search engines. The more often these small sequences of keywords appear on your website, the more likely it is that people will find your website.

Identifying your ideal keywords is not that difficult, especially if you have a niche and you know your ideal students well. If you have done the client collages and answered the key client questions earlier in this chapter, then you will find this step much easier.

Select a training offer that you want to write a great sales page for, or choose an existing sales page and improve that.

When identifying the right keywords, you are not looking for single words but a sequence of between five and seven words that sum up your course and define its niche.

You can download a handy checklist from the Toolkit to help you identify your keywords.

Get your notebook and write down around 15 specific and detailed keywords. Think about the kind of words that people would put in a search engine to find your training. Aim to write three different sequences (about five keywords each) in your notebook. **Group the keywords into a sequence** that's easy for humans to read.

For example:

- **Your training title:** pottery weekend in Devon; online brush-lettering course; photography workshop for ceramicists;
- **Your training topic or technique and who it is aimed at:** raku firing for professional ceramicists; medieval embroidery techniques for beginners; an outdoor wild clay family day;
- **The training location:** watercolour painting in Cornwall; a weekend knife-making workshop in Sheffield;
- **Theme or season:** summer watercolour workshop, textile wreath-making for Christmas;
- **Is it giftable?** When and for whom would this make a great gift?

Below Textile artist Angie Parker added these tags to her Eventbrite page to increase the chances of her one-day weaving course being found.

Related to this event

United Kingdom Events   North Somerset Events   Things to do in Bristol   Bristol Classes

Bristol Hobbies Classes   #craft   #weaving   #bristol   #weave   #weavingworkshop

#weaveworkshop   #bristol_events   #weave_class   #learntoweave   #weave_a_cushion

SEO ranking is about more than just keywords ...

Although keywords are very important for enhancing your website's ranking, there are other techniques you will need to use to show search engines that your content is relevant and valuable:

- **Create informative blogs and high-quality videos.** Regularly update and add new content to show that your website is active and current, as the search engines love that. Try to increase the time that your visitors spend on your site by posting internal links to other articles or including video content.
- **Make the user experience for your website visitor as good as it can be.** Ensure your website is mobile-friendly, improve page load times, reduce bounce rates, switch to https: to ensure a secure connection, fix bad links, use Yoast SEO or another SEO plugin.
- **Your ranking will improve the more visitors you get** and the longer they stay. Use other techniques such as email and social media to drive traffic to your site.

For SEO to work, you need to be specific. If you select very popular keywords, e.g., 'jewellery workshop', you won't be found.

Use professional terminology if you are looking for more advanced students, and more generic terms for beginners or those looking for a general pastime. If you then add your location as well, you are very likely to be found.

Top Tip

Organise a keyword party! Get some people together (ideally those with an interest in your topic) and share your training idea with them. Ask them which keywords they would put into search engines to find training like yours. It's fascinating the different words we use depending on our age, gender and knowledge.

Spend some time researching keywords on Google, Eventbrite and other online course providers. Use your own keywords to see what search results you get. What keywords do your competitors use? Use this research to specify or improve your keyword selection.

2 Using these keywords

Keywords are essential for search engines to know what a specific page or website is about. The more frequently certain words appear on a site, the more relevant the page will be. Repeat your keyword sequences across your website to increase your chances of ranking higher for these words.

The positioning of keywords is also important. For example, including them in your website URL or title ranks them higher than if they appear in the main body text.

Opposite Ceramicist Catherine Lucktaylor uses different blog topics to get found and build her profile and credibility.

Go back to the keywords you identified in Step 1, and use them in:

- **Your course or blog title:** aim for a title 5–10 words long. Don't forget to include words like 'workshop', the venue and the location, e.g., weekend glass blowing taster session in London.
- **Your categories:** naming a category more specifically shows the search engines exactly what you do. Your webpage URL for that category will automatically include these keywords too.
- **Your sales page:** use your keyword sequences frequently, but as naturally as possible. Don't overdo it – 'keyword stuffing' will harm your visibility. Try to include your sequence in the first 50 words of your sales page, the title and main headers, tags, and in the names of your images.
- **Your blog posts:** as well as titles of your free videos on YouTube.
- **Backlinks and social media:** post your training on Eventbrite or LinkedIn, or do a guest post or podcast. On your own social media use these keywords as hashtags. On Pinterest especially, people search for creative tips so it's a great place to post and use your keywords cleverly.

Now take some time to (re)write your sales page and include these keyword sequences regularly in these strategic places before you publish it. In the future, when you are writing or creating any content for your website or social media, be conscious about including your keywords strategically. It will save you a lot of time if you do this when you are writing, rather than having to return later to fix this issue. Over time, your SEO and ranking will improve.

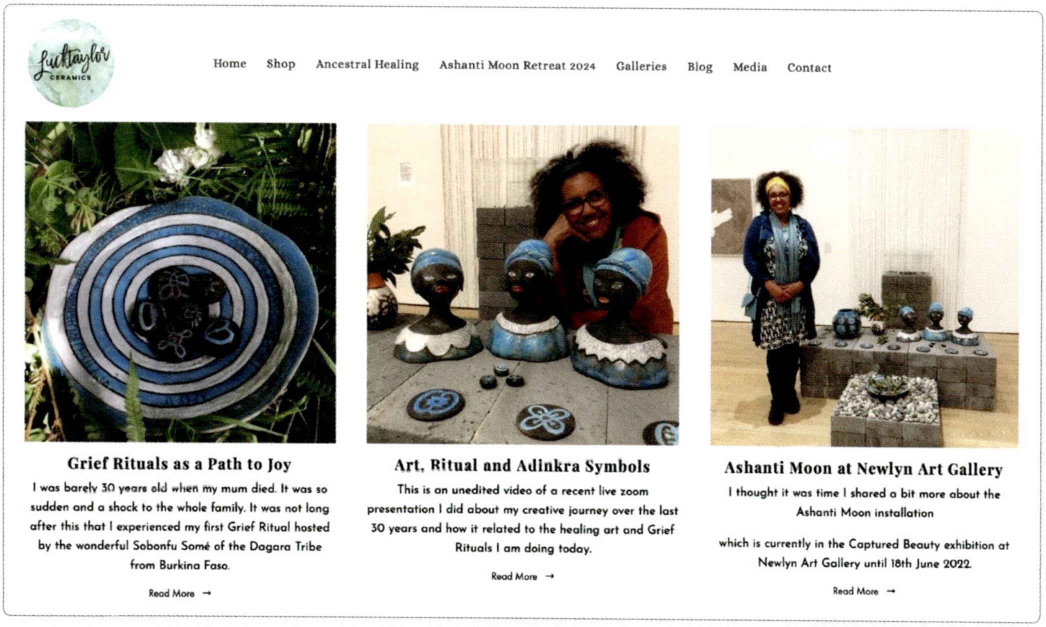

Traffic driving tool 2: Email marketing

If you have existing customers for your products or training, then **email marketing is the best way to drive traffic** to your website, and to get bookings.

Did you know that email marketing is about ten times more effective than social media when it comes to making sales? This is especially true when you craft beautiful, short, well-timed and useful emails, and use them to communicate with your existing clients.

Why is email marketing so effective for getting bookings? There are some very simple reasons:

- People who have signed up to your email database are **much more interested** than your social media followers. It's very easy to get a 'like' or 'follow' on social media, but people who sign up for your mailing list are more interested in receiving further details and are more likely to book.
- Many more people have an email address that they **check daily** than are on social media. You might think that everybody is on TikTok or Instagram, but do your potential students use these as frequently as you? Engagement across all social media platforms tends to fluctuate unpredictably, while nearly everyone has an email address that they access regularly.
- Email marketing is seen as a **more neutral communication and marketing tool.** Email has been around for longer and is used for personal communication and business promotion. Many consumers dislike being interrupted by hard sells on social media.
- **You own your database.** You are in control of your clients' data. You do not have access to your social media followers' data. If your account is compromised or the app closes down, you will lose all your contact data.
- **Reach and engagement is higher** with email marketing. Using professional email marketing software lets you track click and open rates to see what works and what doesn't. When we send an email to The Design Trust's 15,000 email subscribers, we often have an open rate of more than 50 per cent. When we share on Instagram to our 25,000 followers, less than 100 of them usually see our post. That's an incredibly low return on investment.
- **Email marketing can be much more targeted and personalised.** Social media is very much a mass medium, and you are dependent on the platform's algorithm, which controls which of your followers will see your message. Segmenting your email database will ensure that selected groups of contacts will get specific messages.

Common mistake: Worrying about contacting your customers

Many creatives do not like email marketing. They often have a database with names and email addresses, but then avoid sending any emails as they don't know what to write about, or worry about spamming their contacts.

Your email subscribers are much more committed than your social media followers, and therefore, much more likely to buy from you, but instead of building relationships, educating potential clients and staying in touch, many creatives business owners completely ignore their email list. A very big mistake indeed, especially as email marketing is made for creative teachers. Find out why on the next page with my nine tips.

People who signed up for your email list are much more interested in what you do, and want to find out more about your training, your work, and you. Stop avoiding them. They should be treated as VIPs!

Below Email marketing is the best way to stay in touch with existing clients and students, and to get bookings.

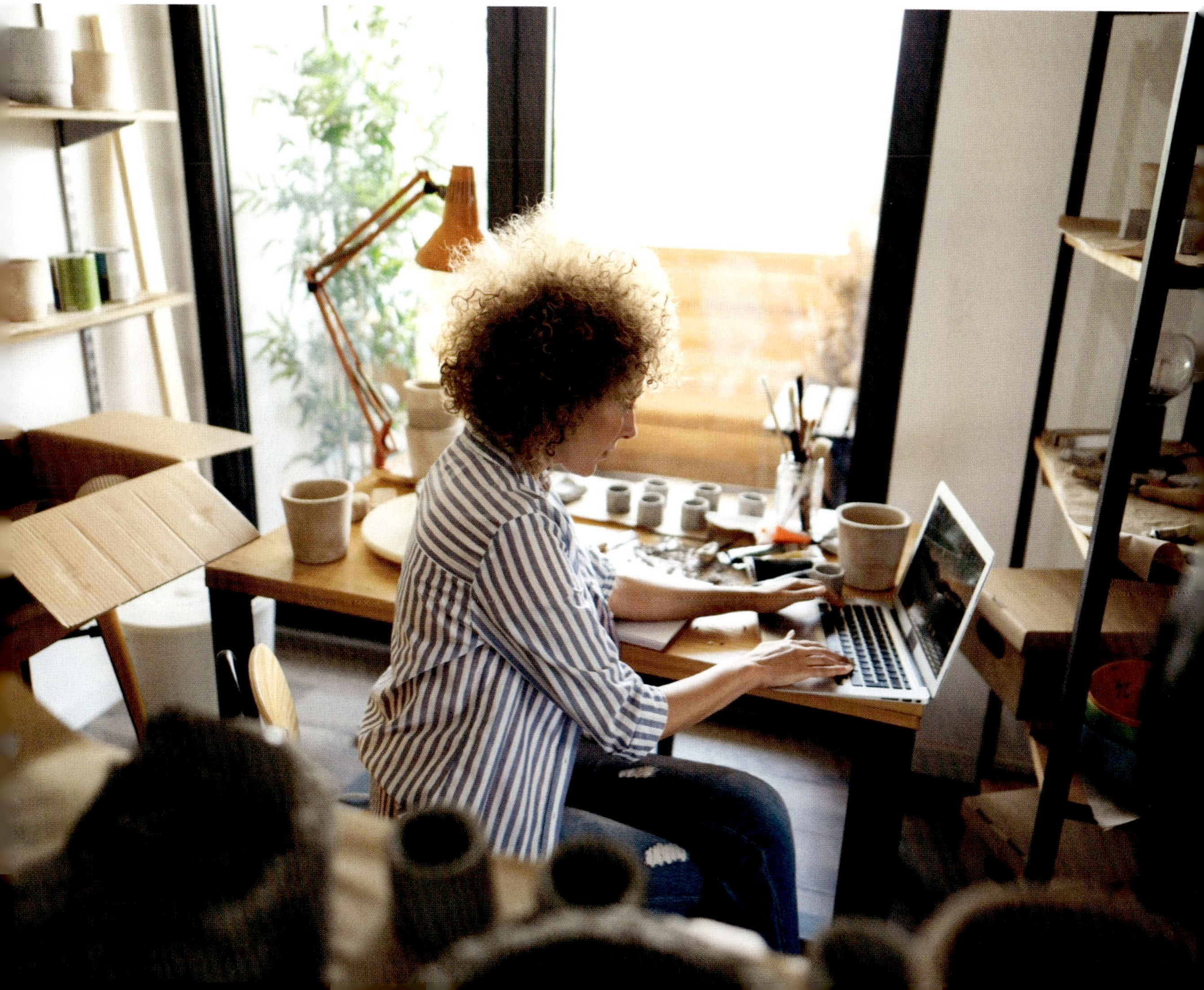

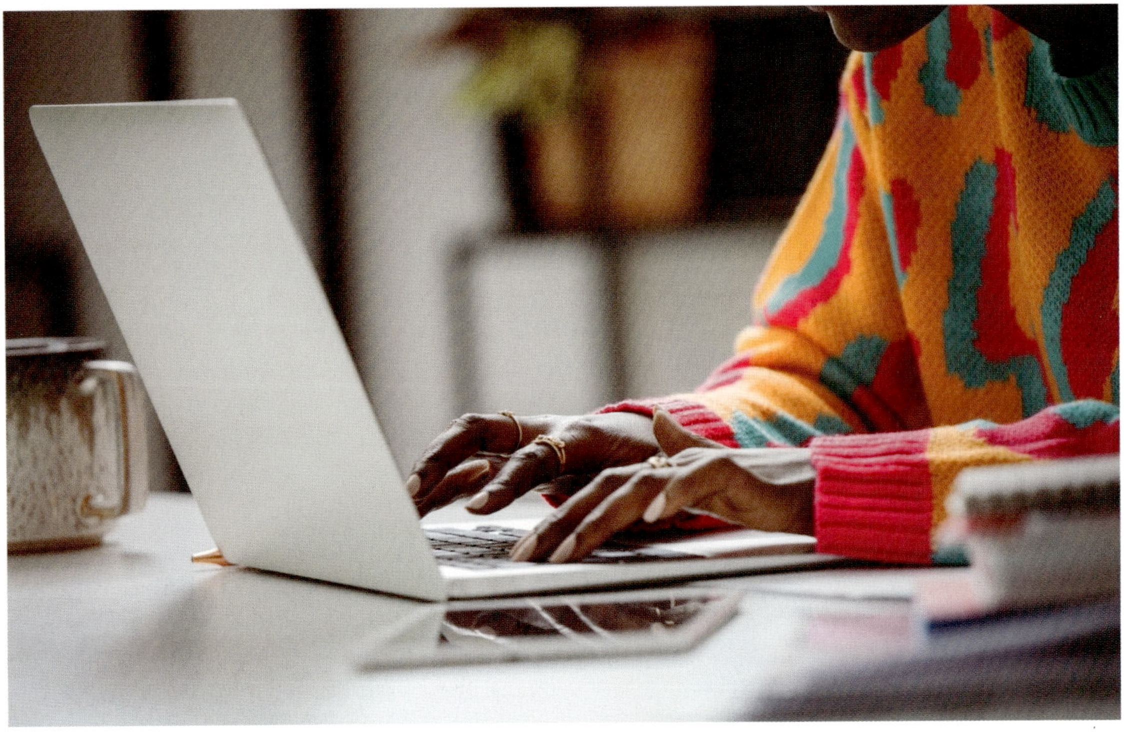

Nine tips to make the most of email marketing

Email marketing is *especially* useful for creative teachers as it's very easy to share tips and additional resources and to educate your audience from the start, while building your credibility and profile.

1 **Use professional email marketing software** such as Mailchimp, Flodesk, or Squarespace Email Campaigns. Do not send bulk emails through your personal email software such as Gmail or Windows Mail, as it looks unprofessional and it's much more likely to end up in your contact's spam folder. Professional email software makes it much easier to personalise and target specific groups (segmentation), track opening and click rates, and create emails using your brand colours, fonts and images.

Very importantly, when you use professional email marketing software this will ensure that your customers' data will be processed and protected more securely, which is a legal requirement.

2 **Personalise your email lists using segmentation.** Rather than sending one email to everybody on your list, you need to plan which groups you want to reach. Start to segment your contacts into different groups based on their interaction with you. To start with, split your contacts into rudimentary groups such as: 'workshop client', 'workshop interest', 'commission interest', 'galleries and shops', or 'media'.

Create segments based on your contact's location – especially useful if you run local in-person workshops – or create tags for specific training that your contact has attended and in which year. That way you can email them specific details about follow-up workshops,

Top Tip

Although segmentation might sound like a boring job (and it is), it's one of the most effective marketing activities that you can do. It will enable you to interact with your contacts on a more personal level. For example, you can contact last year's students to announce your latest training offer, and give them first dibs.

or you can exclude them from marketing campaigns that promote training they have done already.

To segment your groups, you will need to create a specific new tag and either manually upload a CSV file containing the contacts that need this tag afterwards, or you can add a tag automatically when they click on a link or sign up to a course.

Professional software companies usually provide resources around segmentation, so use this to find out the best way to segment your email list.

3 **Add your previous clients to your database.** You can add them to your database, and tag them with the course, workshop or product they purchased.

Many creatives are not aware that this is allowed and often worry about the General Data Protection Regulations (GDPR) that were introduced in 2018. However, the rules are clear that you can stay in touch with clients about their purchases. I wouldn't advise adding customers who purchased something small ages ago, but you can create a list of students on last year's training, and upload and tag them manually afterwards.

You can ask their permission if you prefer, but you do not have to. If you do, ask them to click a link or to reply to the email so that you have proof of their permission.

4 **Boost your open rates.** Your subject line is key! It's worth spending a bit of time on crafting more inspiring subject lines. On average, people take less than two seconds to decide whether to delete an email from their inbox.

Make your subject line inspiring, short and relevant. Understanding the motivation and psychology of your ideal students, and targeting the right segments is crucial. Why might they want to do your training now? Asking questions in your subject line can be very impactful.

5 **Make your emails beautiful and brief.** Nobody has time to read long, boring emails.

Beyond your inspiring subject line add a great image of you or your workshops, and a personalised greeting, using their first name. Use clear headlines and bullet points, and clear calls to actions to book your training. Keep your emails short to encourage them to click to go to your website, where they can find all the details.

6 **Stay in touch to build your relationship.** Email marketing is a fantastic tool for building your profile, credibility and trust with both existing and future students.

Top Tip

Be very careful not to simply ask clients to sign up to a 'general' email list without providing additional information. You will get many more positive responses if you spell out the benefits of signing up.

Top Tip

Marketing is essentially educating your potential and existing clients. This gives you as a creative teacher many great opportunities to stay in touch. Create free resources to attract the right people to your mailing list (lead magnets), and use email marketing really creatively with extra tips, downloads and additional resources to build your relationship and show that you understand your audience. Marketing and teaching are close partners.

Letting your subscribers know that you have got new courses or workshops coming up is a given, and forms part of your launch. But email also works very well to alert them to new relevant blog posts, or when you organise a Q&A or take part in an event where you showcase your products or skills. You could regularly email your interested contacts with specific tips, or tell them about new tools.

7 **Use automation to welcome your clients** to your email list or when they have just booked. It looks professional and will save you tons of time. Create a welcome sequence which you'll write once, and your email marketing software will automatically send these emails. Find out what your email software offers in terms of automation.

Start with a 'thank you' email as soon as they have signed up. Include a brief outline of what they can expect. Follow this up with emails with more tips around your topic or their booking. It's a very friendly way to build a supportive relationship from the start.

We will look more at launching and onboarding in Chapter 9.

Below Example of several lead magnets on Kara Leigh Ford's website.

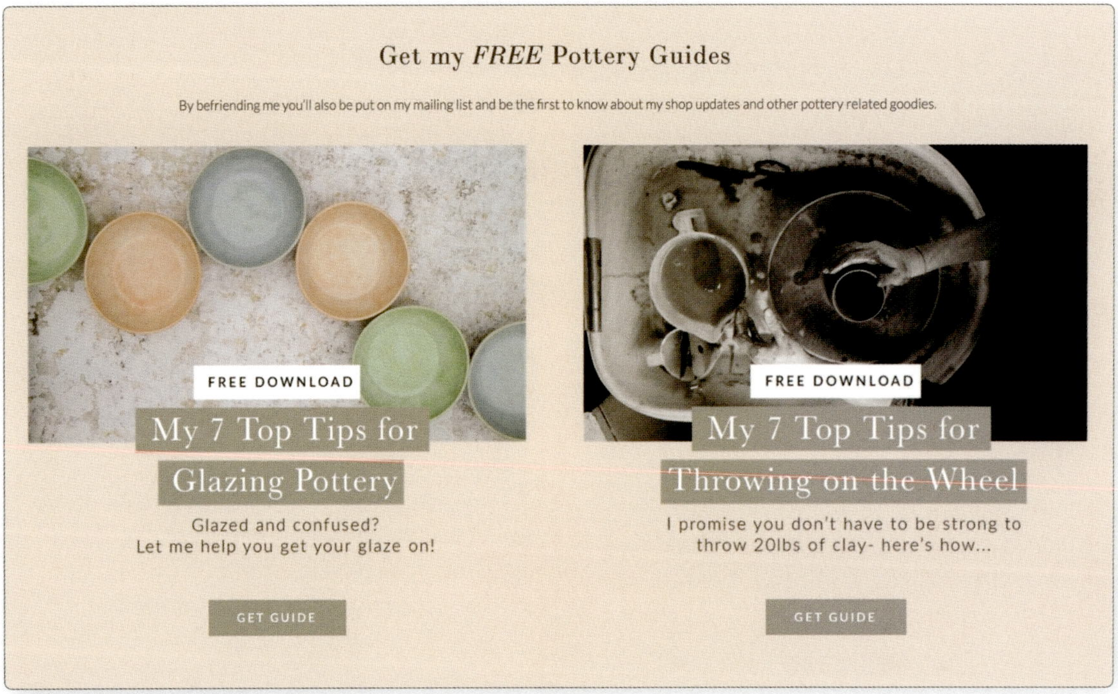

Expert Tip

Create a lead magnet; a piece of valuable, downloadable content that your potential students can get in return for their name and email address.

It might be a beautiful e-book with practical tips to get started in your subject, a short training video around different tools you use, or a checklist or toolkit list.

Be clever with what you think your potential students are looking for online, and what their questions might be around your topic. Lead magnets can be really creative. They might take a little time to produce beautifully, but then they can work really hard for many years to get sign-ups for your training. And you can easily promote these as 'evergreen' content on social media too.

See the page opposite for a great example by Kara Leigh Ford.

8 **Keep it legal.** It's a legal requirement in most countries that businesses sign up to their national Data Protection office. If you have a client database of any kind, you will need to sign up with your national body, and you often need to pay an annual fee.

In the UK the ICO is responsible for the Data Protection Act. Businesses must register with them and pay an annual fee. On the ICO website you will find useful tools and advice to understand what you will need to do to protect and maintain your contact's data. You can receive a fine if you do not register or pay this annual fee while maintaining a database.

9 **Create a paid-for or subscription newsletter.** Asking people to pay to receive your emails has become more popular recently (have a look at platforms like Substack and ConvertKit), and offer great marketing and revenue-generating opportunities.

The trick is to provide content that your subscribers will find valuable and useful, such as recommendations within your field, your opinion, extra tips and advice, special offers from you or related companies or materials. You could publish a beautiful and useful monthly or quarterly newsletter with written, audio or visual content, and charge a small membership fee. It's a great way to stay in touch and build your community, while sharing your knowledge and getting paid for it.

'Once every month I send out a Mailchimp email to about 1,300 subscribers. At the beginning, I found it difficult when people unsubscribed. Now I think it's great because I don't want to be bothering people who don't want to hear from me.'
Sam Marshall, printmaker

FAQ: How do I get more people to sign up to my email list?

This is a very popular question indeed! Try the following:

- **Offer short free training or Q&A sessions** that clients need to sign up for. The Design Trust's number one way to get more subscribers is to host free, live sessions on Zoom, around 10 days before a course starts. We often run Q&A sessions or a short presentation about specific challenges, such as selling online or costing and pricing, and we share some solutions and exercises before we introduce our upcoming course. Participants need to sign up to join or watch the recording afterwards. We regularly add more than 100 new names to our email list! These are good-quality recruits, as they are interested in that specific topic at that time. We tag and segment them so we can stay in touch to sell our online courses.
- **Surveys** (see Chapter 3) are a great way to get email addresses too. We regularly use surveys, especially when developing new courses. We happily provide an extra discount to people who fill these in and ask them to leave their name and email address so we can get in touch when we launch. These are often highly interested new contacts who are very likely to purchase a course.
- **Promote your training at events.** Many creatives often forget to do this! Do a demonstration at an event, display your training leaflets, or ask them to sign up for your waiting list. Or run a competition where visitors can win one of your workshops if they put their name in a bowl. Always check with the event organisers if this is allowed.
- **Work with partners** who have a similar but non-competing audience. Ask if your training can be included in their newsletter, or if they can promote it on their social media. Pitch to write a guest blog post for them or do a free session for their audience, maybe including a special offer. If you return the favour, this will likely cost you nothing.

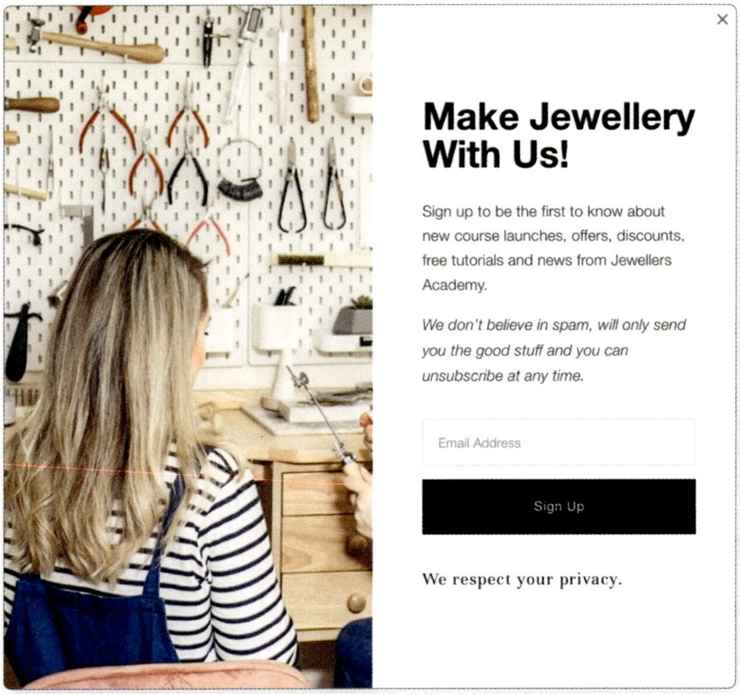

Right Is your sign-up pop-up as visual and purposeful as this? A great example by the Jewellers Academy.

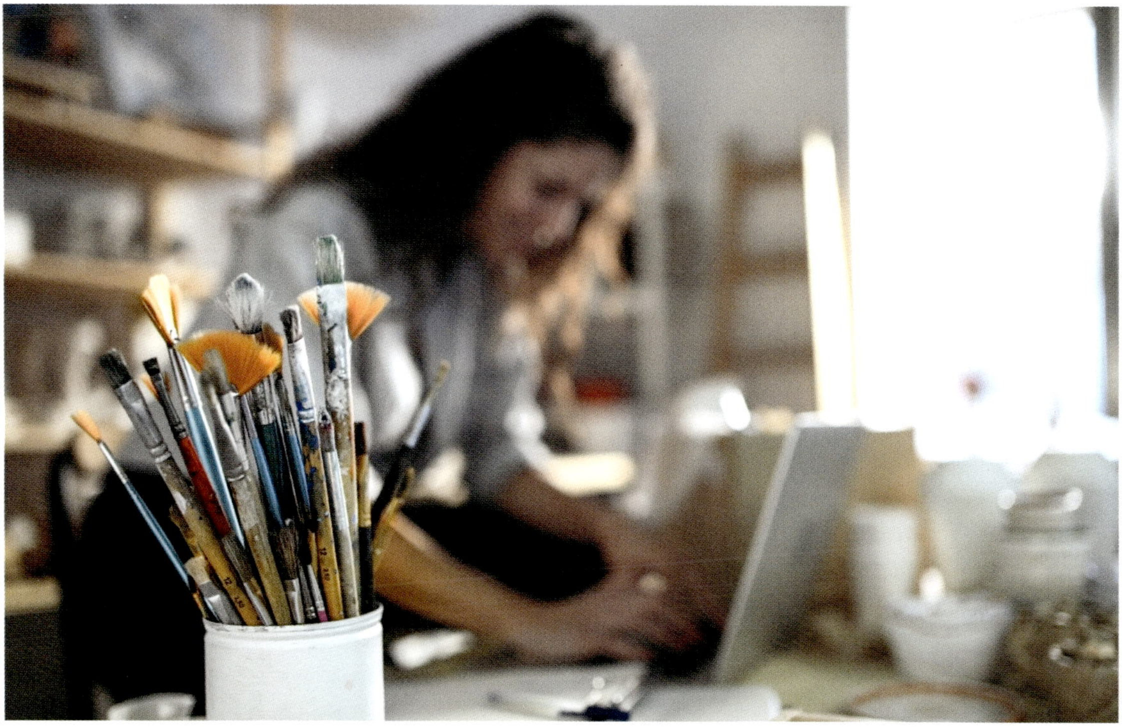

Time to pause

Get your notebook and take time to reflect on how you can improve your email marketing.

- **What do you need to work on?** Do you want more subscribers, need to improve your writing skills, or create a content calendar with topics? How can you treat your email subscribers as VIPs and give them special treatment on a regular basis?
- **How can you use email marketing to drive traffic to your website?** Promote relevant blog posts or free lead magnet videos on your website to your email list. How can you get your social media followers to sign up to your email list?
- **Which emails do you like to receive?** Which newsletters have you signed up for? There are very useful, practical, beautiful examples out there. Use them to inspire how your email marketing could look.
- **How many people do you have on your email list right now?** How many do you want to have in six months' time, and in a year? Identify some actions you will take to attract more subscribers for your training.
- **Have you segmented your email list yet?** It's crucial that you split your contacts into different groups as clients for your creative products are not necessarily interested in your training, and vice versa.

Traffic driving tool 3: Social media

Social media is a very popular promotional tool for in-person and online training. It works especially well to raise your profile and credibility with potential students if you **use keywords and hashtags strategically.**

Social media loves videos! Use short films to promote your training and to share your knowledge and experience to build credibility and trust. Include short videos with tips on your topic, do a Q&A with a student or a behind-the-scenes tour of your online course.

Your images need to attract attention. Add text to your images with Canva or Picfont for clearer 'calls to action' or to include the location and dates of your training. Sharing testimonials or images of your students' results will show others that they can expect similar results.

It's very easy to get likes and followers, but do **encourage them to sign up to your email** list so that you can engage with them more personally.

Below Alison Bick uses Instagram creatively with different types of posts, including an invite with date and location, her portrait and inspiring images.

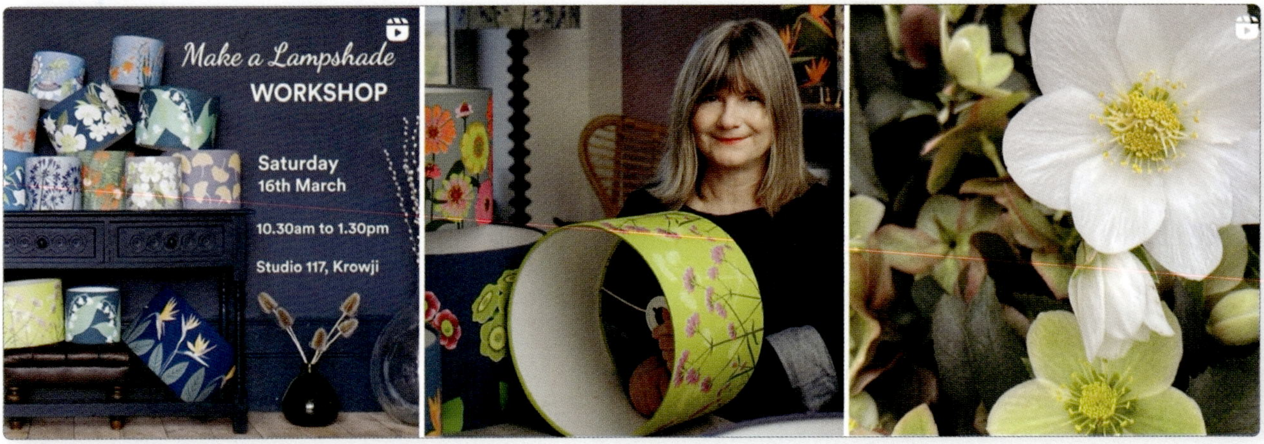

Top Tip

Make the most of your social media bio. Regularly update your profile picture or avatar, ideally with a portrait of you or recent work. Include your keywords, website and location too.

Use tools that can expand your bio, and link to your latest training, e.g., campsite.bio or Linktree.

FAQ: What's the best social media platform for creative training?

At the time of writing, the best social media platform for hobby course promotion is Pinterest, which might surprise you. People spend a lot of time on this platform looking for ideas, so share top tips with beautiful pins that connect to your blog posts or lead magnets. Pinterest works like a search engine, so you will get traffic depending on what people are looking for, rather than how many followers you have. Specific keyword sequences are crucial for driving traffic on Pinterest.

Pinterest is a longer-term investment, which will slowly build your presence and drive traffic. The Pinterest algorithms prefer it if you post regularly: 5–10 pins a week can really boost your traffic. Its big advantage is that pins have a far longer lifespan than Instagram posts. If you use the right keywords, people will find your posts weeks, months or even years later.

Depending on the age of your participants and students, you might want to look at using Facebook (over 45 years old), Instagram (30–55 years old) or TikTok (18–25 years old) to promote your training.

LinkedIn is very valuable if you're offering professional development training, have corporate clients or work with venues. Spend half an hour improving your LinkedIn profile to include details about your teaching, career highlights and your niche to make it easier for professionals to find you.

LinkedIn is also useful for posting upcoming **professional development training,** publishing professional articles – perhaps repurposing some of your blog posts – or creating an online business community for discussions around your topic.

Don't forget to **use the recommendation** feature that LinkedIn offers. You can ask for a testimonial from a venue or organisation immediately after you have delivered training, which can be a very good credibility booster.

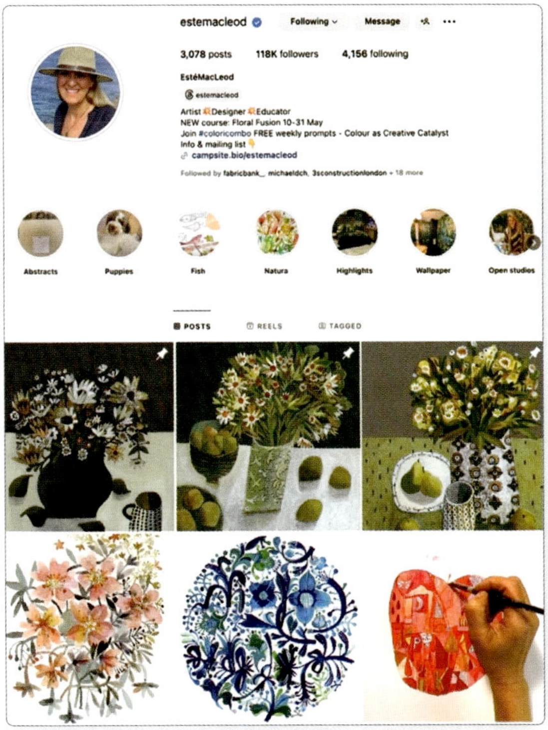

Above Esté MacLeod uses Instagram very effectively with keywords in her profile, regular reels and highlighting her #coloricombo challenge.

Time to pause

Get your notebook and reflect on how you can improve your social media marketing. Identify some specific actions.

- **Do you need different social media accounts** for your products and your training?
- **Do your social media profiles include keywords** and links to your website?
- **Which platforms do your ideal students use,** and which ones could you focus on and improve? Don't try to do them all.
- **Can you increase engagement by asking questions** or starting discussions, organising regular live sessions, or using polls?

Traffic driving tool 4: Traditional marketing

This is one of my favourite types of marketing, and it can be very creative.

Before the internet existed, marketing techniques included posters and banners, sending a flyer in the post, and being featured in the press or on local radio. You can even use your vehicle, if you have one, to promote your creative training using vinyl stickers.

And do you promote your training at craft fairs or exhibitions with flyers?

All of these marketing activities can still be very effective, and are often much more memorable and impactful than social media or online marketing.

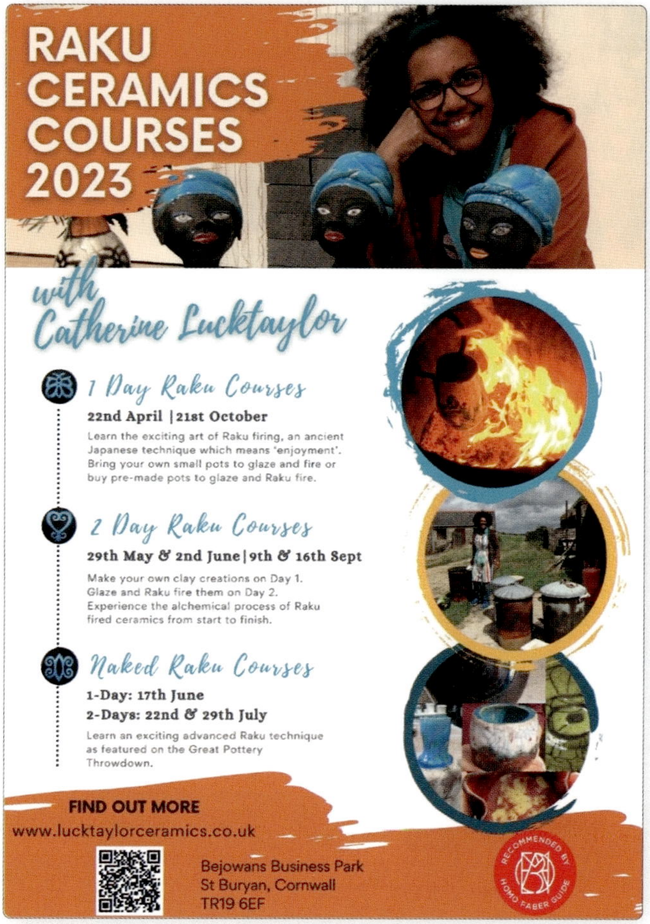

Right Catherine Lucktaylor uses flyers to promote her raku courses locally and at events.

Expert Tip

Local marketing is especially important for in-person training:

- **When you are teaching in a wonderful location or venue,** it really contributes to the overall feel and experience, and therefore the perceived value, and what your students are willing to pay. Use local hashtags and keywords on your sales page and social media such as #thingstodoincardiff or #craftworkshopinyorkshire.
- **If you are planning a longer, recurring in-person training course,** as it's more likely that your students will live locally. It's rare that somebody will travel long distances for a two-hour evening course run over six weeks. In this case, it can really help to distribute flyers and posters locally in bookshops, independent coffee shops or art material shops, or hang an outdoor banner at your venue. Don't forget to segment your email list for local people to send targeted emails to them only.

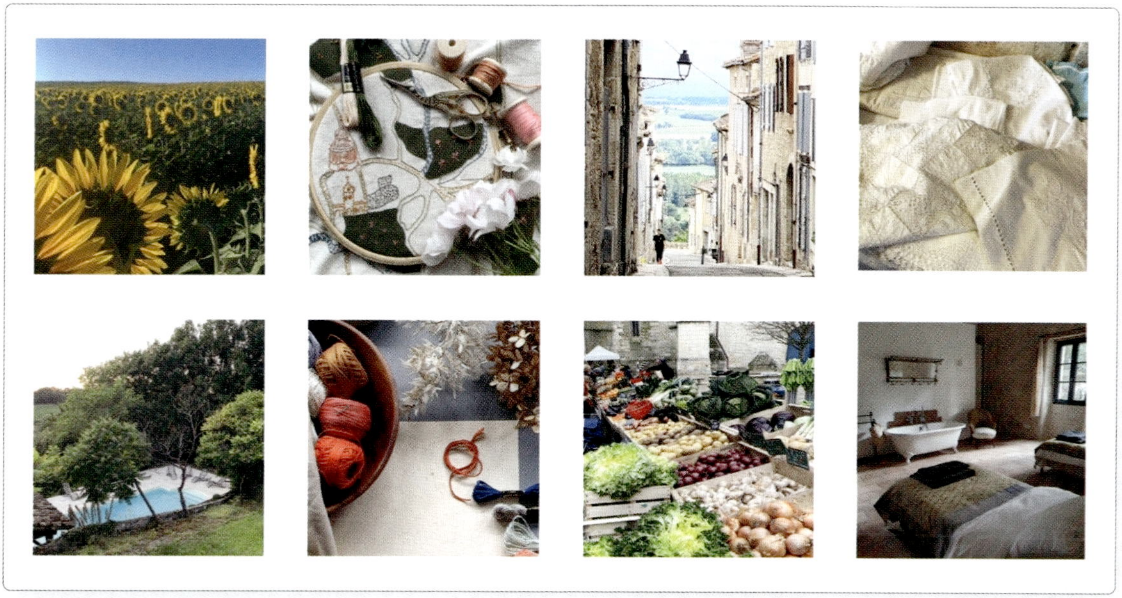

Above When teaching in a beautiful location or venue, really show that off with gorgeous, inspiring images – like Ekta Kaul promoting her international retreats on her website.

Time to pause

Get your notebook and take time to reflect on the following questions:

- **What promotions would you do if the internet didn't exist?** Time to get creative! Can you use your existing craft selling events or get press for your training? Or post an invite or annual brochure to previous students?
- **How relevant is local marketing for you?** Can you make more of your location and venue? Which clients would be attracted to this location? What local marketing opportunities are available for your recurring in-person course?

Identify some specific actions.

We have covered a lot of ground in this chapter! From the fundamental marketing concepts and my personal marketing secrets, to the importance of your website and how to drive traffic to it. There are some really key creative exercises in this chapter: client persona and collages, competitor research, your website, branding and pages, and finally keywords and SEO.

In the next chapter we will continue to look at promoting yourself and your training, focusing on a successful launch, and student onboarding.

But first an inspiring Creative Case Study from Esté MacLeod, whose website is a masterclass in branding and who uses Instagram very creatively indeed. Enjoy!

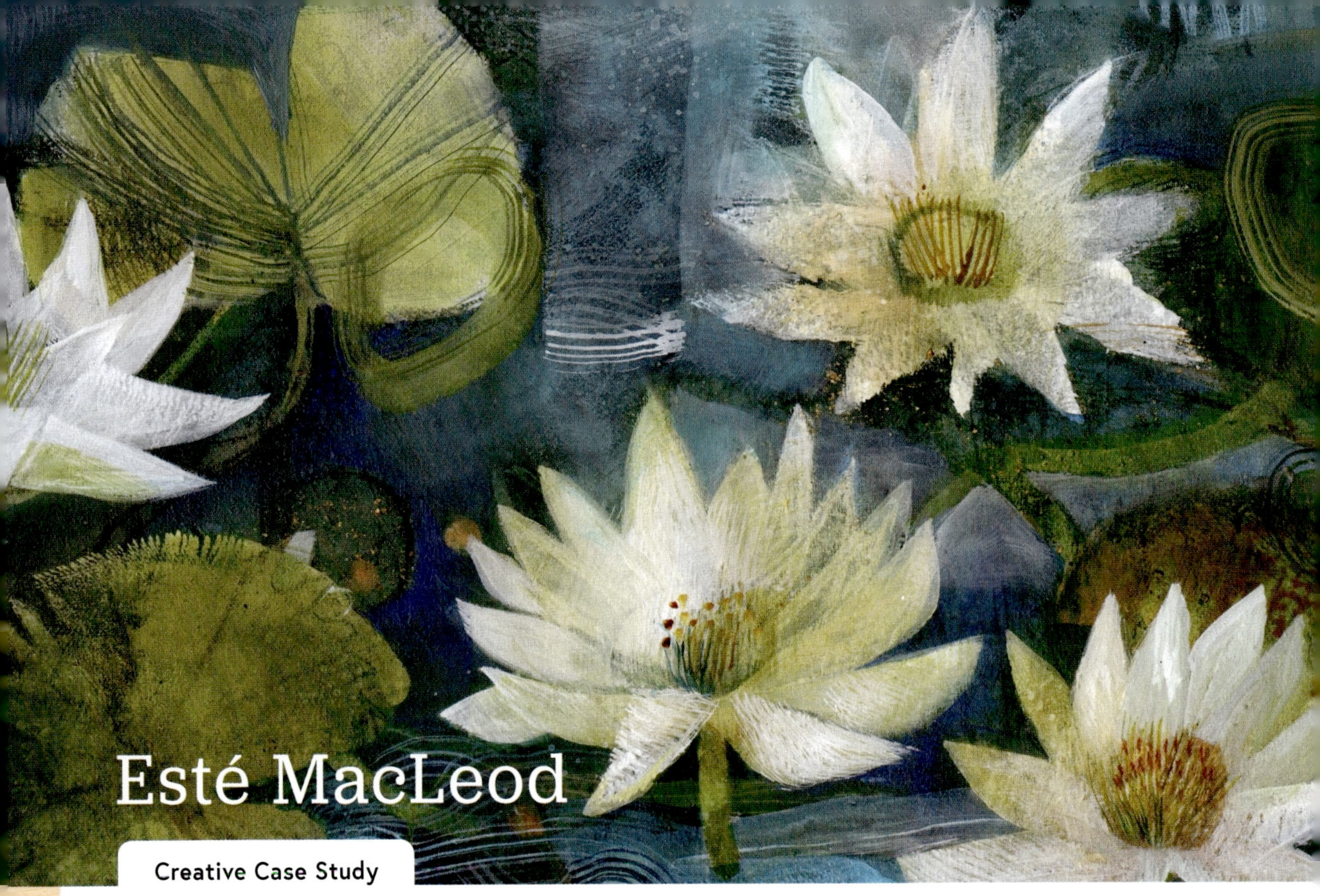

Esté MacLeod

Creative Case Study

Esté MacLeod is a successful fine artist, designer and educator. She is represented by galleries in the UK and abroad, and works with various international licensing brands who feature her art and designs on products including textiles and wallpaper.

Working in a semi-abstract, imaginative style, Esté incorporates a vocabulary of shapes alongside bird and floral motifs. Her studies in textile design and fine art printmaking laid the groundwork for her signature artworks. A degree in ceramics and glass followed by an MA in jewellery design have contributed to her evolving career as a fine artist.

Esté began teaching online in 2015 and in 2021 started teaching on luxury creative art retreats in locations such as Sri Lanka, Morocco, Greece and Bali.

You can find out more about Esté MacLeod on her website www.estemacleod.com

How did you get started with teaching?

In 2014 I enrolled on a six-month art and business bootcamp course called *Make Art That Sells*. Most of my fellow students were working as illustrators, digitally or in gouache and watercolour. In contrast I was a fine artist, painting in acrylics and mixed media on canvas. Given the different approaches to coursework, students asked whether I could offer an online painting course and I thought, 'OK, if there are 60 people interested, I'll do it.' Deposits were taken (with refunds offered just in case!) and the planned course sold out quickly.

I now just had to figure out how to create an e-course! Luckily my husband works in IT and with his help I managed to host my first course on a very simple platform, basically a blog with a password.

'I hadn't considered before then just how valuable my accumulated artistic knowledge was. I realised that there was a lot that I could pass on'

Why and how do you teach?

I have an inherent ability to teach: it's in my DNA. As a curious person I love to learn new things. I come from a family of academics and I have always loved sharing ideas about creativity and artmaking with others. Passing on knowledge is a wonderful experience – it's an absolute joy to see how students develop, become more confident, and embrace their own imagination. I find this very rewarding.

After that first painting-focused course, I noticed that students often copied what was taught directly when step-by-step processes were shown. Shifting the focus towards creativity became the aim of my subsequent courses.

In 2016 I developed a process called the Creative Leap Method™ where both handwriting and the Roman alphabet are used. This is now part of all the courses I teach, regardless of subject or materials.

The Creative Leap Method™ uses letters and numbers as anchor points for drawings. This simplifies processes and encourages 'out-of-the-box thinking', making the creative experience more playful. This catalyst for drawing drives enthusiasm, and students enjoy the process of discovery as they embrace an intuitive and authentic way of creating.

Opposite An Esté MacLeod painting made on a retreat in Bali.

Right Esté MacLeod.

Tell me about your online courses

I now usually develop two new courses each year – a five-day mini-course and a longer, more in-depth three- to five-week course.

There's no real limit to the number of students, but somewhere between 100 and 250 works well for me as I've enough time to answer queries and to provide feedback, and there's a great sense of community and sharing.

Since 2015 I've offered courses covering a variety of creative processes, techniques and media using acrylic and watercolour paints. Weekly modules consist of daily projects that build upon each other and conclude with a

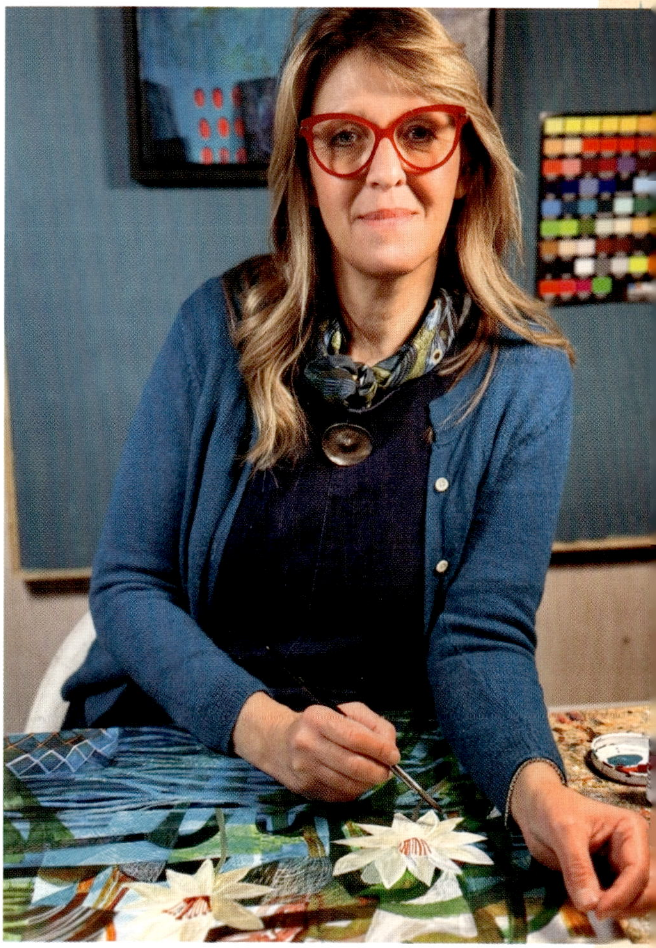

larger, more comprehensive assignment over the weekend.

Courses are sold via my website and social media channels and taught on Kajabi, a dedicated learning platform. Scheduled courses have a start and an end date and remain accessible for at least a year afterwards.

Giving everyone enough time to complete all the course's modules is very important to me, but I feel that if you haven't made any time in that year that you're unlikely to start later on. I continue to develop new courses with fresh content and shelve older courses after a few years.

Mini courses and some older courses are also available as evergreen self-paced options on my website.

Why did you choose the recorded online teaching format?

When I started teaching online, I always included a live teaching element as a weekly check-in to make sure everyone was on track. However, with a global audience it was difficult to coordinate a time to suit everyone. I now make sure all relevant information is included in the recorded course and as accompanying notes. There's always an exclusive Facebook group where students can post outcomes, ask questions and get feedback. It is an additional valuable element of each course.

What I really love about pre-recording my teaching is that I can put a lot of content into a video lesson. It's always edited with clear instructions and it can have sequences removed or slightly sped up so that you don't have to watch paint dry in real time. The result is a condensed lesson where I can show all the processes done over several hours cohesively in 20–40 minutes. Students can watch it when it suits them, and can go back and forward in the lesson themselves. It is my goal to pass on as much information as is practical, in a concise way so that students feel informed and stay motivated.

Online teaching really suits me and lets me reach a large global audience.

How do you plan your online courses?

Some courses take years to develop – the *Explore Abstract* course launched in 2023 and took me more than two years. There's a lot of experimenting as I want to offer something unique and different from other online art courses. The way I work is influenced by my eclectic background, with training in design and printmaking impacting on how I work and teach.

When I start planning, I research options and do a brain dump of what I want to teach specifically. All of that is then broken down into modules where, for example, specific paint techniques or colour mixes are the main focus. I use a grid drawn on large piece paper, with each day as a block to figure out how to deliver the content in manageable chunks.

Each module's projects have detailed demos to show how all the processes come together with clear outcomes and good ideas for expectations. I believe, as a teacher, that strong and sometimes tight guidelines are helpful to teach effectively. Having these parameters means that students can focus on specific components or tasks, and they can progress faster.

> *'Because courses have a set start day, I have a deadline to finish recording. Being under pressure creates a scenario where I hyper focus and in doing so feel creatively in tune and "in the moment". This way of working, where everything comes together in a dynamic way, works for me.'*

What marketing advice do you have?

One effective way of self-promotion is to start sharing your knowledge freely. Do regular short demos on social media and then move on to offer something bigger – YouTube, for example. If 10 people sign up to a course, you've made a start. Teach what you know in your own authentic way.

When I am thinking about doing a course, I often ask my online audience for feedback, or I'll send out a newsletter outlining my plans with a sign-up link for more information. This is a really useful way to see if there will be a demand for a specific course. I've offered mini courses at no cost to see what the uptake might be for a certain topic before I go ahead with a bigger course. I regard this as a kind of soft marketing with less pressure on me and a place where prospective students will get an idea of how I teach.

When a course is launched, I like to engage with students in a dedicated Facebook group. I answer questions promptly as it's important for students to know I'm accessible. The course group remains open indefinitely as some students will take a longer time to do the projects, and I'm genuinely interested in seeing what students do with the course's projects.

Soft marketing is something I prefer to a big advertising campaign. At the start of 2022 I started to share a weekly colour prompt to my Instagram audience using the tag #coloricombo. Each week, I'll choose a small selection of colours based on an artwork, illustration or image by a featured artist. In a weekly email to thousands of subscribers I share the artist's backstory and the colour palette. I encourage people to use the limited colours to get creative, to make art in any medium and to share it in the dedicated Facebook group or on Instagram.

Converting your social media audience into your personal audience is essential. Your mailing list is so important because you can speak to people directly, without relying on algorithms and other external factors. There are over 25,000 people on my mailing list, which makes direct communications easy.

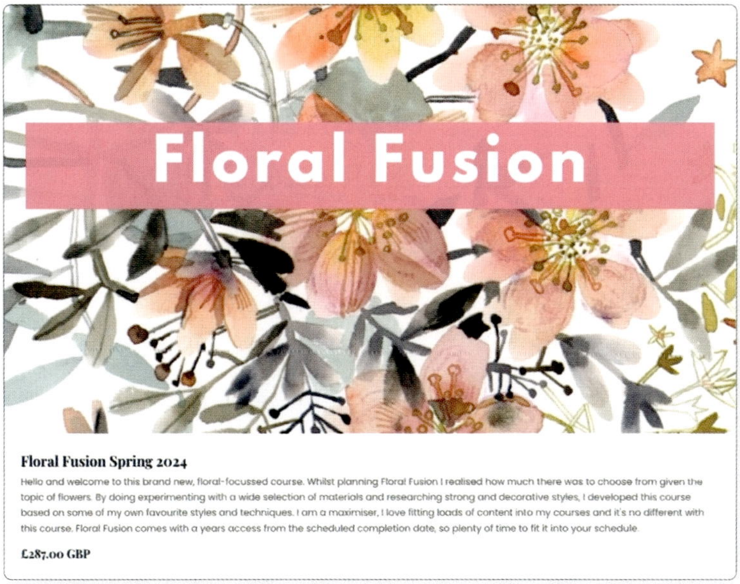

Left Esté creates beautiful banners to promote her online courses on her website and social media.

CHAPTER 9

Launching, onboarding and evaluation

In the previous marketing chapter, you spent time on preparing all the tools and techniques that you need to have in place to sell your course.

This chapter is split into three parts. First, we look at **launching in more detail**, and you will create a launch plan for your training. Once you've launched, you'll need to think about **onboarding your students** – giving them a warm welcome and making them feel confident in and excited about your training. Then we will look at **how you evaluate** your training, before it starts, while it is running, and after it ends.

Why launch?

When you run live training (either online or in person) you will need enough 'bums on seats' to run it. Launching your training at the right time and with a bit of fanfare will really help you to get more bookings.

- **Setting a deadline will give you a planning framework** – what needs to be done and by when – and as we saw in Chapter 8, launching early can be really beneficial. Many creatives admit that they need a deadline to take action and stop procrastinating!
- **It takes as much time to promote one workshop as it does a whole series.** If you have a broader offer that includes different dates and topics, your clients are much more likely to sign up, and you are more likely to create some buzz around a whole programme than for a single workshop.

FAQ: When is a good time to launch?

This very much depends on you and your ideal students. Teaching is often very seasonal. There are some specific times in the year when people are more likely to want to learn.

- **January is a great month as many people want to learn something new.** Winter is the time to be indoors, and new year vibes often encourage people to learn a new skill or start a hobby. People also often have a bit of extra cash in January that they like to spend on themselves. Creative workshops make great Christmas gifts so you can sell these in December and run the training at the start of the year, when often your product sales are low so it's great for your cash flow.

- If you offer family workshops, outdoor activities, or workshops aimed at tourists, **spring is an ideal time to launch summer programmes.**
- **September is 'back-to-school' month.** People are getting back into their normal routines, so it's a good time to launch creative training for the autumn.

When you will launch often depends on how long your training is. The longer your courses are, the more likely your students need to plan in advance. Half- or full-day workshops can be launched several weeks in advance, but long weekend or five-day retreats are often booked at the start of the year when people are planning breaks and holidays. You could offer an early-bird discount to encourage early bookings.

Creative Exercise

Put together a launch plan

Launching new training can be really stressful, and a launch plan will help you juggle everything.

You can see a launch plan example on the next pages, and download the *Launch Plan* template from the Teach Your Creative Workshop Toolkit.

Return to your annual training plan. Start with the end in mind – when you will run your training – and work backwards. Will you have one launch, or several launches through the year? How many weeks before you start the training will you launch?

Identify your specific marketing goals, and make them SMART (specific, measurable, achievable, relevant, time-bound), e.g., 'Get 20 people to sign up to my mailing list by 4 May.'

Break each marketing goal down into smaller actions. This will help you stay on top of your workload. Some launch activities you can include in your launch plan:

- **Add all the details of your annual training programme to your website** at once, or create a summer/spring and autumn/winter calendar. Link to this page in your promotional materials.
- **Create a promotional flyer** that you can send to previous students or hand out at events. For local events, think about banners or posters too.
- **Offer a free online Q&A to answer questions** about the training, share your knowledge and help build your profile, credibility and trust. Don't forget to take

email addresses when people sign up, so you can add them to your database and follow up afterwards. Promote your free session via email and social media.

- **Offer a short, free creative challenge.** Running a three- or five-day challenge around your technique gives people a feel of what your workshop will be like. Much of this can be prepared in advance and automated.
- **Send a launch email offering an early-bird discount** to previous students or contacts who have already shown an interest. Send different emails to different segments of your database, and tailor your message depending on how well they already know, like and trust you.
- **Follow up with additional promotional emails** highlighting the different features and benefits of your training. Include a 'your questions answered' email to overcome any doubts or worries they may have.
- **Finish with a short 'final call' email.** You can send this just days or hours before your training starts. Very often people are busy and think 'I will do this later' and then genuinely forget. Here at The Design Trust we get up to 30 per cent of our students through our 'final call' emails, so they really work. Don't forget to include 'final call' in your subject line.

Once you have a launch plan, you will know when you need to start your launch activities.

What's your SMART marketing goal	What are your marketing actions?
Get 50 existing clients to subscribe to my new course mailing list	Create a sales page
	Email my existing clients
	Do a survey
Get 30 new people to sign up to my new course mailing list	Create a sales page
	2× blog posts on my website
	4× posts on IG
	Guest blog post on wedding site
Create a short intro sales page for my new course	Short description and image and connect to my Mailchimp
Create a short intro video	Record a short video of me talking about the course (3 mins)
Email campaign with 4 emails	Write and send 4 emails out to new and existing people on database

Above Example of a launch plan – you can download the template from the Teach Your Creative Workshop Toolkit.

Who is this aimed at?	What's the story or angle?	Deadline	How long will this take?	What are the costs?	Who can help?	Done?
Existing clients	Excited that I am now finally launching my new course … online!	1 May	4 hours 2 hours 3 hours	None	Clare?	
New people (brides)	Interested in doing my contemporary calligraphy for brides workshop?	30 June	4 hours 2 x 4 hours 4 x 30 mins 4 hours	None	Sue?	
New and existing clients	Sign up now if you are interested and be the first to hear when my course launches (and get an early-bird bonus)	1 May	4 hours	None	Jon	
New and existing clients	Intro, why I created this course, what you will learn, who it is for, my credibility	15 May	2 hours	Micro-phone?	Jen	
80 people who have shown interest	1 Survey 2 Launch now 3 Your questions answered 4 Last call email	1 April 14 May 19 May 21 May	4 hours 3 hours 3 hours 2 hours	None		

FAQ: How do I promote online evergreen training?

Do you have online training that's always available? This can include pre-recorded training and memberships. These formats can be really beneficial for your students, as they can start their online training when it suits them, throughout the year.

However, the downside is that potential participants then **never really have a reason to start your training**, and often delay signing up. On top of that, many creative teachers forget to promote their evergreen training, sometimes because they are bored with it, sometimes because there is no natural time to promote or highlight it. And there is no opportunity to launch.

> *Remember that repeat business is crucial for a successful training business. Promoting what is already available rather than creating new content can be a really quick way to make some money.*

Some marketing ideas for selling your evergreen training include:

- **Promote it at a specific time of year.** At The Design Trust, we do an annual Business Club sale at the start of the year, when members can sign up for the entire year. We give our annual sale members a very good deal, and generate nearly half of our members then. Great for your cash flow too at an often quiet time in the year.
- **If you run in-person workshops,** add online content as an extra bonus that students can access either before or after the training. It often doesn't cost you much extra, but it allows you to stay in touch with them. Or offer access to basic skills training and you can refer to this to save time during the live training.
- **Create a bundle.** When launching a new course, consider adding an older (online) course, and charge a special price for both for a limited period. If you have a new craft show, related commission, or are publishing a book, promote your evergreen training then.
- **Upgrade the existing content and relaunch it.** For example, add new resources, update some of the recordings, or add a free Q&A session for students who book by a certain date.
- **Identify partners such as craft organisations** who can promote it to their members, perhaps with an exclusive discount or a free Q&A session.
- **Bring back the va-va-voom** and create a marketing plan for your evergreen content. Very often we forget what we have and we simply don't promote it properly. Create a marketing plan especially for your evergreen training or membership.

FAQ: How do I fill last-minute places?

One of the big challenges when you run a creative training business is getting bums on seats. This is true especially for live training, as you will have paid a fee for the venue, and you need a certain group size to make the group dynamics work and cover your costs. You really want to avoid having to cancel your training because of low ticket sales.

When you created an annual training budget (p.149), I advised that you cost your training based on selling 80 per cent of your tickets to give yourself a financial cushion.

Checking regularly in on your actual sales versus your forecasted sales will help you to create a more profitable creative business. Do you have a system in place for checking ticket sales against your forecast? This might be as simple as checking in once a month to see how ticket sales are going. If you notice that you still have too many tickets available a few weeks before the training, you will need to become proactive and do some extra marketing:

- **Last-minute emails really work.** If you have segmented your email list, you can send a targeted 'final call' email to local or previous students. Could you get in touch with people who have already booked to see if they want to bring a friend?
- **Have another look at your launch plan.** Have you done everything you listed?
- **Are there any local organisations you can partner with** to promote your training, e.g., a local newspaper, gallery or social club? Put leaflets in local cultural venues, libraries or independent bookshops.
- **Can you negotiate with the venue** to see if you could get a smaller space at a lower cost? Can they help to promote your workshops to their mailing list too?

'I am lucky. My workshops all run at capacity. There is only space available for six people per workshop. I don't want to saturate the market and only offer a limited amount of workshop days. Only when workshops are nearly full do I release new dates.

If there are any last-minute places available, I will send an email or the venue will include it in their monthly email, but this is very rarely needed.'

Angie Parker, textile artist

Below Weaver Angie Parker creating a rug in her studio.

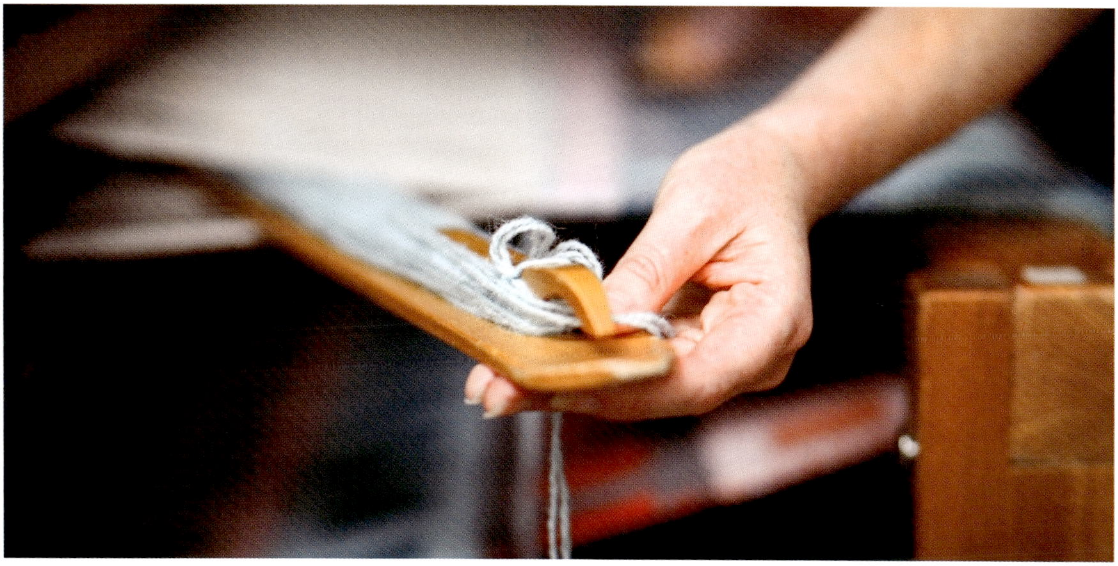

A nice welcome: How to onboard your students

So, people are booking your course; now you need to welcome them. The time between booking and starting might only be minutes (for pre-recorded online training) but if it's in-person training or a significant online course, students might book many months in advance.

Between the moment your students pay for their training and the moment they start is a beautiful opportunity for great customer care. Welcome your students and quickly set the scene for a unique learning experience.

Good communication at this stage will set expectations, immediately develop a good relationship, and often helps to avoid problems later on.

Depending on the length and format of your training, you might provide different levels of communication and support, including, for example:

- **Information about preparation and access:**
  - Is there homework for students to do?
  - **What materials or equipment** might they need? Do you provide them with a list or send them materials in advance as part of a package?
  - Online courses might have specific **technical requirements.** How will they make sure they have these in place?
- Follow up personally with anybody who indicated **special needs or requirements.**
- Offer an individual or group introductory session online prior to the training, whether it is in person or online.

Using email to onboard students

Emails are a great way to welcome your students from the moment they book. Very often you can automate the process to minimise the time it takes to send them.

Email 1: Confirmation email

- Send this out immediately after your student has booked.
- Include the course name and your business name in the subject line, and state that it is important.
- Put your logo or name at the top of the email so that they recognise it immediately.
- Start by thanking them for booking, confirm the name of the course, the date and times, the location and who it is for. Tell them you are excited they booked and give a bit more detail about you or why you created this training.
- What tools, materials and equipment will be provided and what they need to prepare or bring, including any preparatory homework. Provide links to websites or brands that sell the right tools and materials.
- **For in-person training:**
  - Provide venue information with full address and directions by car and public transport.
  - Clearly state arrival time and start time.
  - Suggest local accommodation or food options.
- **For online training:**
  - Describe how to access the training, and any technical requirements.
- Include a link to your T&Cs, code of conduct and cancellation policy.
- Tell them the best way to get in touch with you.

Email 2: Get ready for your course!

Send this out up to four weeks in advance of your live workshop, depending on how much preparation they will need.

- As with Email 1, make the subject line clear, and include your logo at the top of the email.
- Thank them again and tell them how much you are looking forward to meeting them and teaching them. Perhaps give some more details, e.g., how many other people have booked.
- Remind them of the day, date, arrival and start times.
- Provide venue information again, with the full address and travel instructions, and possibly a map. If you are using a large venue, give specific instructions where to go.
- Give them details of how to get in touch with you on the day in an emergency, e.g., if they are running late or lost.
- Remind them of the materials and tools they will need to bring. Ask them to label their tools with their name. Tell them of any arrangements you've made for participants who can't bring their own.
- Remind them of any preparation work they will need to do.
- Include some details about yourself and refer to your website, social media and newsletter.
- Ask again about special needs or dietary requirements.
- Link to your T&Cs, code of conduct, and cancellation policy.

Time to pause

Get your notebook and take time to reflect on the following questions:

- **How can you start to connect with your students** and welcome them as soon as they have booked?
- **How much of this process can you automate?** Check with your booking or email marketing system and save yourself a lot of time.

Start to draft your welcoming emails.

Below Tools used by Chloe Savage for traditional and couture embroidery.

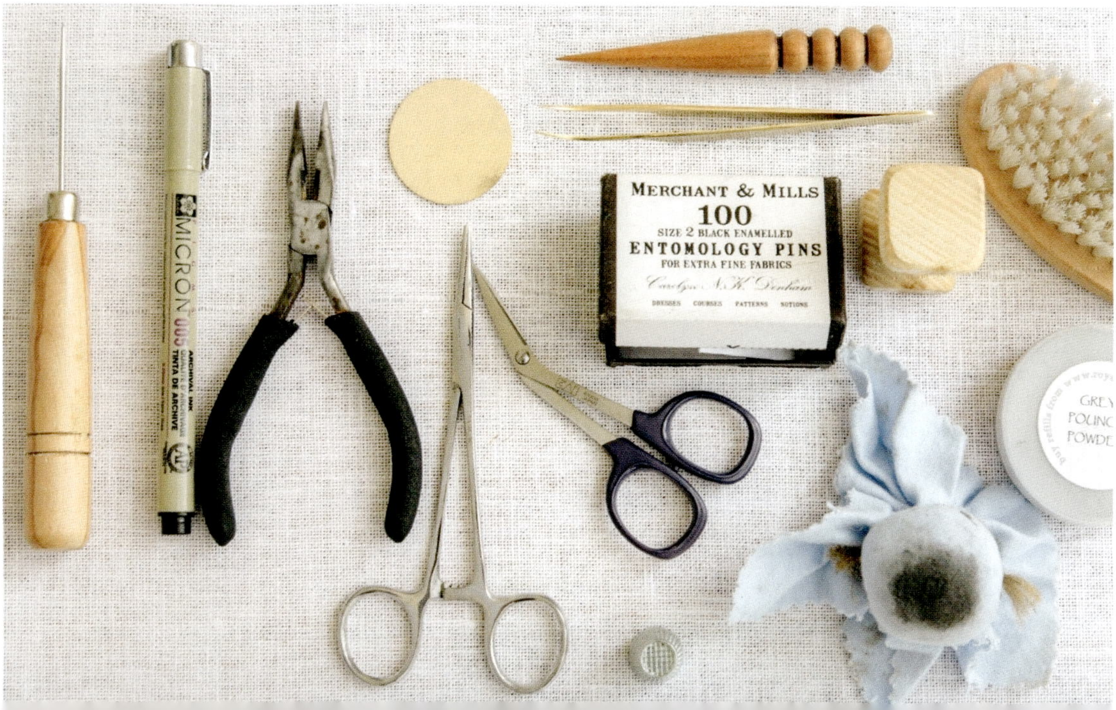

Evaluation

Evaluation and feedback are vital research tools that will help you refine your courses and marketing, yet people often struggle to ask for it effectively. Many creative teachers leave their evaluation until the end, and hand out forms for students to fill in, which can often feel a little awkward.

However, you can **integrate evaluation into your training from beginning to end,** making it continuous and much less formal. (Remember the customer survey exercise, test run and your own evaluation throughout or at the end of training that I suggested earlier in this book? Those are great examples of continuous evaluation.) Regular checking in will help you to **adjust what you do as you go along.** It can also encourage your student to self-evaluate and track their progress so that they start taking charge of their own learning journey.

First, decide what you want to evaluate:

- **The content:** the suitability of the topic, teaching format and methods.
- **The teaching:** your approach and teaching style, and the learning environment.
- **The learning:** what has changed for them because of the training, whether they achieved their goal and how they felt throughout the process.

Informal evaluation techniques

Before the training:

- **On the registration form, ask questions** that will give you insight into their existing knowledge and what they want to learn:
  - Why have you signed up for this course?
  - What's your number one question or challenge around [fill in your topic]?
  - What do you want to get out of today?
  - If you could ask me one question about [topic] what would you want to know?

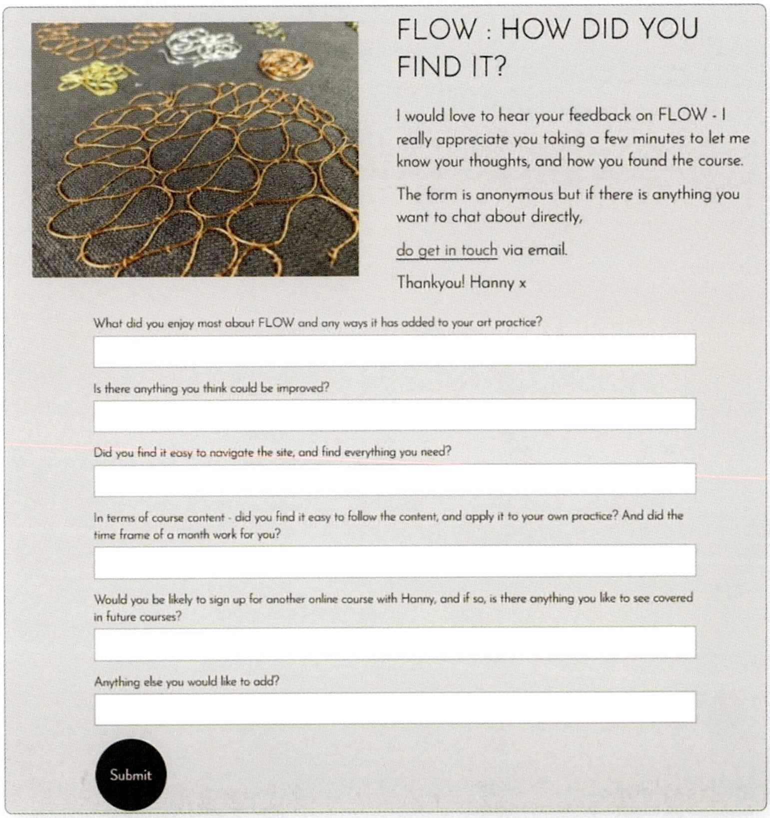
FLOW : HOW DID YOU FIND IT?

I would love to hear your feedback on FLOW - I really appreciate you taking a few minutes to let me know your thoughts, and how you found the course.

The form is anonymous but if there is anything you want to chat about directly,

do get in touch via email.

Thankyou! Hanny x

What did you enjoy most about FLOW and any ways it has added to your art practice?

Is there anything you think could be improved?

Did you find it easy to navigate the site, and find everything you need?

In terms of course content - did you find it easy to follow the content, and apply it to your own practice? And did the time frame of a month work for you?

Would you be likely to sign up for another online course with Hanny, and if so, is there anything you like to see covered in future courses?

Anything else you would like to add?

Submit

Left Hanny Newton uses a short and simple online survey to get feedback on her online course.

During the training:

- **Be aware of the mood in the room** or from individual students. Ask them for one word to describe how they feel and what they enjoyed about certain exercises. Acknowledge that learning can be hard, and pay attention to what questions they ask.
- **Make sure all students have the basic knowledge required** by asking questions about specific techniques.
- **Encourage students to share their work** in progress. Celebrate different approaches. Identify any challenges and look for solutions together. Make time for reflection on what they have learnt or what else they could have done.
- **Ask students about how they will use this technique in the future.** This will get them thinking about application and future development.
- **For online training, get students into action** by questioning them: e.g., 'what five activities will you do before the next session?'

Create and share an evaluation sheet

If you want feedback or testimonials, including a more formal evaluation can work well. You can give people an evaluation sheet at the end of an in-person workshop, or send a link to an online questionnaire. **Include questions such as:**

- Why did you sign up for this course?
- What did you enjoy the most?
- What was the number one thing you learnt?
- Did this training fulfil your expectations? Give a score between 0 and 10. Tell us why you gave it this score.
- What could we do better?
- How would you assess the venue? In terms of location, access, cleanliness/atmosphere? Give a score from 0 to 10 and tell us why you gave that score.

Evaluate yourself

Making some time to reflect during or after any training you do can help you improve. Do your own review before you read any of the student feedback, so that it doesn't influence you. Look at your lesson plan and consider the following questions, ideally within a day of finishing the training:

- What went particularly well?
- Which exercises worked?
- What was challenging? (Rather than who was challenging!)
- What could you do better next time?
- What do you need to take out or add in?
- Were there any particular situations that you could have avoided?
- Did you run on time? If not, why not?
- What was the energy in the room? Were students distracted, relaxed, chatty or bored?
- Look at your goals and objectives again. Did you achieve them?
- Have a look at your students' forms and see what they got from your training. Are there any surprises?
- Did the venue and space work? If not, what could you do next time? Do you need to be better prepared? Does the layout of the space need to change?

Evaluation is a key part of offering great training, and becoming a better teacher.

You can download the *Evaluation Sheet* template from the Toolkit.

Following up after your training

'The follow-up email is so important. It's very effective and people really appreciate the information. I quite often get "thank you" notes and emails.'
Rob Jones, Japanese textiles expert

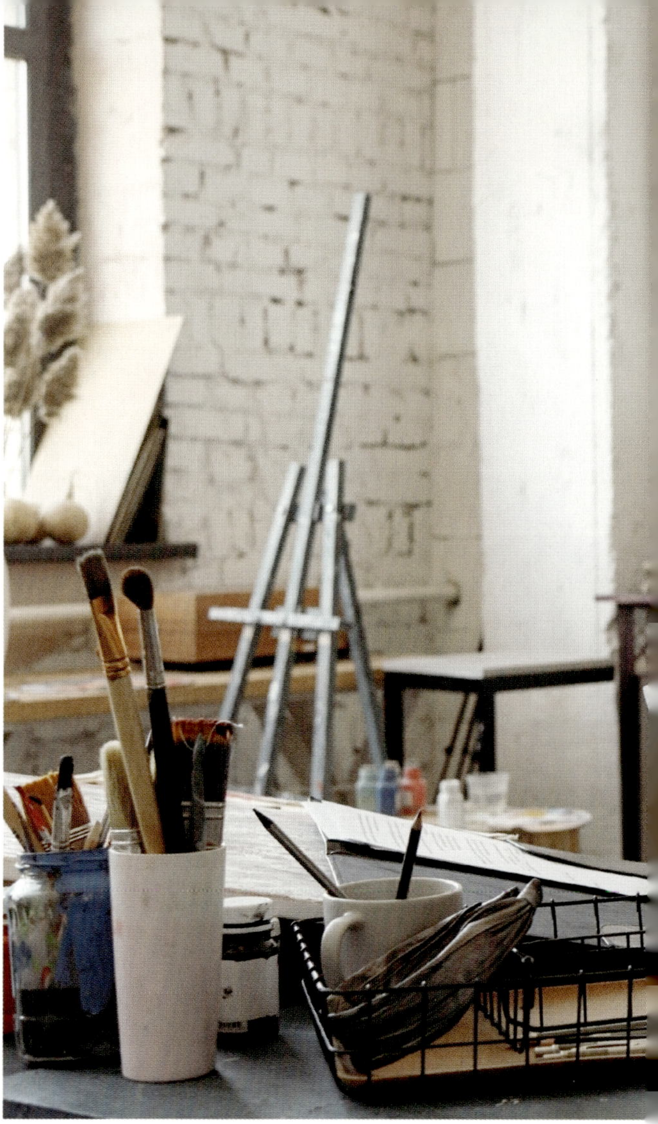

An important part of customer care is the follow-up communication you have with them after the training. As Rob Jones says above, people really appreciate the information, and it is a great opportunity to get them interested in future training, attending events or even to purchase your work.

In your follow-up email, make sure that you:

- **Clearly state in your subject line** that this is related to the training they just completed.
- **Thank them for coming** and share some of your own highlights or observations.
- **Let them know if you posted any images on your website** or social media, and where to find them.
- **Tell them how they can share their own images,** and any hashtags you would like them to use. Point out potential copyright issues before sharing.
- **Share a student list with names** and contact details, if you have permission from all your students.
- **Answer any questions** that you were not able to answer during the course, or summarise the most common ones.
- **Share any useful tools, tips or resources.** For example, you could provide a reading list, a crib sheet for specialist terminology and jargon, a summary of techniques, a list of step-by-step actions as an aide-mémoire, a list of tool suppliers, or links to any relevant blog posts you have written.
- **Tell them about any upcoming training** or other opportunities to see you or your work, such as events or exhibitions. Do you sell any related kits, books or materials they can purchase? Could you give them a loyalty discount?
- **Tell them of any follow-up training or support you offer,** e.g., online community, access to online courses or a content library, or one-to-one support.

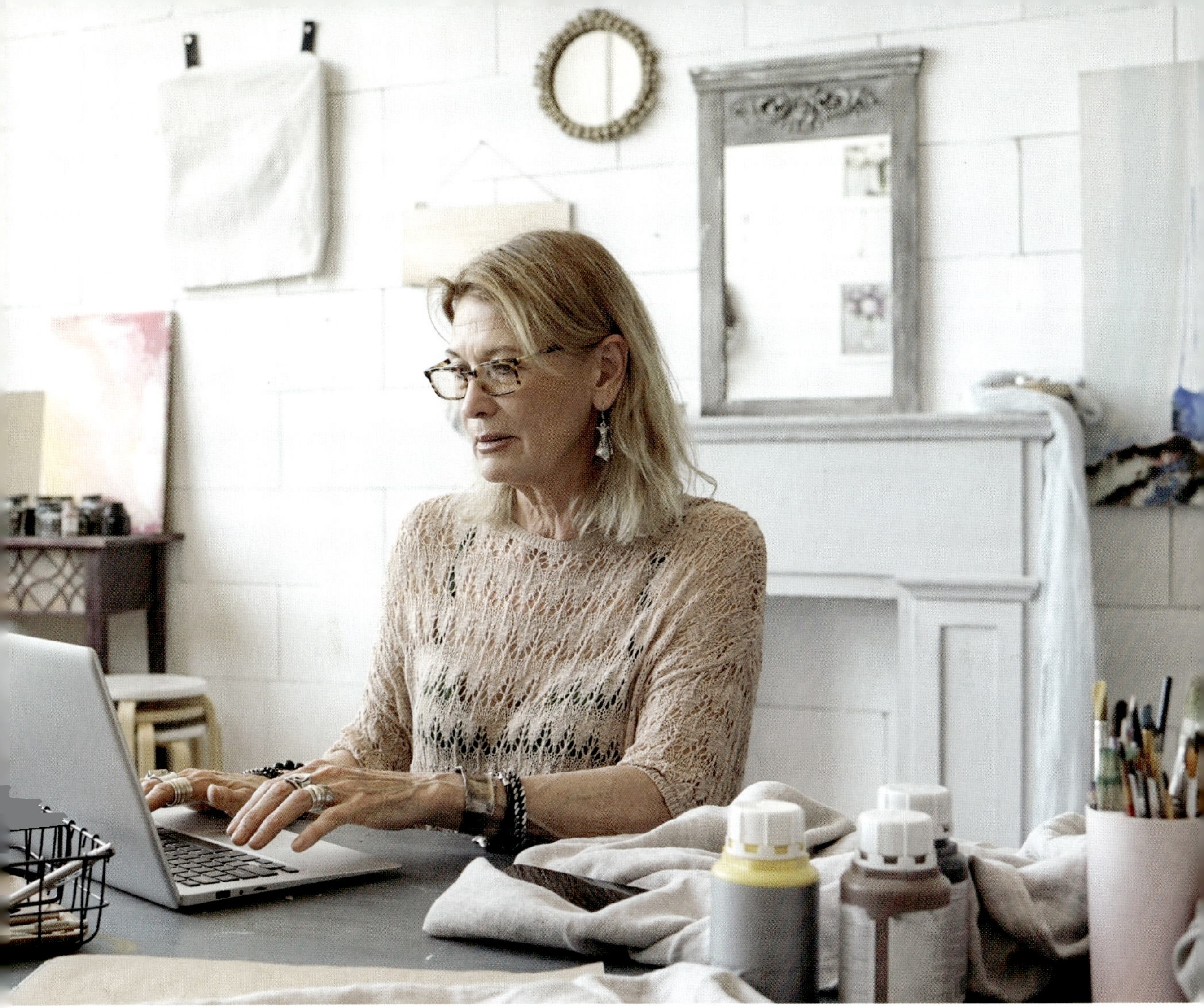

Don't forget to **add your students' details to your database and tag them** with the relevant course name and year. You don't need their permission for this and it means that you can stay in touch about future training or events.

With pre-recorded online courses you could create an automated sequence so that you send an email when your student finishes, or when they are expected to finish the course.

And that's it! You have done it! Now repeat, improve and keep working on building your training business, which is the focus of the last part of this book.

But first, our final Creative Case Study! Jessica Rose is one of my role models as a creative teacher. It's unbelievable what she has achieved with the Jewellers Academy in terms of classes, size and impact. She is a huge inspiration to me, and I hope she will inspire you too.

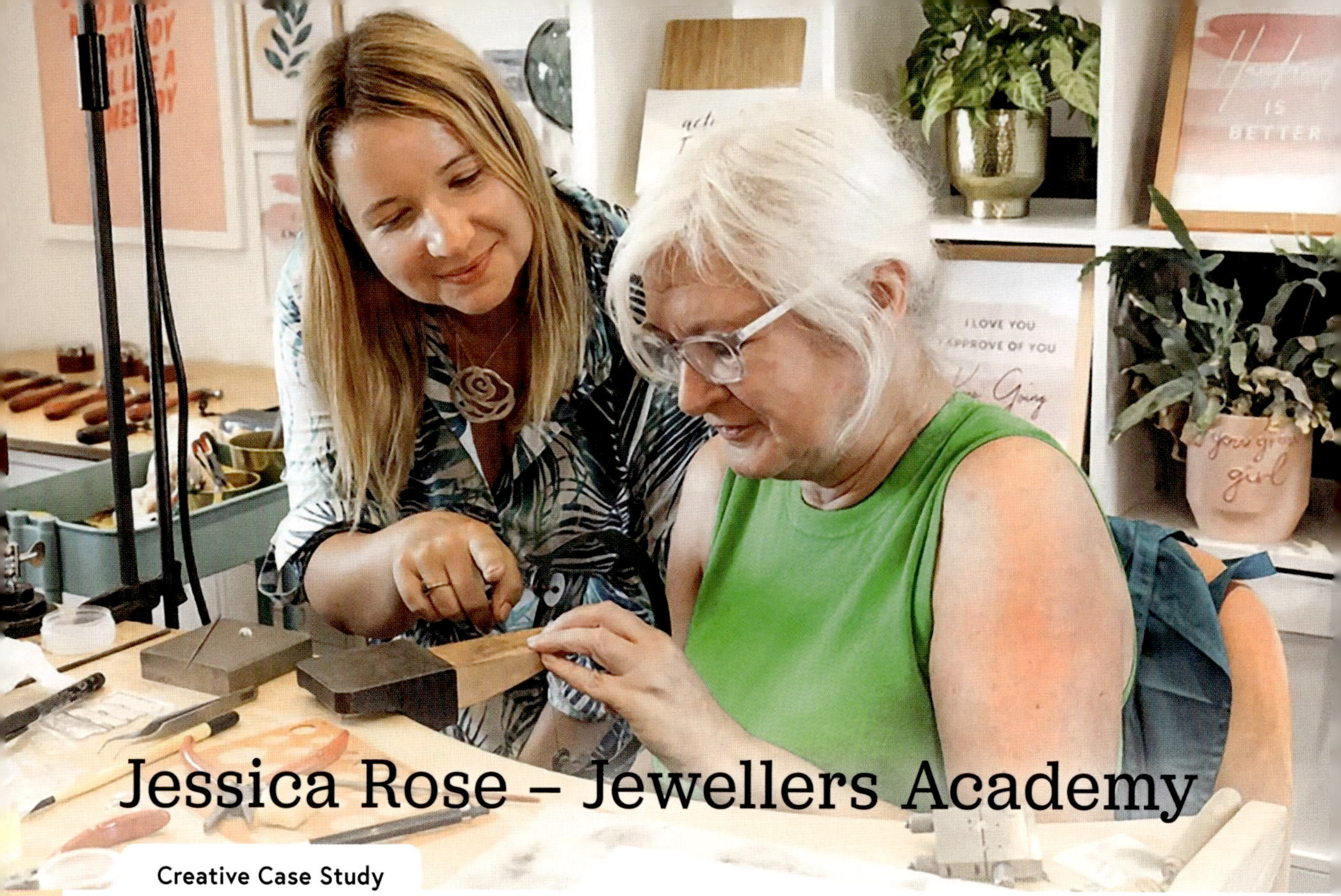

Jessica Rose – Jewellers Academy

Creative Case Study

Jessica started teaching in 2008, founding the London Jewellery School, which was based in Hatton Garden, London's jewellery quarter. The school taught around 40,000 students over 13 years.

In 2018, Jessica launched Jewellers Academy, which is fully online. At the time of writing, there are around 60,000 active students learning jewellery making online through a wide range of pre-recorded and live sessions. Skill levels range from absolute beginners through to professional goldsmiths. The core training consists of four diploma programmes, which combined have around 400 students each year. More than 5 million people have watched Jewellers Academy YouTube tutorials.

Jessica manages a team of around 40 people, most of whom work part-time, with a community and marketing team, film crew and around 30 jewellers who teach and mentor the various programmes.

You can find out more about Jessica Rose and the Jewellers Academy at www.jewellersacademy.com

You are now a big business, but where did it all start?

When I started the London Jewellery School, I wasn't planning to have this big business. My main motivation was not doing a nine-to-five job. I just wanted to make enough income to pay my bills. I was 19 when I started. It just grew very organically because people would come to the beginner class, and then say, 'When can we do the next level?' It just took on a life of its own.

'The growth from the start has come from getting other people involved. From the very beginning, I wasn't the main teacher. Hiring has probably been one of the keys to growth.'

I also hired admin staff early on. I employed someone one day a week to begin with, and within a month she was doing three days a week. That allowed me to get out there and teach and encourage people.

Why do you teach?

I love learning. I'm always doing courses. I've always been curious – it's what keeps life exciting for me.

And then once I've learnt something I want to pass it on, because I then get to see that joy and fulfilment in someone else. It doubles my own enjoyment and it also reinforces my own learning.

'It's so nice to teach people that want to learn what you're offering. And jewellery and business are two things I'm really passionate about.'

You started as a jeweller yourself. Do you still make?

Not as much as I thought I would, although I'm sure I will more in the future. I can't do everything. For me, the passion for teaching and running a business was stronger than the need to make. I love making and occasionally I do, but it's not my main job.

Who are your ideal students?

People that come to us have started making jewellery or are professional jewellers who want to take it to the next level. They want to develop their technical skills, or want to learn how to be profitable and grow.

The key element is that they really want to learn and have a strong passion for jewellery. It doesn't matter what they know, where they are, their age, their background, anything like that. If they have the passion, then we can help them with anything else.

What and how do you teach?

Our diplomas are the core of our business. We offer four of them, and three are progressive – similar to a degree but more practical and technical, delivered using a mixture of live and recorded sessions each week. Three times a year they send their work to us for marking. Throughout the year they are supported by an individual mentor and are part of small mentoring groups. A lot of involvement and accountability is built in.

The Jewellery Business Academy focuses on core business skills. It's a rolling programme, and we offer masterclasses, pre-recorded content, interviews, group coaching, individual mentoring and downloads, covering topics such as selling, websites, finance and social media.

We also offer an eight-week live Business Bootcamp each spring as part of the programme. Students sign up for a year and we open currently in October and January, so they start in a group at the same time.

On top of the diplomas and the Business Academy, we offer many stand-alone courses with lifetime access. These are self-directed and self-paced. For many of our courses we have Facebook groups, and our community team manages these groups six days a week, answering questions and giving feedback.

What are the benefits of learning and teaching online?

The biggest advantage for the student is being able to see everything magnified. We film with macro lenses that get into detail that you can't see with the naked eye. You simply can't see what's really going on if you've got an in-person class with 10 people crowded around someone setting a 2mm diamond.

Students also love learning at their own pace. Some people need longer, especially when it gets more detailed and fiddly. In an in-person workshop they might lose confidence.

What about pre-recorded vs live online training?

Pre-recorded training is great for what we do because we can achieve really close-up angles that you can't do live because it needs editing.

> *'You can create a piece of high-quality content that's really engaging, and as a teacher you can get your energy up for that limited time, which is much easier than having to teach the same thing week in week out.'*

I love teaching live sessions too. When we teach live online there's a different energy in the room, and I often teach with someone else, so there's more discussion, more spontaneity. Students can join in on the chat, or we can see them so there's more interaction.

How do you encourage students to keep going and finish your longer online courses?

With our diplomas there is built-in motivation, because at the end of each term they send their physical work to us for marking, and we're quite strict with those deadlines. We've had extremely high rates of completion for all the diploma programmes. With the making courses it's high too, because once you've started making something, you're in a flow.

The most challenging ones are the self-direct business courses. We deal with that by running sessions live and creating a community. We say, 'For the next three weeks, we're going to work through this course together. Who's joining us?' People are committing, and sharing and getting feedback from other students creates a kind of built-in FOMO. Accountability, feedback and motivation are key.

How do you plan your courses?

I spend between three and six months with a tutor planning the course. 'What's it called? What skills are we teaching? What samples will there be?' I take the role of the ideal student and focus on what I don't know and what I would want to learn. The teachers make the samples in advance and we pay for all of that.

We then break it down into videos or chapters. We're not too strict with this, because some teachers have long lesson plans, and others just turn up and it just comes out. The main thing is that on the filming days we work together. My job is to listen, observe, look at all the camera angles, and make sure that if I were a student, I could do this.

I've worked out that it costs us around £10,000 to make a course. Obviously, it wasn't that much at the start, but our diplomas are like

30 courses put together. We really invest in it. We have a film crew who are experts in getting the right angles, and we get professional sound. They bring in their expertise, strategy and suggestions.

What makes life a lot easier for me is that all these people are just great at what they do, and they care about it. I don't even have to worry about any of it, and I can focus on content production. It's taken time to build up that team. Initially I did all of those things, and then gradually outsourced.

Below Jessica Rose with her book, *Start & Grow a Profitable Jewellery Business*.

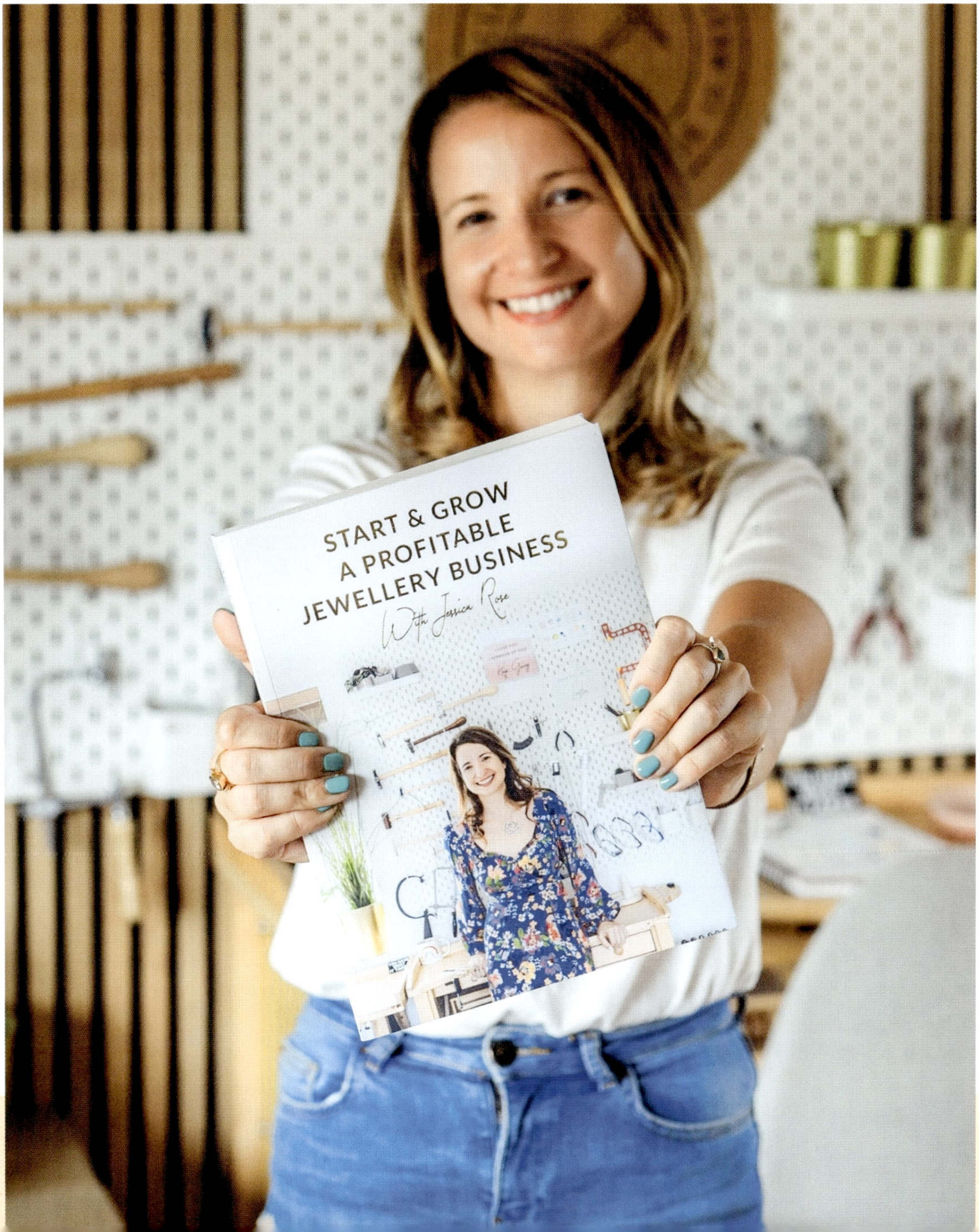

3

Part Three: Taking your teaching to the next level

CHAPTER 10

Going beyond training – what's next for you?

So, here we are, getting close to the end of our journey together.

Throughout this handbook I have shared loads of advice, tips, tools and templates with you to help you make your teaching more creative, to make more money from your teaching skills and to promote your training to your ideal students, to create a useful and beautiful brand and website, and take bookings.

In this final, shorter chapter **we will look ahead**. Firstly, what the growth opportunities are for creative teachers, with the final creative exercise of the Growth Matrix. We will look specifically into creating a membership and expert Chloe Savage will tell you how to create craft kits as part of your offer. We finish with a kind goodbye.

So, what's next for you?

Growth opportunities for creative teachers

Once you have established your regular training programmes, you might want to make improvements to keep yourself inspired and motivated, or to grow your business financially, or in profile or impact.

Growth option 1: Expand who you want to work with or teach

Is your confidence growing? Then get bolder or more niche with who you work with:

- **Work with larger cultural venues or educational organisations** such as museums or universities, or with companies. Can you hire teaching space, or pitch yourself so they pay you? This can have a huge impact on your profile and credibility.
- **Think beyond clients or venues.** Create partnerships or collaborations with other artists or experts to teach together, or approach suitable brands for an affiliate

partnership or to sponsor you or pay for materials.

- **Provide consultancy services or advice to other creatives,** businesses or educational organisations around your creative, business or teaching skills. For example, at the start of COVID-19, I was consulted by various creative and educational organisations, advising them on how to teach online, and ran several 'Teach the Trainer' sessions focusing on online training.

Time to pause

Get your notebook, take time to reflect and answer these questions:

- **Why do you want to teach?** We started this book with that big question. How would you answer that now? What has changed for you?
- **Look ahead, and think about life five or ten years from now:** how old will you be then? What will have changed in your life? Can you picture what you will be known for then? What does success look like for you – as an artist and as a teacher? Write down your big dream for the future. What would you do if you couldn't fail?
- **How do you want to grow your teaching business over the next five years?** What are your ambitions? What turnover or salary do you want? Do you want to work with a team? Many of the creatives featured in this book shared their business dreams too. Have a look at their stories and let them inspire your own teaching dream.

Growth option 2: Expand what and how you teach

Throughout this book we have looked at a wide variety of teaching and marketing opportunities.

Here is a refresher – read though the list, and think about how you can build on them in the future:

- **Create hybrid models** for both in-person and online learning, e.g., you could offer an online community or forum via Facebook. Accountability groups can provide support to implement improvements and encourage students to keep developing their skills.
- **Create a membership** where existing students and alumni can ask questions or provide answers, network, receive discounts on affiliated or your products or services, and access training recordings.
- **Publish a paid-for newsletter:** many creative teachers use Substack or other paid-for newsletter options to stay in touch and generate regular income.
- **Publish and sell e-books** or other digital downloads: write a short downloadable book in PDF around a specific teaching topic or provide patterns, cheat sheets or workbooks. Remember to think about VAT MOSS when selling digital products.
- **Podcasting:** this is a great way to share your expertise regularly to a wider audience. Don't forget to pitch to popular podcasts in your niche to broaden your marketing reach.
- **Add upgrades** from group training to individual mentoring, advice or coaching: provide online, personalised, confidential one-to-one sessions at a higher price point.

- **Upgrade to teaching more advanced students:** offer creativity training or transformational experiences (See Bloom's Taxonomy). You could provide one-to-one sessions tailored to their specific needs, or offer retreats or masterclasses on specialist topics.
- **Work with larger groups:** could you do talks or demonstrations at industry conferences or trade events, or reach out to a well-known podcaster?
- **Accredited training:** to add more credibility to your training you could work with an accreditation body to create a curriculum and tests to adhere to specific teaching qualifications. The Jewellers Academy provides accredited in-house training.

Growth option 3: Sell related products

- **Write a book!** Many creative teachers also publish their own self-published e-books or get commissioned to write a book.
- **Sell tools and materials:** can you do a deal with your tool or material suppliers to use, recommend or sell their products in exchange for an affiliate payment? At in-person training, you can set up a shop, or you can recommend or sell affiliated products online. Even recommending books on your blog (with an affiliate link) can bring in additional passive income. Always be transparent when you use affiliate links and let your readers know that you get a commission.

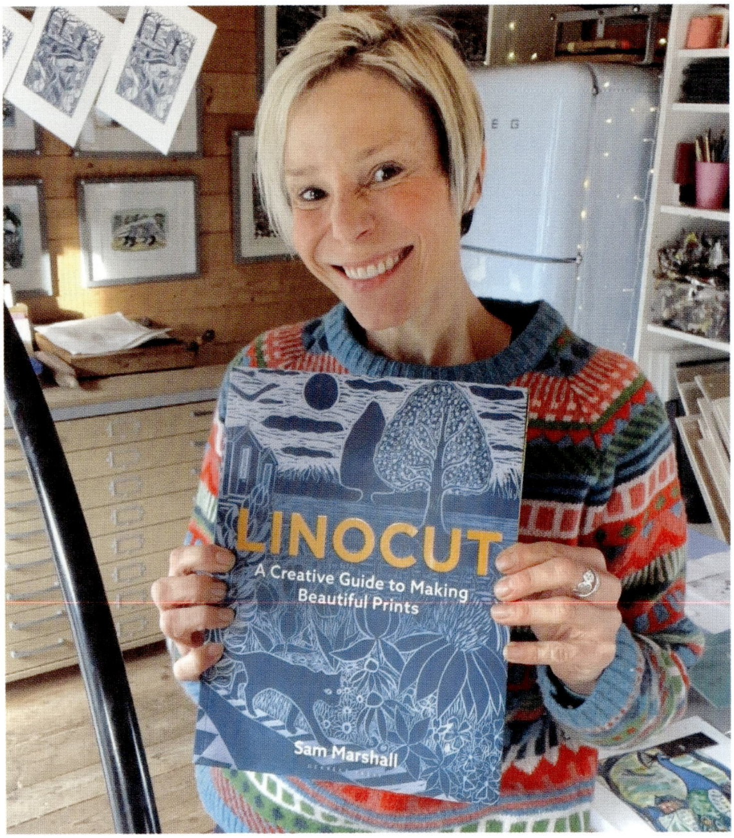

Left Sam Marshall with her book *Linocut*.

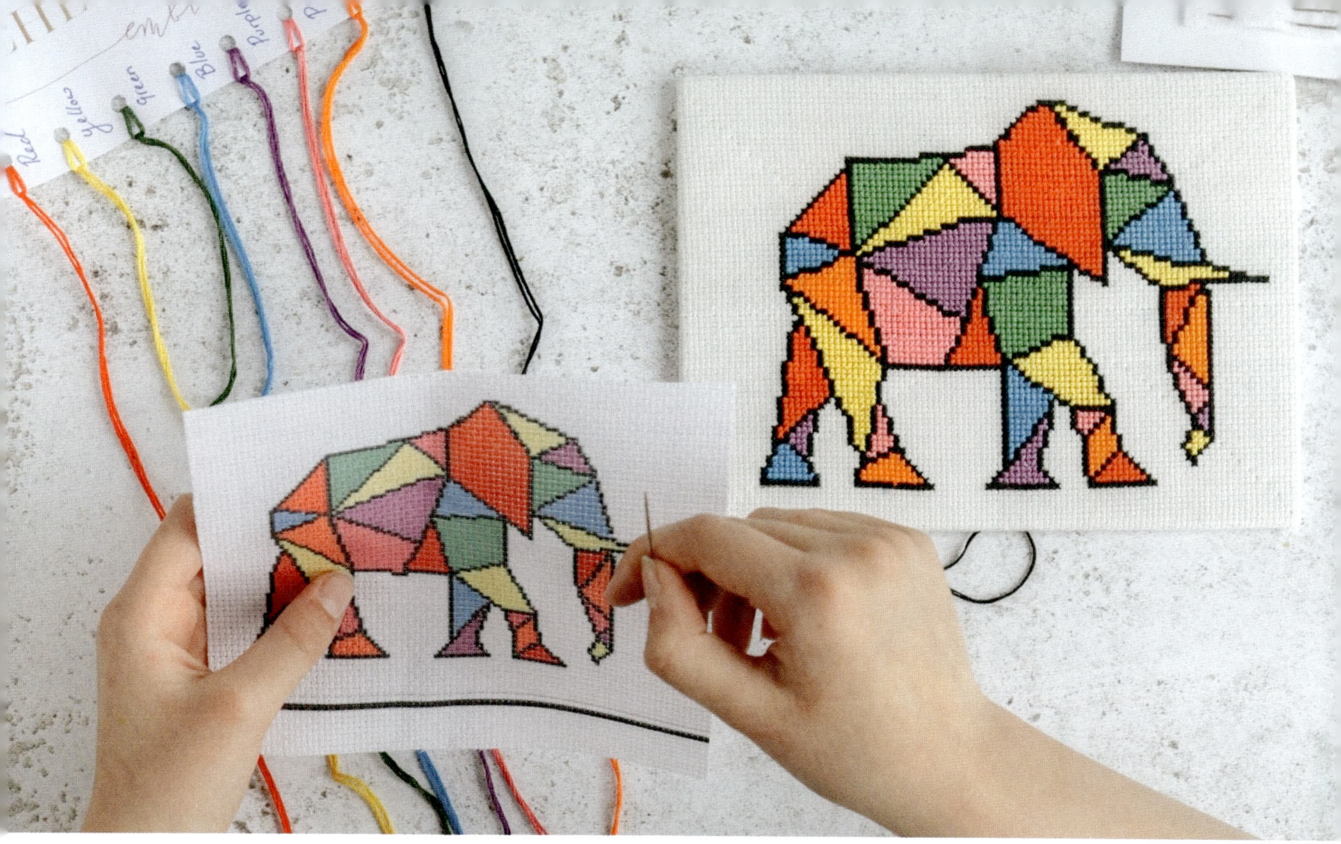

- **Creative kits:** design a creative project and provide all the materials and instructions in a box that clients can purchase online or at events – these are very popular.
- **Subscription boxes:** create recurring revenue by creating and sourcing creative kits that can be sold as part of a membership.
- **Merchandise:** if you are creating a strong community and brand then you could monetise your fame by selling products like badges, tote bags, materials or clothing with slogans or images.

Above Embroiderer Chloe Savage offers a wide range of embroidery kits.

Growth option 4: Use your intellectual copyright

- **License your training materials:** if you have created a unique system of teaching, you could consider licensing your methods to others, who would pay you a regular fee. Teach licensees your approach and provide them with teaching materials. You can trademark your training method, which provides legal protection.
- **Franchising your business:** you grant the right to operate a business under your brand name to a third-party franchisee in return for a franchising and licensing fees. They agree to run it exactly in line with your operational standards and standards of customer care. In the creative teaching sector, franchising is more common with providers of children's classes e.g., The Creation Station, Crayola® Imagine Arts Academy™ and Splat Messy Play.

The Growth Matrix

So, what do you want to do next? How will you grow or scale your training business?

Download the *Growth Matrix* template from the Toolkit. This is based on the Ansoff Matrix – a well-known strategic framework for future growth planning.

Start the exercise by filling in square one with your existing training and who your existing students are.

The next level of growth is to look at your existing students and think about what else they might like to learn and how you can teach them. Earlier in this chapter, I shared loads of potential ideas with you. You might also want to do some market research with your existing students, and consider different formats or activities. Could you upgrade to provide one-to-one support?

The third level is expanding and looking for new students for your existing training. Are you promoting yourself properly? Review your client collage and persona exercise. Do you need to drive more traffic to your website or launch better?

The most risky growth strategy is the last one, and I would recommend that you only do this after you have tried the second and third strategies. In this strategy you start a completely new training offer, with a brand new audience.

1. Existing training offer and existing clients = your current situation E.g., in-person ceramic workshops and courses in London for beginners to professionals	**2. New training offer and existing clients** = what else or how else would your ideal students like to learn? E.g., more technical and business courses e.g. on glazing, building kilns, costing and pricing ceramics or starting a ceramic business, or online training workshops.
3. Existing training offer and new clients = identifying new client groups who might be interested in what you teach E.g., clay workshops for children, hen parties or corporate events.	**4. New training offer and new clients** = most risky E.g., creativity retreats in the UK or abroad, or online membership for creatives.

Above An example of the Growth Matrix with some details filled in.

Time to pause

Get your notebook and make time to reflect and answer the following:

- **Do the Growth Matrix exercise.** Start with what you currently do, how you can expand through the second and third strategies, or offer something completely new through the fourth strategy.
- **Look back at the business dream you wrote down at the start of this chapter.** What do you need to do to make this dream happen? What, how and who will you teach? Who will your ideal students and partners be? Use the annual training plan (p.148) and annual training budget (p.149) and use the templates to sketch out your training up to five years from now.
- **What do you need to do, learn or create to make your dream possible?** What do you need to stop doing?

These planning exercises can help you to visualise your future, which in turn can help make it happen.

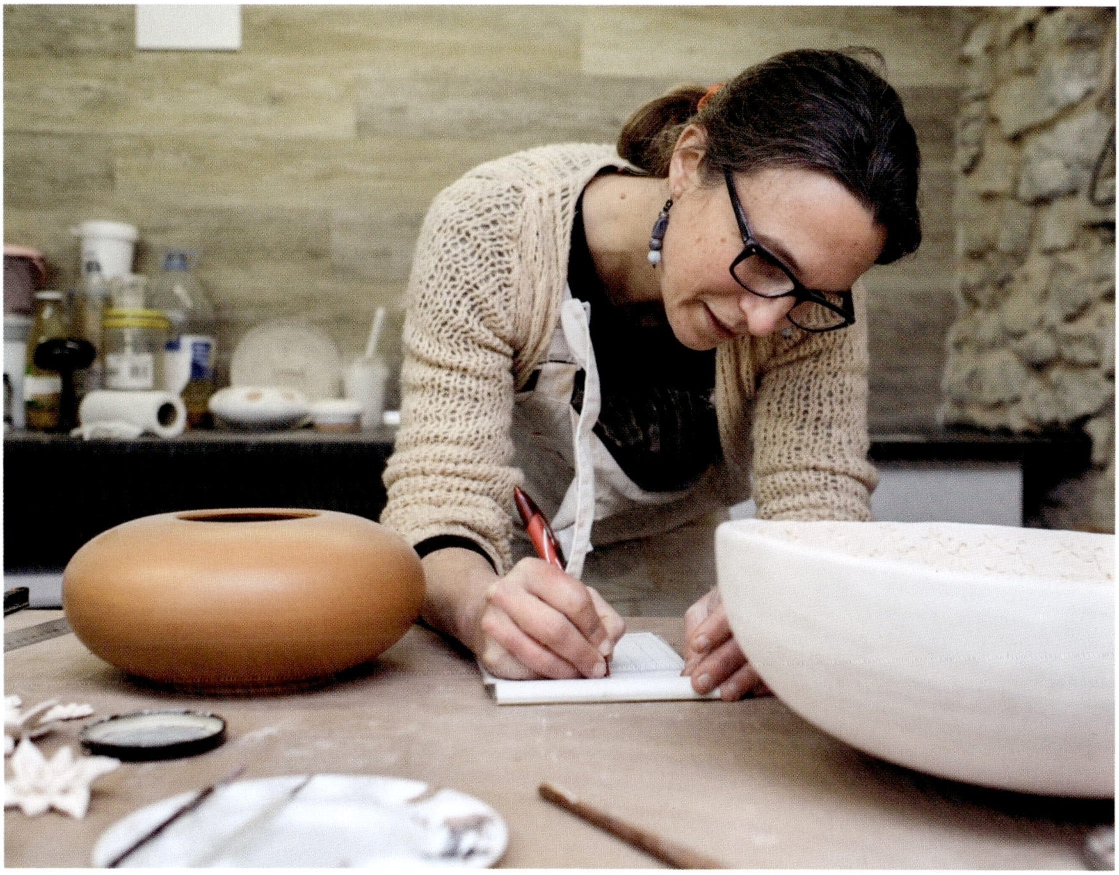

Starting a membership

A great way to grow your training business is by including an online membership, as this can provide a very predictable, recurring source of income for you. You can often reuse existing content, and it's a great way to build community and engagement with potential, existing and past students, often at a low cost to you. Memberships are also very scalable as you can accommodate an unlimited number of members.

However, memberships are not an entirely passive income stream!

Do not underestimate the time and energy it can take to set up your membership online, to keep your content fresh and your members engaged. **To avoid cancellations and low engagement** you will need to provide regular new content and put some time into answering questions. You will also need to promote your membership to attract new members.

A membership is a longer-term commitment, so make sure that you know what you are taking on and that you have enough content planned out to cover several months.

Below Online memberships are a great way to stay in touch, and to create a community around your business.

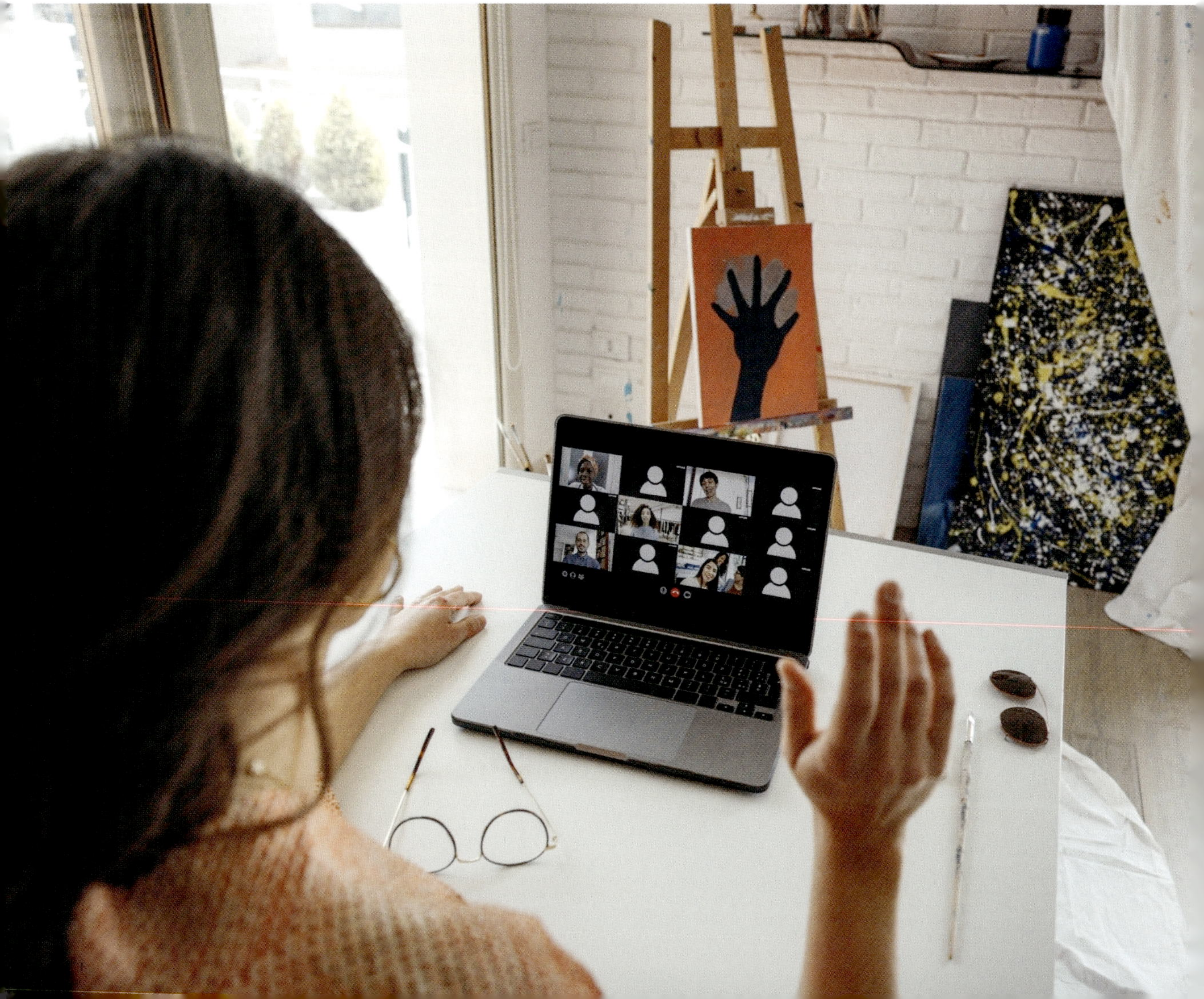

Setting up your online membership programme

There are several steps involved in setting up an online membership programme.

1 Define your membership offering
Who is your ideal member, what are their needs and interests and what will they get?

- Think about exclusive content and live workshops.
- Set up a community forum.
- Will you provide discounts on your products and services, or trusted partners?
- Do some market research to refine your offer, and check competitors' membership fees.

2 Select an online membership platform
Many online training platforms also have an option to create membership sites, which will make it much easier for you to manage members, forums, content and payments. Look at Kajabi, Thinkific and Teachable, or use MemberPress for WordPress websites. You can find more details in the Resources section at the end of this book.

3 Set your membership levels and prices
Offer different tiers with varying benefits, and have monthly, quarterly or annual membership options. Start at a lower price point to get started, and you can always increase your membership levels as your content and offer grows.

4 Design your membership site
Create a user-friendly site that's easy to navigate, and that reflects your overall brand. You might need some additional technical expertise to ensure that your site is mobile-responsive, secure and optimised for SEO.

5 Create compelling content
Develop high-quality content to provide value to your members, including video tutorials, downloadable resources, challenges, live Q&A sessions or guest expert interviews. Try to plan ahead or use monthly themes to be more efficient.

6 Launch and market your membership programme
Create a buzz when you launch by offering early-bird discounts, limited-time bonuses or exclusive perks for founding members. Continue to promote your membership through your website, email marketing, social media, free webinars, guest blogging and partnerships.

7 Provide ongoing support and engagement
Create a sense of community and belonging amongst your members through regular communication and member-exclusive events and benefits. Set clear guidelines around forums and encourage members to support each other too.

8 Keep going!
Use analytical tools to track member engagement, retention rates and member feedback to continuously improve your offer. Scale your membership by attracting more members, launching new tiers or adding other offers.

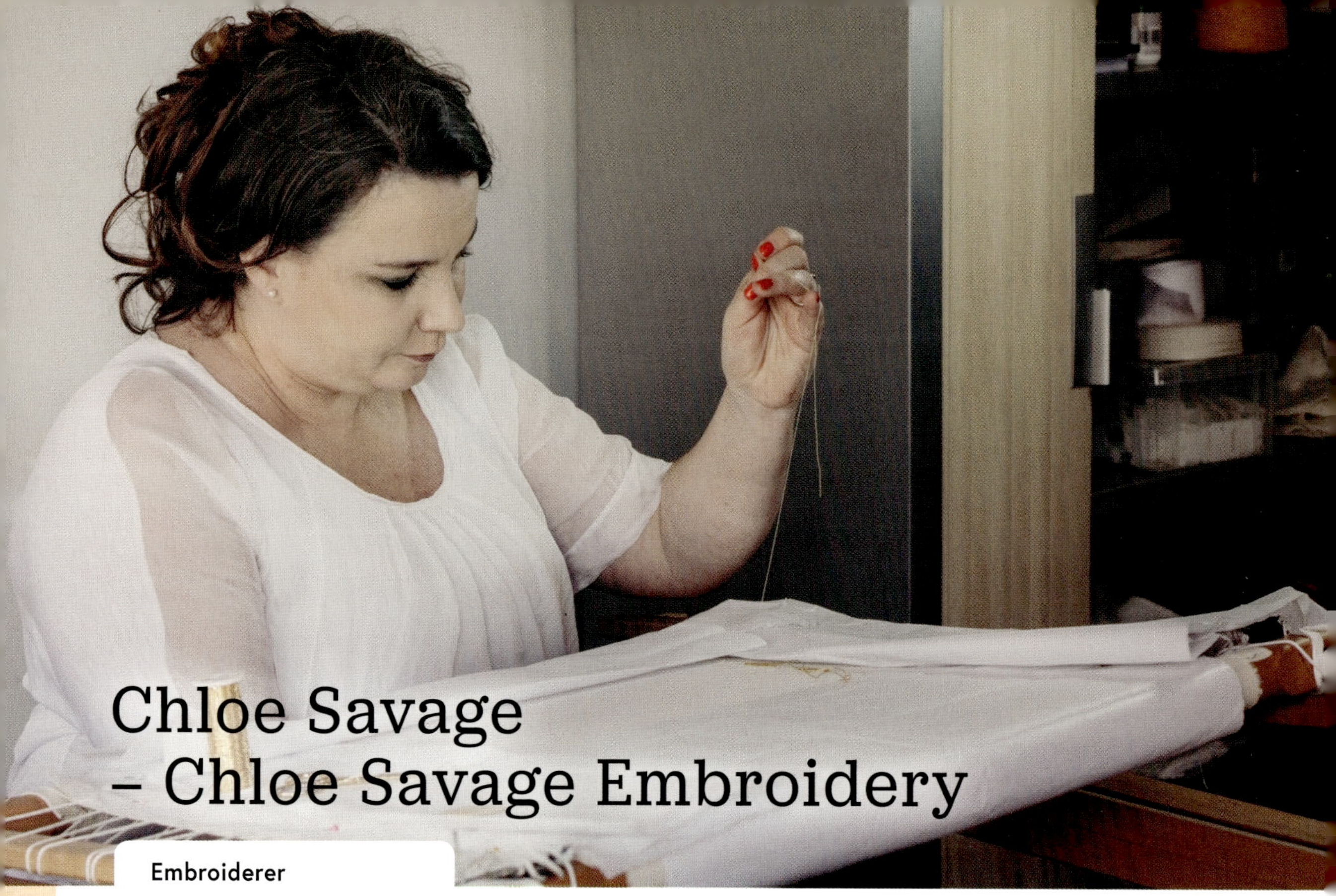

Chloe Savage – Chloe Savage Embroidery

Embroiderer

Expert Tips: Creating craft kits

Chloe Savage is an expert embroiderer, based in Bristol, UK, who often receives embroidery and top-end conservation commissions. Chloe teaches embroidery skills in person and online, runs a membership, and has developed a thriving business in embroidery kits for children, teenagers and adults.

You can find out more about her on www.chloesavageembroidery.com

As Chloe is an expert in designing and selling kits, as well as workshops and courses, **we asked her to share her expert tips with us.**

Above Chloe Savage at work.

1 For me, **designing a craft kit is similar to a science experiment.** 'Is it crewelwork, goldwork or needlepoint? Who is it for? A child or an adult? What level?' We sell mostly beginners' and children's kits.

2 You need to be **honest about the amount of time they need to spend on it.** It should be something they can pick up on evenings or weekends, and it shouldn't take more than 8–10 hours. Size matters too, and price is important. Beginners' kits need to be between £9 and £25, while intermediate and advanced kits often sell for much more because they are more committed.

3 You'll need to **work backwards** and think about the materials you use and the packing and promotional time, and add

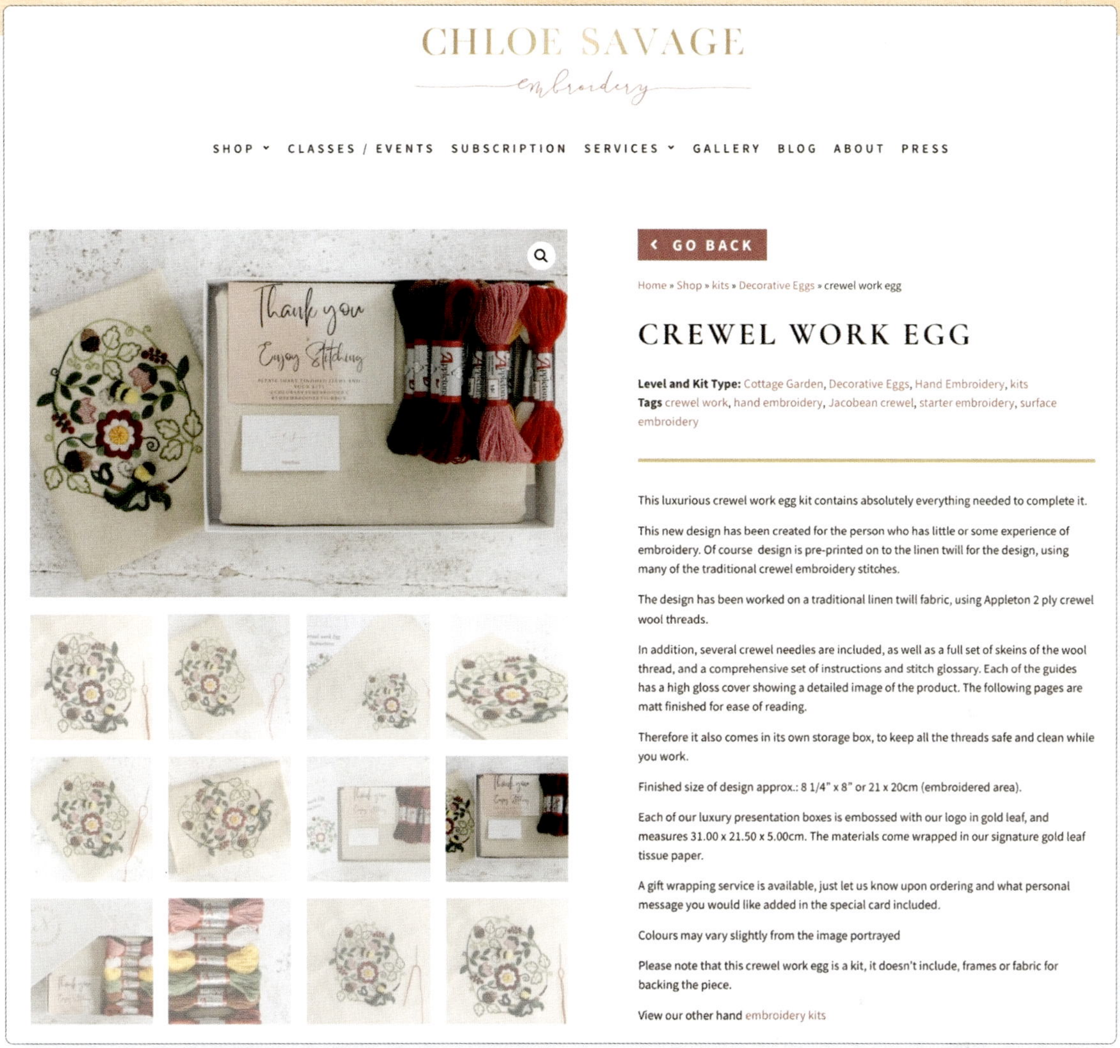

Above Chloe's sales page for one of her kits.

something for your overheads too.

4 **The cost of packing is a big consideration.** Packaging is really important, because it's a gift and needs to sell itself. Our children's kit is a white paper bag with a sticky print label. Children aren't that bothered, as long as it's bright, clean and shows what's in it, and clearly shows the right age range. The children's collection includes kits for ages four and up.

5 When writing your instructions, you need to **get them tested and assume that people do not know the basics.** It's very easy to miss a step. We include more images in the beginners' and children's kits, but you need to be really clear with your written instructions.

6 **We also include a series of sample stitches** with each kit. We have built a bank of stitch diagrams, with lots of different pictures of hands doing different stitches. Don't forget to include instructions on how to finish the project.

7 **A lot of work goes into developing a kit,** but you can sell a large quantity of them, especially if you have a collection. We have the very popular geometric animal collection, and our egg kits that use very different techniques.

A final note

So, here we are, at the end of this book. But this is definitely not the end of your training journey.

Maybe you are at the start of your teaching career or training business, or maybe I have given you some very useful tips to make your training better or to make your life, training and creative practice more sustainable, both financially and in terms of your own energy levels.

I hope you will return to this book often as a source of inspiration, to make notes and truly treasure it, and that you recommend or lend it to good friends and fellow creative teachers too.

What you do next, in the days, weeks, months or years ahead, is **up to you** – but then it always was! What you do with all this new knowledge and inspiration will make a huge difference to you and your future students.

You don't have to do it alone. Do get in touch with me at info@thedesigntrust.co.uk and check out how I can help you to become a fire starter too.

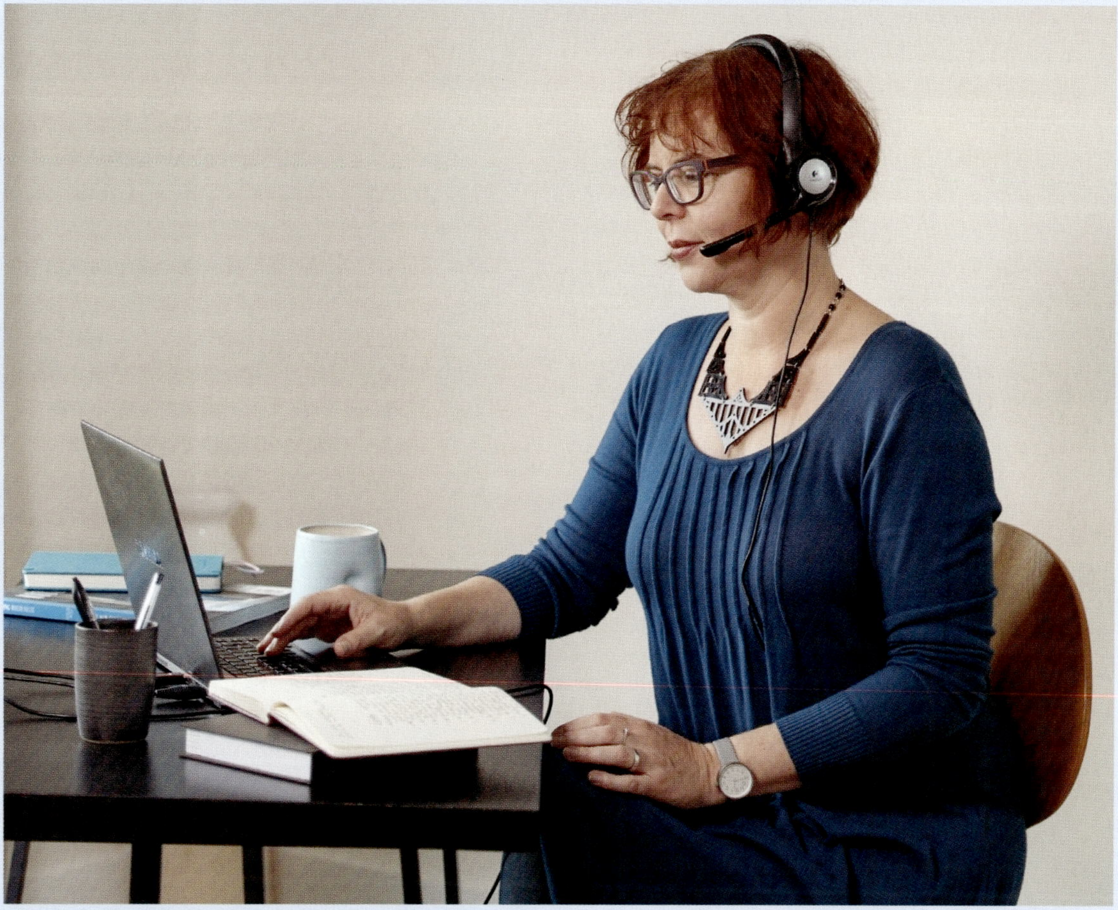

Acknowledgements

This book would not have been possible without the support, passion and advice from many people over the last few years. It truly has been one of the most challenging yet inspiring projects and journeys of my life.

Thank you to Commissioning Editor Clare Martelli at Herbert Press for inviting me to write this book and for her ongoing patience and advice throughout the last two years. Assistant Editors Caroline Guillet and Sara Simper did a great job with organising all the details. Thanks to editor Rachael Prest, who turned a 100,000 word monster into a much more digestible and enjoyable book! And Austin Taylor for designing a beautiful but functional action-taking book. I hope we created something special together.

A huge thank you to all my students and clients over the last three decades, especially those that signed up in March 2020 to my then new online course *Teach Your Creative Skills Online*. Your comments, support and enthusiasm for online teaching at that bizarre time showed me how important it is to be flexible and creative with teaching, and how immensely powerful it is to share your creative skills and passion with others.

Thank you to all the professional creative teachers that contributed to the research for this book through surveys, the creative workshops I attended, and the many people who I interviewed. Your answers, questions, insights and passion for why, what and how you teach and create a successful career through teaching and making are really at the heart of this book. Unfortunately, I couldn't feature everybody who I interviewed, but your stories and advice are woven throughout. Thank you to Alison, Catherine, Chloe, David, Ekta, Esté, Hanny, Lindsey, Jessica, Kara, Lilla, Linda, Rauni, Rob, Ruby, Sally, Sam and Yeshen for your enormous creative and teaching gifts, your wisdom and passion that you shared with me, and now the rest of the world. A special shout out to Angie Parker who became my writing buddy and got me through some tough times.

I couldn't run The Design Trust without Anne-Marie Shepherd, who with her practical support and advice, humour and regular tears keeps me focused, picks up the balls I drop and kept the show on the road while I was working on this book. Thank you. I hope we will be a team that grows old together!

It all really started over 30 years ago when doing a work placement for an arts and creative education organisation in Belgium. Bedankt Ludo en Michael. It's all come full circle.

I am deeply grateful to my family, Guy, Isobel, Emily and Jet who keep me grounded, make me laugh when I need it most, and who support me regardless. I am so proud and humbled to see you grow into loving, creative human beings. You are my rocks. And my fire.

Resources

Books on teaching

DeJean, William, *Make Learning Stick for Everyone: Learn the System for Online, Face-to-face and Blended Learning Environments*, Armedia, 2020.

Frost Cuevas, Rebecca, *Course Design Formula: How To Teach Anything To Anyone Online*, Learn and Get Smarter, Inc. Riverside, CA, 2019.

Goldstein, Mitch, *How to Be a Design Student (And How to Teach Them)*, Princeton Architectural Press, New York, 2023.

Halsey, Vicki, *Brilliance by Design: Creating Learning Experiences That Connect, Inspire, and ENGAGE*, Berrett-Koehler, San Francisco, 2011.

Heijnen, Emiel, and Melissa Bremmer, eds., *Wicked Arts Assignments: Practising Creativity in Contemporary Arts Education*, Translated by Leo Reijnen, second print, Amsterdam: Valiz, 2021.

Honary, Ethan, *Course Design Strategy: The Art of Making People Learn*, Skills Converged Publishing, 2021.

Iny, Danny, *Teach Your Gift: How Coaches, Consultants, Authors, Speakers and Experts Create Online Course Business Success in 2020 and Beyond*, Mirasee Press, Montreal, Quebec, 2020.

Kneebone, Roger, *Expert: Understanding the Path to Mastery*, Penguin Books, London, 2021.

Natalenko, Rie, *Share Your Skills: The Ultimate Guide to Running an Art or Craft Workshop*, The Write Impression Publications, Middletown, DE, 2015.

Nelson, Ken, David Ronka, and Lesli Lang, *Designing & Leading Life-Changing Workshops: Creating the Conditions for Transformation in Your Groups, Trainings, and Retreats*, Cliffhouse Press, Kittery Point, Maine, 2020.

O'Neill-Blackwell, Jeanine, *Engage: The Trainer's Guide to Learning Styles*, Pfeiffer, San Francisco, CA, 2012.

Rose, Dr Carrie, *The Completed Course: The Secret to Creating Lasting Impact, Raving Fans, and Increased Profits With Online Courses*, Kindle Edition, 2018.

Organisations involved with improving teaching

Craft Educators: www.facebook.com/groups/crafteducators The Crafts Council craft educators group.

Creative UK: www.wearecreative.uk

Digital Culture Network: digitalculturenetwork.org.uk

Heritage Crafts: www.heritagecrafts.org.uk A UK charity that provides training grants and opportunities for endangered crafts.

Kaos Pilot: www.kaospilot.dk An international disruptive education provider and facilitator of creative learning experiences for individuals, communities and organisations.

Learn & Get Smarter: www.learnandgetsmarter.com Set up by online teaching expert Rebecca Frost Cuevas with useful courses and community.

Life-Changing Workshops: www.life-changingworkshops.com Training organisation focusing on transformational workshops, which offers a useful newsletter and toolkit.

Mirasee: www.mirasee.com Online school to teach you how to create and launch online courses profitably. With useful free resources, books, podcasts and regular training programmes.

NCACE (The National Centre for Academic and Cultural Exchange): www.ncace.ac.uk Champions knowledge exchange and collaboration between higher education and the arts and cultural sectors.

Queen Elizabeth Scholarship Trust (QEST): www.qest.org.uk Charity dedicated to excellence in British craftsmanship that provides training grants for professional makers.

Stu McLaren: stu.me An expert in membership sites whose site offers free resources and an online course.

Skills and Education Group: www.skillsandeducationgroup.co.uk

Online creative teaching marketplaces or online creative schools

CreativeLive: www.creativelive.com A leading USA-based online school for creatives to learn technical, creative and business skills. Teachers are often well-known experts who teach in front of a live studio audience, with recordings available to members.

Domestika: www.domestika.org A popular website for pre-recorded creative skill training, mainly delivered in English and Spanish. They are looking for professional creative teachers, who then earn royalties.

Etsy: www.etsy.com Leading international handmade and vintage product marketplace. You can promote online courses only if they include a physical element, such as a handout.

MasterClass: www.masterclass.com An American online education subscription platform with well-known experts teaching classes.

Skillshare: www.skillshare.com A leading online education platform. Membership gives access to thousands of online classes. Looking for creatives to teach against royalty payment.

Wecandoo: www.wecandoo.uk Promote your in-person creative workshops through this online artisan marketplace that covers France, Belgium and the UK.

Websites to promote your training

Airbnb Experiences: www.airbnb.co.uk

ClassBento: classbento.co.uk

Courses.com: courses.com

Craft Courses: www.craftcourses.com

Eventbrite: www.eventbrite.co.uk

Find A Craft: findacraft.co.uk

Homo Faber: homofaber.com

Into the Blue: www.intotheblue.co.uk

Software and online tools for online teaching and businesses

AccessAlly: www.accessally.com Popular Wordpress plugin to create online courses and memberships.

Adobe Photoshop Elements: www.adobe.com Leading photo editing software.

Adobe Premier Pro: www.adobe.com Leading video editing software.

Book Like a Boss: www.blab.co Simple landing page builder to simplify booking administration and take payments.

Buy Me A Coffee: www.buymeacoffee.com An alternative platform for creators and creatives to get financial support and create memberships.

Camtasia: www.techsmith.com/store/camtasia Very popular video editing software.

Canva: www.canva.com Graphic design tool to easily add text or designs to images and presentations.

Capcut: www.capcut.com A free video editing and graphic design tool.

Circle: www.circle.so Platform to build online community and memberships.

Convertkit: www.convertkit.com A useful email marketing software which also offers easy landing page designs and the opportunity for paid-for-newsletters. Useful free resources including e-books on a broad range of online business topics.

Crowdcast: crowdcast.io Popular webinar and screensharing software.

DaVinci Resolve: www.blackmagicdesign.com Post-production editing software to add special effects.
Educate Me: www.educate-me.co Online platform to create collaborative courses.
Filmora: filmora.wondershare.com Easy-to-use film editing software.
Google Classroom: edu.google.com Popular webinar and meeting software.
GoTo: www.goto.com Popular meeting and webinar software.
GumRoad: www.gumroad.com Easy-to-use ecommerce platform to sell digital and physical products, incl. Online pre-recorded courses and e-books. Fully VAT MOSS compliant for creators in UK and EU.
Kajabi: www.kajabi.com Popular platform to create, market and sell digital content.
LearnDash: www.learndash.com WP plugin for learning management systems.
LearnPress: thimpress.com/learnpress Comprehensive WP plugin to create online courses.
LearnWorlds: www.learnworlds.com Popular online course platform to create, sell and promote online courses.
Lifter LMS: www.lifterlms.com Leading WP plugin to create highly online courses and membership websites. Very customisable, therefore probably needs a WP or LMS expert to install.
LightWorks: www.lwks.com Free video editing software.
Livestorm: www.livestorm.co Popular video conferencing software.
Loom: www.loom.com Free screen recording software, advanced editing and video storage.
MemberPress: www.memberpress.com Leading WP plugins for membership, online courses, subscription and community management.
Membership Academy: www.membershipacademy.com Very useful online courses, network and templates to start an online membership community successfully.
Mighty Networks: www.mightnetworks.com Leading software to create online communities including memberships and courses.
MS Teams: www.microsoft.com Popular app to connect and manage.
Otter: www.otter.ai A transcription and subtitling software to make your online videos more accessible.
Patreon: www.patreon.com Leading platform to create paid-for memberships or sell digital products.
PayPal: www.paypal.com Leading payment provider to take payments online, or to pay in instalments.
Podia: www.podia.com All-in-one platform for selling online courses, webinars and digital downloads.
Procreate: www.procreate.com Graphics editor and digital illustration app.
Rev: www.rev.com Creates highly accurate automated subtitles to Zoom recordings.
Ruzuku: www.ruzuku.com Easy-to-use online training platform to host and organise online training and administration easily. Has built-in webinar software.
ScreenPal: www.screenpal.com Screencasting and video editing software.
Squarespace: www.squarespace.com The leading ecommerce website has added useful tools to create, host, manage and promote online courses.
Stripe: www.stripe.com Leading online payment software, alternative to PayPal.
Substack: www.substack.com Leading platform to support subscription newsletter content creators.
Teachable: www.teachable.com Leading online course platform to build, sell and administer online courses and digital content.
Teachery: www.teachery.co Customisable online teaching platform.
Thinkific: www.thinkific.com Leading online course platform with advanced features such as quizzes and forums.

Thrive Apprentice: www.thrivethemes.com Leading WP membership and course building software.
Videoleap: www.videoleapapp.com Video editing tool.
Vimeo: www.vimeo.com Leading video hosting and storage platform, an alternative to YouTube.
WebinarGeek: www.webinargeek.com Popular webinar platform.
WishListMember: www.wishlistmember.com Leading WP plugin to create membership site.
YouTube: www.youtube.com Leading video sharing and hosting, and social media platform.
Zoom: www.zoom.com Popular software for video meetings and webinars.

Intellectual property organisations

AIPLA: American Intellectual Property Law Association
ACID: Anti Copying In Design
BIPC: British Library Business & IP Centre
EUIPO: European Union Intellectual Property Office
IPO: Intellectual Property Office (UK)
IPSANZ: The Intellectual Property Society of Australia and New Zealand
WIPO: World Intellectual Property Organization

Disability resources

Microsoft provide resources, Ask Accessibility, and a useful Accessibility Checker to make their technology accessible for all. www.microsoft.com
WebAIM (Web Accessibility in Mind) is a very useful online resource to create more accessible online content for people with disabilities. www.webaim.org

UK: **Craft Courses** has posts on how to make your workshops more accessible. www.craftcourses.com/blog/how-to-make-your-workshops-more-accessible-advice-for-creative-tutors
Sense offers inclusive and accessible arts training designed for those delivering and supporting people with complex disabilities in creative settings. www.sense.org.uk

USA: **University of Oregon** offers Accessible and Inclusive Teaching Workshops. teaching.uoregon.edu/accessible-and-inclusive-teaching-workshops

EU: The **European Disability Expertise** is an initiative financed by the Rights, Equality and Citizenship Programme of the European Union. ec.europa.eu/social/main.jsp?catId=1532&langId=en

AUSTRALIA: **Accessible Arts** is a leading disability, access and inclusion training provider for the Arts and Culture sector. aarts.net.au

Endnotes

1. Sinek, Simon, *Start With Why: How Great Leaders Inspire Everyone To Take Action*, Penguin, London, 2011, p.39.
2. Albers, Anni, *On Weaving*, Wesleyan University Press, Middletown, Connecticut, 1965.
3. Gardner, Howard, *Frames of Mind: The Theory of Multiple Intelligences*, Basic Books, New York, 1983.
4. Kolb, David A., *Experiential Learning: Experience as the Source of Learning and Development*, Prentice-Hall, Englewood Cliffs, New Jersey, 1984.
5. Rose, Carrie, *The Completed Course: The Secret to Creating Lasting Impact, Raving Fans, and Increased Profits With Online Courses*, Kindle Edition, 2018.
6. Kneebone, Roger, *Expert: Understanding the Path to Mastery*, Penguin Books, London, 2021.
7. en.wikipedia.org/wiki/Brand

Picture credits

1: Jess Bailey via Unsplash; **15:** Jo Hounsome Photography; **18, 19, 20, 21:** Stephen Heaton Photography; **28:** Barbara Chandler © Linda Bloomfield; **29:** Linda Bloomfield; **31:** Ben Boswell © Linda Bloomfield; **32:** Lourdes Balduque via Getty; **34:** Maskot via Getty; **35, 191:** MATS team; **36-7:** Gilaxia via Getty; **40:** South_agency via Getty; **44, 183:** Deborah Parkes; **45, 47, 77:** Patricia van den Akker; **48, 85, 141, 177, 197 (bottom):** Yeshen Venema; **50, 56, 57:** Joshua James Photography; **52, 119, 198, 212:** Jewellers Academy; **53:** Mihailomilovanovic via Getty; **59, 79, 100, 103, 174 (top), 230:** Hanny Newton; **64, 94, 97:** Andrew Hobbs Photography; **66:** FilippoBacci via Getty; **68, 71, 87, 205, 216:** Catherine Lucktaylor; **69:** Caroline Marwood; **72, 203:** Angie Parker Textiles; **80, 81:** Holly Cook Photography; **82, 83, 132, 192, 242:** Sam Marshall; **89, 123, 125:** Sally Goodden; **91, 178, 181:** Lindsey Campbell; **96, 176, 194:** Ruby Taylor; **105, 120, 234, 237:** Vicki Knights Photography © Jewellers Academy; **108:** Teo Della Torre; **113, 115:** David Smith; **118:** Karen Young © Jewellers Academy; **122:** Martin Hyett © Sally Goodden; **126:** Twenty47studio via Getty; **131:** Dougal Waters via Getty; **140:** Tas Kyprianou; **143, 217:** Ekta Kaul; **158:** NickyLloyd via Getty; **162, 165:** Dan Rushworth; **169:** Simon Williams; **173, 201, 210:** Kara Leigh Ford; **174 (bottom), 184, 214:** Alison Bick; **185:** Rauni Higson; **186:** Luke Holland; **188:** Lilla Rogers; **193, 200, 215, 218, 219, 221:** Esté MacLeod; **197 (top):** Rob Jones; **207:** SrdjanPav via Getty; **208:** Izusek via Getty; **213:** Halfpoint Images via Getty; **227:** Alice Hendy Photography; **229, 243, 248:** Catherine East © Chloe Savage Embroidery; **233:** Shironosov via Getty; **245:** Abraham Gonzalez Fernandez via Getty; **246:** LeoPatrizi via Getty; **249:** Chloe Savage Embroidery; **250:** Dolly Clew

HERBERT PRESS
Bloomsbury Publishing Plc
50 Bedford Square, London, WC1B 3DP, UK
29 Earlsfort Terrace, Dublin 2, Ireland

BLOOMSBURY, HERBERT PRESS and the Herbert Press logo are trademarks of Bloomsbury Publishing Plc

First published in Great Britain in 2025

A catalogue record for this book is available from the British Library
Library of Congress Cataloguing-in-Publication data has been applied for

ISBN: PB: 978-1-7899-4178-4; eBook: 978-1-7899-4182-1

10 9 8 7 6 5 4 3 2 1

Typeset in IBM Plex Serif and Jubilat
Printed and bound in China by RR Donnelley Asia Printing Solutions Limited

MIX
Paper | Supporting responsible forestry
FSC www.fsc.org FSC® C144853

To find out more about our authors and books visit www.bloomsbury.com and sign up for our newsletters